Praise for Ne

LIGHT THI

"Alan Shepard captured the imagination of America perhaps more than any other astronaut. I was so proud he was our friend, and even more proud of the example of courage that he set for so many people around the world. He was a good man, and Barbara and I loved him." **—President George H. W. Bush**

"Just a wonderful and gripping biography . . . meticulously reported in the best tradition of David Halberstam. It is written with eloquent grace. Most satisfying of all, *Light This Candle* is the can't-put-it-down story of a modern swashbuckler determined to conquer the universe whatever the risk. In Thompson's hands, an amazing life, the ultimate American life, comes alive so exquisitely." **—Buzz Bissinger**, *New York Times* bestselling author of *Friday Night Lights*

"Just what a biography should be: sharp, evocative, and brisk." **—*Kirkus Reviews***

"Shepard was a very complicated individual. He had all the attributes to be successful, but he always lived on the edge. He had the perseverance to live through his medical problems to finally fly to the moon, but he didn't always follow the rules. *Light This Candle* captures the many facets of Alan Shepard." **—Captain James A. Lovell**

"Thompson shows that Shepard was an immensely complicated and conflicted man whose many passions drove him to feats of extraordinary bravery and accomplishment, but also to dangerous flirtations with self-destructions." **—*Smithsonian Air & Space***

"Story-telling at its best . . . Every page is alive."
—**David Hartman**, U.S. Naval Institute *Proceedings*

"Tough to say what's cooler: that Alan Shepard was the first American in space, or that he hit a golf ball on the moon. *Light This Candle* chronicles the amazing life of the brashest, funniest astronaut ever." **—Men's Health**

"The fullest portrait [of Shepard] yet. Does much to illuminate the life and personality of perhaps the most private and complex member of the Mercury Seven." **—Library Journal**

"The thoroughness of his research is impressive, and his fast-paced narrative keeps the pages turning." **—Paul Stillwell**, director, History Division, U.S. Naval Institute

"Journalist Thompson reveals another side of this all-American navy pilot with the right stuff. A snappily written, factual counterbalance to Tom Wolfe's sometimes poetic renderings of the heroes of the early space program." **—Publishers Weekly**

"Neal Thompson has taken a larger-than-life figure about whom we thought we knew all we needed to know, subjected him to rigorous investigative reporting and dogged shoe-leather research, and produced a gripping, highly readable tale that makes Alan Shepard, one of the iconic figures of the past half century, even more fascinating without diminishing his heroic dimensions."
—**Robert Timberg**, author of *The Nightingale's Song* and *State of Grace: A Memoir of Twilight Time*

"A valuable addition to the library of books on the space program." **—The Houston Chronicle**

"Thompson has thoroughly researched Shepard. . . . [The] first full-dress biography of a complex space pioneer." **—Booklist**

"A quick and thoroughly captivating read."

—*Leatherneck* magazine

"A fine book that depicts Shepard vividly. [The] prose crackles with the kind of energy Americans remember from those first broadcasts from space itself. Thompson's persistence in interviewing Shepard's surviving colleagues has bared Shepard's soul in ways the man himself seemed incapable of doing. *Light This Candle*, in contrast to the swagger of Wolfe's *Right Stuff*, exposes Shepard as a complex individual who had to battle his own ambition and ego to become a better man." —*Kansas City Star*

"An illuminating look at America's first spaceman. [Thompson] writes with eloquent grace. This is one of the finest books ever written about our space program. The thoroughness of the author's research is impressive." —*The Indianapolis Star*

"An extremely readable account of the life of a Navy pilot and America's first astronaut hero." —*Dallas Morning News*

"A highly readable effort to explain this remarkable American." —*The Charlotte Observer*

"The story remains irresistible, no matter how often it's told. . . . Thompson's biography hits all the right notes . . . professional, conscientious, and honest." —*The Buffalo News*

"A rare, warts-and-all portrait—and Shepard had a lot of warts. Thompson does a stellar job painting a real-life figure who never really showed his true self to anyone." —*The Vancouver Sun*

" 'Light this candle' is a phrase that tells us a lot about the way America's first spaceman lived his life . . . an enjoyable composition spiced with humor and anecdotes."

—*The Charleston Post and Courier*

"Alan Shepard comes through as ambitious, cold, and often selfish. He also comes through as competent, determined, and brave."
—*The Washington Times*

"A well-researched biography [and] a long overdue account of Alan Shepard . . . A welcome addition to the history of the nation's space programs."
—*Sea Power*

"This excellent biography . . . attempts to explain how such a remarkable personality could remain almost invisible to public scrutiny. Thompson's thorough research has uncovered a surprising amount of information about Shepard. This book is long overdue and a fitting tribute to America's first man in space."
—*Flight Journal*

LIGHT THIS CANDLE

THE LIFE AND TIMES OF
ALAN SHEPARD

///

NEAL THOMPSON

 THREE RIVERS PRESS • NEW YORK

Copyright © 2004
by Neal Thompson
Foreword copyright © 2005
by Chris Kraft

All rights reserved.
Published in the United States by
Three Rivers Press, an imprint of the
Crown Publishing Group, a division of
Random House, Inc., New York.
www.crownpublishing.com

Three Rivers Press and the Tugboat
design are registered trademarks
of Random House, Inc.

Originally published in slightly different
form in hardcover in the United States by
Crown Publishers, a division of
Random House, Inc., in 2004.

Library of Congress Cataloging-in-Publication Data
Thompson, Neal.
Light this candle : the life and times of
Alan Shepard / Neal Thompson.—1st ed.
Includes bibliographical references.
1. Shepard, Alan B. (Alan Bartlett), 1923– 2. Astronauts—
United States—Biography. I. Title.
TL789.85 .S5T49 2004
629.45'0092—dc22   2003015688

ISBN 1-4000-8122-X

Printed in the United States of America

Design by Barbara Sturman

2 4 6 8 10 9 7 5 3 1

First Paperback Edition

For Mary

✦

CONTENTS

PART III /// AFTER SPACE

FOREWORD

Today, it is all too easy to think of the first 15-minute ballistic flight of Project Mercury as a mere blip on the history screen of manned space flight. In 1961, believe me, it was anything but a simple thing to do. The buildup to this flight by the media, Congress, the White House and, frankly, the entire world was overwhelming. The space race with the Russians had been heating up for some time, and the technical reputation of the United States hung in the balance.

Add to this the fact that the reliability of a rocket-propelled system in 1961 was not much better then 60 percent and you may begin to have a feel for the anxiety all of us were experiencing. All but the most optimistic flight surgeons questioned the human response to being at zero gravity for extended periods of time. Many learned doctors in the medical community predicted dire results, such as total disorientation, loss of vision, and a lack of capability to perform the smallest task. Skeptics who thought we were venturing beyond the state of the art were many. *And* we were informed several weeks before the flight that it was to be done with real-time coverage of the world press.

All of us in flight operations came into the space program with varied backgrounds and education. My personal background was from the airplane flight test group of the NACA at Langley Field, Virginia. My entire career had been spent interfacing with new and high-speed airplanes. We were accustomed to exploring the outer edges of the envelope of an airplane's performance. But we had no idea what we were getting into in the realm of space.

I was familiar with the personalities one could expect from men who recognized they worked in a dangerous and sometimes unpredictable business. In the time period that Alan Shepard participated in the U.S. Space Program, there were many astronauts who performed outstanding feats. But among the first seven chosen in 1959, Shepard almost immediately stood out as the leading candidate to be the first man in space for the United States. He appeared to many as an egotist bent on being first, and his sometimes aloof attitude left an impression that he was a cold and distant individual. However, to those of us with whom he worked and trained for one of the most grueling tasks as a space test pilot, he was always the pilot who we knew would not only excel but perform precisely as advertised.

Shepard came to the NASA Space Task Group as a veteran and proven airplane test pilot. His experience as a flyer was well documented, and his reputation at the Navy Flight Test Center at Patuxent River, Maryland, was exemplary. Therefore, as we began training for the first manned flight of the Redstone, it was no surprise to me that he was all business and ready to make his mark on history. I must say that from day one of our meeting in mission control to begin the detail training for the first manned flight, I was impressed with Shepard's desire to do it right. He was intelligent, well versed in the Mercury spacecraft systems, ready to perform all of the tasks required, and totally committed to the purpose of proving man's capability to work and survive in the rigorous environment of space.

Put yourself in the seat with Alan Shepard as you sit on the top of a rocket standing on the launchpad fuming gaseous oxygen and resting on three solid rockets to be used for reentry into the atmosphere, and an escape rocket above you triggered to slam you away from a system that could be headed in a direction other than planned or exploding while you hope that the escape rocket will automatically carry you away from the resultant fireball. On top of that, you are inside a spaceship that is about to carry you straight up to about 115 miles and then deposit you in the Atlantic Ocean more than 300 miles downrange. If you can imagine that experience, then you can understand the type of man Alan Shepard was.

The other thought you should have as you venture into this story is the impact that the success of one of man's first space flights had on the country and the world at the time. It was this singular event that prompted President Kennedy to challenge the technical and scientific communities of the United States to land men on the moon and bring them safely back to earth in the decade to follow.

Alan Shepard's life is documented in this book to help the reader understand who this American hero was. It is a tremendous read about a great human being that dedicated himself—not just once, but many times during his life—to extending the frontiers of flight.

CHRIS KRAFT, August 24, 2004
NASA's first flight director, former director of the Johnson Space Center, and author of the *New York Times* bestseller *Flight: My Life in Mission Control*

> Man must rise above the Earth—to the top
> of the atmosphere and beyond—for only
> thus will he fully understand the world in
> which he lives.
> —SOCRATES, 500 B.C.

PROLOGUE

John Glenn was furious. He thought he'd played it just right, made all the right moves, and that he would surely become the first American in space. It's what they all wanted, all seven men who'd been chosen to vie for the job.

When Glenn wasn't picked first, or even second, he tried to tell his bosses that they'd made a mistake. You don't want Alan Shepard, he said. You don't want this guy, the one we call the Icy Commander, with his egotistical insouciance, his questionable morals, his disregard for authority, and disdain for the press. Glenn moped, fumed, and bitched, wrote letters, and complained to family and friends. But it was no use. NASA ordered him to stop "backbiting" and deal with it.

When the decision finally became public a few months later, on May 2, 1961, the press wanted answers, too. They had adored John Glenn from the start and expected all along he'd be America's first spaceman. So they pestered NASA's gruff little spokesman, Shorty Powers, for an explanation. Why Shepard?

Shorty, in his mellifluous and condescending military voice, tried to explain how the Mercury Seven astronauts were all exceptional men and among the nation's most dauntless test pilots. But one had to go first, and Shepard, he said, "had what all the others had, with just enough to spare to make him the logical man to go first."

Whatever that meant. The truth, which NASA chose not to acknowledge at the time, was simply this: Alan Shepard was the most capable of the bunch. In 1961—at the height of a seething cold war against a seemingly evil empire, and in the early days of a young president's tentative new administration—NASA couldn't take any chances. As one NASA official involved in the Glenn-versus-Shepard decision put it: "We wanted to put our best foot forward." So they picked the best of the best of the best.

///

A few minutes past 1 A.M., six hours before launch time, Bill Douglas, the astronauts' gentle and soft-spoken physician, poked Alan Shepard on the shoulder.

"Come on, Al," Douglas said. "They're filling the tanks."

"I'm ready," Shepard said, rising and pulling on a white bathrobe. "Is John up?"

"John's awake," Douglas said. "We're all awake. Did you sleep well?"

"Very well," Shepard said. "No dreams."

Shepard whistled as he took a brief shower, shaved, then shuffled into an adjacent office where Glenn, already wide awake and wearing an identical terry-cloth robe, sat waiting for him. The cook brought in two nearly identical trays of food.

"Here we go again," Glenn said. "You ready?"

Shepard nodded. The breakfast menu was the same as it had been for a week: filet mignon wrapped in bacon, toast and jelly, eggs and orange juice—a so-called low-residue diet, so Shepard wouldn't find himself in need of a toilet in space.

"What a tough life, huh?" Glenn said. "Filet mignon every morning."

Shepard appreciated that, preferring jokes to any of Glenn's "maudlin sentimentality." He didn't want to think about the importance of the coming event, only about the technical tasks at hand. When asked later about his feelings at breakfast, Shepard said that when you're preparing to roost atop many tons of high explosives, "the last thing on your mind is being a page in a history book."

But May 5, 1961, was a day for the history books. The entire earth was watching. A battle between the world's superpowers was being fought in strange new nonmilitary ways, and the Soviets had struck first three weeks earlier when cosmonaut Yuri Gagarin had circled the Earth—a stunning achievement that could have, should have been Shepard's. Now it was the United States' turn and they couldn't afford any mistakes. Shepard kept reminding himself of that: *Don't fuck up.*

To Shepard's relief, the weather report looked good. No signs of rain.

As he finished eating, Shepard became vaguely aware that people—technicians, photographers, and doctors—were milling around him, watching him. Some were more nervous than he was; they didn't want to screw up their part of the mission, either. Yet they were amazed that the guy headed for the hot seat appeared so poised and rock-steady.

After breakfast, Glenn rode out to the rocket to make final preparations on the capsule. Shepard strode into Bill Douglas' exam room, took off his bathrobe, and let the doctor survey every inch of his sinewy, five-foot-eleven, 165-pound, thirty-seven-year-old body. Douglas asked how he felt, and Shepard acknowledged a few butterflies—but happy ones. When he finished looking down Shepard's throat one last time, Douglas rapped his patient playfully on the chin, and Shepard broke into a toothy smile.

A little past 2 A.M., Shepard went to the astronauts' office and called his wife, Louise. "I was hoping it was you," she said. She had wanted to be down at the Cape watching the launch, but he'd suggested she avoid the hype and the media crush and stay in Virginia Beach. Louise had decided ever since the first days of his Navy career, during the final year of World War II, that it was best to give him space to do his job. Theirs was a relationship built around long distances and lengthy separations; telephone calls had become their lifeline.

Three days earlier—when NASA finally announced that Shepard, not Glenn, had been chosen to ride a Mercury Redstone rocket into space—the press found Louise anyway. Reporters cawed and pecked like a flock of crows outside the squat brick ranch house until Louise, hunkered inside with her daughters, taped a note on the front door: *There are no reporters inside. I will have a statement for the press after the flight.*

When her husband called, Louise had a dozen things to tell him—about their girls, the house, the pesky press, her golf game—but she forgot them all. None of it seemed important now. She knew it could be the last time they spoke. Ever. "We'll be watching you on TV," she said. "Be sure to wave when you lift off."

"Right," he said, and laughed. "I'll open the hatch and stick my arm out."

Shepard, uncharacteristically, didn't have much else to say that morning, either. Finally, Louise told him to "hurry home."

"I will," he said.

"I love you."

Shepard hung up, then walked into the suit-up room. Technicians and engineers avoided any conversation with him. If he wanted to talk, he'd have to be the one to start. Suit technician Joe Schmitt barely shared a dozen words with Shepard as Schmitt worked himself into a sweat squeezing Shepard into the tight, silvery space suit.

Just before leaving the hangar that housed the astronauts' quarters and exam rooms, Shepard winked at Dee O'Hara, the astronauts' kewpie-doll-cute and devoted nurse, who stood near the exit clutching her rosary beads. "Well, here I go, Dee," he said, and Dee just waved, fighting back tears.

Shepard climbed into a transport van, leaned back in a reclining chair, and placed a portable oxygen tank on the floor beside him. He looked and acted like a space-alien businessman riding a commuter bus, with his silvery briefcase by his side.

The van pulled up at the foot of the Redstone rocket, bathed in floodlights, plumes of blue and white oxygen fumes venting from its wafer-thin sides. At eighty-three feet, the rocket was no taller than a mature birch tree. It would take nearly seven of them stacked end to end to reach the height of the Washington Monument. But Shepard was proud of his little capsule-topped rocket and called her "that little rascal." As he approached the rocket, he asked Mission Control for permission to exit the transport van ahead of schedule. He knew he'd never see the "bird" again, so he stopped to symbolically kick the tires.

She's got an air of expectancy, he thought. *A lovely sight ... long and slender.*

Suddenly the crewmen behind him broke into applause, and for a moment the emotions of the day caught up with Shepard. *Life* magazine photographer Ralph Morse, the scrappy little New Yorker who had become a good friend, began snapping away, and one of his shots would occupy half a page in the *New York Times.* Shepard turned to speak to the crew but his throat choked up and he just waved.

On the elevator ride to the top, Douglas gave him a box of crayons—"So you'll have something to do up there." Shepard laughed loudly, almost fogging his visor, but grateful for the tension breaker. He handed the box to Douglas, telling him he was going to be a little busy. At the top of the gantry—in an antechamber whose translucent green walls, like those of a beachside motel, earned it the nickname Surfside 5—stood Glenn.

Glenn wore sterile white coveralls and a paper cap like a butcher's. He greeted Shepard as he exited the elevator, then helped him squeeze through the two-foot-square opening of the capsule Shepard had named *Freedom* 7. As Shepard settled into the couch that had been contoured to his body, he looked up at the instrument panel and laughed into his visor. Taped there was a sign that read No Handball Playing in This Area. Beside that was a centerfold ripped from a girlie magazine. Shepard took one look at Glenn's giggling face, impressed that the Boy Scout was capable of such a crafty gotcha.

///

Right from the start—in 1959, when NASA had chosen seven test pilots to train to become the first astronauts—it was clear the two front-runners and competing leaders of the group would be Shepard and Glenn. The bad boy and the altar boy.

Glenn, the silver-tongued, freckle-faced all-American, spoke eloquently to the press about God and family and serving his country. The others just shook their heads at him, disgusted at his pandering but secretly impressed by his locution.

Shepard, on the other hand, epitomized the cynical, smart-ass fighter jock. You could see it in the strutting, superior way he carried himself. He didn't grin like Glenn; he smirked. Instead of cloying the press, he snapped at them; when asked why he wanted to be the first astronaut, he quipped, "I want to be first because I want to be first."

The opposing personalities of Shepard and Glenn reflected the duality of veteran military men who emerged from cloistered military fraternities to become overnight celebrities. They were, as John Kennedy called them, men of a "new generation" who would compete in "a race for the mastery of the sky." They were also adventurous, combative, indulgent thrill-seekers who performed ludicrous, death-taunting feats in supersonic jets, then rewarded themselves with whiskey, women, and fast cars.

Tensions between Shepard and Glenn came to a notorious head in late 1960. Glenn was sound asleep early one morning in his San Diego hotel room when the phone rang. Shepard, calling from nearby Tijuana, Mexico, explained that he'd been out drinking, spending time with a female friend, and had let his guard down, allowing a reporter and photographer to tail him. "I need your help," he told Glenn.

Glenn handled the situation with a frenetic round of phone calls that kept the story from ever reaching newsprint. The next day he told the other six astronauts they had dodged a bullet and should start thinking about keeping their pants zipped. A few weeks later the astronauts were asked to cast a vote for the man—besides themself—they'd like to see become the first American in space.

Glenn knew who the others would pick—the bad-ass, not the kiss-ass. He was right, and when NASA made it official—on January 19, at a secret meeting the night before John F. Kennedy's inauguration—Shepard just stared at the floor, trying not to smirk and offend the other six as their boss announced that he would get the first flight. In the toughest competition of his contest-filled life, Shepard had won—the bad boy had prevailed. And Glenn had no choice but to take an enormous gulp of pride and serve as Shepard's sidekick.

Shepard, meanwhile, just loved calling Glenn "my backup."

///

On the morning of May 5, 1961, one of the greatest crowds Florida had ever seen descended upon its beaches. Men and women skipped work, pulled their children from school, and to the north and south of Cape Canaveral arrived early, carrying lawn chairs and binoculars, hoping for a glimpse of history.

Across the nation, millions sat glued to their televisions. President Kennedy stood in his secretary's office with his wife and brother by his side. Shepard's parents sat side by side in their New Hampshire living room; even though Shepard's father had opposed his son's decision to become an astronaut, he now sat in an easy chair, watching calmly and proudly. Louise Shepard kneeled before her television, reaching to touch the frail image of the thin rocket that would soon carry her husband.

At that moment John Glenn's hands were reaching into Shepard's cramped capsule. Glenn retrieved the handball sign and the centerfold, then helped strap Shepard tightly into his couch and attached the many hoses, wires, and sensors from his suit to the capsule's dashboard. In the months leading up to that morning, a certain dignity had befallen the relationship between Shepard and Glenn. They were inseparable during the final weeks of training. To escape the tension-filled cacophony of Cape Canaveral, they'd jog on a nearby isolated beach, chase sand crabs, and dive into the cool waves of the Atlantic; at night, they'd sit for hours after dinner, discussing each detail of the up-coming flight, then retire together to the same room, sleeping just a few feet apart.

Just before they closed the hatch Glenn reached in one last time and shook Shepard's gloved hand. Shepard was suddenly moved by how gracious Glenn had been. He thanked his col-league and then jerked a thumbs-up.

"See you soon," he said, his voice muffled inside his helmet.

"Happy landings, Commander," Glenn responded as the crew standing behind him shouted good luck and goodbye.

Technicians closed and bolted the hatch, and Shepard was alone. Monitors showed that his heartbeat quickened a bit as they shut him inside, and Shepard thought, *Okay, buster. You vol-unteered for this thing. Now don't screw up.*

It was dawn. He'd been awake five hours, and the rising sun began to shine through the periscope screen two feet from his face. He started going through his checklist—a newspaper the next day would accidentally print that Shepard was reviewing his "chick list." Then he started through all the procedures he and Glenn had practiced for months. As he did this, he began to think about where he was and where the others were.

some of Shepard's military records and his FBI files, what emerges in response to those questions is a large, energetic, and aggressive life. A life that, before and after space, pulsed with mystery, romance, and adventure. Shepard was the military version of what Elvis was to music, what James Dean was to Hollywood, what Kerouac was to literature. Today's man was once a boy who wanted to be Alan Shepard. But, until now, his true story has never been fully told. It's the story of life fully lived, and entwined through it is—somewhat surprisingly for a man so famous for philandering—a love story.

His beautiful wife, Louise, might have told the story. But after fifty-three years of marriage, she followed him into oblivion, dying suddenly and mysteriously, five weeks after he did, on an airplane, forty thousand feet above earth.

BEFORE SPACE

///

1

"Alan was really kind of a loner"

Alan Shepard confounded people. He angered, intimidated, and embarrassed them; insulted, taunted, or—worst of all—ignored them. Yet for all his maddening iciness, people were drawn to him, because just beneath his cold shell was an intelligent, curious man who could be charming, hilarious, warm, inviting, generous, and even sexy.

There was no way to anticipate which of Alan Shepard's personalities would emerge on a given day: aloof and remote one day, buying you drinks the next. Possibly the only consistent aspect of his character was its unpredictable duality. That and the obsessive drive to be, as one astronaut put it, "better than anyone else."

At every stage of his life, Shepard's effect on family, friends, and colleagues was that of a competitor in a hurry, constantly lurching forward, with no stomach for delays or incompetence. He was attracted to people with something to offer, those with skills, information, or money who could help him achieve his goals. But if you had nothing to offer, "you'd better get out of town," said one longtime friend.

"He was hard to get to know. But once he put his arm

around you, you knew he was there," said astronaut Deke Slayton's wife, Bobbie. "If you were a friend of Al's and you needed something, you could call him and he'd break his neck trying to get it for you. If you were in, you were in. It was just tough to get in."

Shepard's frenetic, unreadable personality churned behind a pair of wide, wild eyes, his most prominent facial feature. Googly, buggy things. Heavy-lidded, they distended out from deep sockets. When he wasn't smiling—he could ignite a huge smile, too, with long, askew teeth framed by meaty lips—it was the eyes people noticed first. Icy blue and intense sometimes, other times warm and watery, but always open wide.

Throughout his life, friends and family spoke of the "infamous stare" Shepard could inflict. Confidence, smarts, ego, anger, hunger all poured through his bulgy eyes. But, like mirrors, they worked only one way, giving nothing back.

Behind the mirrors burbled a mysterious stew of contradictions. He was swaggeringly cocky, often referring to himself in the third person or as "the world's greatest test pilot." And yet he could be humble and self deprecating. Despite a notorious impatience, Shepard also displayed an attention to detail that earned him key assignments as a Navy pilot. "He didn't do anything until he had studied it, tested it, and made damn sure he could do it," said James Stockdale, a onetime test pilot colleague of Shepard's.

In the cockpit of an airplane, Shepard flew with confidence, without fear, always in control, and with an uncanny spatial awareness that can't be taught. "He could fly anything," one colleague said. Another called him "the best aviator I've ever known." But Shepard also had a persistent habit of infuriating superiors by flouting Navy rules, flying dangerously low over beaches, beneath bridges, and upside down. He was "flamboyant" and "indulgent," growled one former supervisor.

Though his flamboyant indulgences once took him to the brink of a Navy court-martial, those same flinty qualities earned him a spot as one of the nation's first seven astronauts. "He was an egotist" and "a typical New Englander . . . hard, cold," said one NASA official, Chris Kraft. "But he was all business when it came to flying."

When he joined the other Mercury Seven astronauts, the same question constantly simmered: Who was Alan Shepard? One astronaut considered him "bitterly competitive, to the point of being cutthroat." Another once accused Shepard of "swindling" him in a business deal. And one astronaut's wife said Shepard "really didn't want to have anything to do with the rest of us, the common folk."

Indeed, he worked hard at setting himself apart. He'd attend casual backyard barbecues in a suit and tie, and he drove a flashy Corvette for the better part of thirty years. He befriended race car drivers, comedians, pro golfers, and millionaires, collected celebrity friends like Frank Sinatra, Bob Hope, Mickey Rooney, and Clint Eastwood. Then again, while he often acted the part of a self-sufficient loner with little need for others' company, he was just as often a party boy who loved good pranks and nights of drinking with buddies. Shepard cherished good times and pursued them vigorously. Some guessed that his need for a good time was a necessary counterweight to his constant, annoying competitiveness. Al Neuharth, who founded *USA Today*, said Shepard "wanted to win, whether it was pool or cards or whatever. He wanted to win, to be number one."

The privacy fence Shepard erected around the perimeter of his personal life shielded another of the contradictions of his persona: that of a ferocious womanizer and, at the same time, a devoted family man and an unashamed admirer of his wife, Louise.

Like many Navy men of his day, Shepard successfully navigated among exotic women in the barrooms of international ports of call. He perfected those skills as a celebrity-astronaut; one NASA colleague called him "the biggest flirt in the country—but it went beyond flirting." A fellow test pilot said, "He had a beautiful wife and family. I just never quite understood it. But this was his compulsion."

And yet, while he rarely spoke of them to his peers, Shepard loved and doted on his wife and two daughters. Few colleagues knew that Shepard also informally adopted a niece (the daughter of his wife's dead sister) and treated her like one of his own. But his strong if imperfect fifty-three-year marriage quietly survived while so many other astronauts' marriages crumbled around him.

One family friend said Louise grounded her husband: "She was the rock." Astronaut Wally Schirra agreed: "She'd bring Al down to earth a lot."

In the end, she was probably the only one who really knew him.

One of the Mercury Seven astronauts once told *Life* magazine, "You might think you'd get to know someone well after working so closely with him for two years. Well, it's not that way with Shepard. He's always holding something back."

For all his vexing complexity, however, Shepard was exactly the kind of man NASA wanted. At the height of the cold war, the space agency sought nothing less than "real men . . . perfect physical and emotional and aesthetic specimens."

In Alan Shepard, NASA got all that and more. A guy who'd fought an evil empire in World War II, landed planes on aircraft carriers during storms and at night, bailed out of test jets ten miles above the earth, downed cocktails or swatted golf balls with celebrities, water-skied barefoot, raced Corvettes, slept with beautiful women, and become a millionaire—all the things boys and teens want to do when they become men.

Shepard was a man's man, and others strived to be like him, even if they didn't necessarily like him or considered him an "asshole" or a "son of a bitch," as many did. If Shepard's character was a study in paradox, that's possibly because, as a boy, he was pulled in two directions by parents with opposing but oddly complementary temperaments.

Both parents came from old-guard New Hampshire stock, with impressive lineages to the seminal Colonial days. But when Alan was born, on November 18, 1923, in an upstairs room at 64 East Derry Road—with its ornate molding, glass doorknobs, and gas lamps in each room—he was immediately positioned between two loving but dissimilar parents, one of them grim and duty-bound, the other boisterous and spirited.

///

East Derry, forty miles northwest of Boston in the southeastern tip of New Hampshire, was a town where everybody knew everyone. Family roots ran deep in such towns, but the Shepard family's roots were among the deepest.

One side of the family sailed from England in the 1690s, their carpentry and blacksmithing tools in tow, then trekked inland from the coast to the folds and foothills along the Merrimac River. Later they helped draft the Declaration of Independence and fought in the Revolutionary War. Ancestors on the other side of Shepard's family transited with the 102 passengers of the *Mayflower*, then helped govern the Plymouth Colony.

Along with Scotch-Irish settlers seeking religious freedom, Shepard's English ancestors carved rural hillsides into potato and dairy farms, which later birthed linen, hat, and shoe factories in a triad of manufacturing towns—Derry, East Derry, and Londonderry.

The landscape of Shepard's youth was a succulent Americana playground of barnyards and swimming holes, apple orchards and blueberry fields, stone walls framing fields of wildflowers and shadowy forests of white pine carpeted by fern and moss. The unpredictable New Hampshire weather could be both fierce and lovely in a day. Winter brought biting winds and mounds of snow that arrived early and stayed late. Summers were brief, hot, and humid, followed by crisp and spectacularly colorful falls.

That landscape was sensually depicted in the poems of Robert Frost, who in 1900 bought a farm not far from the Shepards. "To a large extent, the terrain of my poetry is the Derry landscape," Frost once said. "There was something about the experience at Derry which stayed in my mind, and was tapped for poetry in the years that came after."

The people also made a profound impression: seriously religious, ultraconservative, and snobbishly wary of newcomers. Frost once cashed a check at the Derry National Bank—owned by Shepard's grandfather—and forgot to sign his middle name on the check. The teller sniffed, "Since it doesn't cost you anything, we would like your *full* name."

Frost often felt like an interloper among haughty, superior people. After being rebuffed by the Derry school board for a teaching job, he found work at the prestigious Pinkerton Academy, where Shepard's grandfather was a trustee. Among his students was Shepard's father, Bart, a man steeped in that hard-edged New England culture.

Throughout his life Alan would rankle friends with the imperious and crusty attitude he inherited from the tight-knit, fiercely loyal, and wealthy Shepard clan.

In town, the Shepards wore the nicer clothes, drove the newer cars; they kept a vacation house on a nearby lake. A hue of wealth tainted the other kids' perceptions of Alan, and many peers assumed he lived a coddled life of privilege. He did, in fact, absorb a sense of entitlement and the self-assuredness that privilege engendered. But Alan—and his sister, Polly, who was two years younger—were far from pampered rich kids. Their father valued work and made sure each child performed their share of domestic chores.

Each morning, for example, Alan grabbed a flag from the front hall closet, poked the rod into the front lawn, waited for his father to come out, and then stood back to salute. After cleaning his room, he might lug one of the last, half-melted, sawdust-coated blocks of ice from the icehouse in the woods and put it in the ice chest. Then he'd deliver newspapers to half the homes in town. On Saturday nights he'd sit in the foyer buffing and polishing every last shoe in the house, lining them up to gleam on the stairs.

Bart Shepard was a stern and serious disciplinarian, and Alan inherited a stoicism and toughness of character from him—traits that Bart had inherited from his own prosperous and industrious father.

Alan's grandfather Frederick "Fritz" Shepard was one of the most powerful local businessmen of his day. He owned Derry National Bank and Derry Electric Light Company, ran a stage-coach service and an electric rail line, and built the town library. Fritz Shepard was also a prominent Republican, East Derry's town treasurer, and a colonel in the National Guard. He served as aide-de-camp at the historic month-long Russo-Japanese Peace Conference, organized by President Theodore Roosevelt in Portsmouth in 1905 (which ended the war between Russia and Japan and earned Roosevelt the Nobel peace prize). Until the crash of 1929, Fritz Shepard was a very wealthy man.

He and his wife, Nanzie, fairly lorded above the town in their enormous house on a high knoll off East Derry Road, a Victorian mansion with a tennis-court-sized ballroom where the Shepards entertained such dignitaries as President Howard Taft.

Though Fritz's Derry empire was battered by the Depression, causing him to lose the bank and the rail line, he subsequently threw his energies into making his own line of sodas, tonics, and ginger ale, which allowed him and Nanzie to keep in their employ the African-American couple who served for decades as their maid and butler.

While Fritz tended to his business enterprises, his wife governed the family as its rock-steady matriarch. Nanzie Shepard's lineage was also seriously old guard, and she became an important influence on her grandchildren—especially Alan.

Short, redheaded Nanzie was an equally important social and political figure in East Derry. She led the New Hampshire Daughters of the Revolution, became the first female president of the Republican Club of New Hampshire, and as one of New Hampshire's presidential electors cast her vote for the Republican Calvin Coolidge in 1924.

She and Fritz had high expectations for their sons, imbuing in them an ethic of success and the expectation that they would get a good education and make their mark in the world. Two of their sons, Henry and Frederick junior, went to the Massachusetts Institute of Technology, en route to careers as successful businessmen in Massachusetts.

But Alan's father, Bart, chose a different course. He joined the National Guard in 1915 and then shipped off to France with an infantry division of the American Expeditionary Force in World War I. When he returned home in 1918, he joined the Army Reserves and began working as an assistant cashier at his father's bank, Derry National. Bart took his military service quite seriously and eventually rose to the rank of colonel, which was how Alan and his sister, Polly, addressed him—that or "sir." Bart was enormously proud of his military rank and leaped at any chance to wear his uniform.

When he wasn't in uniform, Bart wore a suit and tie—even on weekends. He kept his thin mustache neatly trimmed and never smoked or drank. Most workdays he ate a thirty-cent cheese sandwich at a downtown Greek lunch counter, and once in a while he splurged on pie. His lone hobby was music—across six decades, he played the organ at nearly every 10 A.M. Sunday service at the First Parish Church, the oldest church in town.

Bart lost his bank job when Derry National followed five thousand others into oblivion after the 1929 crash. When his father then started a family insurance company, Bart took a job and worked there the rest of his life. Bart had the same large eyes as his son, but they appeared more sad than eager on his long face, above a pinched, downturned mouth.

One day Alan would appreciate how his own character was shaped by his father's work ethic, the consistency and simplicity of his demeanor. But those realizations were many years off. As an energetic child, Alan often looked at his father and asked: *Why?* It just wasn't Alan's idea of a life. Bart had none of the qualities Alan admired as a child: bravery, a sense of adventure, a determination to be the best. Instead, his father seemed happy doing his plodding darnedest in a town Alan considered "a small pond."

Alan and his father were hardly chums. Not in the way Alan was close with his mother and his grandmother, Nanzie. Alan and Bart shared few common interests and spent little one-on-one time together, except for tuning the church organ together once a month. It nagged at Alan that his father simply wasn't . . . fun. "He appreciated a chuckle once in a while," Alan once said. "But I can't say he had a playful side."

The sense of playfulness that became one of Alan's more notable attributes derived instead from his mother, Renza. As powerfully as Bart's side of the family had influenced Alan, his emotional temperament was shaped more by his spirited mother.

Renza Emerson's family owned Derry's largest shoe factory and had built a home beside Fritz and Nanzie Shepard's mansion. Bart and Renza barely knew each other as children; he was a decade older and had gone off to war. When Bart returned from war, he noticed that the girl next door had grown into an energetic young beauty who seemed to have qualities that he did not—a sense of fun, a sense of humor. Bart fell in love and, at age thirty, proposed to his twenty-year-old neighbor. The local paper gushed at the engagement of "two popular and prominent young society people." After a honeymoon drive through Vermont and Montreal, dancing at Lake Placid and Niagara Falls, the couple built a two-story Colonial on a plot of land smack between their parents' houses.

To maintain the fine balance of their opposites-attract marriage, it made perfect sense to live with each other's families, like parentheses, on either side. While Bart's side of the family hammered in the value of seriousness and determination, Renza taught her children the value of a good time. Renza, nearly the polar opposite of Bart Shepard, cherished fun and laughs and was, in short, the radiant and playful luminescence of Alan's boyhood.

An example of her high energy and lust for life was her choice of religion. In a sharp counterpoint to the Shepard family's Protestantism, Renza was a Christian Scientist. While Bart attended church as a matter of duty, Renza attended the local Christian Science church for its preaching on positive thinking, its unshakable insistence that happiness is the lone antidote to illness.

The Christian Science Church was founded in 1879, twenty-five miles north in Bow, New Hampshire. Controversial from the start, the church lured many independent-minded New Englanders with its commonsense doctrines. Renza approved of the fact that the religion had been founded by a strong-willed woman, Mary Baker Eddy, who believed in self-reliance and self-healing.

Like her husband, Renza eschewed smoking and drinking, but then again, she didn't need stimulants. She loved the outdoors and throughout her life remained spry and active. She gardened avidly during the spring and summer and in winter joined her children for toboggan rides down steep backyard hills. She had a plain face, but it was made attractive by her natural ebullience. "A people person," Alan called her. "Just a happy, loving individual."

Renza taught her children that it was up to them—not God, not fate—to make things happen in life. Alan admired and emulated his mother's assertiveness, much more so than his father's stoic passivity. While Polly was Bart's little girl, Alan was his mother's boy. Whereas he called his father "Colonel" or "sir," his mother was always "Mum" or "Mumma." And in time he came to exhibit plenty of what one cousin referred to as Renza's invigorating and infectious "pizzazz."

///

The amalgam of influences inherited from his parents would serve Shepard perfectly through his career. His determination, smarts, and skill, combined with an upbeat and positive attitude, would carry him first into the elite upper ranks of the Navy and then to NASA.

But to Shepard's peers, the somewhat contradictory mix of qualities could be jarring.

Fellow astronaut John Glenn called Shepard "an enigma . . . One side of him was cool, competent, and utterly dedicated, the other ready to cut up, joke, and have fun."

From a young age, Shepard struck most people as something of a mystery. He made friends easily enough and could be gregarious. Starting up conversations with strangers came naturally. Classmates felt special when he spoke to them, as though they'd been chosen. But then a week would go by and they'd see him at school or in town, and he'd walk right past, his eyes straight ahead, as if they'd never met—and they'd realize they weren't his friend after all. Friends were people Shepard needed for fun or adventure. But for the most part he could take or leave them and quite often preferred to be alone, biking, skiing, or hiking through town, swimming, sailing, or skating on a backwoods pond. He had a deep capacity for solitude and a self-propelled energy that, whether alone or with buddies, kept him constantly busy—sometimes industriously, sometimes mischievously.

If a few boys wanted to tag along after school, that was fine. He didn't entirely exclude people; it's just that he didn't need the company of others the way most people do. "If he wanted to talk to you, then you'd have a conversation," one friend recalled.

"Alan was really kind of a loner," said his childhood friend Harold Moynihan.

To most of his peers, Shepard seemed to exist in a world separate from theirs. He could be a clown, could be friendly when he wanted to, but he didn't hang around after school for clubs and sports. He could be a flirt, but he wasn't known to have girlfriends. Classmates were intrigued by him, but he was not one of the "in" crowd. It was obvious in the way he carried himself, though, that Shepard didn't seem to care if he was "in." Instead of the downcast eyes and timid gait of a shy, self-conscious loner, Shepard strutted around confidently, with his head back, chin up, and eyes wide.

That quality of self-confident aloofness would follow him through life. Few people would ever consider themselves true friends. "You only got so close to Alan and then he shut you out," said Dee O'Hara, the astronauts' nurse.

Another lifelong quality, which began in childhood, was Shepard's taste for physical challenges. Because he was small for his age, he shied away from team sports, but he excelled at solo sports. He learned to sail, swim, canoe, and ice-skate on Beaver Lake, down the hill behind his house. When the lake froze over in winter, cars with spiked tires raced in ovals around it, and Shepard sometimes skied behind a car, towed by a rope tied to the bumper, once reaching sixty-eight miles an hour. When it snowed, he and his friends built ski jumps on a steep hill behind his house and measured their distances, striving to beat each other. Shepard's personal best was thirty-five feet.

Shepard's favorite form of entertainment, though, was spending time beneath his grandparents' mansion next door, in a basement full of his dead grandfather's tools and machines—a dank hideout that hosted Shepard's most glorious childhood moments.

His grandfather Fritz had been a tinkerer, drawn to the technology of his day: radios, electric-powered tools, a wind-up phonograph. When he died, those techno-toys collected dust until Alan discovered them—along with Fritz's workshop, racks of tools, a treadle-powered band saw, and a cider press—in the stone-walled, dirt-floored basement. As Willy Loman says in *Death of a Salesman:* "A man who can't handle tools is not a man." And in that regard, Shepard—like many of the engineers, pilots, and astronauts who became his colleagues—was all man. With his school friends or all alone, Shepard spent many lost hours in that basement, dismantling and rebuilding small engines or sawing and shaving wood scraps into model boats that he'd launch into naval skirmishes on Beaver Lake.

Fritz and Nanzie's basement was also the sanctum sanctorum where Shepard hatched naughty schemes. From an early age Shepard was attracted to the type of fun that had a whiff of danger or mischief about it. In that basement, for example, he learned to transform apples into alcohol.

He and some friends would collect apples from the small orchard out back—only those that had fallen, because they were more ripe—push the apples through a hand-cranked apple grinder, then dump the mashed apples into a press, beneath which they'd collect the strained juice in ceramic jugs and wooden caskets. Shepard would let the jugs and caskets sit a few weeks in a corner of the basement, fermenting. When the cider ripened and turned boozy but not yet vinegary, he'd invite a few classmates down into the basement and they'd all get loopy drinking his hard, slightly alcoholic cider.

In his pursuit of devil making, Shepard sought the thrill of attracting attention, but he worked hard to minimize any chance of implication. His hard cider parties, for example, were relatively safe affairs because Grandma Nanzie was hard of hearing.

He didn't shoplift or get into fights or openly defy his parents or do drugs. But he did fall in love with the buzz that came from a perfectly executed, low-risk, high-impact prank. Later, as a Navy pilot, he became infamous for his high-speed devilry, such as ripping terrifyingly low across a crowded Maryland beach in a jet or flying beneath a bridge. As an astronaut, he raised such stunts to an art form as he and his colleagues regularly taunted news reporters, innkeepers, politicians—and each other. They put rotten fish in each other's cars and sabotaged the engines, always striving for the perfect "gotcha."

Shepard's love of a good prank created many tensions between him and his stern father. One Christmas he gave a cigar to Bart's older brother, Fritz. After dinner, Uncle Fritz lit the stogie only to have it poof in his face. While Shepard was happily amused by the gag, his cousins were shocked. Not until Fritz broke into a grin did they laugh, too, though a bit nervously. Bart, sitting at the head of the table, didn't even crack a smile.

Within an otherwise serious clan, Shepard's mold-breaking pranks stood out, as did his total lack of fear and his indifference to reprisal—as one cousin observed, Shepard was "not awed by authority." Renza often struggled to keep her son focused, and she once acknowledged how difficult it was to "keep a teenager with boundless energy out of mischief" and to channel "Alan's great vitality" toward productive ventures.

///

Fortunately for both Shepard and his mother, his elementary-school teacher, Berta Wiggins, saw something special in his kinetic young personality, and she worked to convert his scattered, unfocused energy into a sharp beam of brilliance.

Wiggins was a severe, hard-faced woman with rimless glasses, almost always dressed in black, with her white hair pulled back into a tight bun. Like a benevolent prison warden, Mrs. Wiggins for decades single-handedly ran the Adams School, a white two-story building topped by a bell tower where she taught grades one through six, about twenty students in all, in a large second-floor room without electricity or running water.

Wiggins expected much from her students. She stalked the

aisles with a birch rod, ready to whack any daydreaming slackers into compliance. Days were tightly scheduled, and she moved quickly from lesson to lesson. Thirty minutes allotted to Shakespeare, 15 minutes to a piece by Chopin, an hour to math, and so on. Generations of Derry kids forever shared memories of those agonizing moments standing on a platform at the front of the class, called upon to recite a passage of prose or their multiplication tables or a historic speech word for word.

Wiggins took a curious and particular interest in Shepard. She perceived in him a promising young mind with a special perception for math, but noted how quickly he became bored and restive. He'd finish lessons before the other kids and sit fiddling at his desk, distracted and fitful, itching to pull his harmonica out of the flip-top desk. So she often assigned him extra work: a paper on James Fenimore Cooper's *The Last of the Mohicans* (on which he got an A), a report on the Middle Ages (B+), a stamp collection.

When Shepard was eleven, Wiggins asked him to write and bind his own book, and he decided it was time to compose his autobiography. At the time, Alan had become enamored of Charles Lindbergh and kept on his bedside table a copy of Lindbergh's autobiography, *We*. In a show of how strong Shepard's ego had already become by age eleven, the book was titled "Me."

Later, as a test pilot and astronaut, Shepard would need to absorb huge amounts of highly technical information, and could often do so without needing to write things down—a capacity he credited to Mrs. Wiggins. "Mrs. Wiggins was tough," Shepard recalled for a reporter many years later, adding that she had seemed "eight feet tall."

Shepard performed so well under Wiggins' tutelage that by the time he was in fifth grade, she suggested that Shepard skip sixth grade and go right to middle school. Then, after just a year of middle school, his teachers advised that Shepard skip eighth grade, too.

When Shepard arrived at the ivy-covered, redbrick Pinkerton

Academy in the fall of 1936—where his father had sat in Robert Frost's poetry class and his grandfather, as a school trustee, had signed Frost's checks—he was only twelve years old, the youngest and smallest kid in the freshman class.

High school life did not come easy at first. Shepard lagged in both sports and academics his first two years there and struggled to keep up, probably for the first time in his life. Being younger and smaller would become annoying themes of Shepard's young adulthood, forcing him to work more aggressively to stay ahead. After his freshman year, Shepard tried to pack more muscle onto his wire-thin frame by swimming back and forth across a nearby pond with a rope harness around his shoulders and pulling an empty rowboat.

A bitter childhood taste of being the underdog, and learning to persevere during such tough times, would serve Shepard well in the coming years—especially during his mid-1960s battle to reach the moon. Dogged determination and a steely, obsessive pursuit of his goals became his most exceptional qualities. In future years he'd not let anything or anyone get in his way. He'd step over people, even friends if he had to. He even had a determined manner of walking—instead of following sidewalks, Shepard usually walked quickly and in a straight line, stepping over shrubs and across lawns to get where he was going.

But as a boy, the most distinctive sign of that determination was his precocious fascination with—and pursuit of—flying airplanes, an interest that bordered on obsession.

///

Even without his historic flight across the Atlantic in 1927, stories of Charles Lindbergh's aerial daredevilry were enough to thrill a generation of boys like Shepard, who collected airplane magazines and read and reread Lindbergh's autobiography, *We*.

We recounted Lindbergh's earlier adventures, such as barnstorming from town to town in his open-cockpit biplane, offering $5 sightseeing flights, dropping straw-filled dummies from his plane, or even standing on a wing while a copilot flew.

Lindbergh (whose grandfather was also a tool-loving tinkerer, an Army colonel, and a town father) wrote with muted beauty of the bird's-eye perspective: "The fog broke into patches. . . . Numerous shorelines appeared, with trees perfectly outlined against the horizon." His book sold like few before it; within a month of its release in 1927, two hundred thousand copies had been sold, and for years it remained the nation's most widely read book.

Shepard was only three when Lindbergh's plane was spotted by the crowds outside Paris on May 21, 1927, at the end of his spectacular nonstop journey from New York. Though Shepard was not in the crowd the day Lindbergh and his *Spirit of St. Louis* swooped low over Elm Street in nearby Manchester at the start of a historic cross-country victory tour, Lindbergh's celebrity carried over well into Shepard's teenage years. A *Literary Digest* survey found in 1938 that eight-year-old girls wanted to grow up to be movie stars while boys wanted to be cowboys, army officers, or aviators. In a way, Shepard wanted to be an amalgam of all three, but it was Lindbergh first and foremost who inspired the dozens of balsa-wood, rubber-band-powered model airplanes dangling from his bedroom ceiling.

"He was always my hero," Shepard once said, never dreaming that he'd meet Lindbergh, would stand by his side the morning Apollo 11 launched to the moon. "I was just fascinated by planes. They were going somewhere. They were doing things. They were getting faster every year and they were flying higher every year."

Human flight had begun just twenty years before Shepard's birth, when the Wright brothers first caught air on December 17, 1903. A hundred more flights followed in 1904 as the bicycle makers from Ohio improved their flying machine. A witness to the flight of an aluminum-skinned Wright brothers plane described it as "a locomotive that has left the track, and is climbing up in the air right towards you." But it wasn't until Lindbergh's fame, from the late 1920s into the 1930s, that the flying machine began to more fully capture the imagination of an entire generation of boys. As Lindbergh put it, in the air "man is more than man."

Shepard's youth coincided with almost daily new feats of aviation, such as "Wrong Way" Corrigan "accidentally" landing in Ireland during his alleged attempt to reach California, and millionaire Howard Hughes circling the globe by airplane in less than four days. Still, by the late 1930s, aviation had barely reached adolescence. Race cars could still travel faster than most planes, which were still dangerous and unreliable. Will Rogers and his friend Wiley Post died in one; Amelia Earhart was lost in hers.

As Shepard followed the progress and developments of aviation, he gravitated toward boys doing the same, and in time created the Airplane Model Club. Like him, they were boys who read Lindbergh and built model airplanes that dangled in their bedrooms. Shepard was intensely loyal to his fraternity and invited them often into his grandmother's basement, which became their clubhouse, where his grandfather's wood shop provided heaps of scrap wood and cool-to-the-touch tools to cut and drill the struts and rudders of their model airplanes. Beneath a hanging bare lightbulb, the boys glued together strips of balsa wood, wrapped them in tissue paper, and painted the fuselages.

One member of the club, Al Deale, actually owned a boy-sized, homemade glider, which he kept in a dark corner of his father's barn. Deale resisted frequent pleas from Shepard and other classmates to fly the thing, but Shepard was more persistent than the others. He nagged and nagged until Deale finally relented one Saturday morning.

Shepard took the glider to a hill behind the Moynihan boys' house and bolted the two wood-framed, canvas-covered wings to the fuselage, also built of thin wood strips sheathed in off-white canvas. Shepard stepped into the narrow cockpit and pulled straps over his shoulders, so the entire rig hung around him like a crude hang glider. He sprinted down the hill, and just as he jumped a few inches off the ground a zephyr of wind caught one wing and flipped the glider upside down, sending him tumbling into the grass. The lightweight wood cracked and splintered all around him, and the canvas ripped to shreds. Sixty-plus years later, Deale was still a little ticked off at the memory of what remained: "matchsticks."

Throughout his life, if Alan Shepard wanted something, he rarely worried about the consequences. Astronaut colleagues would similarly feel stung by Shepard's me-first attitude, especially his determination to get space flights—at their expense.

///

Six months after his glider flight, in early 1938, Shepard entered the lobby of Manchester Municipal Airport for the first time. For his Christmas present the previous year, he had asked for a *real* airplane ride, and his mother was making good.

While waiting for the flight, Shepard walked curiously through the cross-shaped Art Deco building with a steel-and-glass control tower that looked like a British telephone booth sticking up above the roof. It had been just ten years since the tiny airport had hosted its first commercial flight. The airport had been built at a time when thousands of runways were being paved into the nation's farms and fields.

Until the early 1930s, the majority of planes flying in and out of those airports had carried either mail sacks or military men. Not until the post-Depression years, when manufacturers began adding cushioned seats and carpeting and airlines started serving meals, did the general public begin paying—often exorbitant amounts—to ride a flying bus. By the time Shepard prepared to board his first flight, the airlines had learned a few tricks to attract more customers. They started serving hot meals and had learned that dark carpeting on the floor gave passengers a feeling of strength and security, while light-colored ceilings and walls evoked airiness and freedom.

The young commercial aviation industry was becoming profitable, too, thanks to a wide-bodied plane with plush seats and plenty of legroom that, after its introduction in 1936, soon became the most impressive airplane of its day. The DC-3 established itself as the first workhorse of passenger aviation. It could carry twenty-eight people, and on long flights the seats folded down into beds. The Douglas Aircraft Company (whose future partner, McDonnell Aircraft, would one day build Shepard's space capsule) had found just the right balance of interior colors to prevent airsickness. The DC-3 hosted the first cross-country flights, during which chicken Kiev was served on fine china. Flying was still largely an indulgence of the rich, but as Amelia Earhart put it shortly before her disappearance, an "inventor's dream" had in a few short decades become an "everyday actuality."

As he walked up the rear drop-down DC-3 staircase that day, into the cabin, and up the aisle, Shepard must have felt like he was walking through the nave of a holy place. He claimed years later that as the half-full DC-3 became airborne and rose slowly above southern New Hampshire—above the geometry of stone walls and the shimmer of the Merrimack River—he thought dreamily of a poem Mrs. Wiggins had compelled him to memorize: "The Swing," Robert Louis Stevenson's account of a boy on a swing who imagines he is flying: *Up in the air and over the wall / Till I can see so wide / River and trees and cattle and all / Over the countryside.*

It took less than half an hour to reach Boston, but Shepard's face never left the square window. It was a crystallizing moment, and years later he'd realize how that short ride confirmed everything he'd previously imagined about flying—the gut-flopping sensation when the wheels left the tarmac, the ecstasy of traveling at such speeds, the giddy half terrors of descending for a landing.

At Logan Airport the Shepards got right back in line, boarded another plane—another twin-engine, Douglas-built DC-3—and flew home. Two halves of an hour in the sky was a rare and generous adventure for a fourteen-year-old boy in 1938. Lindbergh once described what Shepard must have felt that exhilarating day: that he had tasted "a wine of the gods of which they"—the poor suckers on the ground—"could know nothing." In a plane, Lindbergh tried to explain, a man "explored the cloud canyons he had gazed at as a child. Adventure lay in each puff of wind." Shepard had gone someplace that, it's safe to say, few if any boys in East Derry had gone. From that day forth Shepard simply knew that he wanted to—*needed* to—fly airplanes.

As his father drove home that day, Shepard sat quietly in the backseat, ruminating. A few weeks later, while sitting in Nanzie's kitchen, he told his grandmother about a plan he'd worked out.

It was twelve miles to Manchester Airport, he had calculated. But the route was hilly—too hilly for his clunky old one-speed bike. If he had one of those new English bikes, the kind with variable gears, he could make the trip easily. Then he could watch as mail planes, military cargo planes, and sleek and silvery DC-3s launched and landed.

Despite her industrious husband's heavy losses in the Depression, Nanzie was still a wealthy woman and could have purchased for Alan the fanciest bike in New England. But being a model New Englander who saved pieces of string, paper bags, and cellophane, instead of buying the bike she offered her grandson some chickens. If he wanted a bike, he'd have to work for it, she told him.

Nanzie fronted Shepard the cash for fourteen Rhode Island Red chickens and a rooster. His father then pitched in and bought chicken feed and a water trough. Shepard dutifully fed and tended the chickens, and by the fall of 1938 he was selling eggs at twenty-nine cents a dozen. Shepard would forever credit Nanzie for the talent he'd one day discover to make a whole lot more money.

Shepard finally got his bike on February 15, 1939, exactly a year after his round-trip flight to Boston. Heedless of the snow mounds and cold outside, he began riding the bike immediately, bundled in winter clothes and slip-sliding on ice, and in two weeks had already traveled a hundred miles.

On Sunday, February 19, 1939, he made his first bike trip to Manchester Airport.

///

Carl Park had a youthful energy that school and sports couldn't quite satisfy. He often skipped his classes and caught rides from the barnstormers—World War I–trained flyers who traveled the country in cast-off military planes—who touched down in the fields outside his hometown of Lewiston, Maine. Park was smitten by the derring-do lifestyle of those pilots, who—like Lindbergh—scratched out a living by giving rides, taking aerial photographs, performing stunts at air shows, and creating a new method of advertising: writing the names of products or businesses in smoke. The lure proved too strong, and Park quit school and began playing drums in a jazz band to earn money for flying lessons. That led to a job with a traveling orchestra; Park gave flying lessons during the day, then flew off to a gig somewhere in New England at night. One of his flying students was a textile worker named Rene Gagnon, who in World War II would be photographed with five other Marines hoisting an American flag atop Iwo Jima.

Park eventually found a job at Manchester Airport and by the late 1930s was managing the place. He slept there, and at night when he heard a plane approach, he would run upstairs in his underwear to the control tower to switch on the runway lights.

Small airports like Manchester's became magnets for flight-smitten boys, aspiring aviation mechanics, and veterans of World War I's limited air fleets, leather-jacketed men looking for work as instructors. On weekends the hillside along Manchester's two runways was crowded with local boys and their bicycles, a spellbound audience for the various take-offs and landings of single-engine Piper Cubs, dual-wing stunt planes, and—the best show in town—the long and bulbous DC-3s.

After a few weeks on the hillside, Shepard began loitering around the tarmac, which is where Park found him one Saturday. "What do you want, son?" Park asked him.

Shepard told Park that he didn't have any money but he wanted to learn how to fly. Park sensed that Shepard was "a good kid," and fell for his "great big grin." He offered Shepard a deal: If he wanted to help wipe down the airplanes and keep the hangars clean, Park would give him a couple of flying lessons in lieu of pay.

The lessons were informal—more like free rides with a few pointers thrown in—but Park recalled that when he began letting Shepard take the control sticks, in no time Shepard had a feel for keeping the plane level. There is no comparable earth-bound exercise—except maybe sailing—that can prepare someone for flying, and many students learn the hard way that they have no aptitude for flight. Some get airsick, their bodies unable to reconcile the imprecise relationship with gravity. Others find the lack of visual cues—ground, walls, ceilings, and such—so disconcerting as to induce vertigo. And many can't wrap their head around the counterintuitiveness of flight, how it's safer to fly fast and high than slow and low, how the best way to save an out-of-control plane is to point the nose straight toward the ground. Instructors tell their students right from the start to distrust their earthly instincts, to resist common sense. Flying, as one 1930s pilot-writer noted, "has no similes in our life on the ground."

But Shepard seemed to have no difficulties in learning how to fly an airplane like an airplane, not like a car or a horse or a bike or a sailboat. Maybe all the model airplanes of his youth embedded in his brain some intuitive sense of the characteristics of a wing. Or maybe his sailing talents afforded him some extra knowledge of the wind. Whatever it was, Carl Park noticed from the start that Shepard was "a natural."

In time Shepard was working so hard around the airport to pay for his next ride that Park expanded his duties from just cleaning the planes to helping the mechanics change spark plugs and repair fuel lines. Shepard considered himself the airfield's "fix-it kid." Park even let Shepard taxi planes from one part of the field to another.

The leap from passenger to pilot is an immensely empowering one. Most adults can recall receiving their driver's license and feeling the newfound freedom of driving wherever you want, whenever you want. In a plane, the freedom is many times more profound than in a car. There is no road, no speed limit, no barriers, no earthly restrictions . . . it is the freedom of the birds.

Shepard was enthralled, swooping down over his town in the passenger seat of a single-propeller, high-winged Voyager or Reliant, the predominant private planes of the day. When Park let him take the controls and Shepard held that stick, he knew he was hooked. Shepard loved to be in control—of people, of situations, of himself. But in a plane, he was in control of everything: of up and down, of the entire world beneath him. One twitch of the control stick, and the whole world tilted. A slight, slow pull on the stick and the world disappeared, unveiling nothing but sky and space and clouds—nothing and yet everything.

New Hampshire produced a few home-brewed aviators of note in those early decades of human flight. Manchester Airport had been christened in 1927, with its first landing and takeoff by Robert S. Fogg, who that summer delivered mail twice daily to Vermont towns marooned by a massive flood. By 1940, just two years after Shepard's first lessons, the airport would be renamed Grenier Airport, in honor of a daring Army Air Corps pilot from Manchester, Jean Grenier, who was killed in 1934 while scouting a dangerous new airmail route across the Rocky Mountains of

Utah. New Hampshire also produced a daredevil named Carmeno Onofrio, who once landed his J-3 Cub, outfitted with skis instead of wheels, fourteen times in one day on the snow-covered peak of 6,288-foot Mount Washington, known for clocking two-hundred-mile-an-hour winds.

But even more profound feats would soon be performed by the men who'd replace Lindbergh as Shepard's driving inspiration: the aviators of World War II.

///

On September 1, 1939, as Shepard began his last year of high school, German soldiers—having already occupied Czechoslovakia—marched into Poland. Hitler had already allied himself with Italy and the Soviet Union, which would become his partners in the Nazi dictator's subsequent trouncing of the better part of Europe.

At the Shepard household, Alan's father began discussing some options for college the following year. Alan had managed to find his place at Pinkerton and had studied hard, and by his senior year he ranked eighth in his class of fifty-five, with all A's or B's except for a C in French. With the escalation of war in Europe, Bart strongly suggested that his son consider the Army's military academy at West Point. It was free, and it would perpetuate a proud heritage of Shepards in the Army. Besides, with the growing likelihood that America would someday join the fighting overseas, Alan might have the chance to do what many Shepards had done before him—to serve his country on the battlefield.

Bart was the type of guy that newspaper columnist Ernie Pyle would call, admiringly, a grunt. He believed in the ethos of the dogface soldier, which he'd been in World War I. But to Alan, the Army life seemed dirty and degrading. Alan loved his father and respected his simple New Hampshire lifestyle, but he had no interest in the Army soldier's life. Alan knew all too well that the United States would likely soon join the war. He saw it at

Manchester Airport, whose runways were becoming busy with military cargo planes. Indeed, before long, the Army would take over Manchester Airport, nudging aside Alan's instructor friend Carl Park as it turned the place into a sprawling military air base.

In the coming conflict the Army would be no place for an aspiring pilot. Thanks to a $2 billion infusion from President Roosevelt, the Navy was buying thousands of planes and training pilots for previously unthinkable feats. They had been welding flight decks atop ships, and Navy pilots were taking off from and landing on these wildly dangerous makeshift landing strips. In the mid-1930s the Navy began building a new generation of aircraft carriers, an entirely new type of ship whose sole purpose was to serve as a floating runway for pilots crazy enough to attempt such risky landings. The Navy was becoming *the* place to fly.

One Sunday in late 1939, Alan's uncle Fritz came to visit and—picking up on the disagreement between Bart and Alan over West Point—suggested Alan consider the U.S. Naval Academy. Alan immediately saw the perfection of his uncle's suggestion. In the Navy he could indulge both his love of the water and, more importantly, his love of the air.

The decision to allow his son to pursue the Navy instead of the Army must have weighed heavily on Bart. Yet at some point he realized: Maybe he would not have a colonel for a son, and a long-established tradition of Shepard men as Army officers would cease, but then again, maybe he would someday have an admiral for a son.

In 1940 Alan notched the second-highest score in New Hampshire on the Naval Academy's preliminary exam. But because he had skipped *two* elementary-school grades, the family learned that, at sixteen, Alan was too young for the academy. Rather than alter their course, they sent Alan for a year to Admiral Farragut Academy, a military prep school in New Jersey. Bart wasn't taking any chances. He wrote to Farragut's superintendent: "Appreciate you putting more pressure on him to study."

After a year at Farragut, Shepard was ordered to report to Annapolis.

When he arrived there, on June 19, 1941, he was again among the smallest in the class. And at seventeen he was again one of the youngest. Though he had been something of a self-sufficient loner in East Derry, he had also been surrounded by family and friends and was never truly alone. Now, as he found himself suddenly thrown in among bigger and older young men, Shepard embarked on a difficult transformation from gangly teen to naval officer—a transformation that, from the start, he seemed almost intent on sabotaging.

2

"I think I love you"

Teams of uniformed, rock-faced upperclassmen ushered Shepard into his new world, a regimented and hierarchical military domain for which he was ill-prepared.

The U.S. Navy had first attempted to create a training academy in 1842 aboard a Brooklyn-based training ship, the American Brig *Somers*. But during the inaugural cruise a student and two enlisted sailors rebelled against their strict captain, were found guilty of mutiny, and were hanged. The Navy decided to replace its floating school with a land-based one, which it built beside the remote fishing village of Annapolis, Maryland, where students—called midshipmen—would be taught far from the distractions of city life.

From the start, in 1845, the U.S. Naval Academy was an institution where no rebellion or insubordination would be tolerated. Its founders never again resorted to hanging, but the plan—"to develop midshipmen morally, mentally, and physically," the founders said—was, bluntly put, to create hardened officers by first breaking their will.

The Naval Academy's spectacular, ivy-covered gray granite buildings, most of them built in the sturdy but elegant French Renaissance style, occupied a picturesque stretch of waterfront along the Severn River, which flowed into nearby Chesapeake Bay. Separated from Annapolis by a ten-foot stone wall, the grounds were known as the Yard. The academy looked like a pastoral Ivy League college campus except for the occasional military cannon or war hero's statue. Beneath a copper-domed chapel lay the body of John Paul Jones, and midshipmen quickly learned the words to an irreverent song about how Jones "lies around all day, body pickled in alcohol."

More than three thousand midshipmen lived in one of the world's largest dormitories—Bancroft Hall, known as "Mother B." When Shepard arrived, construction crews were adding yet another wing to the imposing granite building, which would soon house five miles of hallways and nearly two thousand rooms—so big that Bancroft Hall would eventually earn its own zip code.

In a tradition of antagonistic first-day routines honed across the school's first century, upperclassmen subjected the incoming class to a torrent of insults, screams, put-downs, and various other forms of physical and emotional abuse. For starters, freshmen are known as "plebes." The term comes from the Roman word *pleb*, which means "crude, low, vulgar."

In Shepard's first hours as a plebe, upperclassmen marched him through dank basement hallways from one orientation checkpoint to another. After an exhaustive physical exam, Shepard was told to strip off his coat and tie and was issued a stack of new uniforms—the clothes he'd wear each day until Christmas. They taught him how to salute, then screamed in his face when he did it wrong. After hustling him into a barber's chair, his hair was unceremoniously shaved down to a stubble. Shepard was then taught how to adopt the subservient posture of the plebe—back straight, chin down, and "eyes in the boat," meaning that plebes were to keep their eyes straight ahead, never making eye contact with upperclassmen.

Finally, after a long day of insults and indoctrination, Shepard stood in his white pajamalike plebe uniform, sweating amid rows of fellow plebes, and raised his right hand, promising to "support and defend the Constitution."

Some of the rules weren't difficult, just annoying. Shepard and his fellow plebes were ordered to call all upperclassmen "mister" or "sir"—and to become their servants. Plebes scrambled each morning to spit-shine their black shoes, to make their beds so a coin could bounce off the taut blanket, and, while getting dressed, to memorize the day's meals so they could recite a "chow call"—that is, stand in the hall barking out the menu of the day for the benefit of their elders. Just getting to and from class carried its own set of rules: Plebes had to march down the center of the hallway, "square" each corner with perfect right-angle turns, and slam their backs against the wall and salute when upperclassmen approached. Plebes had to always be aware of how many days there were until graduation day; seniors would demand without warning to know the number, and those who failed had to drop and do forty-five push-ups (because they were the Class of '45).

There was no escape from the small cruelties of plebe life, not even at mealtime, which plebes dreaded. In the cafeteria, plebes served the upper-class midshipmen first. When they sat down to eat, plebes had to sit only on the front few inches of their chair and eat only one bite at a time, chewing and swallowing it before taking another bite. Every now and then, a senior midshipman might yell, "Fire in the paint locker," and the plebes would have to dive under the table and cower as upperclassmen dumped water, ketchup, or milk on them to douse the imaginary fire.

When Shepard was forced to dive under the table, he often tried to smear butter on his protagonists' shiny-clean shoes, in a typical Shepard prank.

Plebes learned the hard way that breaking academy rules could hurt worse than all the memorizing and protocol. While most plebes felt some of the hallowed traditions and rules were silly and useless, few were impudent enough to defy them. Shepard was among those who at times resisted.

One day, a few months into the fall semester, an upperclassman found him yelling out of a second-floor window in Bancroft Hall. Shepard was ordered to shut his mouth and return to his room. He complied, waited until the upperclassman had disappeared down the hall, then went back to the window and began yelling again to his friend. The upperclassman heard him, returned, and punished Shepard with repeated smacks in the ass with a wood-soled shower sandal. Other upperclassmen recalled numerous instances of swatting Shepard in the backside with a broom, making him do push-ups, or forcing him to "shove out," which required a plebe to sit on an invisible chair, his back against the wall, knees bent, until his thighs screamed.

Some upperclassmen who took seriously their job of reshaping plebes found it difficult to make much of a dent in Shepard. For one thing, he'd already, in his own way, been shaped—Shepard had withstood plenty of military protocol from his father. Second, Shepard had the temperament of a mule, refusing to tremble and cower like some of the other plebes. "As an Army brat, conforming to academy procedures was natural—at least Alan made it appear so," his classmate Bob Kirk once remarked.

What troubled some of the upperclassmen, though, was that he didn't seem to take any of it too seriously. Friends called him "Shep" or "Schimpf" (a classmate's young niece's mispronunciation of "Shep," which Shepard and his new friends found hilarious). "Full of piss and vinegar" is how Dick Sewall remembers Shepard, who was three years his junior. Shepard was "pretty crafty," Sewall said, and he often found routes around the academy's rules. Sometimes Shepard would get caught and punished, but half the time he'd talk his way out of it, and Sewall would agree not to report him. Instead of openly resenting his superiors, Shepard had a way of befriending them, adopting them as his allies and protectors. When they did chew him out, he would just smirk. One classmate called Shepard "ratey," an academy moniker for someone who acts as if he rated better than the rest. "He was supposed to be subservient to his master and he was not."

One annoying duty forced upon plebes was waking thirty minutes before the upperclassmen and walking quietly into the older boys' rooms to shut windows so that they wouldn't be too cold when they awoke. One morning Shepard organized a small rebellion—he and a few other plebes stole the left shoe of every upperclassman and hid them in a bathroom. When the firsties learned Shepard was the ringleader, they made him bend over and grab his ankles while they took turns with a broom.

"But he didn't get broken by it," Sewall said. "He was thinking: *Next time I just won't get caught.*"

///

At the time—the late summer of 1941—the two-year-old war in Europe had crept steadily closer to America's shores and minds. German submarines, or U-boats, were sinking British ships in the Atlantic Ocean, and the U.S. Navy had begun patrolling through the Atlantic and Caribbean, searching for German subs and escorting convoys of merchant ships and war supplies across to Europe. Day by day, as Hitler's aggressions stomped further across Europe and then out into the seas, it was becoming obvious that America couldn't wait on the sidelines much longer. Indeed, the United States' alignment with and support of England had put it essentially in an undeclared war with Germany. Shepard and his classmates knew it was just a matter of time before their nation headed to battle, and that they'd play a part in the fight.

Finally, on October 31, 1941, Germany sunk its first U.S. ship—a torpedo that split open a Navy escort ship, the USS *Reuben James*. More than a hundred men died—"Tell me, what were their names?" Woody Guthrie wrote in a tribute song— marking the first U.S. Navy ship to be sunk in the escalating, ex- panding war. Meanwhile, Japan had begun snatching pieces of coastal China and numerous volcanic islands across Indochina, leading to increased frictions between Japan and the United States, which responded with an oil embargo that infuriated the oil-hungry Japanese military machine.

Such escalations soon began to touch Shepard's life at the Naval Academy. On November 29, as German panzer divisions marched steadily toward Moscow, Shepard and his classmates rode a train to Philadelphia for the annual Army-Navy football game. Before ninety-eight thousand fans, Navy beat Army 14–6, capping a 7–1–1 season under coach "Swede" Larson, a major with the Marines. Right after the game, Larson resigned as coach and rejoined the Marines, proclaiming: "There's a bigger game, a bigger battle coming up and I'm going to be in it." A week later, on a lazy Sunday morning, Admiral Husband Kimmel and his fleet of ships at Pearl Harbor were caught completely unpre- pared for Japan's surprise attack. At the academy, the superin- tendent interrupted a tea party with the football team to take a phone call. He returned ashen-faced, closed the doors to the ballroom, and said, "Gentlemen, we are at war."

The news immediately charged the atmosphere of the Yard. Officers strapped on pistol holsters, and the ranks of midship- men buzzed with talk of battle.

The next day President Roosevelt announced that the "day of infamy" at Pearl Harbor put America undeniably at war with Japan. When America's declaration of war was announced over the academy's loudspeakers that afternoon, deafening cheers echoed through the corridors of Bancroft Hall. That was followed by the announcement that the Navy had decided to pull Shepard and his classmates into the imminent conflict by lopping a year off their four-year academic lives. Graduation would be moved up to 1944, and the news further electrified the Yard.

As one classmate put it: "This was war and we had to hurry out to get at least a small share of it for ourselves." Many were ecstatic that their warrior days were nigh. Said one to a reporter: "Hey, that's why we were all there."

But some of Shepard's classmates had to wonder why he was there. For his country? For the war? For the boats? His father? Shepard meandered through his first year at Annapolis and by the start of his sophomore year nine months later was languishing among the bottom-dwellers of his class. Friends and teachers considered him a remarkably smart young man, quick to grasp the most complex of lessons and capable of anything he leaned his head into. At Farragut he had impressed teachers with a 145 score on an IQ test. But through his plebe year at the academy, his head was rarely buried in books. He preferred *Esquire* magazine's special "Annapolis Issue," with sexy photos of Rita Hayworth, an article on "what young naval officers should know about the art of swinging a cocktail shaker," and a cartoon of a topless woman in front of a mirror speaking to her friend: "That midshipman I go with adores slim blondes. Loan me your girdle and hand me that peroxide."

Shepard kept *Esquire* in his footlocker atop his airplane magazines, with pictures of Mitsubishi Zeros and Supermarine Spitfires and "The Story of the Flying Tigers: Japs Are Their Specialty." Instead of his studies, he seemed to work hardest on matters involving women or water.

Shepard found that his childhood love of aquatic sports— sailing, rowing, swimming—served him well at a waterfront school with an armada of sailboats and rowboats. At Annapolis he quickly became a standout sailor, winning many races and even a regatta series at the hoity-toity Annapolis Yacht Club. He methodically learned to sail every type of boat the school owned—small knockabouts, fourteen-foot dinghies, eighteen-foot sloops, and the spectacular ninety-foot schooner *Freedom*. Then, at the start of his second year, called "youngster" year, he signed up to race the school's eight-man sculling boats as part of the crew team. It was a bold move, and more than a few friends scoffed because Shepard would be competing for a spot on the team against rowers six inches taller and thirty pounds heavier. Still, he spent long hours on the rowing machines in the gym, packing on the muscle and increasing his stamina, and eventually made the crew team.

But in the classroom, he showed no such determination, nor any of the intellectual curiosity that had helped him skip two grades back in East Derry. Midshipmen were graded on a scale of 0 to 4, with grades below 2.5 considered deficient. Many of Shepard's grades were between 2.5 and 3.1, barely above that line, and sometimes he dropped below it. In Spanish he had received a 2.37 in the spring of his plebe year; foreign-language classes had dogged him since high school, where French was his only sub-85 grade. In the fall of 1942 he earned another deficiency, a 2.44 in his combined English, history, and government class, called EHG.

In addition to poor grades, Shepard was accumulating conduct demerits for breaking the strict rules of behavior and decorum. By the end of his plebe year he had racked up forty-nine demerits—a large number for a freshman—for infractions such as unshined shoes or being out of uniform. He earned another twenty-two through the fall of 1942, although he managed to talk his way out of many more than that.

By late 1942 Shepard ranked 676th in his class of 1,000. Academics had usually come easy to him; rarely had Shepard struggled like this. Finally he was called before an academic board to discuss his substandard performance. In a subsequent report the board noted that his poor grades made Shepard eligible for "reassignment." That is, he could be dropped from the academy and sent to the Navy fleet—to war.

Shepard knew all too well what that meant. A tuition-free academy education wasn't a free ride. Graduates had to "pay" for the education with five years of service as a naval officer. If they failed to graduate, they'd repay their debt as an enlisted sailor. He'd become just some swab aboard some ship—an anonymous sailor among hundreds of other sailors. And his dreams of flying would be dashed. That day, though, the academic board decided to give Shepard another chance. He had until the end of the academic year—the spring of 1943—to bring up his grades, improve his behavior, and basically get his shit together.

If not, he'd be expelled and shipped to the Navy, which at the time was fighting dozens of bloody battles against Japanese-held islands in the South Pacific.

///

Surprisingly, even the threat of expulsion didn't at first impede one of Shepard's most diligent extracurricular pursuits.

The historic, cove-front fishing town of Annapolis (also Maryland's state capital) was known to midshipmen as "Crabtown." Its women were "crabs" or "crabbies," and the town was teeming with them. As if making up for lost time, Shepard discovered what he'd been missing in high school. And, he learned in Annapolis, he had a knack for it.

Because midshipmen weren't allowed to have cars, the only escape was by foot. Shepard would wait until after lights-out, then sneak out of Bancroft Hall and down to the southern tip of campus. There a bulkhead held back Spa Creek and it was possible to edge carefully around the ten-foot stone wall that encircled the campus. Generations of midshipmen called it going "over the wall." Doing it once was considered a rite of passage, but Shepard made a habit of it. Afterward he'd sneak back into his room, well past midnight, and slip into bed. One night an upperclassman was waiting for him and tacked another few demerits onto Shepard's record.

"He always had some chick he thought was worth the risk," said upperclassman Dick Sewall, who wrote up a number of Shepard's so-called frap sheets; in midshipman-speak, someone busted going over the wall was "frapped" or "fried." Sewall admitted, though, that he often fell for Shepard's diplomatic pleas for leniency and, as one of Shepard's patron saints, ripped up a few of Shepard's frap sheets.

Midway through sophomore year, a year's worth of push-ups and early-morning exercises, which were everyday chores of academy life, had helped fill out Shepard's wiry frame. He was still slender and would remain so his whole life. But with a bit of extra muscle, he now carried himself not as a boy but as a full-chested, strong-armed man.

That physical maturity, combined with a precocious self-confidence, contributed to a reputation with women that absolutely amazed his classmates. And Shepard learned how to position himself in all the right social situations: He religiously volunteered to serve on the committees that organized the academy's dances and hops.

Shepard never missed a school dance and, on weekends and nights off, attended dances or parties in town as well. If he didn't already have a "crab"—also called a "drag"—by his side, he would by night's end. He seemed so at ease around women, able to walk right up to a young lady and almost disarm them with a social grace that made him seem older than his nineteen years. Classmate Bob Kirk said Shepard had "a facility for creating the impression of instant friendship." Shepard once boasted to friends of a girl he met during a weekend trip back home and how he infuriated his father by leaving two sets of muddy footprints in Bart's car—on the ceiling. Kirk said Shepard "appreciated the better things in life" and was "almost as facile (with) the young ladies as he was managing to evade the duty officer's search for would-be jitterbuggers."

Shepard's roommate, Bob Williams, "was in awe of him . . . he processed a lot of women." But during the Christmas holidays of 1942, during a brief trip to the nation's heartland, Shepard would meet the woman who eclipsed any of Annapolis' crabbies.

///

Due to wartime travel restrictions, Alan's sister, Polly, couldn't make it home to New Hampshire for Christmas break that year, so Alan decided to visit her at Principia College, a college for Christian Scientists outside St. Louis, where she was a freshman. He planned to spend the first half of his Christmas break with Polly, then travel back to East Derry. Hopping a Navy cargo plane, he arrived in St. Louis on a Friday night in time for dinner. After dinner, he and Polly walked to Principia's field house, which blinked and glittered with decorations for the annual Christmas dance, with streamers of blue and gold (also the Naval Academy's school colors) hanging from basketball hoops, twinkling lights on a potted pine tree.

Within minutes of entering the room he spotted Louise Brewer, standing with friends across the gym floor. The routine had become second nature for him: quickly sweep the room, find the prettiest girl, make a beeline. But rarely had the prettiest girl looked like this. "Who's that girl over there?" he asked Polly, who told him not to waste his time chasing Louise Brewer, who was beautiful, popular—and had a steady boyfriend. But Alan, looking fit and slim in his dark blue uniform, feeling confident and strong from his early-morning exercises, persisted. Boyfriend or not, he wanted to meet the girl with the narrow waist, long brown hair, and wonderful, radiant face.

At a glance, it'd be hard to call Alan the handsomest in the room; he had a long face, and everything on it was just a bit too pronounced—the eyes, the ears, and the enormous smile, framed by dimples, with his teeth slightly askew. But he had developed a grace, a way of carrying himself, chin up and out, that caught people's eye.

Louise's boyfriend, it turned out, had traveled home for the holidays, so she sat talking with Alan most of the night. Alan told her about life at Annapolis, his childhood in the snowy New England hills, his plans to someday fly airplanes. Louise spoke of her own childhood as a "VIP kid" at Longwood Gardens—a sprawling estate southeast of Philadelphia, owned by chemical baron Pierre S. DuPont, where her father ran the maintenance department. She had a great laugh and was full of confidence and poise. They danced nearly every dance, and met again two days later at a Sunday night Tea Sing at the chapel, where they stood side by side singing carols.

Louise Brewer could easily have been mistaken for Rita Hayworth's younger sister. She had luxurious hair, perfect teeth, and a long, sensuous neck. She was virginal and sexy at the same time. And there was something else—something ethereal about her composure that, Alan would learn, made many men worship her from afar.

Alan joined the club of worshipers, and on Monday's train ride toward Boston he kept thinking of Louise's green eyes and elegant smile. She wasn't like the others he'd dated. She seemed so much more sophisticated than the crabs back at Annapolis.

His parents picked him up in Boston, and he told them all about Louise Brewer on the car ride north. As soon as he got home, he sat at the desk in his room to write a letter in which he boldly invited her to his Ring Dance in June, a highlight of Naval Academy life. That note would be the first in an effusive, sometimes emotional exchange of letters that would continue between Alan and Louise for the next two years.

///

Louise was born, like Alan, in the upstairs bedroom of her parents' house. Her parents, like Renza Shepard, were devoted Christian Scientists who served as "readers" conducting Sunday services at the church in nearby Wilmington, Delaware.

Louise's parents, Russell (called Phil) and Julia, were known as "pensioners" on the DuPont family's Longwood estate. Pensioners tended the estate's sprawl of farms and fountains, gardens and greenhouses. In return they received free housing and many other kindnesses from Pierre and Alice DuPont.

With profits from his family's growing chemical empire, Pierre S. DuPont bought the undulating farmland in 1906 and transformed it into a tribute to nature and beauty. Modeled after French and Italian gardens he had visited, the estate featured water gardens, reflecting pools, a conservatory, and numerous hydraulic-powered fountains, which Phil Brewer helped design and build. In the conservatory, a colorful, sometimes drunken group of master gardeners from England and Ireland grew oranges, pineapples, espaliered nectarines, cantaloupes, and, in a special greenhouse, orchids.

Longwood's hierarchy resembled that of a coal mining town or, in some eyes, a plantation—a self-sustaining community with its own dairy farm and schools, where workers' families lived entirely beholden to their benefactor, DuPont. But the Brewers had it better than most. As superintendent of maintenance, Phil Brewer was one of five department heads—essentially vice presidents—and grew to become one of DuPont's closest advisers, as much a friend as an employee. The Brewers lived in the largest of the pensioners' houses, a large stone manse called the Anvil, which was built especially for them on a secluded corner of the estate. Hundreds of other pensioners, meanwhile, lived down on Red Lion Row, a lane of duplexes built for workers' families.

Louise and her sister, Adele, enjoyed a sometimes magical childhood, witnesses on the fringe of a modern mini Versailles. As daughters of a department head—or "VIP girls"—they received special attentions, such as the dresses Mrs. DuPont bought them in Europe. Louise and Adele attended lavish balls in the glass-encased conservatory, where twelve hundred guests watched ballet and fireworks. At one such party, John Philip Sousa's band performed; at another, nymphs danced in the water garden.

For Louise, it was a conflicted life—she was both the hired help and the inner circle. She mixed with other pensioners' children during the day and at night she mingled with dignitaries or royalty at DuPont dinner parties and concerts. A highlight of the year was the Christmas party. Families lined up in the conservatory to receive their annual gift from the DuPonts; the kids usually received one piece of clothing and one toy. But the Brewers didn't have to line up; they were seated in the balcony of the conservatory when the other families arrived. Each year they received gifts of fine china.

Phil Brewer was a severe, dough-faced man who worked obsessively long hours on Longwood's fountains, leaving the girls mostly in the care of their mother, who dressed her two daughters in identical outfits.

Louise struggled to accommodate what she called her "tomboy streak" and once complained of the difficulties in "being a girl and knowing you can't do all the things boys do." Longwood beckoned like a sprawling playground, with fruit orchards, farm animals, ponds, and fountains. Her sister, Adele, befriended the other Longwood kids (and once created a stir when she became involved with one of the farmhands), but Louise often stuck to herself and, in the other kids' eyes, was cold and standoffish. In fact, some people at first thought she *was* a DuPont, so sophisticated and superior.

When she arrived at Principia, her chilly demeanor earned

her the nicknames "Frosty" and, after the refrigerator brand, "Miss Westinghouse." But there was one classmate who didn't mind—Louise's boyfriend, George Dietz.

A boy whom Alan Shepard now considered his rival.

///

For Alan, the holiday glow of his meeting with Louise dimmed suddenly, awfully. On Sunday, just two days after Christmas, the Shepards received terrible news from Bart's brother, Fritz.

Alan's cousin Eric had been killed in a plane crash during Marine Air Corps training. It was ruled an accident, although some family members whispered that he may have been hotdogging, taking chances in a machine he wasn't yet ready to tame.

Eric was twenty-four and had been eager to join the war. After graduating from the University of Maine, he had joined the Marine Corps and signed up for flight training. He wanted to help other Marine pilots strafe and bomb Japanese ships in the Pacific islands, where the Marines were beginning to turn the tide of the war. Eric had been more than Alan's favorite cousin; he was Alan's hero. They'd been good friends despite a five-year age difference. Alan's spunk seemed the perfect complement to Eric's quiet serenity. Except for his grandfather, Alan had never lost someone so close to him—a rare thing in a family half consisting of Christian Scientists, whose preference for prayer over medicine could sometimes lead to early, unexpected death.

Eric's death struck Alan a severe blow. He knew war was a dangerous and deadly game, and he knew to expect the mounting casualties to begin hitting closer to home. But not this close, and not in this way. If an enemy attack had taken his cousin's life, it might have somehow been easier—he'd have someone to blame. A training accident, though, seemed all the more senseless and wasteful. Alan was deeply troubled and confused by Eric's death. He sent a telegraph to Annapolis asking for permission to extend his holiday leave and attend his cousin's funeral.

Eric was buried in Massachusetts the day after New Year's, and Alan wept openly at the service. Then he endured a miserable train ride back to Annapolis.

Until that time, Alan's year and a half at the U.S. Naval Academy had been unimpressive; he'd even been threatened with expulsion. His most notable achievements were sailing up and down the Severn River in the academy's boats and getting lucky with lovely Annapolis crabbies. But when he returned to Annapolis in January of 1943—whether it was the inspiration of his lost cousin or the promising relationship with beautiful Louise Brewer—a transformation began to churn, one that would culminate in a crucial turnaround. Alan started the spring semester with a new intensity and a gritty sense of determination. He locked in tight on two goals. First, he wanted to salvage his shabby academic record—mainly to graduate and become what his cousin Eric now could not: a military aviator. Eric's death reminded him that he was there to become a flyer.

The other goal was Louise. His desire for her wouldn't stop him from dating other women—one of them quite seriously—but he knew that ultimately he wanted Louise Brewer, and Alan would spend the next few years in a relentless pursuit of both goals.

"I hope I can really accomplish something at Annapolis that will make you proud of me," Alan wrote to his father in early 1943.

///

One of the first signs of Shepard's new sense of determination was his improving performance and rising status on the crew team. Despite an aversion to team sports, Shepard craved the knife-edged precision of rowing the sixty-foot, eight-man rowing shells. He considered the sport "an exacting one" and told a local newspaper reporter at the time that the best aspect of the sport was how "it builds your arms and chest muscles to prime shape."

But, as the shortest member of the team, a full three to four inches shorter than the others, Shepard spent his first two seasons on the freshman or junior varsity squads. He didn't yet have the strength or arm reach to make varsity. Earning a varsity letter in at least one sport was an important feat in the competitive world of the academy. Plus it was required for attendance at the senior-year Letterman's Ball.

In the spring of 1943 Shepard began lifting more weights, rowing harder in practice, doing more push-ups—intent on getting his varsity letter and inviting Louise to the ball.

The team practiced, sometimes at dawn or in the afternoons after classes, under the guidance of coach Buck Walsh, a Naval Academy graduate and an Olympic gold medalist in 1920. After a half-mile walk to the boathouse, they'd climb into their boats as Walsh's deep voice boomed through an amplified megaphone, yelling, "Pull! Pull! Pull!" When all eight men were rowing in sync, gliding across the orangey surface at sunrise, it felt as if they were actually flying above the glassy water. Rowers called such moments of synchronized rowing being "on the bubble," and at the end of practice Walsh would bark, "Let 'er run," and they'd lift their oars and coast to an exhausted stop.

Shepard began to impress Walsh with his strength and determination. What he lacked in size he compensated for with strength and quickness, and Walsh developed a special affection for the short, hardworking young man he called "Shep." Roommate Bob Williams, who rowed on the varsity squad, said Shepard initially "had no business in the varsity shell" but proved himself with "the fastest reflexes of anyone I've ever known."

Once Shepard was hospitalized a few days due to a bout of the mumps. But he wasn't about to let an annoying childhood disease slow his fight for varsity. At 2 A.M. one morning, a nurse entered Shepard's room to check on him. She found him on the floor, and it looked as if he was having some kind of attack. Her shrieks filled the academy's hospital ward until she realized what he was doing: push-ups.

"I thought it was ridiculous for him to go out for crew because he was so small," said classmate J. T. Cockrill. "He really seemed to have more drive than normal guys."

During his rigorous efforts to make the varsity squad, Shepard also started to display more openly his ego and his aggressive competitiveness. A race against Columbia University was once canceled at the last minute due to high winds that had turned the Hudson River choppy. But the two teams continued to row for practice. Shepard's boat—with just six of the eight men rowing—pulled alongside the Columbia boat, then passed it, and Shepard taunted the other team. "Look," he said, pointing at the other rowers and laughing. "We're rowing with six and we're leaving them behind." During some races he tried to psych out opponents with a Bugs Bunny impression: *Nyah . . . what's up, doc?*

"He was like a racehorse," said teammate H. Y. Davidson. "He had that instinct to be out in front all the time."

///

The academy's accelerated three-year schedule meant that in the spring of 1943 Shepard was both a junior and a sophomore; the next school year would be his last, which didn't give him a whole lot of time to achieve the goals he'd set.

At the end of the current school year—during a series of events known as June Week, which culminated with the senior class graduation—Shepard's class would receive their senior year rings and attend their Ring Dance, after which Shepard's class would officially become seniors. Shepard wanted Louise Brewer to be the one to share the symbolic moment with him, and in letters to her he repeated his invitation.

Louise initially declined the invitation, but Shepard

persisted. He sent a Valentine's Day card, which she said was "mighty cute." Louise, in turn, began signing her return letters affectionately, "Weezo" or "Weezer" and "as ever, Louise."

A week before the dance, Louise finally accepted. She arrived in Annapolis early in the week, and the weather was beautiful. After dropping her bags at a downtown boardinghouse that catered to visiting girlfriends, she and Alan walked around the yard, past the statues, the crypt of John Paul Jones, the graveyard of naval heroes. Later Alan took her sailing on the Severn River, and they snuggled—him shirtless and her in white shorts and her hair tied up—in the back of the yawl as he steered.

Alan seemed intent on proving that the Christmas Dance at Principia six months earlier had been no small encounter. He was charming, funny, and attentive, and he introduced her to all of his friends. Alan had, typically, volunteered for the Ring Dance decorating committee, and a yearbook photographer caught Alan and Louise together: she standing on a crate, in saddle shoes and a knee-length white skirt, he handing her a Chinese lantern, wearing a tight T-shirt and looking up at her with a grin.

That night when Alan escorted Louise into the beautifully decorated ballroom, all heads turned. She was stunning in a floor-length sleeveless white gown. "Spectacularly beautiful," they said. "A real knockout." Few who were there would forget the sight of her, or of Alan, in his dress blue jacket, white pants, and white shoes, radiating pride.

A Navy band played moody ballads in the background, and World War II seemed far away. After a turkey dinner, Alan and Louise walked through a giant replica of a ring, dipped his own class ring into a basin containing waters from the seven seas, and kissed.

The next day he rode with her on the train to Baltimore. She hailed a taxi to take her home to Longwood, an hour north. Their goodbye was so fast she felt the need to write him as soon as she got home. "I wish there were some way I could tell you what a really wonderful time I had," Louise wrote on June 14, 1943, on red stationery.

> *Thanks seems like such an inadequate word sometimes. Oh, I was sure I'd have a good time. But the whole weekend— rather, week—surpassed any expectation. Thanks to you. I suppose no fellow likes to be called sweet, so I won't call you that, but that doesn't alter the fact that you were terribly sweet to me. You know, you really don't have to worry about me coming down again, for if the "invite" is still good, I'll be down with bells on. Figuratively speaking, of course. It would be a little noisy the other way.*
> *Love, Louise*

On the heels of his giddy, romantic week with Louise, Shepard climbed up the gangplank of an aging World War I battleship, the USS *Arkansas.* For the next three weeks he'd sleep fitfully in a festeringly hot bunk, eating lousy food, with no land or women in sight and always a chore to do—his first bitter taste of the real U.S. Navy.

Naval Academy midshipmen, in the summer before their senior year, are assigned to a "summer cruise," which exposes them to life aboard a ship. For many it is a shocking experience that quickly dispels notions they might have courted of the romantic life of a sailor. Aboard ships like the *Arkansas*—nicknamed Old Arky—midshipmen often learn, with disgust, about their latent claustrophobia or seasickness.

Because German U-boats still lurked off the Atlantic coast, Shepard and his classmates spent their nineteen-day cruise a bit closer to home: sailing up and down the Chesapeake Bay, which in August can turn as sweltering as a hot bathtub.

At two football fields long, Old Arky easily swallowed up the thousand midshipmen, who got hopelessly lost and

disoriented in her bowels. The chain-smoking and ruddy enlisted Navy men who operated the ship introduced Shepard and
the others to the hard truths of their chosen profession. Some of
those lessons were thrilling, such as firing the *Arkansas'* twelve-
inch and five-inch guns, feeling the concussive explosions and
smelling powder for the first time. Other lessons were sobering
and mundane: scrubbing the wooden decks, standing watch
alone in the dead of night, learning the complexities of navigation, sextants, and stars. Being restricted to Chesapeake Bay
meant that, unlike peacetime academy classes before them, they
would not be able to dock in New York or Boston and spend a
drunken night ashore. Mainly Shepard counted the days until
his return to Annapolis and pined for the occasional twilight
happy hour, whose offering of a few cans of beer made it a little
easier to fall asleep in his cramped metal bunk.

For Shepard, the trip was further proof that the life of a
Navy sailor wasn't for him, sound and convincing evidence that
the Navy pilot's life, instead, was his true calling.

Ever since his uncle had suggested he attend the Naval
Academy, Shepard knew that his real purpose in choosing the
Navy was not to become a sailor but to use the academy as a
stepping-stone toward the elite ranks of naval aviators. At the
time—as he well knew from the aviation magazines in his footlocker—American pilots had begun dropping bombs onto Tokyo,
and for the first time in history entire battles were being won and
lost in the sky. Leading the way in this brash new style of modern
warfare—more so than their counterparts in the Army Air Force
(the Air Force's predecessor) or the Marine Corps—were the aircraft carrier pilots of the Navy. President Roosevelt, sensing that
the Navy was developing the airborne power to win the war, approved thousands of new Navy planes each month, nimble and
nasty fighter planes called Hellcats and Hose Noses. Shepard was
hungry for that thrilling and powerful aviator's lifestyle.

After the better part of a month at sea with a thousand men, he was also hungry for Louise Brewer. Shortly after returning from his summer cruise aboard Old Arky, he called her one night and got her out of bed. She was groggy, and his words were so unexpected she couldn't believe her ears. "I think I love you," he said. It had been on the "tip of my tongue" for weeks, he told her, and he finally had to release it.

The next morning, Louise wrote him a long letter, telling him how "topsy turvy" the world seemed to her. The summer, which she'd spent at home at Longwood, had been filled with air raid drills and blackouts; even church services got interrupted by the sirens. At a time such as this, how could he be so sure of his own feelings? How could anyone? She still considered Alan "almost a stranger."

Their relationship had consisted of a few dates, a few dances, a flurry of letters, and a kiss or two. "Maybe," Louise suggested, "we just better go along and finish our respective jobs and let the future take care of itself?"

Louise was just a girl when her parents sent her to Principia, and her first close friend there was a handsome, athletic boy with "pugilistic" features, named George Dietz. He and Louise dated steadily through high school and seemed destined for marriage. After Alan proclaimed his love to Louise for the first time, she invoked George's name. "Alan, I think a lot of you, but as I said once before, I haven't known you very long," she wrote. "I've known George for 9 years now and how long have I known you?"

But in subsequent phone calls and letters, Alan refused to give up, and Louise began questioning whether she was being too careful and logical. This was all just infatuation, she tried to tell herself. There was no such thing as love at first sight. Then again, she had never known anyone quite like Alan, with his bigger-than-life personality and his puffed-out chest, his jaunty walk and his muscles. He was so exciting, and he seemed to have enough confidence for the two of them. Maybe too much confidence.

In a letter to Louise in the fall of 1943, he invited her to the next year's Letterman's Ball, neglecting to tell her that he didn't actually have a varsity letter yet. A few weeks after that, he sent her a bracelet for her birthday. And his persistence began to unsettle Louise. "I really don't know you too well," she wrote yet again.

Indeed she didn't.

///

In 1943 it wasn't unusual for young men and women to date multiple partners. Testing the waters was an acceptable and prudent preface to choosing a partner for life. And so, while courting Louise from afar, Shepard spent most weekends that fall semester with a pretty young secretary from Philadelphia named Fran, whom he'd met at a dance. She'd ride the Saturday morning train, he'd meet her on the platform of the Annapolis station "at the usual time," and they'd go to football games, dances, the movies. Like Louise, she stayed overnight at Mrs. Chestnutt's boardinghouse in Annapolis. Unlike Louise, Fran let Shepard know that she was flat-out, no-bones crazy about him.

"Oh Shep, you're the most wonderful, handsome, lovable, bad boy this side of heaven," she once wrote. "You've got me all wound up. Love (and I do mean it), Fran."

Fran couldn't have been more different from Louise Brewer. While Louise was regal, refined, composed, Fran was feisty, passionate, a little insecure, but sexy. "Right now I need a little bit of your loving to keep me warm," she wrote during an afternoon break from her job at the switchboard of Episcopal Academy outside Philadelphia. She signed it "your dizzy, datty, drowsy little dame, Fran."

Weekends in Annapolis bustled with young women hoping to spend time with a nice officer-to-be—and maybe find a husband-to-be. In those uncertain times of war, many midshipmen found themselves betrothed to a girlfriend after just a few dates. It was clear from Fran's talk of marriage, children, and grandchildren that she likely wanted more from their relationship than a few dances and kisses.

"When I get married I'll pick a fight with my husband once a week just so we can kiss and make up," Fran said in one of two letters she wrote to Shepard on the same day. "Makes it much more exciting, don't you think?"

As Christmas of 1943 approached—sensing that the fling was cruising toward dangerous ground—Shepard told Fran that he wouldn't be able to see her during the upcoming holidays. He had plans, he said in a letter, without much elaboration. She was crushed that he was, as she put it in her response, "too handsome and popular for this Philadelphia lassie." She'd have been even more devastated had she known that the man she loved would be spending his holidays with the woman *he* loved.

///

Little by little, in his letters to Louise, Shepard was wearing her down. Louise had always been proud of being practical, conservative, old-fashioned. She was so sure she was living a proper life, valuing caution and security above romance. "But Alan, I was *wrong*," she finally confessed in a letter in October.

"I wasn't too sure I believed in love," she wrote. "How could you be in love with someone when you didn't know how they really thought about things of importance or what their standards were? My head did a wonderful job of getting me all confused."

A few days before Christmas 1943—exactly a year from when they first met—Shepard visited Louise at Longwood Gardens. They hadn't seen each other since summer. Still, while skating on the pond one night, Shepard asked Louise to decide: *Is it us?*

When Shepard returned to Annapolis two weeks later, to start his final semester at the academy, he had the answer.

The relationship would never be a perfect one. Like many relationships born during wartime, it was lopsided, with all the power in his court. And while their different personalities would often complement each other, Shepard's zest for good times would just as often grate against Louise's desire for quiet and simplicity. But Louise would decide that it was best to let him chase his dreams.

In late January 1944 Shepard invited Fran to Annapolis for one last dance. He told her about Louise, then spent the rest of the night stanching her tears. He had never meant for things to get so serious, he explained. It was just a few laughs, wasn't it? They'd had fun, hadn't they? But Fran felt "struck by lightning" and fell into his arms, crying and clinging to him, begging him to change his mind.

A month later Fran wrote to apologize for "making a scene [and] building a few castles without a firm foundation." After all, she said, "heartbreaks . . . are a part of life."

George Dietz, meanwhile, had been watching Louise slowly slip away into the arms of another. Louise finally told her longtime boyfriend it was over. George was crushed and would never forget her—or the name Alan Shepard.

///

By early 1944 General Dwight D. Eisenhower had been named supreme commander of Allied forces in Europe and began preparing for a full-scale, all-out invasion of Nazi-held France. Even the decades-old USS *Arkansas* was relieved of its duties as a midshipman training ship and chugged toward the beaches of Normandy.

Meanwhile, the airplanes Shepard so anxiously wanted to fly continued to dominate the course of the war, exhibiting the newfound strength and abilities of naval aviation.

While Shepard attended classes that spring, American planes began round-the-clock bombings on Berlin and dropped paratroopers into Italy. But it was in the South Pacific that the airplane really began to exact some revenge for Pearl Harbor. Men who would in time become Shepard's colleagues were at that moment dogfighting Japanese Zeros, earning the coveted title of ace, awarded to pilots with five confirmed kills.

Shepard, eager to join them and with just months separating him from the war, wrote to tell his grandmother how soundly Annapolis had prepared him for battle. "I could never have been happier in any other place. It has put me on my two feet, entirely independent, and has broadened my outlook and matured me much more evenly than any other college or university could have done in three years," he wrote.

Annapolis had been a strict, demanding training ground—certainly the most challenging experience of Shepard's otherwise pampered life. But in a display of determination that would eventually become the most notable aspect of his complicated personality, Shepard had gotten himself back on track. He had wooed the girl of his dreams and worked his way back from academic failure. His grade in Spanish rose to an acceptable 2.89, and his average in EHG nudged up to 2.73. When the academic board met in the spring of 1944 to determine Shepard's fate, they decided that he was now "proficient."

Meanwhile, Shepard had also impressed Coach Walsh with his strength and hard work, and Walsh finally named Shepard to the eight-man varsity boat. The team would go undefeated that spring of 1944 and be named eastern intercollegiate champions. Although the playoffs would be canceled due to the war, Shepard had become one of the team's workhorses—which meant he would get the varsity letter he so intensely desired. And, he reminded Louise, that meant she had an excuse to come back to Annapolis once more and dance with him at the Letterman's Ball.

Until his senior year, Shepard recalled later in life, he felt he "never really hit my stride." He was always a little behind, a little smaller, a little younger. At first, instead of working harder, Shepard realized that he let himself become a victim of what he called his "insidious complacency."

"I was only twenty when I graduated from the academy," he said decades later in an unpublished interview. "I just really hadn't matured, I guess, until that last year there."

But once he shunned his complacency and began throwing himself at his academic and athletic goals, classmates saw the maturity, too. "Schimpf's big smile and easy laugh made an impression on the class," the Class of '45 yearbook said beneath Shepard's grinning mug shot. "With his personality and ability, he should go far."

Other notable students would make deeper impressions on the school. Jimmy Carter, a freshman when Shepard graduated, would rise to become one of the top-ranking midshipmen. Future millionaire and presidential candidate Ross Perot would, in 1951, help pen the school's new code of honor—"midshipmen do not lie, cheat, or steal."

Shepard wasn't quite at the bottom of the class, which is where a similarly rambunctious midshipman (and future U.S. senator), John McCain, would find himself fourteen years later. Shepard ranked among the academy's mediocrity—463rd out of 915. But he had emerged with Louise Brewer as perhaps his proudest collegiate achievement. Louise came to his Letterman's Ball that spring and stood with Shepard's parents two days later to watch him graduate, on June 6, 1944, just hours after troops had begun scrambling onto the bloody, valorous shores of Normandy. At the precise moment of America's deadliest World War II battle to date—which was being supported by seventeen naval aviators strafing and bombing German strongholds above Normandy's beaches—Shepard and his classmates flung their midshipman caps in the air, an explosion of fluttering white forms, like an ascending flock of doves, signifying the transition from student to officer.

A month later Alan and Louise were secretly engaged to be married.

3

"The kamikazes raised
hell last night"

The Williams home in the too-cute town of Sausalito bustled like an overstuffed boardinghouse that summer, with loud and anxious men in uniform coming and going at all hours. Margaret Williams even put out a guest book to keep track of her son Bob's academy classmates, all of them bound for transport ships departing from nearby San Francisco. "Never even noticed the fog," Shepard wrote in the guest book when he arrived, August 9, 1944.

After graduating from the academy, Shepard had spent a month of aviation indoctrination in Florida before heading to San Francisco, where he was to catch a transport ship that would deliver him to his first assignment: a yearlong tour aboard the Navy destroyer USS *Cogswell*.

Each day for the next two weeks Shepard and his former Annapolis roommate, Bob Williams, drove out from Bob's parents' place to the San Francisco Navy Yard, where they searched for their names on the roster of junior officers scheduled on the next transport. Williams was assigned to the USS *Cleveland*, a light cruiser that, like Shepard's *Cogswell*, was island-hopping from battle to battle throughout the South Pacific. But day after day their names appeared nowhere on the roster, and they were told to come back the next day. Shepard and Williams were then free to ply the Bay Area. By day they hit golf balls; by night they stalked the town, unencumbered, uniformed studs. They'd yet to dip a big toe into World War II and already they had the swagger and chin-up strut of young American heroes. One weekend they drove north to drink and dance—"more than I could report," Williams recalled—with young ladies at the Russian River Resort, a rustic hotel-restaurant-nightclub set among northern California's redwoods. Shepard even found time for a few dates with a friend of Williams', even though he'd slipped an engagement ring on Louise's finger a few weeks earlier and had begun calling her "my fiancée."

San Francisco, more than any other city, churned and pulsed with the business of war. As a major port of embarkation for sailors and soldiers, the steep streets and trolley cars sparkled with the crisp blue-and-white or khaki-and-white of uniformed men, so much so that writers called it "War City." Civic groups urged residents to comfort men headed to or from war with the slogan "Make a serviceman happy." Residents planted victory gardens to raise food for the war effort, bought $18.75 war bonds, and dumped their pennies into collection bowls, which raised money to buy cigarettes, gum, books, magazines, playing cards, and soap for their men at war.

No expectation was spared—San Franciscans donated blood that was sent to the front lines, and the *San Francisco Examiner* conducted a "Save a Life with a Knife" campaign, urging readers to donate knives (four inches or longer) to be delivered to soldiers in the Pacific. Recruitment posters with brawny, shirtless men hung in shop windows: "Man the Guns—Join the Navy." By the time Shepard arrived, the nagging threat of Japanese attack had abated, nighttime dim-out restrictions had been lifted, and the city's thirty air-raid sirens wailed less frequently. Still, people kept their shades drawn at night, listening to Jack Benny or Fred Allen and sometimes picking up snippets of Tokyo Rose's propaganda program *The Zero Hour.*

Shepard's few weeks in San Francisco were both heady and invigorating. Savvy San Franciscans knew the difference between a mere sailor and an officer, and as a newly commissioned ensign, Shepard was treated with deference and respect. Restaurants, nightclubs, and movie theaters showered him with military discounts, and everywhere he went people clapped him on the back, offered encouraging words, and called him "sir."

But, at the same time, a subtle pall of sadness mixed with the wind and fog of the city.

John Dos Passos, in a *Harper's* magazine story entitled "San Francisco Faces West; The City in Wartime," described how men counted the foggy, drizzly days to their inevitable departure from War City to war. Young men—often mere teenagers—sat quietly in restaurants eating a final meal with family, friends, or girlfriends. "No wonder they keep their lips pressed tight when they stare out toward the western horizon," Dos Passos wrote.

Shepard was never one to let depressive thoughts intrude on a good time, and he enjoyed his days and nights in San Francisco, slurping noodles in Chinatown, watching the seals on Seal Rocks from the Cliff House restaurant, hiking the crooked streets of Nob Hill. But he had to know what all departing Navy men knew: These could be his last days on American soil.

Finally, in late August, he and Williams found their names on the roster. Navy veterans must have chuckled when Shepard asked about the transport ship posted beside his name. Though he'd one day command the most intricate and costly machines ever built by man, Shepard's introduction to military life was aboard a stinking, decades-old rust bucket.

///

The USS *Willard A. Holbrook* began life in 1921 as a luxury passenger ship, but in middle age it was demoted to freighter, regularly crisscrossing the Pacific, its holds stuffed with coconut
meat, jute grass, burlap, and other exports from Asia. At the start
of World War II, the U.S. Army took command of the rust-
splotched ship to deliver troops to and from Pacific islands. The
pungent stench of coconut, spices, and rotting grasses had
seeped into the *Holbrook*'s steel frame, and Shepard and the others called her "Stinkin' Old Holbrook."

As they steamed slowly toward the South Pacific, Shepard
shared a tiny room with four other men. Inside those steel walls,
it felt as if he was being roasted alive. Many men, sick of sleeping
in puddles of sweat, slept up on deck beneath the stars with just
a bedsheet—and, if they were lucky, accompanied by one of the
thirty-one Army nurses aboard. For weeks they saw nothing but
open water. They played marathon games of bridge and joked
about how another classmate's enormous penis should earn him
an immediate promotion. As they crossed the equator, Shepard
and other naval virgins ran half clad through a "belt line," the
Navy's ceremonial ass-whooping for those crossing the earth's
midsection for the first time.

One night, as the Holbrook neared an archipelago of
Japanese-held islands, an edgy officer on watch shouted into his
radio, "Submarine on our port side!" The captain gave orders to
douse all lights, even cigarettes, and for all aboard to keep quiet.
Finally, as tensions rose on the unarmed *Holbrook*, the submarine
broke the surface, and all aboard sighed with relief upon realizing it wasn't a submarine at all. It was a whale. It took Shepard six
weeks to reach the island of Biak, a jagged scrap of paradise off
the New Guinea coast that had been recently wrenched from
Japanese hands to become a midsea staging area for American
ships and troops.

Army and National Guard infantrymen had battled Japanese forces for months before gaining control of the island. Evidence of those battles gave Shepard his first whiff of death. Japanese soldiers' bodies, some burned or beheaded, littered the small island, filling the sweltering air with their putrid odors of decay.

Shepard's arrival at Biak almost gave him the chance to meet his hero, Charles Lindbergh. The famous ocean-hopping flyer had spent a few months as a civilian "tech rep" at Biak, showing Navy aviators there how to conserve fuel. Lindbergh, who had initially argued against America's involvement in the war (earning him much scorn), even flew a few bombing missions in the South Pacific and, despite the fact that he was a civilian and no longer an active duty colonel, shot down a Japanese Zero. The sailors and soldiers stationed there enthusiastically told Shepard and his friends about Lindbergh's exploits, although Lindbergh would remember Biak most for the sorrowful smell of dead bodies.

Shepard would one day get his chance to meet the lanky, mercurial Colonel Lindbergh, to stand by his side on one of the most historic days in history. But that was twenty-five hard-fought years away.

Meanwhile, Shepard's efforts to reach the USS *Cogswell* were delayed when the "Stinkin' Holbrook" was unexpectedly smashed by one of its own. Another ship coming into port lost control and slammed into the *Holbrook,* to the cheers of those watching the slow-motion collision from shore. While waiting for another transport ship, Shepard loitered on the beach, drank beer—"he could really put it away," one shipmate said—and more than likely sipped some of the bitter home-brewed moonshine some Army soldiers had concocted.

One day the crew of a B-25 bomber invited Shepard to join them on a practice bombing run. B-25 "Mitchell" bombers had been used—most notably by flying ace Jimmy Doolittle in

1942—to pummel Tokyo with bombs. Shepard jumped at the offer and was allowed to ride with the nose gunner, who sat in a glass bubble in front of and below the pilot. The gunner let Shepard take his machine gun and drill a few holes into an abandoned target ship. As the B-25 banked and turned back toward Biak, the pilot spotted a few straggling Japanese ships. The nose gunner grabbed the machine gun back from Shepard and strafed them. It was Shepard's one and only airborne adventure of the war, and it marked the start of a yearlong and agonizing worship from afar of the Navy's heroic aviators and their aircraft.

///

Two months after leaving San Francisco Shepard finally caught up with the *Cogswell* in late October. As he tramped up her gangplank his eyes took in her horrid condition. The destroyer had been at sea for eight months, island-hopping and making war around the Philippines, New Guinea, and Indonesia. Rust-streaked and waterlogged, the ship looked like the hell it had been through. *Cogswell* had plunged into some of the more impressive skirmishes in naval history and pounded exotic, palm-fringed islands with tongue-twister names like Chichi Jima, Kwajalein, Eniwetok, Truk, the Marianas, Palau, Mindanao, and Yap. Most recently, she had lent her guns to the destruction of Japanese ships at the critical Battle of Leyte Gulf. It was hard to believe the battle-scarred destroyer was little more than a year old. And as soon as Shepard joined the crew, *Cogswell* wasted no time in restocking and returning to the heat of battle.

In recent months, the Japanese navy had begun to crumble, and the United States realized that an all-out assault on Japan itself was finally possible. The *Cogswell* was needed for the next phase of the Pacific war: establishing military bases on some of the volcanic islands south of Japan, which would become staging grounds for the full-scale attack.

The *Cogswell*, built at the famous Bath Iron Works in Maine, was a two-thousand-ton workhorse of a destroyer, capable of reaching nearly forty miles an hour. Her duties were to provide artillery support to ground troops, to find and destroy submarines, and to escort and rescue other ships. She carried more than three hundred men, including up to twenty officers at any given time.

As junior officer of the deck, Shepard's first job was to man the ship's internal telephone circuits. The secretarylike job bored him, and he immediately requested a transfer to the gunnery division, which he considered "a promising prospect." Still, he was so junior—"the junior J.O.," he called himself—and the ship so full, he was forced to sleep in a hammock stretched across another officer's cabin. At first his primary concern was to "get my own bunk."

Japan soon gave him more to worry about.

After two days at sea, a Japanese torpedo ripped into the hull of the USS *Reno*, a cruiser traveling directly behind the *Cogswell*. Men sleeping on *Reno*'s top deck were blown overboard, and the rest of the crew jumped from the fast-sinking ship into the sea. The *Cogswell* U-turned and began plucking sailors from the oily waters as the *Reno* struggled to stay afloat. Shepard recognized two of the exhausted men as academy classmates.

"Have been running into all kinds of people that I know that are in our class," he reported, somewhat nonchalantly, in a letter to a friend. "Why, only a few days ago we picked Joe Schwager up out of the oil-covered waters."

Cogswell pulled 172 of *Reno*'s sailors and officers aboard, then slowly escorted the damaged cruiser away from submarine-infested waters toward safety. Three days later, a vicious typhoon struck the *Cogswell* and its convoy, tossing the ships around like bath toys for two days. That was followed by occasional but thwarted attacks by Japanese suicide planes. When she finally reached the apparent safety of the U.S.-occupied port on the atoll of Ulithi, the *Cogswell* was hit with reports of Japanese mini-submarines prowling the lagoon, and Shepard and the crew stayed at their battle stations through the night. Just before daylight, one of the enemy subs fired on a Navy tanker, and dawn bloomed with the exploding tanker's demise. The crew was killed, but *Cogswell* helped hunt the Japanese submarines, four of which were sunk by U.S. ships. At the end of his first month as a seaman, Shepard's ship was awarded a unit citation for rescuing the *Reno*'s crew and then escorting and protecting the wounded ship.

Admiral William F. "Bull" Halsey, the belligerent, bloodthirsty commander of the Third Fleet, praised the entire *Cogswell* crew for "a brilliant and courageous piece of fighting."

///

The war in the Pacific was the Navy's war. Its ships, its planes, and its Marines (which were and still are part of the Navy) wrenched Pacific islands from Japanese hands, one by bloody one. Far from home and seemingly overmatched by enormous and well-trained Japanese forces, the Navy made surprising progress in its efforts to establish military bases on the islands south of Japan, in preparation for an expected assault on the enemy's homeland. *Cogswell* and the hundreds of other ships in the U.S. Navy's Third Fleet, leapfrogging from fight to fight, island to island, were proving to be one of the greatest fighting units in the history of warfare.

But sometimes opposition came from unexpected fronts. After assisting in assaults on and around the Philippines, in mid-December of 1944 the *Cogswell* was slammed without warning by another violent and unexpected typhoon, this one far worse than the first. She was running low on fuel, which made the top-heavy ship rock violently from side to side. Attaching refueling lines to a nearby storm-tossed tanker become impossible, so Shepard's crewmates held tight to their bunks below as 120-mile-an-hour-winds and thirty-foot waves battered the helpless vessel. The ship ascended wave mountains, then surfed down the other side, one after the other. For two days sleep was impossible—men were slammed from wall to wall and thrown to the steel floors. Cooking was also impossible, so they ate little during the forty-eight hours of hell.

"This is the worst storm we have been in," one sailor wrote in his diary. "We can't steer our course, the seas are too big."

Although personal diaries were strictly forbidden—the Navy didn't want information falling into enemy hands—a few aboard the *Cogswell* secretly kept written accounts of their day-to-day travails. "Several men have been lost over the side," the ship's cook wrote in his diary.

Three other Navy destroyers were capsized and sunk by the typhoon. For days afterward the *Cogswell* pulled near-dead and waterlogged sailors from the calming seas. Nearly 790 young men who had survived Japanese torpedoes and kamikazes lost their lives to the furious Philippine Sea.

"In the light of hindsight it is easy to see how any of several measures might have prevented this catastrophe," Admiral Chester W. Nimitz, the Navy's optimistic fleet admiral in the Pacific (and, like Shepard, a onetime Naval Academy oarsman), said in a follow-up report a few months later. "The important thing is for it never to happen again."

But it would happen again. And again.

When the seas finally relaxed and *Cogswell* finished searching for survivors, she limped back into the lagoon off Ulithi atoll on the morning of Christmas Eve, and the shell-shocked crew began to smell the simmerings of a huge Christmas turkey dinner the galley was planning.

Late in the day, forty-five overstuffed mailbags were lugged aboard from a mail boat. One of the bags contained a letter from Shepard's mother, Renza. Bad news from home: His beloved grandmother Nanzie, the woman who had hatched his chicken operation and in whose basement Shepard had spent half his boyhood, was dead.

She was eighty-three but had been in perfect health. Three weeks before Christmas she slipped on an icy sidewalk in Boston, hit her head, and died three days later. Shepard was not allowed to return home for the funeral. That night, he wrote his parents "to tell you how proud I was and am of Nanzie." Curled up in his cabin, exhausted and frazzled from the recent battles with enemy subs and enemy seas, he wrote:

"You have started me on my way as a Shepard—a way that is exacting in its requirements, a path that is difficult to follow but one that is certainly worth the while and effort. I only hope that I can follow your examples and live my life in such a way that will make both of you proud of me and that will make me worthy of being a Shepard."

///

In late February 1945, five months after Shepard had joined the ship, the *Cogswell* returned to California for a much-needed overhaul. Her hull was rusted, dented, and bullet-pocked. Shepard and his fellow sailors—filthy and exhausted, edgy and sleep-deprived—were given three weeks of welcome liberty. He sent word to Louise that they should make the most of his brief hiatus from war: he wanted to get married, right away. He flew to Longwood, where he and Louise broke the news to her parents on a Sunday morning. Louise's parents had known the couple was serious, but the urgency of their desire to wed just one week later surprised the Brewers. Still, bold times led to bold decisions, and many of Alan and Louise's friends were also leaping into marriage, near strangers choosing each other for lives built on the foundations of a brief courtship. Despite some heavy scowling from Phil Brewer, he and his wife consented.

Shepard called his parents with the news, then hopped on the next train to Boston. When he didn't see his parents at the station, Shepard assumed they had had car trouble and hitch-hiked the 40 miles to East Derry. When he found no one at home, he climbed onto the roof and forced open his bedroom window to get into the house. The next morning his parents called from their Boston hotel room, a bit frustrated that their son hadn't waited for them at the train station.

The Shepards all drove back down to Longwood Gardens later that week. Alan and Louise married on March 3, 1945, at Stephens Lutheran Church in nearby Wilmington, Delaware.

Alan's father, Bart, was the best man. Father and son both wore their uniforms, Alan in dark blue and Bart in brown and tan. Back in 1941 Bart had come back from reserve status and re-joined the Army as a full-time officer. He wanted to do what he could for the war and worked as a recruiter in Manchester, con-vincing young New England men to serve their country.

Louise, age twenty-two, wore a satin gown with a long white train and antique lace; as a corsage, she wore one of Longwood's rare and delicate orchids. Alan looked older than his twenty-one years—in the twenty months since cavorting on the streets of San Francisco, he had matured from a teen into a full-grown man. The couple traveled north, back to East Derry with Bart and Renza, then drove up into the White Mountains of northern New Hampshire for a brief honeymoon.

Their honeymoon was the first time they had spent more than a day or two together, and never had they been truly alone. There was just a small window of time to get reacquainted, to make plans—how many children? what should their names be? where should we live?—and then to watch each other undress, to taste each other, to make love and pretend for a few days that the war, the Navy, and Alan's death-defying career were not about to swallow them both up.

In late March Alan and Louise traveled west to southern California—the first of many cross-country treks in the nomadic life to come—and the clock ticked down toward Alan's scheduled April 5 reunion with the *Cogswell*. Enjoying cocktails, dinners, movies, and sunset walks along the pier, they were briefly, blissfully, carefree young newlyweds. Then, after a final night together, a final taste of each other, Louise drove Alan to the docks at the Long Beach Navy Yard. She waved from the pier as Alan sailed toward God knew what brutalities of battle. Without knowing when or if he'd return, Louise aggressively set about creating a life of her own. She drove to San Francisco, found an apartment to share with a college friend, took a job at Gump's department store, and began attending occasional parties with other Navy wives.

Bob Williams' mother hosted one such party, for Louise and few other wives, at the Sausalito home where Alan had stayed. Louise flipped through the guestbook there to find her husband's strong, neat signature from a year earlier and then signed the book herself.

A reporter from the *Sausalito News* mingled at the party, where the wives all signed a round-robin letter to send to their husbands. In her article, the reporter described how the women reminisced about watching their men graduate the previous summer, about feeling proud to send their brave lovers off to the good and righteous war.

Louise befriended some of the Navy wives, and Mrs. Williams occasionally stopped by the apartment to see if she needed anything. But her real friends, and her real source of strength, were those in the congregation of the Christian Science Church. Wherever Alan's career took them, the Christian Science Church would become Louise's surrogate family.

Alan wrote to her often and asked Bob Williams to check up on her the next time he returned home.

One day, Louise met another of the store clerks at Gump's, a girl named Peggy Duff, and as they got talking they realized they both knew a cute Naval Academy grad named Alan. It might have been the first time that Louise came in contact with one of her husband's flings, but it wouldn't be the last. Peggy Duff—"the rump," Alan once called her—had been one of those attracted to his uniform during what Alan called his "good times" in Sausalito. Alan wrote to Bob that Louise's chance encounter with Duff was "too close for comfort! The old 'rump' certainly gets around."

///

As the *Cogswell* steamed back toward the South Pacific, Shepard received word that a former classmate had abandoned his crippled ship and wound up in shark-infested waters, where he met his doom. Meanwhile, another classmate, a year behind Shepard at the academy, was still exploiting the midshipman's life but was expelled for bringing a date into Bancroft Hall and showering with her. "Wholesale debauchery!" Shepard said in a letter.

Shepard, steaming west in early April 1945, was suspended between those two worlds—the academy life behind him, kamikaze pilots ahead. While in transit from California to Pearl Harbor, the *Cogswell* learned of Japan's increasingly desperate use of suicide planes against U.S. ships. Upon arrival at Pearl Harbor, Shepard was told that he would be one of the *Cogswell*'s primary defenders against such kamikaze attacks—he was being relieved of his telephone duties and promoted to deck officer, helping oversee a cluster of 20 mm and 40 mm antiaircraft guns on the ship's bow. A half dozen such clusters ringed the football-field-sized destroyer, which complemented an array of larger and more menacing five-inch guns. The *Cogswell* cruised off the Hawaiian coast for more than a week, conducting training exercises to give Shepard and the others time to get acquainted with their weaponry and prepare for the fighting ahead.

Pearl Harbor also gave Shepard a chance to firm up his plans for a future that had little to do with ships at sea.

When Shepard had climbed aboard the *Cogswell* back at Long Beach, a new commanding officer was running the show. The *Cogswell*'s beloved first skipper, Commander Harold "Dutch" Deuterman, had been replaced by a man who lasted just a few weeks before breaking his leg, which then opened the door for the gruff and reviled Lieutenant Commander Reuben Perley to take command of the ship.

Tall and slim, Perley was an authoritative and foul-mouthed skipper who seemed to take joy in yelling salty-tongued put-downs into his sailors' faces. One day Shepard was cracking up at another young officer's perfect impression of their scrappy skipper when Perley appeared out of nowhere and strode silently up behind the unwitting performer. Shepard had no time to warn his friend. Perley's mustachioed lips curled into a sneer and he barked into the man's ear before sending him to his cabin for a few days of red-faced punishment. More than once Perley sent Shepard himself to his room as punishment for one of his practical jokes, or for ignoring his duty station to watch planes take off from a nearby aircraft carrier.

Whenever an aircraft carrier cruised nearby or a cluster of planes flew overhead, Shepard seemed to be running for the *Cogswell*'s railing, straining for a better view. Shepard did little to conceal his distaste for the sailor's life. He took his new job seriously and respected the enlisted men in his charge. But at the end of the day he believed there was only one Navy ship worth his while: the aircraft carrier.

"That was very obvious, and he didn't hide it," said John Huber III, who stood many nightly watches by Shepard's side, during which Shepard talked mostly about planes. "He did his job well, but he didn't want to be there. He was basically a free spirit. He wanted to be in the air."

But junior officers such as Shepard were required to serve at least a year at sea before the Navy would consider teaching them to fly its planes. Shepard was more than halfway there, and Huber and other shipmates recalled how obsessively he counted down the days to the end of his first year.

At Pearl Harbor Shepard submitted his request for flight school. He passed the required physical, then waited, checking off each twenty-four-hour step toward his first naval anniversary. "One of these days . . . ," Shepard told a shipmate one night while they both stood watch. "One of these days—if I don't get killed—I'm going to learn to fly."

"Shepard always had his eyes on the planes," shipmate Andrew Atwell recalled. "He was on the wrong ship. His mind was on the carrier."

///

Somewhere in the Pacific, in mid-April, the *Cogswell* received bad news, then good. First, President Roosevelt—the man who had dragged the country out of the Great Depression and then led it into and through the war—had died. Four weeks later, while still en route to the tropical atoll of Ulithi, the *Cogswell* received word that Germany had surrendered. The fighting in Europe was over. But up ahead in the western Pacific, war raged on, more ghastly than ever.

The Japanese, by April and May of 1945, were becoming almost desperately aggressive. In the fight to retain the volcanic island of Iwo Jima, they had adopted a no-survivors strategy: fight until you die. The same strategy applied to the kamikaze pilots who, in the samurai tradition, wrapped hachimaki headbands around their heads, then aimed themselves at U.S. ships. A few of Shepard's old academy classmates were among the victims; their body bags were draped with American flags, then slid overboard for a somber burial at sea.

"Sorry to hear about McBride and Day," Shepard said in a letter to Bob Williams. "We have lost a lot of classmates."

He would soon lose many more.

///

In late May Shepard and the enlisted men he now commanded at his battle station sighted the bombed-out shores of Okinawa, an island 340 miles south of Japan and a crucial stepping-stone toward the expected all-out assault on Japanese soil. Marines had already swarmed onto the north end of the island, spooked by the surprising lack of Japanese opposition.

To help protect those Marines, the *Cogswell* had received orders for radar picket duty. They could have more accurately called it sitting duck duty. It worked like this: To create a buffer zone of ships around Okinawa, the *Cogswell* and scores of other destroyers (and a few battleships) lined up in rows, like slats on a picket fence. The purpose of the radar picket was to intercept approaching Japanese planes and shoot them down before they could reach Okinawa's shores.

These picket ships made tempting targets for the waves of enemy fighter planes that Japanese admirals sent screaming down from the mainland up north. A force of more than two thousand Japanese planes, most of them kamikazes, sat ready to attack the picket ships. That assault began in early April, when seven hundred planes swarmed down upon the U.S. fleet in a two-day span, giving the sea lane north of Okinawa its nickname, "Kamikaze Alley." One Navy report estimated that the average amount of time it took before a picket duty ship was hit by the enemy was eighteen hours. The *Cogswell*'s first picket duty was scheduled for seventy-two hours.

"If we last that long," one sailor quipped.

Another sailor told his diary: "We have a slim chance of coming out without getting hit . . . I will have to admit, I am a little bit nervous."

As the *Cogswell* sailed to her position north of Okinawa on June 1, the crew witnessed charred and mangled warnings of the dangers ahead—damaged destroyers, ravaged by kamikazes and unable to propel themselves, being towed to the nearest safe port. "The smell of burned flesh and cries of pain were overwhelming," a sailor on one such destroyer later recalled. "Many of the wounded men were burned severely when the fuel tank exploded and one man was killed from jumping over the side to avoid the flames and being run over by the ship."

More than thirteen hundred U.S. ships were ordered to support the Marines' invasion of Okinawa, dubbed Operation Iceberg, which had begun April 1, nearly two months before Shepard and the *Cogswell* arrived. The Okinawa invasion—fought on land, at sea, and in the air—would last nearly three months, one of the longest and bloodiest battles of World War II and involving one of the greatest wartime armadas in U.S. history. Although thousands of Marines would die during bitter fighting against a hundred thousand Japanese soldiers entrenched and hidden in caves on Okinawa, radar picket duty was considered one of the most dangerous and terrifying jobs of the campaign.

In addition to facing the menacing kamikazes, picket ships had to confront rockets, bombs, and—hanging beneath some Japanese planes—stocky little glider bombs called *baka*, which were guided toward U.S. ships by a suicide pilot crammed inside.

The *Cogswell* stationed itself in Kamikaze Alley, and it took less than twenty-four hours for the first kamikaze planes to appear from the clouds. One night, with bombs and planes exploding on either side of the *Cogswell*, many of the crew members shook hands, believing they'd not survive until morning.

The *Cogswell*'s prime defenses against such attacks (since her five-inch guns were often too big for close combat) were the 20 mm and 40 mm antiaircraft guns that Shepard and his men operated. When the *Cogswell* nailed its first kamikaze, Shepard's supervising officer—gunnery officer Charles Evans Hughes III, the grandson of the famous Supreme Court chief justice—began screaming, "We got 'em, we got 'em, we got 'em." Surly Captain Perley yelled back, "The war's not over yet!"

Shepard spent his days (and most nights) anxiously scanning the horizon for approaching kamikazes. On the rare nights when he was allowed to sleep, he had to fight back images of Japanese soldiers who sometimes swam from the nearest shore or from a small boat, pushing mines into U.S. ships' paths or climbing aboard to slit the first throat they could find. One night it was the throat of an officer on a ship directly behind *Cogswell*. After that, Shepard began taking turns on night watch, a recently issued pistol clipped to his belt, firing his handgun or his 20 mm guns at anything potentially human bobbing in the water.

Shepard had received only a few days of practice firing his guns during training exercises back at Pearl Harbor. But now, like most World War II warriors, he quickly learned the harsh lesson of kill or be killed. When a kamikaze drew near, he'd stand behind his guns, screaming at his men—some older than himself—to fire and keep firing and bring the bastards down. The noise of his guns, and the occasional report from the nearby five-inchers, was painful and physical. It racked the body and punished the eardrums; very few men at the time wore earplugs.

One morning early in June, shortly after midnight, the *Cogswell* and a few other nearby destroyers helped blast apart twenty-eight Japanese planes that had swarmed around them "like a flock of blackbirds," as one Navy officer described it. One Japanese plane dove straight down onto the nearby USS *Caperton* but missed the deck by just a few feet. Another, flying just forty feet above the water, sped directly between the *Caperton* and the *Cogswell*—which prevented both ships from shooting, for fear of hitting each other—then inexplicably fell harmlessly into the drink. Yet another plane, already damaged by gunfire, came straight at the *Cogswell*, which shot off its wings before it could reach the ship. Shrapnel from the exploding planes washed over the *Cogswell*'s decks. Such nights sparkled with the glitter of bullets and rockets flying, the air roaring with the bursts of exploding planes, the *boof-boof* and *rat-a-tat-tat* of guns, the metallic pinging of fragments bouncing off hulls.

"The kamikazes raised hell last night," one *Cogswell* sailor said.

Shepard chomped at the bit to be up in the air, to be inside one of the mean-looking American F4Us that were gaining a reputation as effective kamikaze-killing machines. Each day brought him closer to flying—if only, he sometimes hoped, the war would last long enough for him to get his Navy pilot's wings.

In the year since graduation he had matured in countless, unexpected ways. He may not have been a pilot or a hero, but he was also no longer just another man in uniform. Shepard was now, at twenty-one years old, a fighter, an officer, a killer—an American warrior. And his diligent efforts, along with the others blasting *Cogswell*'s guns at the enemy, prevented his destroyer from joining ships such as the USS *Porter* and the USS *Pringle* on the ocean floor.

On June 7 the USS *Porter* had relieved the USS *Caperton* as the *Cogswell*'s partner on picket duty. Just two hours later a kamikaze plane broke through U.S. air defenses and dive-bombed straight at the *Cogswell*. Shepard and the other gunners had the plane in their sights, ready to start firing, when it twitched left, then right, and twirled drunkenly down upon the *Porter*. The Japanese plane ticked the *Porter*'s radar tower and splashed into the water beside the ship.

The kamikaze's bombs exploded, which ignited the plane's own fuel tanks, punching a fist of flame into the *Porter*'s hull. The *Porter* gulped up the East China Sea and began to sink, fast. The *Cogswell*'s crew watched as the *Porter* swallowed water, leaned to one side, then went away. All aboard *Porter* were rescued by the *Cogswell* and other nearby ships—one sailor scrambled aboard the *Cogswell* crying like a baby because he'd had to leave $7,000 in poker winnings down below in his locker—but the sailors on the *Pringle* weren't so lucky. A kamikaze strike blew a hole in her side and knocked out the power. The men who jumped into the shark-infested waters were the lucky ones. Many others were trapped in the darkness below deck when, just five minutes after the attack, the ship's bow rose to the sky and the vessel slid backward beneath the sea. "I heard screams as she slipped under the water and disappeared," one of *Pringle*'s survivors said.

"A bottle of whiskey was passed around and everyone took a big gulp," said another of *Pringle*'s survivors, who lost sixty-nine shipmates that day. "My hands shook as I drank and thought of my shipmates, sharks, fire, and the terror of the last few hours."

During the three-month Okinawa campaign, eighteen hundred Japanese planes—mostly Mitsubishi Zeros, stuffed like ticks full of fuel and explosives—made one-way trips toward the U.S. fleet, the greatest concentration of kamikaze attacks of the entire war. Though most were shot down, kamikazes damaged 198 ships and sank 17 of them. More than 3,000 men were killed in those attacks, including 832 aboard the aircraft carrier USS *Franklin* which was struck solidly by two bombs as men scrambled in panic across the *Franklin*'s decks. "The burial of the dead was terrible," the *Franklin*'s flight surgeon said. "They were all over the ship." And Admiral Halsey called the kamikazes "the only weapon I feared in the war."

But by early July the battle for Okinawa—a fight Winston Churchill called one of the most intense in military history—was over, and the island was under U.S. control. Though it was the bloodiest, deadliest battle since Guadalcanal three years earlier, American deaths paled in comparison to the one hundred thousand dead Japanese soldiers. Many preferred suicide to surrender, including Okinawa's top officers, who ate a final meal and then immolated themselves.

As the constant noise of war and its ever-present smoke

subsided, the *Cogswell* was granted a reprieve from picket duty, and Shepard joined his shipmates on the north shore of Okinawa for some much-needed recreation. But instead of relaxing, the men walked gape-mouthed among the ghastly dregs of combat—mechanical wreckage and the twisted and rotting remains of dead Japanese soldiers were scattered everywhere. The men had to watch for booby traps—thin trip wires attached to grenades. "Much evidence of bloodshed and violence," Shepard's shipmate wrote secretly in his diary that night.

Okinawa was the final full-scale battle of the war. But Japan refused to surrender, and on July 16 the USS *Indianapolis* secretly left San Francisco, carrying two atomic bombs. After delivering the bombs to the island of Tinian, the *Indianapolis* was sunk, on July 30, by a Japanese submarine. The death of 883 men was one of the war's worst naval disasters.

Meanwhile, the *Cogswell* spent a month bombarding the Japanese mainland before the ultimate day of bloodshed and violence, a day that convinced the Japanese of their defeat.

That day was August 6, when the atomic bomb nicknamed Little Boy fell from beneath the *Enola Gay* and landed on the city of Hiroshima; three days later, just a hundred miles from where the *Cogswell* was stationed, another bomb fell on Nagasaki (armed by its "weaponeer," naval aviator Frederick L. Ashworth, a fellow graduate of the Naval Academy). The deafening, world-shaking explosion could be heard and felt aboard the *Cogswell;* "an awful bomb," one sailor called it. More than a hundred thousand died in the two cities. A week later, at about 7:30 P.M. on August 15, *Cogswell* received new orders: cease firing. It was a day Navy men would not forget, a day to exhale. Aboard *Cogswell* there were muted displays of jubilation—not the rapturous cheering that spilled into the streets of San Francisco back home, just quiet waves of sad, sober relief.

The war was over, "and much sooner than was expected," Shepard wrote in a letter.

On August 27 the *Cogswell* was chosen to be the first of the Navy's flotilla to enter Tokyo Bay, to prepare for the following week's surrender ceremonies. Behind her steamed hundreds and hundreds of battered ships with weary crews. It was a surreal procession into enemy waters, with Shepard riding on the deck as his ship took the lead. Citizens crowded along the shores, watching their captors flex their might. Most sailors felt not pride but fear—*Is it really over? Is it safe to be cruising so close to the land and people we've bombed and slaughtered?*

At first, in keeping with wartime precautions against night-time attack, the *Cogswell* kept its lights off. Then a characteristically feisty order came down from Admiral Halsey (who once had issued the famous order "Kill Japs! Kill Japs! Kill more Japs!"). Halsey ordered the *Cogswell* to "turn on your lights and let them know the U.S. Navy is here." The cliché-prone Halsey crystallized the World War II experience for his men when he added, "There are no extraordinary men—just extraordinary circumstances that ordinary men are forced to deal with."

Like most survivors, Shepard would speak little of his World War II experiences. "Some struggle," Shepard once wrote to a friend, playing it cool when the war had ended. What colleagues from the *Cogswell* remember most about Shepard was an eager young man, smiling and optimistic, ticking off the days until he could transfer to flight training. But, in the end, Shepard knew in his heart that the *Cogswell*, and he, had been lucky. A total of thirty-four Navy ships were sunk off Okinawa, half of them by kamikaze hits. More than thirteen thousand Navy men, Marines, and Army soldiers were killed in the Okinawa campaign, including Ernie Pyle, who stuck his head up from a trench and caught a bullet, dying like the war grunts he'd lionized.

But the *Cogswell*, after flinging itself into countless battles, had lost but a very few men and—like Shepard—emerged intact and relatively unscathed. Then in mid-September—two weeks after the surrender ceremonies and around the time of Shepard's first anniversary at sea—the mail room received an official Navy letter for Shepard. It contained the orders he'd ached for: to report to Corpus Christi in a month for flight training.

As Shepard hopped a transport ship back to Pearl Harbor, yet another typhoon ripped into the fleet he left behind. Once again thirty-foot waves and hurricane force winds knocked ships into each other and onto the shores of Okinawa, as if they were child's toys; thirty-six men were killed.

This time, the Guam weather station gave the storm a name: Typhoon Louise.

4

"UNSAFE FOR SOLO" in Zoom Town

Many young warriors returned home from World War II
wanting only to put distance between themselves and the
horrific things they'd seen.

What they most wanted now was stability, a steady job, and a
small brick rancher in which to raise children with a college
sweetheart. They put their memories and mementos of dark,
heroic adventures—medals, letters, pictures—into a box and put
the box away. War was over, and there wasn't much to say about it.

Shepard, like many of his fellow veterans, would speak
little during the rest of his life about his year aboard the USS
Cogswell. He never attended the ship's reunions or swapped letters with his shipmates. Yet while he would never dwell on the
effect World War II had on his life, the effect was surely profound. The war invigorated his appetite for thrills and adventure,
and he learned in the Pacific that the best thrills could be found
only in one place: the air.

As he and Louise drove from southern California in September of 1945, across the Arizona deserts, and through the end-
less plains of east Texas on their way to Corpus Christi, luck was
on Shepard's side. His timing was accidentally perfect.

Shepard's assignment to learn how to fly Navy planes coincided with a historic shift in military policy. With its massive floating airfields, the Navy's mighty domination over the Japanese in the Pacific had demonstrated the superiority of an incredible new style of warfare. In the aftermath of the war, a presidential commission and several congressional committees met to discuss how to incorporate the best of naval aviation into the Navy of tomorrow. And despite substantial postwar budget cuts, the Navy saw to it that enough money would be spent on the next generation of Navy pilots and the next generation of planes.

In late 1945, the best and brightest of that next generation— the chosen ones—converged on the sweltering Gulf coast of the Lone Star State.

///

Corpus Christi was a crusty little port and fishing town of thirty thousand. Kissed by the bath-warm waters of the Gulf of Mexico and Corpus Christi Bay on its northern and eastern shores, the city's western flanks bristled with both longhorn cattle ranches and oil fields full of oil pump derricks that looked like dinosaurs. Some big-city folk from up north in Houston might occasionally come to town on weekends or visit briefly on their way to the beaches of nearby Padre Island, but in the days before air-conditioning, there was no escape from Corpus Christi's punishing heat, not even in the tepid waters. So the town had remained a backwater, a hurly-burly mix of dockworkers, cowboys, commercial fishermen, and Mexican immigrants. Then the U.S. Navy arrived and turned Corpus Christi into a city of testosterone, adrenaline, and airplane fuel.

In 1940, when it had become clear that America was destined to join World War II, the Navy decided it needed another flight training facility to back up its air training base at Pensacola, Florida. With a $25 million bankroll from Congress, the Navy picked a waterfront expanse south of downtown Corpus Christi, mostly for its stark, unimpeded flatness and, except for the occasional hurricane, its lack of rain. It took only a year to create a twenty-thousand-acre network of six conjoined air bases that sprawled south of town, consuming vacation cottages and virgin beaches while attracting ten thousand jobs and millions of dollars, which changed the culture and landscape of the region virtually overnight.

The first cadets arrived on March 12, 1941, and graduated with their aviators' wings eight months later. At the graduation ceremony, as cadets stood at attention beneath the brutal Texas sun, they fainted one by one onto the sun-baked tarmac. "They were kind of falling all over the place," one cadet said.

After the bombing of Pearl Harbor, the training schedule at Corpus Christi surged, with six hundred new cadets arriving each month. For the next four years an average of three hundred cadets graduated monthly, taught by a rotating faculty of more than eight hundred veteran instructors. At the height of World War II, Corpus Christi overtook Pensacola as the Navy's main training facility. Construction costs—for bridges, roads, railroads, and housing facilities—swelled to $100 million, a river of cash that poured into the coffers of Houston-based Brown and Root Construction, which was awarded the contract at the urging of a young congressman named Lyndon Johnson. By 1943 Corpus Christi Naval Air Station was the largest aviation training facility in the world.

Among the thirty thousand wartime graduates of Corpus Christi was future president (and Shepard's future friend and neighbor) George H. W. Bush, who received his pilot's wings there in 1943 at age eighteen—the youngest aviator to ever complete its training program. Actor Tyrone Power, as a Marine Corps lieutenant, received aviation training there in 1943, as did actor Buddy Rogers, who had starred in the film *Wings* but found during primary training at Corpus Christi that he suffered from airsickness. Other notable alumni included baseball great Ted Williams, who served as Corpus Christi's physical fitness instructor.

As naval aviators began dominating the battles of the war in the Pacific, Corpus Christi developed a romantic cachet that lured the national media. *Life* and *Collier's* came to town, and both produced long, glowing spreads about the birthplace of America's finest flyers; *Collier's* dubbed it "Zoom Town."

For many newly arrived cadets, the first lesson of Zoom Town was adapting to its simmering heat. The stagnant air smelled like boiled shrimp, and a fishy stink seemed to seep into your skin. First-timers stepping off the train said they felt as if they'd suddenly been submerged in an aquarium. Aviators often fainted during uniformed marches and exercise sessions. A steady wind off the Gulf of Mexico stirred up the dunes, causing a fine coating of sand to settle on every flat surface. An omnipresent humidity hung in the air, a sheen of moisture that clung to walls, clothes, and upper lips.

Some cadets felt as though they'd arrived in a strange foreign land. The annoying cowboy music on every radio station, the tropical coastline, the lazy drawl or rapid-fire Spanish of the locals—all made the place feel more like a Caribbean pirate coast than America. Brief daily rains turned quickly to steam. Some days you'd need a raincoat and sunglasses at the same time. And beneath the incessant sun, cadets quickly developed the burned, peeling faces that would become the telltale symptom of their new career, the mark of an aviator.

Some hated the place. Others looked up into a sky full of airplanes and thought, as one cadet proclaimed in 1943: "Man, I have arrived at heaven."

Corpus Christi's 997 hangars were stuffed with biplanes, seaplanes, single-props, dual-props, tankers, cargo planes, and helicopters. The air swarmed with the smoke and thunder of every size and shape of airplane known to man. On particularly busy afternoons, three hundred planes might share the skies at the same time.

Sometimes there were too many planes and not enough sky.

///

When Alan and Louise arrived in November 1945, there were hardly any planes at all. Most of the Corpus Christi air fleet had been flown inland to Dallas, just ahead of a hurricane whose fifteen-foot waves hurled themselves over the sand dunes and across the airfields, flattening scores of buildings at the base and downtown. A family of four was drowned in their car, and meals had to be delivered by boat to flooded corners of the air base. As the waters receded, they left behind thousands of dead frogs, whose bodies soon began to rot, baked into putridity by the stifling heat.

Alan and Louise moved into a two-story corner apartment at 3601 Ocean Drive, one of the nicer complexes in town, right on the Gulf halfway between downtown and the naval base. The proprietor, Goldy, was a widow who had lost her husband in the war. Tropical gardens encircling the complex had been ravaged by the hurricane, and a hardworking and dignified old Mexican gardener labored to repair the damage.

By late November much of the hurricane damage had been repaired and the planes had returned from Dallas. The morning after their first Thanksgiving together, Alan awoke at dawn, kissed Louise goodbye, and drove off for his first day of training.

For Shepard, Corpus Christi would become much more than just a stop along the way. He and every other Navy flyer who passed through—including future senator John McCain and future astronaut John Glenn—would remember how it all began here. They would recall the blustery competitiveness, the bragging and dirty jokes at the officers' club, and the laughter at the expense of hapless pilots who dumped their plane into the Gulf. Those who had served in the war entertained those who hadn't with stories of the Battle of Midway and the victory at Okinawa. Among the trainers, it was easy to distinguish the aces (pilots with five or more enemy kills)—they were the ones who, in the words of another famous pilot, "exuded confidence the way a lamp gives off light."

The complex of airfields and military barracks resembled many of the naval stations that would become Shepard's future workplaces: flat, dusty, infested with rattlesnakes and mosquitoes, surrounded by scrub oak, mesquite, and sand dunes. But a magical power lurked beneath the daily grind of the Corpus Christi training regimen. If the Naval Academy had turned boys into officers, and the war turned young officers into men, Corpus Christi made men—at least those who didn't flunk out—feel like Superman. Here, they were given the tools and secrets to defy gravity. They "tasted the proud intoxication of renunciation," as one aviation writer put it, and it empowered them, engorged their sense of themselves. Corpus Christi was the launch pad that would propel Shepard toward everything he hoped to accomplish. And it began with an awful bang.

Two weeks into his classroom training, Shepard heard the plaintive wail of the crash buzzer. Two fat seaplanes—one taking off, one landing—had slammed into each other about two hundred feet above the bay. Pieces of wreckage and body parts tumbled down into the water. Of twenty-seven men aboard the two planes, only five survived. Twenty-two dead aviators accounted for the worst accident to ever occur at Corpus. But Shepard would soon learn that losing classmates was a persistent peril.

A few months before his arrival, Shepard learned, a small group of planes was flying in formation when one plane lost control and nicked another, and they all began bouncing into one another. "Finally," a mechanic witnessing the crash from the ground said later, "about five or six planes were dropping down, just like rain." With so many planes coming and going, guided by barely competent young trainees, keeping track of the frenzy was a constant challenge. Planes often shared runways—the right half for takeoffs, the left for landings. One trainee who was conducting ground traffic failed to see a plane come up behind him, and the propeller cut him to pieces. In one twelve-month span, ninety-one men died in 5,532 crashes.

On his way to class Shepard usually walked past some mangled hunk of wreckage from the latest tragedy, deposited prominently outside the hangars as a message from the brass: *Don't let this happen to you.* And every few days the crash buzzer sounded, signifying another young aviator down. Louise, a few miles to the north, could hear those buzzers, and each time she fretted that it might be her husband.

///

Shepard's introduction to Navy flying occurred in the front seat of a single-engine, two-seat biplane called the Stearman N2S. Painted traffic-sign yellow (to warn everyone around that a trainee was inside), the Stearman earned the nickname "Yellow Peril."

Every Navy pilot would forever recall his first moments in the open cockpit of the Yellow Peril, which the Navy used for decades as its primary trainer. It was a dashingly primitive stick-and-rudder aircraft. Future generations of aircraft would be flown with a sophisticated steering wheel system, similar to a car's. But the Stearman—just one generation removed from the Wright brothers' first planes—was flown with rudder pedals and a simple stick jutting up between the pilot's legs. The control stick tugged on cables linked to ailerons—wing-mounted panels that help an airplane bank left and right. The control stick was also linked to the elevators—horizontal panels on the tail that, in combination with a corresponding increase or decrease in power, controlled the ascent and descent of the plane. On the pilot's left was the Stearman's throttle control lever, and at his feet were the two rudder pedals, which steered the plane. The Yellow Perils flown by the Navy had identical controls in the front and back-seats—one for the instructor, one for the student. The instructor communicated with his student via a one-way rubber tube called a gosport, usually used by the trainer to tell his student how badly he was flying. The Yellow Peril was sturdy and reliable but slow (top speed 126 miles an hour), and it had a troublesome rudder and bad brakes, which made even simple maneuvers such as taxiing complicated and dangerous.

After mastering the Stearman, trainees moved up to the low-wing SNJ Texan or one of the silver Valiants left over from the war, fast and powerful single-wing planes that shook like a jackhammer. The Valiant was known as the "Vultee Vibrator." Trainees also logged a few hours in the massive PBY seaplanes. Twice as long and wide as every other plane at the base, the PBY looked like a submarine with wings stuck on. It flew like a truck and, with its small cockpit window, was difficult to land on the water. You had to descend slowly until—*bam!*—you smacked down onto the Gulf. One trainee landed right on a channel marker, killing himself and seven others.

But it was the Yellow Peril that dominated Shepard's first months of training, which began in earnest on January 7, 1946, after a month of classroom instruction. Some trainees had their first brush with death in the Yellow Peril. Others, like Shepard, just got their first taste of shame.

///

For many students—especially someone as impatient as Shepard—the early days of basic flight training were maddeningly slow going. The pace had died down considerably since war's end, and trainees were flying only one or two days each week.

Mornings were spent—often restlessly—inside steamy classrooms, studying celestial navigation, physics, and astronomy, and learning about the seven characteristics of a good pilot: "skill, composure, enthusiasm, judgment, aggressiveness, combativeness and endurance." In the afternoons, students assembled outside the hangars, eagerly looking for their names in white chalk on the large flight scheduling board.

Shepard first found his name on the board on the afternoon of January 10. He was assigned to plane 64 and a thirty-minute hop with Ensign J. C. Pennock, a young instructor who would become his mentor for the critical first months of training.

During the first few flights, Pennock flew while Shepard kept his hand gently on the control stick and his toes barely touching the rudder pedals, which was supposed to give him a feel for how Pennock was maneuvering the craft. If a student felt comfortable after a few introductory flights, the instructor might show him some acrobatics.

Many naval aviators recall in specific detail their first loops, spins, and snap rolls, the abrupt climbs called chandelles, and the up-and-over corkscrew turns called Immelmans. "It was wonderful," one Corpus Christi cadet recalled of his first series of spins above the Gulf. "The beautiful tidewater panorama whirled past my eyes like some gigantic kaleidoscope. . . . I loved it."

Training flights were always shorter than Shepard would have liked, but Pennock wasted no time in thrusting him toward his first solo flight. With Pennock barking in his ear, Shepard learned to taxi to the runway, adjust the fuel mixture, increase the throttle toward full power, keep an eye on the airspeed indicator as he rolled faster and faster down the tarmac, and then, at just the right moment, pull slowly back on the control stick while feathering the rudder. Once clear of the air base, he'd bank out over the gaping expanse of the Gulf. Then he'd do it again and again and again.

Once he was airborne, Shepard displayed some of the natural abilities he had shown Carl Park back home above the Manchester airfield. He seemed comfortable with turns, climbs, glides, and landing approaches. But at first Shepard displayed less-than-perfect technique in reaching the sky. Pennock and a few other instructors noted in Shepard's training records, sometimes with frustration, that he could be too aggressive at the controls. Instead of finessing his plane aloft, he sometimes jerked the nose up too quickly, bringing his plane dangerously close to stalling.

He had his share of other troubles, too, such as the brief taste of fright on January 18 when the power on his Yellow Peril began cutting out in midflight. He and his instructor managed to limp back home in the malfunctioning aircraft, but the experience seemed to have rattled Shepard. The next day, while attempting to land, he approached with his nose too high, drifted unsteadily from side to side, and then slammed hard onto the runway, nearly losing control.

Trainees progressed through a series of stages, A, B, C, and so on. Before proceeding to the next training stage, they had to perform a successful test flight, called a check flight, which earned them a "check" from their trainer—a ticket to the next stage.

To earn a "down check" was considered the ultimate embarrassment. The measure of a top aviator was to fly with absolute precision. Hotdogging and aggressive flying were impressive to the lay person, but a real pilot knew that it was harder to fly a series of perfectly executed basic maneuvers than to swoop and loop.

Shepard's first check flight, on February 2, proved that he still had a long way to go. With Ensign Pennock sitting behind him, Shepard accelerated down the runway but waited too long before pulling back on the control stick. The plane began swerving back and forth as it barreled down the tarmac—"violently," Pennock noted in his report—until Shepard finally pulled the nose up and the plane climbed to safety. In the air, a lack of precision caused some of his turns to "skid" and "whip," the instructor noted.

Trainees were judged on various stages of a check flight—such as taxiing, takeoff, climb, turns, glides, judgment, and landing—and received one of four grades for each stage: good, satisfactory, borderline, or unsatisfactory. Of twenty-four maneuvers Shepard performed that day, Pennock judged only one to be "good"; seventeen were "satisfactory" and five were "borderline." With a less accommodating instructor, Shepard's career might have ended then and there. The truth was that any of those five "borderline" grades could well have been an "unsatisfactory." An unsatisfactory grade—equivalent to an F—was called a "down check" and was often a first step toward washing out of the training program. But Pennock saw something in Shepard, trusted his "good judgment" and desire—"student catches on very quickly," he once wrote—and decided to pass him to the next stage.

Shepard's first solo flight—the next step in the regimen and a liberating, exhilarating landmark in every aviator's life—was almost as sloppy as his check flight with Pennock. And it marked the start of a frustrating period of imperfection in his Corpus Christi experience.

The Navy expected its trainees to score "good" marks at least 20 percent of the time. Through his first stage Shepard had earned "good" marks more than 30 percent of the time. But when he advanced to Stage B, his grades plummeted to a 15 percent "good" rate, and he received as many "borderline" marks as he did "good" marks.

Instructors at Corpus Christi were either Santa Clauses (usually the self-confident war vets) or by-the-book Scrooges (usually those who had been denied the chance to dogfight at war and had something to prove). The latter seemed to feel it was their duty to prevent bad pilots from advancing, to weed out the slackers. "Cadet Brownstein is of quiet, meek disposition," one instructor wrote of his student.

Shepard was hardly meek, and most instructors—such as Pennock, who hovered somewhere between a Santa and a Scrooge—found him "eager to learn," "a fast learner," and "above average." But as the training reached the complicated stages of acrobatics, instrument landings, and simulated aircraft carrier landings (performed on carrier-shaped runways), his grades declined, and his instructors began showing some impatience.

"Student was confused during orientation, causing him to have trouble in making up his mind," one instructor wrote. "Poor taxiing," wrote another. "Very unsteady and erratic . . . DIDN'T THINK."

And one grizzled war veteran issued the ultimate insult: "chases needles." That meant Shepard was staring at the dashboard instruments, using their data as a crutch instead of flying by instinct and feel—like a musician who plays all the right notes, but without soul. By mid-1946, as Shepard entered the challenging stage of intermediate basic instrument training, he needed to sharpen his flying or he would face reassignment to the regular Navy.

///

Flying, like playing music, can be easily taught. Even a thirteen-year-old can learn to fly a plane, which in some ways is easier than driving a car; the barrier-free air can be more forgiving than the highway. But, like playing music well, learning to fly exceptionally is another matter entirely. Shepard knew how to fly. He had a natural sense of his place in the sky. What he lacked was the necessary focus to become exceptional. At times it was hard for him to recognize that his cavalier self-confidence was not enough.

In the postwar Navy, plenty of naturally talented aviators clogged Corpus Christi's runways. In fact, instructors seemed occasionally to go on binges and flunk wide swaths of trainees, apparently in an effort to purge the less-than-exceptional flyers from the air. The Navy wanted razor-sharp precision, and that called for hard work, practice, and diligence. Those who seemed unwilling or unable to sharpen their skills to perfection were known as Dilberts—and Shepard seemed headed toward becoming one.

Dilbert (long before its current iteration) was a comic strip created by two Navy officers during World War II, a mockery of cocky student aviators whom the veteran flyers considered the menaces of the sky. Dilbert himself was usually depicted with a "vacant, stupid smile and irritating self-confidence." With his big nose in the air—like a preening naval Mr. Magoo—he was often oblivious to the perils his sloppy flying inflicted on those around him. One strip showed him flying up above the clouds, unaware that his propeller was shredding the belly of a plane above him. The cartoon became wildly popular among pilots, and for many years *Dilbert* cutouts were tacked to the walls of naval air stations around the world.

Dilbert's problem was that he had little time for the minutiae of flying, including preflight inspections, diligent weather checks, and radio transmissions. At Corpus Christi—which some aviators nicknamed Dilbert College—most Dilberts ended up washing out. They were sent to a separate barracks, the Great Lakes boot camp, far from the airplane hangars, where they'd begin a few painful weeks of transition back to a regular naval officer or enlisted man. Going "to the lakes" was code for the end of a trainee's flying career.

Many otherwise solid officers found they just didn't have what it took to fly. Some discovered, too late, that they suffered from motion sickness. Getting sick during spins and rolls was not a way to impress the instructor. Those were the guys forced to wear a flying-jackass medallion around their necks after a bad flight or a midair vomiting spell.

Sometimes it didn't make sense, who failed and who didn't. Jack Barran, an academy classmate of Shepard's, was athletic, smart, coordinated. But for some reason he just couldn't get the hang of the airplane and "bilged out." The bilge is the depths of a ship's hull where leaking water collects; in the Navy, it means "stupid." His instructor finally gave it to him straight one day: "Barran, you taxi great, but you fly like shit." Meanwhile, others guys who weren't athletic—uncoordinated goons who threw like a girl and tripped over their own feet—flew gracefully and fearlessly, as if all their previous earthly shortcomings had been exchanged for imperturbable poise in the air.

Such incongruities added to the competitive and everchanging pecking order among the students. Indeed, as would be true of many of Shepard's relationships to come, classmates were both his closest friends and his fiercest competitors.

Shepard was flying almost daily and loved it. But except for night flying, at which he excelled, his grades were below average, and so were his skills. The threat of being shipped to the lakes loomed large, and the lessons of Carl Park from his teenage years were no help now. He was up against guys who as boys had also built model airplanes, worshiped Lindbergh, and read pulp magazines like *G8 and His Battle Aces*.

Halfway through basic training, Shepard was losing ground. One day in early June Shepard's instructor ordered him to take the lead slot in a group of other training planes, a formation called a "join up." He was supposed to make a slow ninety-degree turn and the rest of the group would follow. But he turned "IN THE WRONG DIRECTION," as his furious instructor wrote in big, bold letters on his evaluation sheet; as in the children's game Crack the Whip, all the other planes dutifully lined up behind him in the wrong direction as well.

Then on June 13, 1946, Shepard experienced the ultimate Dilbert-esque humiliation. He had reached the end of the first stage of intermediate basic instrument training. An instructor and he climbed into an SNJ to begin a check flight in which he would prove he'd learned his instrument training well. The flight went wrong from the start. Whether it was nerves or overconfidence, he looked only straight ahead as he taxied toward the takeoff runway. With so many planes coming and going, not looking left and right was an unforgivable infraction. His instructor reached down to his clipboard and scratched a check mark in the left-hand box: "unsatisfactory."

Shepard pushed the throttle and sped down the runway, but as the plane rose off the ground he pulled the nose up too soon and high, coming dangerously close to stalling. The instructor reached down and checked "borderline" next to "takeoff." The rest of the flight was uneventful, but on his approach for landing, Shepard "raised the flaps too soon," the instructor wrote before checking once more, this time in the "field approach" box, "unsatisfactory." Afterward he wrote a brief summary that Shepard "taxies in a straight line, does not look for other planes." The instructor then stamped his report in red ink: "UNSAFE FOR SOLO."

To recover from a down check, students had to perform extra flying exercises and then pass two check flights in a row, which Shepard did successfully. But through the summer of 1946 he continued to struggle, earning more than ten times as many "borderline" grades as "good" grades. At the end of basic intermediate instruction he'd earned only 5 "good" grades out of 336—an appalling rate of 1.5 percent, and far below the 20 percent the Navy expected.

Back in 1901 Wilbur Wright had essentially summarized the flyer's credo on death: "If you are looking for perfect safety, you will do well to sit on a fence and watch the birds. But if you really wish to learn you must mount a machine and become acquainted with its tricks by actual trial."

Shepard, with his slumping grades and his down check, decided to get better acquainted with his machine and the sky.

///

Shepard felt that one reason for his poor grades was a lack of flying time. It takes hundreds of hours of training to reach a true level of comfort in a plane. By the summer of 1946, he had accumulated barely 100 hours.

The reason flight time was so scarce was the recurring intrusion of the real world, the nonmilitary world. From the moment Shepard's ship had entered Tokyo Bay for Japan's surrender eighteen months earlier, everything else was categorized as subsequent to the victory of war: the postwar employment boom, manufacturing boom, baby boom. The impact on Corpus Christi was a mass exodus of low-paid, low-morale mechanics headed toward jobs with Ford and General Motors.

The men who had helped repair and maintain the Navy's planes—the same men who had built an amazing eleven airplanes a day at Douglas Aircraft's Long Beach plant during the height of war—were now needed in factories to feed the postwar demand for cars. This hemorrhaging of grease monkeys meant there weren't enough functioning planes for the swarms of Lindbergh wanna-bes. So Shepard spent many afternoons in the hangar, playing bridge and talking about flying while waiting for a plane. They called it "hangar flying."

Sometimes he went eight frustrating days between hops. Finally Shepard decided he could wait no more and drove out to a local airfield, where he signed up for private lessons. The Navy frowned on private training, so Shepard had to do it in secret.

In only a few months Shepard earned his private pilot's license and invited his parents, Bart and Renza, and his sister, Polly, down to celebrate the event and show off his skills. He rented an open-cockpit biplane—similar to the Yellow Peril—and gave each family member an inaugural ride. Louise flew first, then Polly, who squealed and waved wildly at everyone on the ground. Bart wore a leather pilot's helmet and a parachute harness, and Shepard even let him take the controls once they'd leveled off.

Then it was Renza's turn. She had given him his first airplane ride—that DC-3 hop to Boston and back—and now he would give her a small taste of his new world. After a brief tour above town and out over the Gulf, he turned back toward the airstrip but suddenly pulled back on the controls. The plane arched backward and climbed slowly into the Texas sky. Renza gritted her teeth and held tight to the sides of the cockpit as the plane continued up and over—a long, slow loop. Shepard descended back down toward the runway, but just before touching down he pulled up, accelerated, and performed another stomach-churning loop Renza would never forget.

As Shepard accumulated hours of "civilian" flying time, his grades at Corpus Christi steadily improved. Through the advanced stages of training—thrilling exercises in mock dogfights, shooting at towed targets, landing on simulated aircraft carriers, flying at night, and flying in formation—he began showing signs of precision and exactness.

"Good hop," an instructor wrote on one report. "Held attitude and air speed nicely."

Shepard would not receive another down check during his final few months of training. Just as his brush with expulsion from the Naval Academy had snapped him out of the fog of mediocrity, the looming humiliation of failure at Corpus Christi had done the trick. He would say later that he'd learned from his down check that getting ahead required perfection, which meant pointing a finger at the reflection in the mirror each day and saying, "You know something? You didn't do as good a job yesterday as you should have. You goofed off a little bit."

"Every day you've got to say that," he told a reporter in a

rare moment of self-analysis. "That kind of complacency is so insidious. And complacency occurs in everyone. None of us is immune to that."

///

Corpus Christi wasn't entirely about the flying. Instructors also showed the trainees how to walk (slowly), talk (not much), and stalk (for women) like an aviator.

Other unwritten lessons emanated from these alpha male veterans: trust yourself above all others; question authority; get what you want; whet your appetites; be exemplary, heroic, precise; if you choose to be unconventional, don't get caught.

"Naval aviators were not angels, not by a long shot," one aviator recalled.

Indeed, the Trocadero, the Club Swan, and other downtown Corpus Christi bars—as well as the red light district and its infamous Raymond's Gardens Dance Hall—eagerly awaited the nightly arrival of swaggering young suntanned officers in Ray-Bans.

It's possible that the notion of angelic aviators was too high an expectation, that the idea of a by-the-books pilot was an oxymoron. After all, sometimes the temptations were too strong. The earth looked so foreign from on high, rippling in Technicolor beneath, just begging for a closer look. No towns, no restrictive streets, no borders. Just trees, like a forest of hands, reaching upward. Just streams and rivers, like glistening, slithering reptiles. Just softly curving pastures, like the hips and belly of a woman—the world men thought they knew made new and fantastic by the perspective of flight. For many pilots, the early days of flying solo were like "escorting a fervor as tender as if I had just fallen in love."

And many naval aviators of Shepard's day couldn't resist the urge to drop down and taste just a bit of illicit, close-to-the-earth flying known as "flat-hatting."

In future years it would become Shepard's trademark. And while there are no recorded instances of Shepard flat-hatting at Corpus Christi, the practice was comparable to spit-balling in grade school—almost everyone has done it at one time or another.

The name came from an alleged incident in which a pedestrian's hat was crushed by a low-flying plane. To flat-hat is to dive down onto a target and streak past at a terrifyingly low altitude. A popular target for flat-hatting was the WAVES compound. WAVES were "women accepted for voluntary emergency service," who worked as mechanics, tower operators, nurses—and who sometimes sunbathed outside their compound. Pilots would swoop down low for a look, hoping to catch a few WAVES in a stage of undress. The trick was to fly fast enough and escape quick enough to prevent someone on the ground from seeing the plane's tail number. Corpus Christi's administrators even planted newspaper stories asking citizens to report flat-hatters.

The risks of flat-hatting—along with hedge hopping, a variation in which a pilot flew low to chase cows at the enormous King Ranch—were great. Those who got caught were sent "to the lakes." No questions asked, no second chances. Some pilots returned to the airbase with telephone wires dangling from the landing gear and struggled to explain how the wires had gotten there. A few pilots let the ground get too close and were killed; many came close. One famous Corpus Christi story involves the trainee who flew his plane straight into the path of an oncoming train, at night, and then switched on the landing lights. The engineer, thinking the plane was an oncoming train, slammed on the train's brakes.

At this stage in his career, Shepard wasn't known for flat-hatting or hedge hopping, nor for drinking or chasing women or staying out late, nor for arrogance or sarcasm—none of the things that would later comprise his reputation. "He was always happy-go-lucky, smiling, and being funny," said Tazewell Shepard, a World War II recipient of the Navy Cross who would go on to become naval aide to President Kennedy.

"Taz" was a lanky, slow-moving Alabaman, with a drawl that contrasted sharply with Alan's blue-blood New England accent. Some other trainees asked if the two Shepards were related, and Alan would launch into a ridiculous story about how he and Taz had the same father but different mothers, both of them circus performers. It seems their father kept running off with different circus women, he said.

Taz recalled that Alan seemed happy just being with Louise, playing golf with her, dining out in town with her, showing her off to his colleagues. For Alan and Louise, that year may have been one of the purest of their marriage.

Louise hated the succession of 100-degree days—Texas was clearly a world apart from the splendors of Longwood Gardens. But she acclimated to her new Texas life with her usual charm, taking up needlepoint and joining the church and women's church groups. She was bubbly and easy to talk to at parties, and she was well liked by all. "She captivated everyone she ran into," one of Alan's friends recalled. Although she swore that once Alan's training ended, she'd never live in Texas again, she was happy to have her new husband so close by at last.

Alan would leave her each morning at dawn and carpool to the base. But the academic schedule allowed him to be at home for dinner. In the hot and steamy evenings, they barbecued, went to parties, and lounged by the pool on the base, sipping drinks with other newlyweds. On weekends they played golf, a game to which Alan was becoming addicted. No months at sea, no enemy threats. Just the two of them starting a life. And one balmy south Texas night, in the second-floor bedroom of their Ocean Drive apartment, they conceived another life, the first child in a family that was to prove a bedrock of Shepard's life.

///

By early 1947, Shepard's grades had improved enough that his instructors raised his rating from "average" to "above average." He and Louise transferred to Pensacola, Florida, for the final months of advanced training, and this final test of naval flight training was the toughest of all.

It's been said that finding an aircraft carrier at sea is like finding a pencil mark on a white wall. Before the Navy would give Shepard his wings, he had to find that pencil mark and land an airplane on it. Six times. With his father watching from the deck, filming the whole thing.

Before he learned to fly, Shepard was known mostly for his self-assured attitude and occasional displays of aggressive determination. He was one of a quarter of a million naval officers and, at that time, merely a lowly lieutenant j.g. (junior grade)—just one of the crowd. Earning those wings, however, was the first step toward being marked as exceptional.

A naval aviator's "wings of gold" are a pair of wings attached to an anchor. They signify that the wearer has landed a plane on that speck of a carrier, which means, in many pilots' minds, that they are "the best-trained men in the world." One pilot said that after he successfully landed his first plane on an aircraft carrier, "it was difficult to walk without swaggering."

The crazy notion of using ships as floating runways had emerged in the early 1920s. The first aircraft tenders were retrofitted with long tracks that would catapult seaplanes over the edge. The USS *Langley* was the first true carrier, a former coal carrier with steel planks welded into a skinny rectangle on top. By 1930, two more ships—the battle cruisers *Lexington* and *Saratoga*—had been converted to aircraft carriers, and Navy contractors began building planes with folding wings, so that more could fit atop. Carrier aviation evolved through the 1930s with the important addition of arresting gear—cables that snag and stop incoming planes—and hydraulic catapults that shoved airplanes into the air.

But probably the most critical innovation—the one that surely saved many pilots' lives during World War II—was the spontaneous creation of the landing signal officer, or LSO. This was the brave and meticulous man, stationed at the rear of a carrier, who gave signals to incoming aviators with rectangular paddles in each hand. The first LSO was the USS *Langley*'s skipper, Kenneth Whiting, who got frustrated watching a pilot repeatedly miss his landing. He grabbed two white sailors' caps, ran down to the rear edge of the *Langley*, and coached the pilot toward the deck with hand motions to indicate when he was too high or low. That extra guidance proved so helpful that the LSO was immediately initiated into the emerging hierarchy of carrier aviation.

LSOs guided pilots to safe landings by advising them to add power (two paddles held together in front of the LSO's body) or to drop lower (both arms raised overhead into a slight V), or to abort and "wave off" (both paddles waved frantically overhead). A basket of netting over the left rear of an aircraft carrier's deck, a dozen feet below the LSO's platform, provided a place for him to jump and escape a crash landing.

Carrier aviation had indeed come a long way by the time Shepard prepared for his six required carrier landings, and he was set to earn his wings at an ideal time to be a pilot in the U.S. Navy. Though President Truman had signed the National Security Act in 1947, creating a new U.S. Air Force, Navy pilots considered themselves—would always consider themselves—the nation's best pilots. And throughout the late 1940s stories rippled through the insular naval aviation community of various records and firsts performed by ice-in-the-veins Navy pilots: an eleven-thousand-mile, nonstop trek from Perth, Australia, to Columbus, Ohio; the first ejection seat, tested at six thousand feet above Lakehurst, New Jersey; an amazing 170-hour endurance flight. Some records lasted but a blink. The world speed record of 641 miles an hour, set at Muroc, California, by Turner Caldwell, was bested five days later by a pilot who reached 651 miles an hour. Pilots were now even flying *jets* off and on aircraft carriers. It was a whole new world, Shepard's world—*if* he could nail six landings.

On the second day at sea, aboard the USS *Saipan*, Alan and a handful of other trainees prepared to make their six landings. The wind blew steadily that day, making an already complicated maneuver more difficult. Even the takeoffs were rough, with the winds slapping the planes sideways as soon as they were airborne. And the wind played tricks with the trainees' efforts to line up their landings. One pilot came in at a horrible angle and the LSO frantically waved his paddles, sending the pilot away from the ship and back around to the end of the line. Another pilot's wobbly attempts and subsequent wave-offs made the ship's officers so nervous that the pilot was sent back to land on shore.

As Shepard approached for his first-ever carrier landing, Shepard's father, Bart, pointed a 16 mm camera at the approaching dot of a plane, which grew larger as it neared the ship. Shepard had convinced the captain of the *Saipan* to allow Bart aboard for the two-day trip; in his uniform, Bart proudly walked around the deck, saluting all who came near.

Shepard had performed the prelanding pattern by flying ahead of the ship, banking into a U-turn, and then passing at a low altitude, U-turning again, and following the ship's wake until he spotted the LSO's paddles. His descent was slow and steady. His speed was just right—a few knots above the stall speed. Each time the wind nudged Shepard off track, the LSO tilted his paddles to get him straightened out. Finally, when it seemed as though he was going to fly right over the ship, Shepard saw the LSO's paddles drop down and left—the signal to cut power. He pulled back on the throttle, let the nose drop a little, and then pulled it up again. His SNJ dropped to the *Saipan*'s deck, bounced hard, and then caught one of the arresting wires with its tailhook. Pilots call carrier landings "arrested landings" or "traps"—more like a controlled crash than a gentle runway touchdown. Shepard's body was thrown forward into his shoulder straps, and he nearly head-butted the instrument panel—the violent conclusion to every safe carrier landing.

"Absolutely perfect," Shepard yelled. "Right in the center."

His next five landings were also nearly perfect.

The next day Bart pinned on Alan's wings of gold, and the uniformed father saluted his uniformed son. Alan called it "one of the best moments" of his life.

5

A perfectly charming son of a bitch

After receiving his wings, Shepard, like other knighted Navy pilots, paused anxiously at a fork in the road. Both paths led to a career as a naval aviator, but only one offered the full fly-boy package—speed, thrills, danger, and adventure.

On the day he received his wings, he had been handed a one-page form on which to list his preferences for a squadron assignment. Like many of his peers, Shepard wrote "CV"—the Navy's alphabetical code for carrier aviation. Next to that he wrote "VFB" (a fighter-bomber squadron), then "VF" (a fighter squadron), and then "VTB" (a torpedo-bombing squadron). Each of his selections was a request to become a so-called single-engine pilot. Newly winged pilots were assigned to either single-engine or dual-engine aircraft. The latter meant big bombers or transport planes, oafish, lumbering air buses used to transport troops or supplies. Due to their size and the need for a long runway, dual-engine planes were based on land. At the time, the best way to reach an aircraft carrier was to be selected for the smaller, speedier single-engine aircraft.

Single-engine flyers, furthermore, would be entrusted with the Navy's fastest, most sophisticated planes. And if chosen for single engines, they'd be pointed down a path leading to the next generation of aircraft—jets. In the late 1940s the Navy had begun slowly replacing its propeller planes and their piston-driven engines with jet-propelled aircraft. Only a handful of the Navy's top pilots were flying jets at that time (the first U.S. jets were flown in 1942 and 1943). But the next best assignment—which placed an aviator in line for jets—was to serve as a single-engine pilot.

At the bottom of his request form, Shepard added an extra plea, an effort not only to be assigned to single-engine planes but to get the nastiest single-engine of all.

"I earnestly desire to fly fighter-bombers—Corsairs," he wrote.

Shepard had been introduced to the powerful, ugly, and notoriously tricky F4U Corsair during the final year of World War II. He watched from the deck of the USS *Cogswell* as divisions of the menacing planes grumbled overhead, aggressively bound for some aerial enemy confrontation. He'd heard thrilling stories about the Corsair's kamikaze-killing sprees. Still, there was an asterisk beside the Corsair's success. It was an imperfect plane, and only the best pilots could fly it—which, of course, was all Shepard needed to hear.

The Navy made its assignments by reviewing a student's grades and assessing which squadrons needed new blood. Shepard had to worry whether his late surge of improvement during Corpus Christi training had been enough. He knew the Navy wanted careful, "check-happy" pilots—those willing to check and recheck their planes before taking off, in pursuit of error-free flying. Navy airplanes were getting faster, more sophisticated, and more unforgiving by the day. It was not a time for Dilberts.

Shepard did not have to wait long for his answer. Five days after scribbling "CV" and "Corsairs" he received a letter ordering him to report the following week to Cecil Field in Jacksonville, Florida.

But surely the two letters he saw most clearly on the half-page letter were VF—the code for a fighter squadron. Not only had he received his wish to be a carrier pilot, he had been chosen to fly the coolest, most dangerous plane in the Navy.

///

The single-engine F4U had a long snout and V-shaped "gull" wings, earning it various nicknames like "Hose Nose" and "U-Bird" or simply the "Hog." A two-thousand-horsepower engine drove its enormous thirteen-foot propeller. It had terrible visibility; it was difficult to see over the long nose, and early versions had a birdcage over the pilot instead of a bubble canopy. Pilots had to zigzag while taxiing down runways, just to be able to see around the nose and in front of them. The Corsair's fuel cells leaked and had to be taped up. On takeoff, pilots had to practically stand on the right rudder to keep it from turning or "torquing" to the left. The plane bounced hard on landings, which pilots often compared to "milking a mouse"—a delicate feat. As one famous Corsair pilot said, "The air, not the runway, was the Corsair's element." The manufacturer, Chance-Vought, was constantly modifying the plane to correct the problems and even hired the most famous pilot of all, Charles Lindbergh, to work out kinks and teach other pilots how to handle the temperamental plane. Late in World War II Lindbergh had traveled to Corsair operating bases in the South Pacific as a civilian technical adviser; that's where he had nearly crossed paths with Shepard, on the corpse-covered island of Biak.

Despite its maddening and dangerous quirks, the Corsair was also an incredibly successful enemy-killer during the war. It could fly more than four hundred miles an hour and could turn on a dime. During World War II, heavily armed F4U Corsairs shot down more than two thousand Japanese aircraft, most of which had just a fraction of the Corsair's power and maneuverability. In a fast dive, the front edge of the Corsair's wings made a whistling sound, and the Japanese called the terrifying planes "whistling death."

Among the many notable wartime Corsair pilots was an unflappably talented Marine named John Glenn, Shepard's future colleague and friend. Glenn flew fifty-nine combat missions in World War II. Despite being hit by antiaircraft fire five times, he always managed to fly his damaged but sturdy Corsair back home. "Nothing gave me more pleasure than to be flying a Corsair," Glenn said in his memoirs. "You reach a point of oneness with the plane, as if you are the brain and it is the body."

Joining a Corsair squadron was a very sweet assignment for a twenty-three-year-old. Practically every Navy pilot of the day wanted to fly off aircraft carriers, although not all of them wanted to do so in the Corsair. Many of Shepard's colleagues had a love-hate relationship with the temperamental Corsair. But Shepard absolutely loved the plane, calling his Hose Nose a "for real men only" kind of machine.

Even after the war, the Corsair continued to inflict plenty of damage on pilots. The engine sometimes stalled at slow speeds, and if it did, the plane would flip to the right—often too quickly for a pilot to correct. Pilots called this "a bad stall characteristic"—a murky euphemism that meant the plane could spontaneously crash and burn.

One day one of Shepard's classmates came in too high and fast for a landing at Cecil Field, slowed down too abruptly, stalled, and flipped. He was killed in a fireball a half mile short of the runway. Another peer failed to adjust the mixture control (which sets how much air and fuel the engine uses) before taking off; as the Corsair became airborne, the engine quit and both plane and pilot were obliterated.

A dark joke among Corsair pilots was that the schedule in a Corsair squadron was a grueling one: a flight at 6 A.M., a flight at 1 P.M., a funeral at 3 P.M. Some pilots called the Corsair "the bent-wing widowmaker."

Death continued to stalk Shepard in his career, beckoning him and wooing him like a demon chanteuse. It had pursued and taunted him throughout World War II. It had unnerved and mocked him at Corpus Christi, and it now taunted him at Cecil Field. More than three thousand Navy trainees lost their lives in the mid-1940s, and thousands more were injured. The Navy counted thirteen thousand major accidents in one year, half of them resulting in destroyed planes.

Learning to recover from the loss of a fellow aviator was an unwritten part of the curriculum of naval flight training. The solution, usually, was to shun it—and then drink. Acknowledging death was a dangerous thing. It was like acknowledging fear, and fear was unacceptable. So, to fuel their resistance to the fear of death, they imbibed.

Among the notorious imbibers during Shepard's months of advanced training outside Jacksonville were two former Naval Academy classmates, Dick Hardy and Bill Botts, who rented a beachfront house at Ponte Vedra Beach. Alan and Louise lived nearby, and Alan carpooled the twenty-six miles to Cecil Field every day with Hardy and Botts; the threesome, according to Botts, "collected speeding tickets like popcorn."

On weekends, Alan and Louise sometimes attended the infamous Hardy and Botts beach parties together. But Louise was carrying their baby, and pregnancy didn't agree with her; her fragile constitution often left her exhausted and bedridden. So Alan regularly walked alone to the boozy and bustling Ponte Vedra beach house, where cocktail shakers chattered and locals girls in bikinis giggled and danced. Actor Freddie Bartholomew (who had starred in a 1941 movie called *Naval Academy*) lived next door and often stopped by for a drink. Alan or Bill Botts usually rented a small biplane from the local municipal airport and took turns landing on the hard-packed beach, taking party guests up for show-offy spins, loops, and dives. Botts recalled that on one such ride, a cute redhead screamed, "This is the first time I've been off God's green earth!"

As Louise approached her due date she left Jacksonville

and went to stay with her parents at Longwood. Friends recalled that Alan then began occasionally accompanying the other bachelors for nights on the town.

Before long, though, a vice admiral who lived a few doors down the beach caught wind of the weekend parties and ordered them to cease. The owners of the beach house kicked Hardy and Botts out. "And the party was over," Hardy recalled.

After that Shepard and the others were assigned to their first squadrons. Training days were over. It was time to become aviators.

///

In July 1947 Louise gave birth to their daughter, whom they named Laura, in Wilmington, near Longwood. A few months later, after recuperating at her parents' house, she joined Alan in Norfolk, Virginia, where he had been assigned, back in April, to his first squadron.

Fighter squadron VF-42 was awaiting the overhaul of its aircraft carrier, the USS *Franklin D. Roosevelt.* The *FDR* had been commissioned weeks after the end of World War II, the first of a new class of behemoth postwar carriers. When Shepard first spotted her, she was as rusty as a forgotten pickup truck.

Her deck, just shy of a thousand feet, was the Navy's longest, and in 1946 it had been used to host the first-ever test launches and landings of a jet on an aircraft carrier. But when military funds dwindled after the war, the *FDR*'s manpower was cut back to a skeleton crew, which fell behind in maintaining the huge ship. The *FDR* became rusted and filthy until she was finally put into dry dock for a much-needed overhaul. During the overhaul, Shepard's squadron operated out of Norfolk Naval Air Station, exercising their Corsairs out over the Atlantic.

For a brief while longer, Alan and Louise and their baby daughter were a normal family. In the two years since the end of World War II, despite moving from California to Texas to Florida to Virginia, Alan and Louise had enjoyed evening meals together, shared the same bed, played golf on weekends, and acted, for the most part, like a typical postwar couple. But Alan and his Corsair were about to embark on two years of extreme flying far from home and family. And during those two years he would begin distancing himself from his pack of peers, establishing himself as one of the premier pilots in the U.S. Navy. New levels of skill and an even stronger confidence would begin to emerge.

///

With its muscular engine and enormous propeller (each of its four blades was as long and heavy as a man), the Corsair was among the few prop-driven aircraft of the day capable of approaching anywhere near the speed of sound. Reaching the cusp of Mach 1 required diving from thirty thousand feet at full power until the plane reached 350 knots—more than 400 miles an hour, or Mach .76. The speed of sound, or Mach 1, is roughly 660 miles an hour at sea level. At such speeds, the skin would ripple across Shepard's face, breathing would become difficult, and the Corsair would groan, pop, and creak.

At such superhuman speeds, a favorite aviator's trick was to "crack the whip." That meant pulling back sharply on the control stick, which would briefly shove Shepard into his seat at seven times the force of gravity, on the brink of blacking out. Then he'd jerk the control stick forward again, creating an air pocket behind the wings that would slam closed with a loud crack—like a thunderclap or the sonic booms left in jets' wakes. "A rivet or two could pop, skins might wrinkle, but the old bird should still bring you home safely," one Corsair pilot said of such high-speed dives.

While performing those and other feats above the Atlantic Ocean east of Norfolk, Shepard learned to tame the Corsair, and his increasingly precise and confident flying soon caught the eye of the fighter squadron's commander, James L. "Doc" Abbot.

Abbot was an energetic, self-assured pilot from Mobile, Alabama, whose gentlemanly manner shielded a shrewd ability to manipulate the Navy's rules and hierarchies and get what he wanted. Abbot spoke with a crisp drawl—a melding of his home-grown Alabama lilt and the clipped cadence of a Navy officer. That friendly drawl could disarm an opponent and defuse any situation. When Abbot had been chosen to lead VF-42, he visited the Norfolk offices in charge of assigning pilots to squadrons. He affably offered to help them out—then proceeded to handpick each of his pilots.

As a 1939 Naval Academy graduate, Abbot chose to surround himself with other "ring-knockers," most of them from the classes of '44 and '45. After a few weeks of flying together out of Norfolk—impressed with Shepard's solid and skillful command of the Corsair—Abbot chose Shepard to be his wingman. Choosing a wingman is as intimate as it gets in naval aviation. A wingman is a pilot's flying partner, his guardian angel. He flies slightly behind his partner, watching his "six o'clock"—his ass. Wingmen advise each other on speed, direction, altitude. If an enemy approaches, a wingman intercedes. If a pilot is in trouble, the wingman does everything he can to find a solution. But because the Corsair was difficult to fly perfectly level and straight, flying wing in a Corsair was no easy feat. It required finesse and a smooth hand on the controls. In choosing Shepard, Abbot was essentially saying: *I trust you with my life.*

In the purest of partnerships, the trust is mutual. And so Shepard surely trusted his commander one day above Pensacola, Florida, when Abbot decided to have some fun.

A few months after Abbot had gathered his handpicked squadron of flyers, he took them down to the naval air station at Pensacola for some training exercises and mock carrier landings, in which they landed on a carrier outline painted on the runway. One day the commander of all four squadrons that constituted Shepard's air group ordered all ninety planes of the group to take to the sky. Abbot took the lead of his squadron, which flew last behind the other three squadrons. As the ninety-plane gaggle banked left, Shepard held his Corsair steady, just behind Abbot's right wing, and the rest of the squadron followed. The air group commander started calling Abbot on the radio, but Abbot ignored the calls, pulled away, and descended down onto nearby Mobile, Alabama, where he dropped even lower for an all-squadron flat-hat of Abbot's parents' house. Shepard and the others loved it, and the stunt endeared them to Abbot.

Back at Pensacola, the air group commander asked Abbot what happened, and he innocently explained how his men had accidentally missed the turn.

///

VF-42 finally loaded its planes, its men, and its equipment onto the massive *FDR* in early 1948 and left Norfolk for the island-speckled blue waters of the Caribbean. The *FDR*'s shakedown cruise was a chance for the planes and pilots to get acquainted with their floating runway, and for the *FDR* and her crew to accommodate the challenges and dangers of fuel-laden planes landing on her back.

The *FDR* sailed first to Guantánamo Bay, where vast amounts of dark "anejo" rum were consumed, and where the eager pilots of VF-42 tried to figure out how to strap tanks of rum to their Corsairs and fly them back to the United States. One pilot was elected to buy a wooden cask of rum from one of the locals. But back on the *FDR* they realized their what-if scenarios of toting rum on a Corsair were nuts. So they drank it.

FDR then moseyed through the Caribbean so that Shepard and his squadron mates could attempt landings on her 968-foot deck. Most of the squadron were "nuggets"—recently qualified squadron pilots on their first assignment (also known as FNGs, or "fucking new guys")—and that meant they had very little experience with carrier landings. So as they nursed their rum hangovers and cruised past Jamaica, Haiti, and the Grenadines, they practiced landing on *FDR's* armored deck, again and again and again.

Shepard continued to impress Abbot and his peers during the *FDR's* warm-up cruise—especially after getting Abbot's permission to try landing at night.

Landing on a carrier at night is one of the most difficult and dangerous maneuvers in all of aviation—*especially* in the Corsair. Even in calm seas, carrier landings at night are a ludicrous test of a pilot's mettle. (At the time, no other nation even attempted night carrier landings.) One air group commander—Abbot's boss—had been killed while attempting a night launch; he was catapulted off the deck and right into the sea. Of the three dozen pilots under Abbot's command, most, like Shepard, were on their first carrier cruise. Those who were on their second cruise were offered the chance to "qualify" for night landings. At the time, qualifying for night landings was a rare distinction held by pilots in specialized squadrons.

But Shepard insisted that Abbot give him a chance to qualify as well. "He just talked his way into it," Shepard's squadron mate Dick Hardy recalled.

Most cockpits sit directly above or just ahead of a plane's wings; on the Corsair, the cockpit sat *behind* the wings. To see around his Corsair's absurdly long nose, a pilot had to approach the faintly lit outline of the *FDR* while banking steeply to the left, get the ship lined up in his sights, then turn sharply in toward the ship's tail while descending slowly and, at the last second, straightening out and lowering the plane's nose. Eyes bounce from the instrument panel to the string of lightbulbs sewn into the LSO's suit to the fast-approaching runway lights and back to the instrument panel. A precise speed must be maintained— slow enough to land but a few knots faster than the point where the Corsair could stall. Like threading a needle, all the while the pilot had to keep both hands perfectly steady. With a margin of error of just a few feet, the slightest twitch—a sneeze, a cough—meant he'd be dead, along with the LSO and possibly scores of shipmates. Finally, with the deck almost invisible beneath him, he had to pick up the LSO's lighted paddles, wait for the cut signal, then chop off the throttle and drop down onto the deck. Because the Corsair bounced hard on landings, the LSO had to bring the plane in precariously close to the rear edge of the ship, to make sure its tailhook snagged one of the arresting cables.

One dark, calm night in the Caribbean, Shepard earned the rare distinction of being the first "nugget" in the Navy to perform carrier landings at night in the Corsair—another psychological half step ahead of his peers.

Flying at night—"in the confidence of the stars," French pilot Antoine de Saint-Exupéry once called it—would become one of the great challenges and great loves of Shepard's career. And night carrier landings would become his specialty; for the rest of his life he would call those landings the most treacherous feats of his career.

After a few months on the Caribbean, the FDR returned briefly to Norfolk and then, in early 1948, set out for a nine-month cruise to the Mediterranean. Shepard kissed Louise and baby Laura goodbye and walked up the FDR's gangplank. On the top deck he turned to wave to his family but couldn't find them among the crowd of wives, children, and friends milling below. Louise had decided not to drag out the goodbye scene. Why hang around with the other wives to watch the ship slowly, painfully disappear? Instead, she turned around and marched the baby home—the beginning of another long-term separation. Shepard's one attempt at easing the pain of many months apart was a ritual that would continue through the rest of their lives. Whenever he was able, he would call Louise at 5 P.M. (her time) to say, "Hello, I love you, I miss you."

But for him, the separation also offered the chance to be a full-time flyer.

That is, until the Atlantic Ocean snatched away his airplane.

///

The *FDR* was nearly halfway to Europe when the icy Atlantic began tossing her around like an empty beer can on a river. Her engines wailed and whined. Her sailors barfed. Waterlogged airplanes bucked and bounced, straining against their wheel chocks and tie-downs. Shepard hunkered down below, wondering if his Corsair would survive the sea lashing, wondering which was worse: the relentless storm above or the South Pacific typhoons he'd survived in World War II.

The rusty *FDR* had been overhauled in order to be displayed as a new symbol of American military might and to lend backup support to the ongoing delivery of food and supplies to Soviet-blockaded West Germany—the Berlin airlift operation, which was then under way. At a time when communism was still rooting around for new homes in the war-shaken countries of Europe, *FDR*'s role was to be part ambassador, part patrolman. To impress and intimidate its audience, the *FDR* brought along some of the Navy's best fighter pilots. Yet as they neared the Azores in the eastern Atlantic, nine hundred miles off Portugal's coast, Shepard and his colleagues had more on their minds than flying. Amid a monotony of gray—the sky, the sea, the ship, and their mood—not becoming shark bait was what mattered most.

Enormous swells lifted and dropped the *FDR*, all forty-five thousand tons of her. Her skipper pointed the massive ship straight into the oncoming slopes of water. She'd slowly climb a wave, twenty . . . thirty . . . forty feet up, then disappear in an explosion of sea and foam before hurtling down the backside.

Most of the *FDR*'s airplanes were tied down at the front of the ship, in "recovery" mode; with the planes up front, the rear deck was open to "recover" landing airplanes. The ship's officers considered moving the planes to the rear—called "respotting" the deck—away from the crashing seas. But waves were now regularly hulking up and over the ship's bow, deluging the deck. Any man walking up there would get swept overboard as easily as an ant gets flicked off a picnic blanket. Respotting was impossibly dangerous. All Shepard could do was ride it out below in the pilots' ready room, hoping that his squadron's planes were lashed tight enough to withstand the pummeling waves.

But the biggest wave was yet to come. When it did, the men in the *FDR*'s control tower gasped as it rose higher and higher, became a building of water, and then slammed down onto the plane-filled front of the deck. The front quarter of the ship was submerged, and when the water receded, the men in the tower gasped again.

The planes of Shepard's squadron had been parked in rows, five in the front row and rows of six behind that. When the wave hit, the first five planes were torn from their moorings and swept away without a trace. A few planes in the second row survived, but most were mangled beyond repair, so badly damaged that the crew tossed them overboard. Of the eleven planes in the first two rows, only one plane survived. It belonged to Shepard's squadron commander, Doc Abbot, but it would never manage to fly right again.

Shepard was sickened when he heard the news. His plane, his beloved Corsair, had been in that first row, and it was now flying to the bottom of the Atlantic.

///

While waiting for replacement planes to be delivered, Shepard became intimately reacquainted with the simplistic color schemes of man at sea: the flat, drab, and persistent gray paint of his domestic environs, the muddled blue-gray-green of the ocean, the alternating white and blue of the sky, the unobstructed views of celestial light shows and the moon. His four thousand shipmates—a population greater than the entire Naval

Academy student body, or Shepard's entire hometown—were squeezed into a compact steel city three football fields long. Days and nights rumbled with the phlegmy churning of the ship's boilers, the air sweetened by the stench of the Navy's black fuel oil fumes.

But this was not the USS *Cogswell*, and Shepard was no longer restricted to his ship's boundaries. This was a ship whose sole purpose was to launch men like Shepard. And when the *FDR* reached the coast of North Africa, the Navy was asked to help search for a downed commercial plane, and Shepard—in his new Corsair—left the *FDR's* gunmetal gray behind and sped across the Sahara Desert, just fifty feet above the sand.

At the same time, however, continued military spending cuts meant limited dollars for fuel. As the *FDR* toured the Mediterranean Shepard was flying less than he had hoped. He and his squadronmates were sometimes getting just a half dozen hops a month. Even the *FDR's* skipper, Captain Harry D. Felt, expressed his concern about his pilots' lack of flying. "If they lay off too long, you're asking for trouble," he said.

Abbot finally wielded some of his wily influence in Washington, and managed to obtain extra fuel for his squadron. But some of his men had become a bit rusty.

As part of the *FDR's* ambassadorial duties, dignitaries were often invited aboard and sometimes treated to an air show. While stationed in the Greek port of Piraeus, Doc Abbot went ashore and visited the Greek royal palace to ask if the king and queen would be interested in touring the *FDR* and watching its aviators perform.

King Paul, Queen Frederika, and a few other Greek officials came aboard, and the *FDR* sailed a few miles out into the Mediterranean and put on a show. Shepard led his division of Corsairs in formation past the ship. Other pilots fired rockets at targets as the hundreds of crew members and visitors on deck watched and cheered.

Then a pilot named Hal Fish approached and aimed his five-inch rockets at the target, a junk ship moored a few hundred yards away from the *FDR*. When Fish squeezed the trigger, the rocket "pickled"—failed to separate from the wing. It then exploded and ripped the wing off Fish's plane, which flipped and slammed into the sea.

"He didn't have a chance," said Shepard's squadronmate Dick Hardy.

In such instances, pilots learned that fate, not skill, sometimes determined who lived or died in the still immature world of naval aviation.

///

Doc Abbot, after several months of flying with Shepard as his wingman, had decided somewhere in the Mediterranean that it was time for a new assignment.

Amid the choreographed ballet of landing on an aircraft carrier, pilots are graded on how quickly they can land, release their tailhook from the arresting wire, and move their plane to the front of the ship. It's called "time in the gear," and Abbot had VF-42's second-lowest time in the gear. Ranked slightly ahead of him was Shepard.

So Abbot decided to give Shepard command of his own section (two planes). Some weeks after that, he gave Shepard command of a full division (four planes). Putting a nugget in charge of a division was an enormous vote of confidence and an endorsement of Shepard's refined mix of aerial chutzpah and finesse. Division leaders must fly smoothly and gently so that the other three planes can follow. They can't "horse" erratically. They must also always fly in control, and Abbot—who considered himself a superior pilot—saw shades of himself in Shepard.

As his squadronmates watched Shepard take another step up in the hierarchy, some noticed a change in his personality. He started to become, in one colleague's words, "bodacious." He was already known for a big, self-confident attitude. But that wasn't uncommon in the Navy. After gaining his own division, though, Shepard's big personality grew even bigger, and it turned some colleagues off.

"He was a perfectly charming son of a bitch," said Shepard's friend Bill Botts, who appreciated his cocksure demeanor even if others didn't. Everyone who met Alan Shepard over the next fifty years would, almost without fail, describe him as an acquired taste, someone you either liked or didn't—"like Miami, or olives," said Botts.

Carrier aviators owed their lives to the enlisted men who operated the launching catapults, maintained their planes, monitored the weather, and stood on the FDR's tail waving paddles as whirring propellers bore down on them. But the aviators and enlisted men rarely mixed. In the hierarchy of a carrier at sea, the aviators were the big dogs, and the ready room was their doghouse, the place they boasted and argued about this plane and that, about speed and ascent and danger and noise. During the many lulls while the FDR was steaming from one port to the next, Shepard and the others made up for a lack of flying by talking about flying. They could sit for hours smoking and drinking coffee in the ready room. Shepard loved to talk about the Corsair, its eccentricities, and its power, and how landing it on a carrier required the skill of an intuitive pilot. He was fiercely proud of his Corsair and annoyingly proud of his ability to fly it better than most.

But his buddies were learning how to take the hotshot down a peg.

Bob Baldwin, who flew one of the AD Skyraiders assigned to the FDR, loved to rile Shepard by bragging that the AD—a workhorse with one of the more powerful engines of the day—was faster than, tougher than, and far superior to Shepard's Corsair.

Baldwin and his roommate, Warren O'Neil, ribbed Shepard one night at dinner about Shepard's "inferior airplane." During missions, "us AD pilots always have to throttle back and wait for you Corsairs to catch up," they said. Shepard hated that. One night he'd finally had enough and stood up from the table, pointing a finger at Baldwin and then O'Neil, barking, "Baldwin, with you sucking on one end of this ship and O'Neil blowing on the other, we'd have forty knots of wind across the deck." The other two just laughed harder, which made Shepard even madder. "He didn't take any foolishness from anybody," O'Neil recalled.

Although Shepard was earning a strong reputation as a skilled pilot, a leader, and a teacher, the pace aboard the *FDR* sometimes grated on him. And when things got slow the ship's captain ordered VF-42's pilots to perform "collateral duties," demeaning paperwork tasks. Meanwhile, back home, Navy and Air Force pilots were breaking records, flying jets, and crashing through the sound barrier. Guys like Chuck Yeager were screaming above the salt flats of Muroc Lake in southern California, piloting winged rockets with tough names like XP-80 and X-1. Also, the Navy had rcently created its first squadron of jet pilots, who at that very moment were learning to take off and land on the USS *Saipan*—the same aircraft carrier that Shepard had landed on a year earlier to earn his wings.

Furthermore, the Navy had just established the Test Pilot Training Division, a place to train a new generation of pilots who could test the new jets coming off the manufacturers' assembly lines. The Naval Air Test Center (soon to be named the Naval Test Pilot School) was created at Patuxent River Naval Air Station in Maryland. That, Shepard decided somewhere in the Mediterranean, was where he wanted to be—flying the fastest, newest, meanest jets in the world. And he told Abbot so every chance he got.

Meanwhile, the scenery—both terrestrial and human—wasn't bad. The *FDR*, due to restrictions on fuel, parked itself for extended periods of time in some spectacular foreign ports, offloading its men into Naples, Tripoli, the Greek islands, and the swanky beach towns of the French Riviera. Many Navy marriages were battered by the liberties taken during the *FDR's* excessive amounts of shore leave.

Shepard kept Louise in his thoughts. He bought her perfumes in France, leather gloves in Italy, and even a few paintings. He wrote to her often and, when he could, called her and the baby, Laura, at 5 P.M. Eastern Standard Time. Still, when a flyer isn't flying, the next best thing is often found in foreign ports, in the bars inside those ports—on a bar stool.

As if rediscovering the skills he'd honed dating "crabs" back in Annapolis, Shepard displayed no inhibitions in those ports and their bars. He'd walk right up to a beautiful woman, and if she didn't speak English, he'd dig up a few words of French or Spanish from high school and the academy. His foreign-language grades had always been poor, but he knew enough to buy a girl a drink. He wasn't especially handsome, but whatever he had, it worked, and soon Shepard was known as one of the more successful flirts—"a spot we were all trying for," Baldwin recalled. He and Shepard used to each share time with the same French girl at one of the towns along the Côte d'Azur: "It just depended on who got ashore first."

Once an older woman made the first move. Shepard and his roommate, Bill Chaires, decided during a weekend of liberty to take a train north from the port city of Cannes to Paris. They checked into the cut-rate Hotel Pennsylvania and then walked down the Champs Elysées, stopping in the lobby bar of a hotel for a beer. While standing at the bar, a waiter approached and handed them a note—an invitation from two ladies in the dining room to come share a drink.

"Why not?" Shepard said.

The two men entered the dining room and saw Eleanor Roosevelt waving at them. The former First Lady was in town for a U.N. General Assembly meeting (where she would give a famous speech called "The Struggles for the Rights of Man"). After sharing a drink with her, Shepard invited her to come to Cannes and tour the ship named after her deceased husband, the ship she herself had christened in 1945. Mrs. Roosevelt initially accepted, which infuriated Shepard's unprepared superior officers. But she later called the ship and canceled her visit.

Shepard's other European barroom encounters were equally impressive. His shipmates would watch in envy and awe as Shepard left bar after bar with women. What happened after that they could only guess. Shepard's buddies would always assume that the night was not over for Shepard and whichever young woman he befriended. Shepard had a habit of not exactly denying or confirming it. He just let people assume what they would.

"He was sort of proud of his reputation. He just liked girls," Bob Baldwin, a retired vice admiral, says today. "That was just a compulsion he seemed to have. He didn't wear it on his sleeve, though. He was content to let it speak for itself."

///

The Navy was so impressed with Doc Abbot's work in the Mediterranean (Hal Fish's death had been the lone fatality, a rarity for the day) that halfway through the *FDR's* tour there they snatched him away from his squadron and stuck him in an office at the Pentagon. So that's where Shepard addressed his letter. Abbot knew what it would say even before he opened it: *Please, help me get into test pilot school.*

Abbot walked a few doors down from his office, entered the office of the admiral overseeing test pilot assignments, and had a word with him about Lieutenant Alan B. Shepard.

While waiting for a response during the slow-paced Mediterranean afternoons, Shepard would loiter in the ready room, sipping coffee and filling out some overdue paperwork. When he heard voices and spurts of laughter coming from the flight surgeon's office down the hall, Shepard would smile, put down his papers, and walk over to chat with a decorated World War II hero, the man who would soon change his life.

Turner Caldwell, commander of Shepard's air group (known as CAG, for "commander air group"), had become good friends with the *FDR*'s flight surgeon, who had also been a carrier pilot during World War II. Caldwell often walked down from his office to sit with the doctor and swap stories of flying and fighting. Shepard loved to listen in on these conversations, especially when Caldwell spoke of the bright red Douglas Skystreak he had flown into the history books the previous year.

Lean, slight, and deceptively fearsome, Caldwell had been a carrier pilot in the South Pacific, commanding one of the Navy's first night flying squadrons. He once led eleven planes, all dangerously low on fuel, away from battle and to safety when their aircraft carrier was damaged too severely to let them land. After the war, Caldwell was selected to fly the Navy's first experimental jets, which were then the fastest machines known to humankind. On August 20, 1947, he took off in the nail-polish-red, futuristic-looking Skystreak—he called it the "crimson test tube"—and ripped across a 3 km course at the salt flats of Muroc, California (later named Edwards Air Force Base). Caldwell, his body shaking like a loose piston inside the cockpit, pushed the jet to the brink of the speed of sound—640.663 miles an hour. It was the fastest any human had ever traveled, and Caldwell's photograph appeared on the front page of newspapers across the country. Five days later, though, the record was broken, and two months after that Chuck Yeager took his X-1 rocket plane to 700 miles an hour, becoming the first to break the sound barrier. But Caldwell's fame inside the Navy didn't diminish. He rose to become one of the most respected and influential aviator-mentors.

Using the slow pace of the *FDR* cruise to his advantage, Shepard spent every free moment he could at Caldwell's side, peppering him with questions about night flying, the Douglas Skystreak, and the other jets he had flown. Caldwell, patient and relaxed, spent many an afternoon folded in a seat with Alan Shepard figuratively at his knee. Such informal connections, Shepard found, could mean a lot in the insular naval world.

After serving as Shepard's air group commander, Caldwell was promoted to new duties at the Pentagon in early 1949 (ironically, his successor was killed in a Corsair crash immediately after taking off from an aircraft carrier). Shepard, meanwhile, was dispatched to another carrier, the USS *Midway,* for a few weeks on a cold-weather flying mission. Wearing a thick insulated suit that made movement and flying difficult, Shepard conducted flight experiments intended to pave the way for the Navy's new specialty "all-weather" squadrons.

When that brief tour ended, he was scheduled to return to the states for shore duty—most Navy pilots, after their first carrier tour, served some time in an office. Shepard's peers must have gasped when they heard he was headed not for shore duty but to the place they all wanted to be: the hammered-flat waterfront known as Pax.

6

Shepard should be court-martialed

The United States Naval Test Pilot School at Patuxent River Naval Air Station—known fleetwide as Pax River, or just Pax—was created to test the new jets the Navy had begun phasing into its fleet of aircraft in 1949. At the time an intense competition for superiority in the air had developed between the Navy and the coltish new Air Force, which was also testing the world's latest and fastest jets.

To edge ahead of the Air Force, the Navy had circulated "aviation plan 65" in 1948, which called for the best naval aviators—those displaying "outstanding flying proficiency"—to be pulled from fleet duty and assigned to Pax River.

Turner Caldwell told his superiors that Alan Shepard was one of the best, and when Caldwell spoke, people listened. Doc Abbot also recommended Shepard, who in mid-1950 was selected from 150 nominees to join two dozen other exemplary flyers in the next class—class number five—at the Navy's new Test Pilot School. It was more than a sweet assignment for a junior officer, it was unprecedented. At twenty-six, he was—once again—the youngest pilot in his class. But this time his youth was nothing to be sheepish about. It was a badge of honor and his biggest break so far.

For a first-tour pilot to leapfrog his peers and reach the pinnacle of naval aviation required more than luck and skill. It required the kind of help Shepard got from Doc Abbot and Turner Caldwell. Other aviators grumbled that Shepard wasn't a better pilot, just better connected. Indeed, Shepard admitted that he "may not have extra talent." He had learned that an aggressive pursuit of his goals required him to rely heavily on helpers, mentors, and saviors. He would cultivate such men throughout his career. Just like the upperclassmen who "saved his bucket" when he got in trouble at the academy, he gravitated toward such men—because he admired them *and* because they could help him. And in the near future one such mentor-savior would save Shepard's career.

///

Shepard's transfer to Pax in the summer of 1950 coincided with the first shots of the Korean War, which would soon pull many of his Navy peers into battle.

At the end of World War II, the United States had helped cleave Korea in half—an effort to keep the Soviet-backed northern half of the peninsula separate from the U.S.-occupied south. Two separate nations, North and South Korea, were created in 1948, but two years later North Korean troops invaded across the 38th parallel, and the United States—largely due to its commitment to contain communism—joined the fighting.

His transfer to Pax River was both a geographic and psychological divergence from the rest of the Navy. For Shepard, this was good and bad, because while he was headed to an aviators' mecca, some of his Korea-bound peers—such as John Glenn—would soon make names for themselves as heroic combat aviators waging jet-powered aerial battles against Soviet and

Korean MiGs. But Shepard's role as a test pilot was also an integral one in the greater struggle that came to be known as the cold war.

"Pax River," on the shores of Chesapeake Bay in southern Maryland was, like Corpus Christi, a sandy, scrubby waterfront community turned vibrant by the influx of Navy hotshots. There wasn't much of a town—just a grocery store, a florist, a couple of churches, and a grungy roadside watering hole called the Roost, where Shepard "drank cheap booze . . . and almost ended up in jail." The summers were unbearably hot and muggy. Swarms of fat mosquitoes chased people inside at night.

As one pilot put it, "There wasn't much to do in the lowlands of southern Maryland—except fly, and drink. Otherwise, it was a miserable place."

But the flying . . . the flying was unlike anything Shepard had dreamed of.

After an intensive five months of classroom instruction, during which Shepard's head was crammed with two years' worth of technical training in trigonometry, physics, aerodynamics, and more, he was selected to continue working at Pax River for another two years. Assigned to the prestigious tactical test division, he began flying more often, at faster speeds, and at higher altitudes than ever. On the *FDR* he'd sometimes gone several days without a single hop. Now he was sometimes flying five different planes—most of them unproven experimental models—on the *same day*.

By 1950 most of those planes were jets. Fast, complex, imperfect pieces of machinery, these were some of the most complicated mechanical concoctions humanity had ever produced. They allowed humans to travel one, two, and then three times the speed of sound. But they also leaked oil, creaked and groaned, spontaneously exploded, mysteriously spun out at high altitudes, and crashed without warning.

Often there was no time to learn the intricacies of each new plane. With the manufacturers constantly making modifications, the handbooks were often outdated. Shepard usually got a quick rundown of the jet's quirks from another pilot, maybe a brief assessment like "she flies real easy." Then he'd take off and learn the rest in the air.

"Training was very informal, to put it politely," another early Navy jet pilot said. And sometimes that informality cost lives. Three months before Shepard's arrival, two test pilots and two crewmen were killed in an experimental twin-engine Neptune patrol plane. At the time, Pax officials were becoming nervous about the occasional crashes and the many near misses; they raised the requirements for new test pilots (only those with instrument flying experience were accepted) and proposed expanding the classroom and training portion of each Pax tour from five months to eight.

Still, it was considered amateurish if a pilot needed a lesson or asked too many questions before flying any given plane. Such was the ethos of this boys' club, where a man's stock soared with each rejection of death. Shepard's commander when he arrived at Pax, John Hyland, had gained fame during an air show for Navy dignitaries in which an osprey flew into his jet's tail, forcing him to eject at five hundred or so miles an hour. In the days before automatic ejection seats, this required him to pop open the canopy and allow himself to be sucked from the cockpit. Just barely avoiding slamming into the tail, Hyland pulled open his parachute and plunged deep into Chesapeake Bay. A sea plane rescued him and delivered him to Pax. Besides a sore arm, his only injury was a bruised knee, which he banged on the bumper of an ambulance waiting for him on the tarmac. Hyland returned to the air show, took the microphone, and apologized to the VIPs for not bringing back the parachute's D-ring handle as a souvenir.

The plane Hyland had been flying was an F2H "Banshee,"

which in time became Shepard's specialty, the only jet he considered a worthy successor to his Corsair.

The Banshee was a twin-engine, straight-wing jet fighter with twice the power of the Navy's first jet fighter, the FH-1 Phantom. The Banshee carried bombs, rockets, and cannons, could fly in rough weather, and could reach 586 miles an hour, just a hair shy of supersonic. McDonnell Aircraft built 895 of them, and the Banshee helped establish McDonnell as the rising star in the competitive aircraft manufacturing industry.

Shepard also regularly flew an alphabet soup of other jets—the F9F, F3D, F86, and so on, long, sleek, silvery tubes capable of maneuvers he could only dream of executing in his old Corsair. His job at Pax was to push each plane a little further each day. The tests, as he'd note in his log book, included airspeed calibration, stability and control, climb tests, buffet evaluations, and aerobatics. The goal was to get right up next to a "critical area"—that is, the point at which the plane might explode, spin, lose control, or stall—and then write up a report on the plane's limits. Once he found the outer limits, he'd go out the next day and push the envelope a little further.

Shepard once took to the sky in a Banshee carrying full external fuel tanks—extra tanks attached to the jet for long-distance flying. He wanted to see if the tanks could withstand a high-speed roll. They couldn't. As he began twirling his Banshee, the bolted-on tanks broke from the jet's wings and blew two craters in a farmer's field, while Shepard managed to bring the damaged and wobbling jet back to Pax intact. "He could fly anything," one colleague said.

One of Shepard's projects was to fly all over the United States to measure the contrail levels of various jets at various locations. Contrails are the vapor trails that snake behind jets. The Navy wanted to know at what altitudes the contrails of its planes were visible so that, in wartime, they could fly above that level and thereby avoid antiaircraft fire. Shepard spent many happy hours flying forty thousand feet above major American cities.

And when he returned to Pax, he'd usually swoop down over the brick rancher he and Louise had built on the Patuxent River and give her a supersonic heads-up that he was on his way home. Some days these flat-hats reached as low as a hundred feet. His commander told him to knock it off, though, when the manager of a local turkey farm began complaining that Shepard's low, high-speed passes were freaking out his turkeys.

Shepard would soon take the art of flat-hatting—the earth-hugging feat he'd been introduced to at Corpus Christi but had yet to fully explore—to dangerous new levels. But at first he earned a reputation for an analytical mind, a mind that was constantly busy with questions of aerodynamics and engineering. He didn't often show this egghead side of himself, but those closest to him realized that he never performed a test or maneuver (or, later, an illicit stunt) until he was convinced it wouldn't kill him.

Nor was he afraid to sit at his desk and type out a lengthy, detailed, and highly critical report on one of his test planes. Shepard knew his job was to wring out a jet's imperfections and to prevent imperfect jets from being used by the Navy. He spent long hours with Pax River's engineers, discussing the most minuscule idiosyncrasies of a jet. "If it sucked, he'd say so," one of Shepard's commanders recalled. Another commander said Shepard "turned in some of the best reports we had."

Shepard's attention to detail eventually established him as one of Pax River's most conscientious and hardworking pilots, and word of his expertise began to spread. One day an officer named James Stockdale (who would later spend seven years in a POW camp and become a vice presidential candidate) needed a pilot to perform a series of complicated ascents to high altitudes for a study on accelerated climbs. He chose Shepard not for his flamboyance but for his technical ability and precision.

///

Shepard tried to bring that same level of precision to his hobbies, too. He took up waterskiing and progressed quickly from two skis to slalom. With a friend, he built a ramp on the Patuxent River so that they could take turns jumping. Then he began trying to ski barefoot. Friends began to wonder if he was good at everything he did, this hipster with the gorgeous wife, the adorable kids (he and Louise had had a second daughter, Julie, in 1951), the sports car—and the world by the balls.

By that time Shepard already had a strong sense that he could "roll a plane a little better than the next guy," as he put it. But as his luck held out and his superiors began entrusting him with riskier and more complicated assignments, he began to become more deeply convinced that he might be a little better than the rest. He knew deep down that he didn't have more raw talent than some of the others, though he would never have admitted such a thing. He did, however, believe he worked harder and paid closer attention to the details of flying perfect tests. He began to push himself harder, and the goal was always perfection, to show the bosses and his peers that he, in his own words, could "fly the best test flight that anybody had ever flown."

But as soon as he learned to fly perfectly, the power of it seemed to supercharge his already swelling ego, and he began to experiment with flying recklessly, as if straightforward, glitz-free missions were now beneath him, as if he couldn't help but indulge his dark side. His antics would take him to the brink of a premature end to his career.

When construction workers completed the first span of the Chesapeake Bay Bridge, which connected Maryland's mainland to its Eastern Shore across a narrow stretch of the bay, Shepard couldn't resist. A couple of his colleagues had already flown under the half-built bridge. Shepard did them one better and looped the span—he flew his Banshee under it, over the top, and then back under again. John Hyland, head of Pax River's tactical test division, got wind of the stunt and called Shepard into his office. Hyland admired Shepard's skill and his bravura. But he couldn't condone such flights or every yahoo in a Navy jet would try it. He gave Shepard a stern lecture about the dangers of flat-hatting but decided not to report the incident to the higher-ups.

A few weeks later, though, Shepard was returning from a test flight out over the Chesapeake and decided to take a detour up to Ocean City, the bustling beach town on Maryland's Eastern Shore. He flew down low and screamed across the beach, blowing the bikini tops off a number of sunbathing women. He was moving too fast for anyone to get his tail number, but a photographer from a Philadelphia newspaper happened to be taking pictures and caught the stunt on film.

Shepard was summoned before Rear Admiral Alfred M. Pride, the no-nonsense commander of Pax River, who chewed Shepard's ass and then issued a letter of censure, a black mark in his record that would silently follow him the rest of his career.

But apparently Pride's censure wasn't severe enough.

Shepard's favorite jet, the F2H-2 Banshee, had set an altitude record of fifty-two thousand feet in 1949. Shepard was among a select group of Navy pilots trained to fly even higher, and in 1952 he was assigned to an elite group performing altitude tests on the Banshee. One day, a few weeks after Shepard had flat-hatted Ocean City, a project manager at the Naval Aviation Test Ordnance Center on nearby Chincoteague Island in coastal Virginia asked Pax River for a high-flying test pilot. Shepard was sent to help. The mission was to fly above fifty thousand feet—something the Chincoteague pilots and planes couldn't do—and release a missile, to determine the high-altitude effects of missile launches.

Shepard flew from Pax River to Chincoteague that morning, performed the mission perfectly, landed back at Chincoteague for a debriefing with the project manager, and then had lunch with his friends George (an academy classmate) and Betty

Whisler. Shepard returned to the airfield by midafternoon, refueled, and prepared for takeoff.

It was a relatively quiet Saturday afternoon, and a quarter of a mile downrange from the airfield about three hundred enlisted sailors and fifty officers—including Shepard's friend George—had gathered in rows on the tennis courts for their weekly inspection.

As Shepard took off, he radioed the air traffic control tower, seeking permission to make a "low pass." His intent was to boast of a successful mission—an aerial chest thumping of sorts—by streaking above the base and putting his jet into a wing-over-wing victory roll. The tower gave him the okay, but they didn't know his reputation for low passes. "When Al made a low pass, it was really low," said George Whisler, who was standing at attention on the tennis courts as Shepard took off, U-turned, then pushed his twin-engine Banshee to full bore and swooshed down on top of the naval base.

Shepard ripped the air just 150 feet above the ground. Passing over the tennis courts, the roar of his engines scared the breath out of the hundreds of uniformed men standing at attention below. Thinking a jet was about to crash onto their heads, sailors and officers dove to the ground, and hundreds of white hats were swept into the air by the wake of Shepard's jet. The commanding officer of the base jumped to his feet and screamed, "Get that pilot's name. I want to know where he's from. And then I want him grounded." George knew instantly it was his friend but kept his mouth shut.

When Shepard landed at Pax River twenty minutes later, he taxied to a stop and saw Admiral Pride waiting for him. He thought: *Hmmm, I must have done a great job on that mission if the admiral is coming out to greet me.* But Pride's face was locked in a scowl.

Pride was one of the pioneers of naval aviation, having flown off the Navy's first carrier, the USS *Langley,* in the 1920s. He was also a serious, strict, and proper New Englander who was much feared by his men. A test pilot once thought his career was over after he bailed out of a damaged jet during a night flight, landed in the water, shed all his clothes, swam to shore, and rang the doorbell of the nearest house—where the naked aviator was greeted by Pride's flustered wife.

"Were you just over Chincoteague?" Pride asked Shepard.

"Well, yes, sir."

"Did you make a low pass?"

"Well, I guess I did."

Pride had had enough. He dismissed Shepard and then summoned his immediate supervisors. Shepard should be court-martialed, he told them. "I want to straighten this kid out," the crusty old admiral said. "We just can't have this sort of thing."

While Shepard's supervisors pleaded with Pride not to court-martial him, Shepard was grounded and put "in hack" for ten days. Being in hack meant he had to pack a bag, move out of his house, leaving Louise and the girls behind, and live in the bachelors' quarters. While in hack, he wasn't allowed anywhere near an airplane.

H. Y. Davidson, Shepard's old rowing buddy from the academy, saw Shepard drinking alone that night at the officers' club. When Shepard told him the story of the low pass at Chincoteague, Davidson was surprised his friend was so upbeat after apparently sabotaging his own career. Davidson said to himself: *What a waste of a good career.*

When he heard the rest of the story weeks later, Davidson was shocked to learn Shepard hadn't been shipped off to the supply corps. "A lot of us would have lost our wings for something like that," Davidson said. "But he had a way of getting away with it." Once again, Shepard had a couple of guardian angels looking out for him.

///

With his strong jaw, his dimple-framed smirk, his slicked-back hair, and his lithe body language, Bob Elder looked like a movie star playing a fighter jock role. Elder had been born in the wilds of Saskatchewan, Canada, but his family moved to Portland, Oregon, when he was a teen. A longtime love of airplanes led him to enroll in the naval ROTC program at the University of Washington, and he received his aviator's wings just a few months before Pearl Harbor. Elder was among the first naval aviators to join the dogfighting in the Pacific, where he flew combat missions off aircraft carriers in some of the most crucial battles of the Pacific war, including the Battles of the Coral Sea, Guadalcanal, and, most notably, Midway. On June 4, 1942, Elder and his SBD Dauntless flew three missions, spent a total of twelve hours and fifteen minutes in the air, and helped sink the Japanese aircraft carrier *Hiryu*. For his destruction of Japanese planes and ships at Midway, Elder earned *two* Navy Crosses and the Distinguished Flying Cross.

After the war, Elder was among the first Navy pilots to fly jets and among the first to land them on aircraft carriers. By the time he and Shepard met in 1950, Elder was known Navy-wide as "sierra hotel," naval aviator radio-speak for SH—shit hot. (The opposite of shit hot was "delta sierra"—DS, or dumb shit.)

Elder was considered all the more shit hot because he didn't boast or brag and didn't talk down to his inferiors. He was approachable and likable. "Bob was very laid-back," one colleague said. "But he was a great tactician."

Shepard had adopted Elder as his mentor. Just as he had gravitated toward Doc Abbot and Turner Caldwell, he had a way of befriending the shit hot men around him. He soaked up whatever knowledge of flying they were willing to share. When he wasn't conversing with them, he was watching, observing, learning.

Elder had taken a shine to Shepard, too. After Shepard's terrifying low-low pass over Chincoteague, Elder stepped up to argue vigorously in his defense to prevent Admiral Pride from court-martialing Shepard. Shepard's boss, John Hyland, also joined the emotional debate, but it wasn't easy. "He [Pride] was furious," Elder said.

Finally, Elder and Hyland calmed Pride's anger and convinced him that a court-martial would only cast off one of the Navy's most promising young aviators. Pride withdrew his court-martial threat and settled for a strong letter of reprimand. He also grounded Shepard for two weeks and warned that if he ever heard of another Alan Shepard stunt, he would kick him out of the Navy with a bad-conduct discharge.

Afterward Hyland had a long talk with Shepard, warning him that he had gotten caught twice and that getting caught a third time would surely end his career for good.

"Now look, Shep, if you want to fly low and do slow rolls at low altitudes, for God's sake, go out to sea and do it where no one can catch you. But don't get caught again," Hyland said. "Now, do you understand that?" Elder gave him a similar lecture.

"He was pretty flamboyant as a young officer. I had to stick my neck out a country mile to get him out of that one," Elder recalled. "That was a close one on Al's part. It was a dumb thing to do. He shaved the corners a little closer than most."

Secretly, though, Elder admired Shepard's skills—and his exuberance.

"I thought he was a little indulgent," he said. "I was, too, so I could recognize it."

///

A few weeks later, when Shepard was allowed to fly again, he flew back to Chincoteague, where his old boss, Doc Abbot, had recently been assigned. He seemed uncharacteristically subdued, his chin down instead of up as he asked Abbot to borrow his car for a few hours. Though Shepard didn't explain why he needed it, Abbot handed him the keys. When Shepard returned that afternoon, his chin was back up and he was all smiles. He stood on the tarmac talking happily with Abbot, not quite ready to return to Pax River. There seemed to be something on his mind, but Abbot couldn't get him to open up.

Then Shepard spotted on the tarmac a twin-engine bomber plane called a JD-1. He'd never flown one, and he asked Abbot for a ride. Abbot took Shepard up and showed him how to fly the thing. Then they landed and swapped seats, and Shepard flew the big bomber perfectly, even better than Abbot. At one point he put the plane into a hard turn, and Abbot noticed that the altimeter didn't budge—Shepard had just learned to fly the plane, yet he was keeping it absolutely steady. Abbot felt sheepish, but then on the landing, Shepard accidentally braked too hard and the nose slammed down onto the runway. Abbot was secretly thrilled to see his friend, for a change, make a mistake.

Afterward Shepard finally explained why he had borrowed the car. He told Abbot how a few weeks earlier, before the Chincoteague flyover incident, he had flown low over the beach at Ocean City and "scared the hell out of a lot of people." The local sheriff got the number on the plane's tail—presumably from the photograph in the newspaper—and wanted to bring charges against Shepard. Shepard borrowed Abbot's car so he could visit the sheriff and talk his way out of an arrest.

"It was a remarkable piece of work," Abbot recalled. "It surely would have been the end of him."

/ / /

Surviving his brush with court-martial had indebted Shepard to his two superiors, John Hyland and especially Bob Elder. But it also endeared him to them. Military men harbored a built-in distrust of their superiors, and that distrust was especially strong among self-reliant aviators. Escaping an admiral's wrath relatively unscathed only solidified the brotherly bond between Shepard and Bob Elder. Shepard had committed one of the ultimate sins—*three times*—and had gotten caught twice, but emerged with a smirk and a swagger.

The two men began flying together more often, performing tests with each other, such as the dangerous in-flight refueling procedure. They once traveled to the Cleveland Air Races to demonstrate in-flight refueling to the crowd, which included Miss America. The next day's paper pictured Shepard standing on the outside steps of a tanker plane, looking straight down into Miss America's impressive cleavage.

But an in-flight refueling test at Pax River would nearly kill them both.

The plan was to see if a jet could carry ten thousand pounds of bombs. The test had been designed by the Air Force, but the fledgling service didn't yet have a plane that it trusted with that much weight.

"Let's show them how to do it," Elder suggested, and came up with an idea.

To reduce the total weight and allow the plane to lift its ten-thousand-pound payload, he'd take off with an F2H Banshee's fuel tanks near empty. Then he'd refuel in the air as soon as he reached a safe altitude. Shepard would fly right beside Elder in a "safety" plane, to observe everything up close. Top officers from Patuxent River, the Air Force, and the Pentagon were invited to watch the test from the deck of the USS *Leyte*.

Refueling in air is an extremely difficult maneuver, and in the early 1950s the Navy was still learning how to do so safely with its jets. Both planes—the powerful jet and the slower tanker plane, usually a propeller-driven aircraft—had to fly at exactly the same speed, almost exactly the same altitude (the rear plane flew slightly lower), and just a few feet apart. The low-fuel plane then extended a long, stiff refueling pipe, called a probe, and inserted it into the drogue in the rear of the tanker. Pilots often defused the danger with jokes about the sexual nature of midair refuelings. Shepard once took the joke a step further. He painted pubic hair around the drogue on the theory that the other pilots' probes would be more likely to reach the drogue if the target looked like a vagina.

Shepard's boss, John Hyland, took off first in an AJ tanker

plane loaded with jet fuel, followed by Shepard in the safety plane, an F9F. Finally, Elder took off in a new Banshee just delivered from the factory. When the trio reached eight thousand feet, Shepard tested the AJ's drogue by refueling from the tanker, topping off his own tanks. But the F9F had a special tip on the end of its probe, and—unbeknownst to Shepard—when it disconnected from the tanker, it damaged the drogue. When Elder plugged his Banshee's probe into Hyland's tanker, hundreds of gallons of fuel gushed out. The volatile cloud smothered his plane and was sucked into the engines' intake ducts. Elder felt his plane "shuddering like a dog passing pee seeds." Pockets of fuel began to explode. Part of Elder's landing gear was blown off. Wing flaps were shredded, and one engine was nearly blown off its mounts. "Literally, it was blowing the airplane apart," Elder said. In the understated language of a naval aviator on the brink of destruction, he added: "I had my hands full."

Shepard pulled away from the fireball, thinking he'd never see his friend again. Elder's communication system was destroyed, so Shepard couldn't contact him. All he could do was fly alongside as Elder's Banshee flipped upside down and slid into a spin, plummeting toward the Chesapeake. A pilot's instinct is to save an airplane at all costs. It's a fine line, and many pilots cross it, thinking they can save a plane only to find—too late to bail out—that they cannot. Elder considered bailing out but continued systematically trying every trick in the book, whipping the control stick this way and that, stepping on the right rudder, then the left. Suddenly, just a few hundred feet above the water, Elder gained control of the crippled plane, straightened it out, and limped toward the nearest airfield, at Oceana, Virginia. Elder wasn't even sure if the landing gear was intact, so he came in slowly, gently.

Shepard looked down in awe, watching Elder land roughly but safely.

Bravo Zulu! he thought. Translation: good job.

///

What distinguished Shepard from his colleagues, beyond his precocious command of flying jets, was an aptitude for the theories of flight. He spent many hours flying out over the Atlantic, scribbling notes about air speed, distance, and altitude onto a clipboard in his lap, all to test a theory he called "total momentum."

The goal was to find new ways to give Navy pilots an edge in a dogfight with an enemy. Shepard gathered enough data to compile a report that advised pilots in the fleet to always fly a little higher and/or faster than their opponent, because the combination of speed and altitude—the "total momentum" of the airplane—would give them the advantage in a dogfight, helping them reach the desired position behind and above an enemy plane, where they could take aim with their guns and rockets. "I don't know what a genius IQ is, but he had it," Shepard's boss, John Hyland, once said.

One of Shepard's final projects as a test pilot was a lengthy series of ridiculously dangerous tests in 1952 above the hard-packed sands of dry Muroc Lake, the California air base made famous by such record breakers as Chuck Yeager, the Air Force pilot who five years earlier had broken the sound barrier there.

Shepard's mission: to deliberately disable his jet in midflight, then try to land it.

The intent was to come up with emergency flying procedures that Navy pilots could use if their jet ever flamed out—a so-called dead-stick landing. Shepard and Hyland took turns flying up to about forty thousand feet, where they'd intentionally shut off their engines and then try to wrestle the plane to the ground. Most Navy pilots were familiar with the procedures for dead-stick landings in a propeller plane. But in the early 1950s very few Navy pilots had flown a jet, let alone landed one with a flamed-out engine. Also, jet engines at the time were notoriously unreliable, and flame-outs were a common concern—especially in Korea, where the Navy and especially the Air Force had begun introducing jet fighters to take on the powerful, supersonic Soviet MiG-15 jets.

Shepard compiled an extensive report on dead-stick jet landings that was circulated among aviators—largely it required a long, slow, meticulously controlled descent—and, according to Hyland, was "very, very well received all around the fleet."

///

By the end of his Pax River tour, Shepard had to feel luck on his side.

Scores of test pilots found themselves, like Elder, spinning upside down in a "wounded bird" but, instead of escaping, rode the bird into the earth. In fact, the whole point of Pax River—to push jets beyond their limits—was designed to accommodate death. Test pilots were the 1950s equivalent of crash-test dummies later used by car makers, but they were obviously no dummies.

The paradox of Shepard's job was that his planes—prototypes and experimental models—were *supposed* to blow up, spin out, and crash. That's why the Navy needed the best pilots in the world to test them. And when an aviator emerged from two years of such flying, with a trail of dead buddies behind him, he was a changed man, absolutely convinced of his own invincibility.

Shepard would claim years later that he survived test piloting by staring in the mirror each day—just as he had begun to do during his struggles back at Corpus Christi—to "look for signals." *Did you goof off yesterday? Did you get complacent?* In his mind, he had to put such pressure on himself because atop the naval aviation dog pile every day is a competition. And the competitors happen to be your best friends, who, as Shepard once put it, "are going to run right over you on the way to the same target." But when his two-year tour at Pax came to an end in 1953, Shepard had begun to realize that he had become a seriously "sierra hotel" aviator—shit hot.

"Maybe you are a little bit better," he once told himself.

Years later, he'd admit: "I believed I was the best graduate of the Navy Test Pilot School to ever come down the road. Obviously I wasn't, but I believed I was."

In early 1953, with the Korean War still raging, Shepard was plucked by a World War II hero to serve in a new carrier-based jet squadron bound for Korea—a chance to apply his test pilot theories, reflexes, and guts against a formidable foe.

7

"Do you wish to declare an emergency?"

Alan, Louise, and the girls pulled up one Sunday afternoon at the Sunnyvale, California, home of Alan's friend Bob Elder and his wife, Irene. It was early 1953. Dwight D. Eisenhower was the new president, America was finally tiring of Senator Joseph McCarthy's Red-baiting, and thirty thousand Americans had been killed in Korea.

Pack up and move, pack up and move. It was becoming the family routine. At the end of the weeklong drive across the country, the Shepards had arrived with no place to stay and just a few dollars in their pockets. The Elders let Alan and Louise and the kids live in their extra bedroom until they were able to find a place of their own amid the cherry and apricot orchards of nearby Palo Alto.

They had learned to travel light, put down shallow roots, and expect change. During eight years of marriage, Alan and Louise had already moved across the country and back once and lived in half a dozen houses. The girls, at five and two, were adapted to the peripatetic lifestyle, and the family made the most of whatever months or weeks they could all be together. In Palo

Alto Louise quickly found a Christian Science church, and for a few months they lived as a normal, social, church-going family, although at Sunday services Alan usually stood at the back of the church with two other reluctant Navy men.

Alan even agreed to join Louise and a dozen other couples in a small drama club called the One-Nighters, which met on Friday nights to rehearse. The other members were surprised that Alan, normally so aloof, played his parts with gusto. Once they performed on Academy Awards night at Woodside's Pioneer Hotel, and they laughed and carried on so much that the waiters thought they were all drunk.

The comfortable family routines came to an abrupt end when Alan and his new squadron boarded the aircraft carrier USS *Oriskany* in San Francisco, bound for the coast of war-racked Korea. They were shipping out for the first of two conjoined tours that would keep him separated from the family for more than a year. Just prior to his departure, Louise and the girls visited the ship, touring the floating village and dining in the officers' mess, which had been decked out with white tablecloths and silver, with white-gloved stewards serving the food. As Louise and the kids drove home, one of the girls asked, "Mommy, how come Daddy is so rich and we're so poor?"

///

Shepard had tamed the brutish Corsair, nailed scores of carrier landings and wrung out some of the Navy's first jets, but the lone blank on his aviator's resume was aerial combat. As his squadron and the USS *Oriskany* churned toward Korea he had to be praying for a chance at one-on-one combat with a "Red."

U.S. newspapers would soon pick up stories about the first Navy and Marine aces—aviators with five kills—and would quote Marine Major John Bolt and his lively description of chasing down two MiG jets and, within five short minutes, shredding both "dudes" to pieces, calling it "a pretty good return on the investment." Another Marine aviator, John Glenn, flying an F86 jet with baseball great Ted Williams as his wingman, earned the nickname "Old Magnet Ass" for repeatedly attracting North Korean antiaircraft fire. One night an enemy shell blew a two-foot hole in Glenn's tail; another night he ran out of fuel and glided across the 38th parallel to a dead-stick landing. Before the war's end Glenn would blast three MiGs from the sky.

In mid-1953, the Navy still lagged behind the Air Force in its use of jets in the Korean conflict. The Navy was having some success with its F9F Panther jet fighters, but its pilots were flying mostly Corsairs and other propeller planes. Air Force pilots, meanwhile, were flying supersonic F86 Sabres.

Back at Moffett Field, during training exercises before joining the *Oriskany*, Shepard and his colleagues loved to stage mock dogfights out over San Francisco Bay. But while Shepard chafed for a dogfight, his expertise from flying jets at Pax River made him the perfect candidate for a much broader role: to introduce jets to the underpowered naval air fleet. Shepard was selected to usher F2H Banshee jets into VF-193, an all-weather fighter squadron nicknamed the Ghost Riders. All-weather squadrons were a relatively new concept in the Navy, created to fly in the volatile, low-visibility conditions of Korea and East Asia. The F2H would became the most versatile all-weather aircraft of the 1950s.

The Ghost Riders were one of four squadrons that constituted Air Group 19, which was commanded by James David Ramage, a tall, broad-shouldered figure of a man who was a World War II dive-bomber and (like Bob Elder) a Navy Cross recipient. During the war, Ramage's initials, J.D., according to Navy call signs, had translated to Jig Dog. Later the Navy changed its call signs so that Ramage's initials became the much less manly Juliet Delta. But Ramage would always be known as Jig Dog.

Within days of his arrival at Moffett, Jig Dog had ordered a "group grope"—to get a full view of his air group, he wanted to see every bomber, jet, and tanker airborne. Unlike some commanders, who were largely ground-based administrators, Jig Dog was a talented aviator, so he joined his men in the air. After that, he endeared himself even further by hosting cocktail parties at his house. Shepard enjoyed himself so much, one of those nights he had to "slow-roll" his car home at half the speed limit.

At the time, the Navy was buying up hundreds of new jets, planes that Shepard had tested and critiqued back at Patuxent River. Even more than World War II, the Korean War invigorated the American economy, marking the origins of what Eisenhower would one day call America's "military-industrial complex" and making corporations such as Douglas and North American increasingly powerful and wealthy. As part of its transition, the Navy was retiring most of its propeller squadrons and replacing them with new jet squadrons. Air groups typically consisted of four different squadrons, and Air Group 19 was among the first groups to switch from three squadrons of propeller planes and one squadron of jets to the reverse: three jet squadrons (including Shepard's VF-193) and just one prop squadron.

Jig Dog had tried to handpick talented jet flyers for his new air group, but there weren't many to choose from. That's because most were reserve pilots who hadn't flown since World War II. Very few had flown jets at all. "I was lying, cheating, and stealing to get the best aviators," Ramage said. He chose Shepard partly on the advice of Bob Elder, who after Pax River had been named commander of Shepard's sister squadron, VF-191, another of Air Group 19's new jet squadrons, nicknamed Satan's Kittens.

It's hard to explain to a nonpilot what makes another pilot great. It's not like in sports, where speed or strength can be timed or measured. In flying, expertise is assessed in subtle ways. It's based on trust, and people trusted Alan Shepard. "At that time, friendships were strong and you knew who the good pilots were," Ramage recalled. "Pilots know pilots. Elder was a pilot's pilot."

And if Elder said Alan Shepard was a good pilot, that was enough for Jig Dog. "Al was very much in demand," Elder recalled.

As the *Oriskany* set sail and training missions began, Jig Dog quickly discovered that few of his men had Shepard's aerial finesse in a jet. The F2H Banshee—soon to be celebrated in James Michener's novel *Bridges at Toko-Ri*—was designed to be an all-purpose jet fighter. During his rigorous testing of the Banshee at Pax River, Shepard had proven to the Navy that the jet could fly high and low, fast and slow, at night and in the cruddiest of weather. But when it came to landing softly on the deck of a moving ship, the Banshee wasn't an ideal match for the *Oriskany*.

The Oriskany was a "straight deck" aircraft carrier, an elongated, moving football field with hydraulic catapults punching aircraft into the air in one end zone, and in the other end zone, nine rows of cables to catch the tailhooks of landing aircraft and snap them to a halt. One problem with the straight deck was that if a plane's tailhook missed the landing cables, the plane barreled ahead toward rows of parked planes. Barriers were supposed to catch such errant planes, but sometimes those barriers snapped, or the incoming plane bounced or rolled over them, and the planes slammed into other fuel-laden jets, scattering (or sometimes slaughtering) sailors. Years later the Navy would replace carrier decks like the *Oriskany*'s with angled decks—such as those Shepard had tested at Patuxent—that had separate lanes for takeoffs and landings.

The inexperience of Jig Dog's men was betrayed by the deeply gouged landing area of the *Oriskany*'s hardwood deck, whose pitted and chunked teak planks had to be constantly replaced. The men were coming in too high and fast, cutting their power too close to the ship, causing their planes to drop too hard.

In the complicated hierarchy of an aircraft carrier, the aviators were the big dogs, but they were essentially guests of the *Oriskany*'s captain, Charles Griffin, who assembled the pilots on his banged-up deck one afternoon. Tall and thin, with a triangular face, Griffin was generally a quiet man, a history buff who liked to read history lessons over the ship's loudspeakers. But this day he loudly chewed out his pilots. "Stop damaging the flight deck," he told Air Group 19. Jig Dog then coined a phrase that became the mantra of the group: "Don't dive for the goddamn deck." Shepard, who'd performed more carrier landings—in jets and on straight decks—than just about any other aviator in the air group, helped teach the others how to approach slower and lower, to avoid stalling and land gently without killing themselves or their colleagues.

Although two of Shepard's colleagues would nearly lose their lives in bizarre landings on the *Oriskany*, Air Group 19 eventually developed an outstanding record—a low fatality rate and a limited number of lost planes. Jig Dog would credit Shepard's leadership and mentoring for that success rate, and although he would see occasional signs of recklessness in Shepard, he came to trust him enough to choose him as his wingman, just as Doc Abbot had. That decision would ultimately save Jig Dog's life.

///

Aviators practically lived in their "ready room," their office/clubhouse/kitchen and, as Jig Dog put it, "the place where you go to drink coffee and tell lies." Pilots picked up weather reports from the teletype or sat in the theater-style leather seats for mission briefings. They kept their gear stowed in lockers—helmets, boots, and insulated rubber "poopy suits." Similar to a diver's wet suit, poopy suits were worn under aviators' flight suits and designed to keep them from freezing if they had to eject and land in the water. They not only sweated profusely inside the skintight suits but occasionally were forced to relieve themselves during long flights—hence the nickname.

Enroute to Korea, life aboard the *Oriskany* ticked along, a metronome of routines. Breakfast at 6 A.M. A morning of launched props and jets. Maybe pull alongside a transport ship to exchange supplies and pick up new men and bags of mail. An afternoon of postflight storytelling in the ready room. Maybe a basketball game or a boxing match. At night the men might get haircuts, take showers, or crowd into the library for magazines and books. Sometimes movies were shown in the so-called hangar bay, one level below the flight deck, where aircraft were stored.

The *Oriskany* bustled with three thousand men, each with a job. For most those jobs were painfully routine. Some spent the entire day in the ship's bowels tending to its engines and boilers, washing the laundry, or baking the thousand loaves of bread consumed by the *Oriskany*'s crew each day. But the pilots—especially the jet pilots—were the celebrities. They dressed differently, with sunglasses and baggy flight suits. They spoke their own cool, clipped language, full of jargon, acronyms, and euphemisms. They told each other to "check your six," which meant watch your six o'clock position—your ass. They complained about a Charlie Foxtrot in the air—code for CF, or cluster fuck. And just before taking off, they'd hit the head for a "combat dump," also called "sending a Marine to sea." They talked of vectors and air speed and thrust, about weather and "cat shots" (catapult shots off the deck) and "go juice" (either coffee or jet fuel). And they never talked about fear or death. Instead they'd use euphemisms like "He went in," which meant "He crashed his fucking plane into the water and died."

In the blustery weather of the Sea of Japan, a routine day could quickly turn deadly. An unexpected blast of wind, a small mechanical error, a lapse in timing or judgment, and you'd be gone. For Shepard, luck would be a constant copilot. He would forever argue that skill, discipline, and attention to detail protected him. As he liked to say, "There are old test pilots and there are bold test pilots, but there are no old, bold test pilots." Still, there are events that are simply out of a disciplined pilot's hands.

///

Even without the help of enemy planes and missiles, a twenty-seven-thousand-ton aircraft carrier capable of moving at nearly forty miles an hour—fast enough to pull a water skier—is a profoundly dangerous vehicle, and the *Oriskany*'s cruise toward Korea was not without its mishaps. Billy Lawrence, a short, tough Naval Academy football player from Nashville, was one of the few "nuggets"—pilots on their first assignment—in Air Group 19. One day, off the coast of Hawaii, Lawrence experienced what was blandly called a "partial catapult."

Two hydraulic-powered catapults were built into the forward deck of the *Oriskany*. A plane's front wheels attached to the catapult's tow bar, which whipped the plane forward like a slingshot to help it become airborne. But hydraulic catapults were infamously temperamental. The explosion of a hydraulic catapult aboard the aircraft carrier USS *Bennington* killed a hundred crewmen. In subsequent years hydraulic catapults would be replaced by stronger and safer steam-powered catapults.

Billy Lawrence hooked his Banshee to a catapult tow bar, pushed the jet to full throttle, and prepared for the jolt of the catapult's shove. But the catapult inexplicably lost power halfway through the launch, and the plane belly-flopped two hundred yards off the bow and began to sink as the fast-moving ship bore down on it. Lawrence was able to escape from the crippled jet, and a helicopter—which always hovers nearby during takeoffs—was able to drop a safety line. But Lawrence realized too late that he had forgotten to unstrap his parachute. The helicopter barely lifted him and his waterlogged parachute to safety.

When Captain Griffin later summoned him to the bridge, Lawrence expected to get chewed out. Instead, Griffin told him, "Well done." Lawrence later learned that Shepard, as the officer assigned to investigate the mishap, had written up the accident report and instead of crucifying Lawrence praised him for handling the emergency with poise.

Other aviators weren't so lucky. One landed too hard on the deck, and a bomb attached to the wing exploded, killing him and several others. One pilot took off perfectly one morning, banked left, and just kept going left—into the sea. Another was killed when his propeller plane's wings, which folded in toward the cockpit to allow more planes to fit on the carrier deck, inexplicably folded in the air.

Still, with advice and training from Shepard, who took on a mentoring role during the cruise toward Korea, the hard landings declined and Griffin's deck required fewer repairs. As the *Oriskany*'s record came to outshine that of most other ships in the Pacific, colleagues began marveling at Shepard's expertise. He had more experience at twenty-nine than most aviators a decade older. "He had an aura of confidence that was unbelievable," said squadron mate John Mitchell. "Whether it was in a roomful of admirals or in mixed company, he just exuded it. And that confidence carried over into his flying. He was fearless."

///

As the *Oriskany* neared the coast of Korea in the summer of 1953, significant progress had been made in the armistice talks, and the aviators began to suspect that war would turn to peace before the *Oriskany* reached the scene. Still, the stormy seas complicated many otherwise routine landings, forcing the LSOs to wave off incoming jets, which then looped around for another approach. While waiting for his chance to land one afternoon, Shepard's squadronmate Frank Repp began running low on fuel and received permission for an emergency landing. Alighting on an aircraft carrier in calm seas is difficult enough. But in foul weather the ship might rise and fall as much as fifteen feet and would rock from side to side as well. Landing on such an unstable target was like trying to thread a needle held by a drunk.

Pilots were told to time their approach so that they would land precisely as the deck was falling into a trough between waves.

Repp approached slowly and, in an effort to touch down before the next wave lifted the ship's rear, lifted the Banshee's nose a bit to slow it down. But he had slowed down too much, and his Banshee flamed out and stalled. Repp was now a falling brick, and despite the LSO's frantic wave-off signal, it was too late to veer left or right. All he could do was coast—a hail Mary dead-stick landing—and pray for the best. The deck was still too high, and for a second it looked to Repp as if he was done for, as if he was going to slam right into the backside of the *Oriskany*. Then, slowly, oh so slowly, the deck began to fall into the trough be-tween sea swells.

In the game of inches that is an aircraft carrier landing, Frank Repp came up a few inches short that day. His Banshee hit the rear edge of the deck and cracked open like an egg. The plane split apart just behind the cockpit—feet from Repp's head—shredding the tanks where the last few hundred gallons of fuel sloshed around and unleashing a fireball that shot flames two hundred feet into the sky. Two-thirds of the plane—wings, en-gines, tail—stopped dead on the edge of the ship's fantail, then slid back into the water. Bouncing forth from the flames, at more than a hundred miles an hour, was the front third of Repp's Ban-shee, less than fifteen feet of nose and cockpit, which had some-how escaped without being blown to pieces. Inside, Repp held his hands tight to his chest—he remembered that in similar acci-dents men had lost limbs by bracing themselves against the cock-pit walls. The wingless tube tumbled and flipped across the deck until a barrier caught and stopped it. Repp thought he was dreaming when he saw the figure of a man wrapped in a puffy as-bestos suit, who pulled him free of the wreckage.

Most of those on the ship who saw or heard the explosion assumed the worst. Jig Dog had even picked up the telephone to call Captain Griffin and report another fatality. Then he saw Repp walking across the deck.

"Frank!" he yelled. "I thought you were on that airplane."

"I was, Jig," Repp yelled back. "Pretty colorful, wasn't I?"

The next day Repp was flying a new Banshee.

Shepard's colleague John Mitchell once found himself in a similar dead-stick landing, bearing down fast on the *Oriskany*'s tail. Just the night before, Shepard had told him not to let his speed drop too low on approach or, like Repp, he'd stall. But when Mitchell tried to accelerate, there was no response. Instead of trying a "colorful" landing, he jerked the Banshee down and left at the last second, hoping he'd hit water, not steel. But the jet slammed into an open section of the ship's rear end, just below the flight deck, an area called the "spudlocker." The plane burst into flames, and Mitchell heard the screams of five men who were sleeping nearby. The screams made him realize: *I'm not dead.*

After crawling from the wreckage and helping carry the other injured men to the ship's hospital, Mitchell phoned the ready room to tell his colleagues he was okay. Another pilot picked up the phone and Mitchell said, "Hi, this is Mitch." After a moment of silence an angry voice on the other end said, "That's a pretty sick joke, whoever you are." And Mitchell realized: *They think I'm dead.*

Another officer grabbed the ready-room phone and began screaming at Mitchell, "You fucking son of a bitch, you sick fucking—"

"Willie!" Mitchell yelled, recognizing the voice of a craggy, forty-five-year-old warrant officer, Willie Williamson. "Willie, Willie, Willie! It's me." Finally Mitchell convinced Williamson he wasn't dead. Shepard rushed down to the doctor's office, where the doctor had touched up Mitchell's miraculously minor scrapes and cuts and was offering him a shot of whiskey to calm his nerves. He took a glass of whiskey for himself and told Mitchell to rest up and give him a full statement tomorrow. "And Mitch," Shepard said, "good to have you back."

///

In July 1953 an armistice was signed by the United Nations, North Korea, and China. Even though South Korea refused to sign the treaty, the Korean War began winding to a close. Shepard's chance to blast the enemy from the sky had passed. Instead of dropping bombs or chasing MiGs, he and his squadronmates remained in "alert posture" and spent their days patrolling the skies, like cops on a beat.

Korea had been Shepard's last, best opportunity to reach the exalted ranks of certified combat aviators. But Shepard would not, in an otherwise stellar career, earn a single kill. That fact would haunt him years later when his record was stacked against that of his fellow astronaut, John Glenn, who five days before the cease-fire was flying with his four-plane division when they encountered and downed three MiGs. Glenn painted another red star beside the words "MiG Mad Marine" on his jet. Three stars for three kills—not quite an ace, but close. Glenn's last MiG turned out to be the last of 792 Soviet-made MiG jets downed by U.S. aviators in the war.

Arriving too late to join that elite group was a disappointing twist of timing for Shepard. But he was never known to mope or complain about things. Like his optimistic mother, Renza, he rejected dejection. Even during bad times his colleagues would notice his "irrepressible spirit." Shepard could be insensitive, dismissive, and pithy. Sometimes he was distant and contemplative, other times pedantic and overbearing. He had a low boiling point and could easily explode into noisy anger. But an emotion he never displayed was melancholy, as if even a brief submission to woe was the ultimate sign of weakness. Besides, Shepard always found ways to enliven a disappointing situation.

At the end of its patrol duties off the Korean coast, the

Oriskany returned for a brief stop back in San Francisco. During the Pacific crossing, VF-193 practiced some formation flying. Four-plane divisions returning to the ship usually bypassed the carrier in the echelon formation—each plane a little behind and below the other, like steps, so that each pilot could see the next. They'd then separate and land one by one. Shepard one day convinced his three other divisionmates to assemble in a tight diamond formation and pass low over the ship. It was a trick borrowed from the Navy's four-year-old stunt team, the Blue Angels. Formation flying requires incredibly steady hands, but disassembling a tight-packed diamond formation is even more difficult and dangerous—and, without prior approval, completely against the rules. As Shepard's quartet roared past the *Oriskany*, the deck crew cheered its approval. Captain Griffin and Jig Dog, however, weren't amused. Shepard was put in hack—just as he had been back at Patuxent River. He had to stay in his tiny room for an entire week.

Billy Lawrence, John "Mitch" Mitchell, and the other younger pilots visited Shepard at mealtime so that he wouldn't have to eat alone. But, just like those swats in the ass at Annapolis, Shepard took his punishment with a smirk. In fact, he seemed proud to have distinguished himself from his peers. Soon after the flyover stunt his squadron commander wrote in his fitness report an assessment that could have easily applied to Shepard's whole career: "LT Shepard is a very fine Naval Aviator, but he occasionally strains the bounds of good flight discipline." In time, however, Shepard convinced Jig Dog that his skills were valuable enough to outweigh his indulgences.

Jig Dog was a perfectionist and not one to suffer incompetence. He frequently had lesser pilots transferred off the ship, in keeping with a note he wrote to himself at the start of the cruise: "You are not aiding the individual or the Navy by retaining a weakling. Get rid of him early. He will only cause you trouble in the end." But he realized Shepard was a keeper, and over time he decided to look the other way when Shepard broke the rules.

Once, during a change-of-command ceremony just west of San Francisco, Jig Dog chose Shepard to lead a ceremonial four-plane flyover. With all the *Oriskany's* officers and crew assembled on the deck, Shepard had gotten approval from air traffic officials in San Francisco to make a low-altitude pass. But as the four planes approached the ship in an echelon formation, Jig Dog could hear a change in the pitch of the roaring jet engines, and he knew something was amiss. Then he saw the planes' noses start to tilt upward. All heads on deck started tipping back as Shepard's quartet soared up and over for a spontaneous—and unauthorized—loop-the-loop before coming in for the low pass. Air traffic control called the ship to ask about the changing altitude of the jets on their radar screens. But Jig Dog talked his way out of it, and Shepard escaped unpunished. Again.

Another time the commander of the entire seventh fleet was aboard the *Oriskany* during exercises in the Sea of Japan. One by one, each four-plane division of Air Group 19 passed by the ship. Then Shepard's division roared past—upside down. Again Shepard was spared the rod, but just barely. "It was pointed out that that type of aviation was not necessarily the way the fleet commander liked to see his planes flown over the flag ship," Jig Dog recalled.

The way Jig Dog saw it, Shepard was flamboyant but not dangerous. He was a hotshot, always looking to stand out from the crowd, but he was never extreme. Sometimes Jig Dog would hear mumbles of complaint from other aviators—those whom Shepard might reprimand for deficiencies in their flying while he was out there breaking Navy rules. But Jig Dog had decided to let Shepard get away with his "idiosyncrasies." They boosted the air group's morale, broke up the tedium, and made the flyers momentarily forget the occasional fiery wrecks and funerals at sea. "He always had a lot of protection," Jig Dog said. Looking back, Jig Dog realized that by keeping Shepard on board and keeping him happy, he may well have saved his own life.

///

A winter night over the Sea of Japan, the Korean coast off to the west, the ship somewhere east, and a storm brewing overhead. Flying solo on a night mission, Shepard learned from the *Oriskany* that unidentified planes had been spotted on the ship's radar, and he needed to find out who they belonged to. The mission looked to be a quick one. As he approached the "bogey," he realized they were friendly—U.S. Air Force jets. Shepard made a wide turn back to the ship. He was above the clouds, but as he descended through them he was surrounded by a surging storm and couldn't see a thing. He began flying by his instruments, following the ship's homing signal on his radar screen. Just then the blip on his screen that represented the *Oriskany* disappeared, and the control stick in his hand became mushy. A quick calculation told Shepard that a lightning strike had probably zapped his Banshee's electrical system; a backup system kicked in, but flying under backup power was much more difficult, especially inside a raging storm. Then the jet's navigational system quit, followed by the radio, essentially severing Shepard's connection to the *Oriskany*. He was many miles out, and as he approached a spot where he thought he'd find the ship, it wasn't there. A thought crossed his mind: *I might be in real trouble.* He was burning fuel fast and considered that he might have to ditch in that dark, cold water. In an effort to steady his thoughts, he checked his systems again, and realized the radio was flickering on and off.

He tried calling the ship. "Malta Base, this is Foxtrot Two. Do you read? Over." The reply was faint.

"Foxtrot Two, this is Malta Base. I just barely read you."

Shepard explained that his navigational aids were "erratic" and he might need assistance. The ship couldn't find him on its radar and asked, "Do you wish to declare an emergency?"

Shepard did not reply, and the ship asked again: "Do you wish to declare an emergency?"

"No," he said, knowing what a declared emergency—and a lost plane—might do to his record and his reputation. *Declaring an emergency means I can't handle my airplane without help. To admit that means I failed. It means I can't fix my own problem.*

"No emergency, Malta Base. I want to try a couple of things. I'll get back to you."

The famous French combat pilot and poet Antoine de Saint-Exupéry—who disappeared in a storm during a reconnaissance mission—likened the feeling of being lost in a storm to being "alone before the vast tribunal of the tempestuous sky." Saint-Exupéry, who delivered mail from Spain to Africa before World War II, wrote often of such moments, when "fog and sand and sea are confounded in a brew in which they become indistinguishable, when gleaming flashes wheel treacherously in these skyey swamps."

At such times, the pilot "purges himself of phantoms at a single stroke [and] brings sanity into his house." And that's what Shepard did. He ignored the "black dragons and the crowned crests of a coma of blue lightnings" and settled down.

Flying to the spot where he thought the ship should have been, he turned left, and left again, and again. He flew in ever-expanding boxes, each box a little bit wider than the last—a textbook search pattern. Dropping low over the water to improve his visibility, he was burning fuel at a horrendous rate.

As he turned into one of his squares, he saw a dim red light ahead. He flew nearer and through his rain-spattered windscreen saw the *Oriskany*'s faint outline emerge in the darkness. His final fear was that the plane's electrical problems would prevent him from lowering the landing gear. But three green lights on the control panel assured him that the wheels were down.

The ship pitched and yawed in the rough sea. At 888 feet long, the *Oriskany* was nearly 100 feet shorter than Shepard's previous carrier, the *FDR*. Subtract from that the front half of the deck, where the rest of the *Oriskany*'s planes were parked, and the actual landing area of the ship was about as long as a football field and half as wide. In the seven years since Shepard's first carrier landing, he had nailed that tiny runway scores of times without incident. But never before had it looked so faint, nor had it bucked and heaved so violently.

To complicate matters even more absurdly, Shepard had less than five minutes of fuel left as he neared his ship. He had only one shot at making the landing.

Through the heavy rain and "scud clouds" he could barely make out the dim, lighted profile of the brave LSO who was standing on the *Oriskany's* tail. His one final concern was that the electrical problem had jammed the jet's tailhook, which should have been lowered from the jet's tail, ready to grab one of the arresting wires. To make sure the tailhook caught, he slammed down hard onto the deck, the force of it jarring his teeth and bones. Then came the satisfying shove forward as the tailhook snagged a cable. He roared to himself as the plane came to a stop.

Climbing out of his plane, Shepard strutted across the soaking wet deck, straight toward the ready room, and joked that it was just a "normal carrier landing." Later, Shepard admitted to his squadronmate John Mitchell that it was the first and only time he'd thought he was done for. "It scared the pee out of him," Mitchell recalled.

Years later, when asked about the highlights of his piloting career, Shepard said without hesitation that flying on and off carriers at night "was the hardest kind of flying I've ever done or ever expect to do . . . It's what separates the men from the boys."

///

Colors also separated man from boy aboard a Navy aircraft carrier.

Brown or black—one or the other was the shoe color of every man on the ship—immediately identified the wearer as somebody or nobody. More than 90 percent of the three thousand men aboard the *Oriskany* wore black shoes. Aviators wore brown, and the term "brown shoe" was nearly equivalent to "sierra hotel"—shit hot. "Black shoes," meanwhile, were looked down on. The aviators sometimes called them just "shoes."

But there was an even hotter color than brown. Blue belonged to the uniforms and the jets of the men who performed maneuvers few other Navy pilots were allowed to fly. They snapped and rolled and looped and spun. They were called the Blue Angels, and every brown-shoe Navy man harbored a secret desire to be one of them. Shepard did little to hide his desire to be blue.

The Navy had created the stunt-flying Blue Angels in 1949, and for years Shepard nurtured a simmering envy of the studs chosen to be the Navy's stunt men. Once, while ashore in Spokane, he and Frank Repp watched a Blue Angels performance, and afterward Shepard asked Repp to introduce him to the leader of the Angels, Ray Hawkins, with whom Repp had previously served. "He always wanted to be one of them," Repp recalled. "He just liked being around them."

In late 1953, one of Shepard's colleagues—the commander of a sister squadron in Air Group 19—had been picked to become the new leader of the Blue Angels, and Shepard wrote to Doc Abbot and Turner Caldwell, asking them to help get him a gig as an Angel, too. But the Navy crushed Shepard's dream when it decided in 1954 to start using the acrobatic team as a recruitment device and to allow only naval aviation cadets to become Blue Angels. The reasoning was that young men, with dreams of someday becoming an Angel, would want to join the cadets.

Shepard's response was not to sulk or complain, but to turn around and surreptitiously organize his own acrobatic team, comprised of the *Oriskany*'s best flyers. He chose his friend and mentor Bob Elder, young Billy Lawrence, John "Mitch" Mitchell, and Preston "Spook" Luke. With Jig Dog's reluctant permission, they became a poor man's Blue Angels and during lulls in the schedule practiced formations, wingovers, and loops. Once they were proficient enough, Jig Dog even let them put on a few shows for visiting guests. In time, they earned the nickname Mangy Angels. They performed many of the same maneuvers as the Blue Angels, "except we took a few liberties the Blue Angels couldn't," Elder recalled.

They'd fly straight at each other and, at the last fraction of a second, twist 45 degrees left into a knife edge and pass canopy to canopy, with just a few feet between them. They'd fly horizontally past the ship, slam into a chandelle (a maneuver with a sharp left or right twist and then a climb), shoot straight up like rockets, let their jets coast to a stop, and then tumble back toward earth like a wounded bird before kicking in the thrusters again and soaring back to the sky. "It got a little dicey," Elder said. "I wouldn't do it with any old pilot."

One Sunday afternoon the Mangy Angels performed for the entire Pacific task group. Cruisers, destroyers, and carriers lined up at sea to watch the acrobatics. "The star of the show was Alan Shepard," Charles Griffin, the Oriskany's captain, said later. "He was a magnificent pilot and he really put on a show."

Once, the Mangy Angels made plans to get a photograph of themselves flying vertically in a four-plane diamond formation with Japan's Mount Fujiyama in the background. They envisioned making the cover of Life magazine, or at least the Naval Aviation News. They took off from the Japanese air station at Atsugi, flew a couple of practice loops, then headed south toward Mount Fuji. John Romano, one of the ship's photographers, followed behind in the backseat of another Banshee. As the four-plane formation prepared to go vertical, with Shepard in the lead, they called to make sure Romano was ready. His response was garbled gibberish. They called him again but got no answer. Finally Romano radioed back that something had come up and he was headed back to Atsugi. When the other four landed, he confessed that he'd gotten sick in his oxygen mask. "We were very disappointed," Bill Lawrence said many years later. "Because the country was probably denied the greatest aerial photograph in history."

///

When the Korean War ended, the Navy cut costs by taking many planes off the carriers and leaving them ashore. It was cheaper to fly in and out of an airbase, so the *Oriskany* regularly parked on the shores of one of America's World War II enemies, Japan. After that war the Navy had taken over the port town of Yokosuka, south of Tokyo, and turned it into a massive military base. Shepard and his pals spent much of their free time in that infamously seedy harbor town, one of the great havens of drunkenness and debauchery, a sailor's dream port, a cheap and X-rated Disneyland.

It was familiar ground for Shepard, who had visited Yokosuka a decade earlier, in the dying days of World War II. But by 1954 a sprawling naval shipyard had grown around the harbor. It had a well-known officers' club, the Clover Club, which was often full of attractive young "DACs"—Department of the Army, civilians. Beyond the shipyard, amid the wooden structures of the low hillsides, lay a town of hoods, hustlers, and whores.

For months, the all-male city of the *Oriskany* had been at sea, with no taste of romance except maybe a girlie magazine and a rare private moment in the showers. Young men bubbled into Yokosuka, an explosion of bar hopping and beer swilling. And if you happened to find a knowledgeable cab driver, he'd take you to the Green Eyes, Club Denen, the Casbah, and Mama-san's. For an extra few yen, he'd take you further.

Yokosuka's shopping district wasn't the only place where things came cheap. Bargains were also found crowded along the dirt roads at the edges of town, in the "hotsy" bathhouses and geisha houses, neon-lit clubs like the White Hat, and the bordellos, where a kimono-clad girl would meet you out front and invite you inside. "Guys would go there like flies," one sailor recalled of his days on liberty at Yokosuka. "For a carton of cigarettes, you could be king."

The *Oriskany's* crew spent so much time in port that Captain Griffin worried that his men—especially Air Group 19—would all become infected with venereal disease. He threatened to call a "short-arm" inspection so that the ship's doctor could check every man's geisha-befriended penis. Jig Dog intervened, telling Griffin that if he forced his men to submit to such an inspection, he'd have to check Jig Dog's "short arm," too—and his own. Griffin called off the inspection.

In ports such as Yokosuka, the code among the brotherhood of naval aviators was to look the other way, don't ask questions, and mind your business. How a man behaved in port was his affair. It had nothing to do with the family back home. It was, in some ways, part of the job—an entitlement after serving months on a ship full of men.

Shepard was no different. In fact, he enjoyed himself more than most of his peers in ports such as Yokosuka, downing cocktails, smoking cigarettes, and meeting women. Friends called him a "snake," a "roué," and a "liberty hound." He'd stay out late, night after night, then get up and do three flawless hops in his Banshee. But few could recall seeing him drunk. When he and a group of pilots went out for the night, Shepard had no interest in chugging beers at the bar. He was a man with a plan, and the plan was to meet some attractive woman. Shepard's Mangy Angels partner Mitch Mitchell said Shepard, relying on some "inner sense," could scope out a bar crowd and "pick out just the right one." It might take one drink, it might take all night, but more often than not he'd walk out with her. "He never said a word, never bragged," Mitchell said. "You never knew what happened. His lips would peel back from those big beautiful teeth and he'd just smile. Shep never revealed anything—where he went or who he screwed."

Shepard was hardly an anomaly of the 1950s. Alfred Kinsey's pioneering study *Sexual Behavior in the Human Male* found that 80 percent of successful businessmen cheated on their wives. At the time, new icons of masculinity and sexuality were replacing old ones. The subtle charms of Cary Grant got swept aside by the raw sexual energies of Marlon Brando, James Dean, and Elvis Presley shaking his ass on TV. A young man named Hugh Hefner had begun publishing a magazine that, in addition to pictures of beautiful nude women, told men how to mix a cocktail, buy a sports car, have fun. Within three years, nearly a million men subscribed to *Playboy*.

Men and women were breaking free all over America at the time. The Beat poets and comedian Lenny Bruce began breaking new ground with their words; women (helped by the pill) began expanding their own sexual boundaries. And men like Alan Shepard, who had watched their Depression-scarred fathers deny themselves and who had survived World War II and the Korean War with their optimism and virility intact, began to break free of the old cultural and moral restrictions, to convince themselves that forbidden pleasures were their due. It seemed to some peers that he simply couldn't help himself. When Shepard wasn't flying, he was chasing.

"The other women in his life were significant," said former academy roommate Bob Williams. "They were always there."

Then again, some colleagues considered Shepard an otherwise devoted spouse. "I know it sounds contradictory, but I think Shep was a good husband," said former academy classmate and test pilot Bill Botts, who attributed the philandering not to a bad marriage but "because he had more wild seeds in him than most people."

Shepard's duality gave some colleagues whiplash. He didn't talk much about his wife and kids, and they'd be shocked to see him at family events, attentive and respectful with Louise, playful and fatherly with his two daughters.

And while some of Louise's friends wondered why she stayed with him, she knew about and apparently accepted what was happening. She may have pretended at times that Alan was different. But she wasn't stupid—she knew. Still, they tried, really tried, to be a family. The deep and complicated truth was this: Alan loved Louise and she loved him. If his indulgences hurt her, she kept it to herself and created a selfless role as her husband's anchor. Without her, he might have gone off in who knows what reckless directions. Louise grounded Alan. She was his tether to earth.

///

With his impressive performances in port, his Mangy Angels exploits, and his precision flying, Shepard became a celebrity aboard the USS *Oriskany*. He did calisthenics and sometimes jogged on the flight deck to keep fit. He could give an hourlong lecture on the intricacies of some aircraft without any notes. One night, he took a Banshee up to fifty thousand feet and dove straight down toward the Philippines, intent on pushing the plane beyond Mach 1; he knew the Banshee wasn't built for such speed, but he still managed to reach Mach .93, more than 600 miles an hour.

He was a natural and had what pilots call "situational awareness." Like a basketball star who knows intuitively where everyone is on the court at all times, Shepard had a keen, bird's-eye sense of the space around him—where the other planes were, where the ship was, how fast and high he was flying, how much fuel he had left. Most pilots keep a "check-off list" on their knee, which is like a to-do list to remind them to put all the switches and handles in the right position. Shepard never used one, and once scoffed when he learned that Mitchell religiously used his. "You use a check-off list?" he asked after a cross-country flight with Mitchell.

Shepard patiently shared his knowledge with eager, younger flyers but could cut someone to ribbons if he sensed incompetence. He hid his emotions and kept his distance from those who wanted to become friends, seeming not to need or even want that kind of relationship. And yet, while he liked being alone, in a crowd he was graceful and swaggering and funny and smart.

He was the *Oriskany*'s own movie star, and when some real celebrities came aboard, his friends weren't surprised to learn that Shepard had befriended a few of them. To avoid paying union wages to extras and stuntmen back home in Hollywood, Paramount Studios convinced the Navy to let it shoot a film aboard the *Oriskany*, where it would be freed from union restrictions. *The Bridges at Toko-Ri*, based on James Michener's bestselling novel of the previous year, would become one of the more famous depictions of Korean War dogfights. It starred William Holden as an aging fighter pilot and Mickey Rooney as a daring young helicopter pilot.

Captain Griffin had some reservations about Rooney, who was known as a real wild man when he got drunk. But Griffin didn't allow alcohol on his ship and felt sure that Rooney would behave in the absence of booze. A few days into the shooting, he even came to like Rooney, who performed for two and a half hours one night in the hangar bay, playing drums and telling jokes for the *Oriskany*'s crew. When the ship docked in Japan, though, and the crew went ashore, Rooney "got a few drinks under his belt and he was just a little stinker first class."

During the filming, there was a lot of juggling of airplanes. The planes, flown by Navy aviators, waited on other nearby aircraft carriers until their cue from the movie's director, Mark Robson. The planes would then approach and land on the *Oriskany*, with Robson's cameras rolling. One of the pilots was one of Shepard's former Naval Academy classmates, Bill Geiger. After landing and parking his plane, Geiger roamed around the ship until he found Shepard, and they made plans to meet that night in Shepard's room.

When Geiger arrived in Shepard's cramped, cluttered stateroom, Shepard had a small cocktail party waiting. He'd set up a folding table covered with a tablecloth and put out some hors d'oeuvres—cheese, crackers, nuts—some paper plates and napkins, and, despite the captain's no-alcohol-on-the-ship rule, a cocktail shaker. Shepard beamed with pride at his little unauthorized happy hour and mixed them each a martini—straight up, with olives. They were sipping their drinks when there was a loud knock on the door.

"Enter," Shepard called, and in stumbled Mickey Rooney and another member of the cast. Rooney had clearly found another happy hour somewhere. He was bombed.

"Hey, Mickey," Shepard said. "Come on in. Have a drink and meet my friend Bill Geiger."

Geiger was speechless. He was both starstruck and disgusted by Rooney's drunkenness, and he was amazed that Shepard was on a first-name basis with a movie star. Rooney stumbled over and offered Geiger a sweaty handshake. "Hey, fella," he slurred. "Shake the hand that held the tit of Ava Gardner."

///

Shepard's love of cocktails never seemed to affect his flying or his nerves, however. That fact was never more clear than on the dark, cold morning of March 15, 1954, as Shepard's squadron prepared for a simulated attack on the battleship USS *Iowa*. Jig Dog, with Shepard as his wing man, would lead a two-division group of eight Banshees and meet up with a dozen AD Skyraiders, propeller planes that would take off before the faster Banshees. Together they'd stage a coordinated mock attack.

The Skyraiders took off into the predawn blackness just as a heavy snow began falling. Jig Dog could barely find his Banshee on the stormy flight deck and was sure the mission would be canceled. Then he heard the call: "Man jets." And soon after: "Start engines." Even after he and Shepard launched and rose toward twenty-five thousand feet, he thought that at any moment the orders for a return to the ship would crackle into his headset. "I'd never been out in weather like that, before or after," he recalled.

Once all eight Banshees were airborne, Jig Dog started climbing in an effort to get above the clouds. But in a matter of seconds "things began to unravel." First his windshield froze over and he had to crank up the heat to full blast. Then it became unbearably hot. The heater had at least cleared a small opening in the ice, but it didn't matter much because there was nothing to see but black sky filled with monsoons of snow. Jig Dog's squadron kept flying, not by sight but by monitoring their instruments.

Then, about half an hour into the flight, Shepard noticed that Jig Dog was beginning to veer off course and was soon leaning into a 45-degree bank, with the rest of the formation following him off in the wrong direction. Just like that childhood "crack the whip" game, Jig Dog was whipping his squadron dangerously off course.

A wingman's job is, foremost, to stick with his leader. To watch his six o'clock. So Shepard "snuggled in" next to Jig Dog and began calling on the radio.

"CAG! CAG!" (CAG is Navy-speak for "commander, air group.")

Jig Dog's mind was fuzzy. He wasn't sure what was going on or how to correct it. Even worse, he didn't care. He heard Shepard's voice and tried to adjust his position. But he had an "uncontrollable urge to roll over on my back and dive into the ragged overcast." He could see "the glow of light from the sun." He was climbing and turning left. If he kept heading in that direction, the plane would soon spin out of control.

Then he heard Shepard's voice again—calm, not panicky, but urgent. The voice seemed far away, but it was insistent. And it drew him back from unconsciousness.

"CAG. CAG. CAG," Shepard almost yelled. "Nose down, CAG. Nose down. Wings level. You're going in." Jig Dog heard those last two words: "going in." That snapped him out of it. He grabbed the stick with both hands and flattened out his jet.

But then, almost immediately, he felt nauseous. He vomited into his mask and then into his lap. His reactions on the control stick were sluggish. The instruments all looked fuzzy. But Shepard's voice kept pushing into his headset, and Jig Dog could feel his wingman's presence just off his right shoulder. He finally descended to a lower altitude and regained his wits. The air tasted better, "and I began to care." He cleared out his mask as best he could and began communicating with Shepard and the ship. The mission, he learned, was canceled and all planes were to return to the *Oriskany*.

Jig Dog wasn't sure whether to call an emergency, which would require the *Oriskany* to clear the deck of all planes, or try to keep flying. He talked it over with Shepard, who could tell his commander was emerging from whatever fog had confused him. They decided that Jig Dog should go ahead and land. The storm had blown past, and the sun was even poking through the clouds. Shepard kept talking, keeping him engaged. Jig Dog brought his plane in slowly and landed, snapping to a safe halt without incident.

The inside of the Banshee was disgusting, and Jig Dog looked like shit. An inspection of the plane found that the oxygen system had failed. Cranking up the heat had probably exacerbated the problem. Jig Dog collapsed in the ready room and waited for his wingman. When Shepard saw his boss, he just shook his head.

"Just wasn't my day to buy the farm," Jig Dog said. "Shep, I owe you one."

He'd get his chance to return the favor a year later. And Shepard would need it.

It would make all the difference in his career.

8

"That little rascal"

In late 1954, near the end of his second tour on *Oriskany*, Shepard was promoted to lieutenant commander—a significant step up the naval ladder to a rank that can take 15 or more years to reach but which he had reached after a decade, at age 30. During a boozy celebration at the Yokosuka officer's club, Mitch Mitchell and the others razzed Shepard about becoming an old man. As the taunts increased, Shepard's face began to turn red and he called the others a "bunch of pussies." "He didn't like to be needled," Mitchell said. "He was very conscious of his manliness." Finally, at night's end, they threw him into the club pool, fully clothed—a baptism of sorts for a full-blown brown shoe.

By the mid-1950s, naval aviation had reached the other side of a remarkable postwar transformation. Supersonic and technologically sophisticated jets were now the norm, and Shepard had contributed to nearly every phase of that transformation. He had stellar, enviable credentials: among an elite few to become a test pilot as a lowly lieutenant junior grade; first in-flight refueling tests of the Banshee F2H-2; first carrier landings with Banshee F2H-3; among the first Navy pilots to land on the new angled-deck aircraft carriers; among the first night-flying carrier pilots. He had flown numerous flights above seventy thousand feet, just shy of space it-self. And his flight logs reflected a total of nearly five thousand hours of flight time—more than half a year in the air.

But even more impressive than his credentials were the immeasurable qualities that only another aviator could appreci-ate, subtle skills and instinctive abilities that emerge only after hundreds and hundreds of flights. Shepard had uncanny spatial sense, a light but accurate and decisive touch with the controls, and an almost physical union with any plane he flew. He could make an airplane do anything he wanted. He was, in short, one of the best pilots in the U.S. Navy. Where he once thanked luck and hard work for his success, he now began to believe it was more than that. He *was* better than the rest, and he wore that self-satisfied poise on his sleeve.

It was in his voice, too. When he now spoke about flying, he did so with unwavering authority. In his New England accent, with its unpronounced r's and long a's, he peppered conversa-tions with pronouncements of finality. "In the final analysis" and "at the end of the day," he liked to say. Another favorite was *actu-ally*, as in, "Actually, Mitch, the best way to land a Banshee is . . ." He was suave and assured—not movie star slick, but confident and comfortable with himself, with his body and his clothes. People trusted him. He was a leader and a role model to younger pilots, who hung around him in the ready room, asking his ad-vice and seeking his approval. "Probably the best aviator I've ever known," said Bill Lawrence, one of the Mangy Angels, who would fly off and on with Shepard for a total of five years.

But there was a flip side to many of Shepard's traits, as if every good quality had an evil twin. The dark side of Alan Shep-ard the precise, technical flying genius was Alan Shepard the hotdogger, the showoff, the flat-hatter. Then again, some of the brass liked a little spunk in their men, and at the end of Shepard's tenure with Air Group 19, Adm. Jack Whitney requested that Shepard become his aide. Maybe Whitney wanted to tame the bronco flyer, or maybe he thought he was doing him a favor. Shepard, however, was disgusted by the thought of trading jets to work as an admiral's gofer. A Navy man is supposed to follow orders, especially those of an admiral. But Shepard wanted to fly. So he called Jig Dog.

During World War II Jig Dog had similarly impressed his superiors, and at war's end an admiral requested that Jig Dog become his aide. But Jig Dog had encouraged his boss to convince the admiral that he wasn't right for the job: "He's got attitude problems," his boss had said. So when Admiral Whitney requested Shepard as his right-hand man, Jig Dog called the admiral's office to put in a bad word for Shepard. "Admiral, in no way do you want Al Shepard as your aide," he said. "I don't think he'd be useful in the job. And besides, he's a hellraiser."

That's why, in 1956, instead of becoming an admiral's aide, Shepard was called back for another tour as a test pilot and instructor at Patuxent River.

///

When Shepard returned for his second tour at Patuxent River, he resumed flying the newest, fastest, hottest jets ever made. In the few years he'd been at sea, experimental jets had continued to emerge. His old straight-winged Banshee now seemed like a toy compared to bullet-fast and bat-winged jets named Demon, Crusader, and Skyray.

But he would soon learn that, at the end of the day, every jet had its flaw. Usually those flaws became violently apparent when the planes reached the extreme region of plane-against-air friction, the invisible wall known as the sound barrier.

To break the sound barrier, you have to fly anywhere from 660 to 760 miles an hour. That range is due to the fact that sound travels roughly 740 to 760 miles an hour at sea level but as much as 100 miles an hour slower at higher altitudes and in lower temperatures. When Chuck Yeager broke the sound barrier in 1947, he was cruising at 700 miles an hour at forty-two thousand feet, becoming the first human to reach Mach 1.

The tough-sounding Mach number got its name from Austrian physicist and philosopher Ernst Mach, who had studied ballistics and sound waves in the late 1800s. The Mach number is the ratio of an object's speed in relation to the speed of sound, so that Mach .7 is 70 percent of the speed of sound (or "subsonic"), Mach 1 is the speed of sound (or "transonic"), and Mach 2 is twice the speed of sound. Anything above Mach 1 is considered "supersonic," but prior to Chuck Yeager's feat, scientists had presumed the human body was incapable of withstanding the extreme forces of supersonic speed. Some scientists ventured that a pilot hitting the sound barrier would be squashed like a bug, his body flattened by the pummeling of pressure waves.

Six years after Yeager proved those theories wrong, a test pilot named Scott Crossfield, part of the fledgling NACA (National Advisory Committee for Aeronautics—the predecessor of the space agency, NASA), sat in the cockpit of a rocket-propelled Skyrocket—slathered tip to tail with wax to reduce drag—and was dropped from the belly of a B-29 bomber. Crossfield lit up his engines and then tipped his plane into a shallow dive, watching the "mach meter" until, at 1,291 miles an hour, it reached the number 2.

Three years later, another rocket-boosted aircraft, the X-2, reached 126,000 feet—the fringes of space. And a few weeks after that, a pilot named Mel Apt reached Mach 3 (2,094 miles an hour), but then immediately spun out of control and was killed. That was the problem with high-altitude supersonic flight—while knocking on heaven's door, unpredictable and deadly things could occur quickly. Which is exactly what was nearly killing any pilot who tried to blast through Mach 1 in the Grumman F11F-1 Tiger, the Navy's vexing and expensive new jet fighter.

The Tiger was designed to be the first Navy jet fighter to go supersonic, with an enormous turbojet engine that could easily shove it toward unprecedented heights, a dozen miles above earth. An experimental version of the Tiger reached 1,386 miles an hour (Mach 2 plus some), and the Tiger would soon be adopted by Shepard's beloved Blue Angels. The jet was so fast that a Grumman test pilot, while testing the plane's machine guns, caught up to his own speeding bullets, which smacked into his windshield and damaged one of the engines, forcing a crash landing.

But early models of the Tiger, also being tested by the Air Force in 1956, had a troubling little tic. When the F11F Tiger reached Mach 1, any effort to turn would cause "reverse yaw"—a violent, out-of-control spin in the opposite direction. Shortly after Mel Apt was killed in his Mach 3 flight at the former Muroc airbase (which had been renamed Edwards Air Force Base in 1949), Shepard was sent there to help "wring out" the Navy's troublesome Tiger. A little more than an hour north and east of Los Angeles, Edwards was the desert testing grounds made famous by Yeager and by Shepard's mentor, Turner Caldwell, and other pilots in their record-breaking matte black or bright red rocket-powered jets. In the aviation fraternity, it was also famous for the broken-down, wood-floored local dude ranch/bar, the Happy Bottom Riding Club.

Even though it was an Air Force base, Shepard loved flying in and out of Edwards, which he called "a beautiful airfield." After landing so many planes on the minuscule "floating runway" of an aircraft carrier, it was liberating to have the entire hard-packed dry lake beds on the edge of the Mojave Desert as his runway.

The night before his scheduled tests on the Tiger, Shepard paid a visit to the Happy Bottom, which was run by Pancho Barnes, a legendary and foul-mouthed daredevil aviatrix of the 1920s, who once earned a cameo beside Clark Gable in the movie *Test Pilot*. There Shepard ran into a group of regulars—a few Air Force pilots stationed at Edwards. One of them, noting that a Navy pilot had entered the bar, began loudly asking his colleagues how they could recognize a Navy formation. Answer: four planes flying in the same direction—sort of.

Shepard smirked, trying not to show his anger, then fired off his standard retort: "I'd like to see you 'blue suit boys' land on an aircraft carrier ... at night ... in a storm." Shepard teased the Air Force guys about their inability to fly the F11F Tiger, then boasted that he'd tame the Tiger and prove it wasn't the plane's fault—it was the pilot's.

Behind his dark-lensed sunglasses and inside a pressurized suit that would allow him to function in the low-pressure air of high altitudes, he took off from Edwards one sunny California morning and ascended alone up above sixty thousand feet, a slow, spiraling ascent that took the better part of an hour. Once he reached the designated altitude, he tipped the Tiger forward into a dive and opened up the throttle. He was watching the airspeed indicator rise toward seven hundred miles an hour and the Mach meter rise toward 1 when, without warning, the engine flamed out and all power was lost. He had a split second to take a quick breath before the cabin pressure disappeared, and without the necessary heat from the engine, the thick-glass canopy enclosing the cockpit immediately frosted over.

The Tiger began falling "like a Steinway piano," Shepard said years later. Fortunately, the powerless plane had seized with its ailerons and rudder in good positions—Shepard was in a slight turn and able to keep the Tiger from spinning completely out of control. The plane corkscrewed toward earth, and Shepard decided to let it, to wait until he reached the denser air at lower altitudes. At forty thousand feet he tried to restart the engine. Nothing. Ten thousand feet later, in still denser air, he primed the fuel pump and tried to start the engine again. Nothing. Shepard laughed—one of those involuntary "oh shit" laughs—and through the frosted canopy watched the Sierra Madre grow closer.

There are a number of reasons a pilot stays inside a dying plane longer than he should. First, his confidence lets him believe he can save what is lost. Second, his pride keeps him from admitting defeat and parachuting to safety. Third, bailing out is a risky and sometimes deadly alternative. Yet, more aviators—especially test pilots—have been injured or killed as a result of the decision to stay with a wounded bird than because of any other factor.

Shepard knew he was "using up the sky in a terrible hurry," but he decided to stay, to try one last time to start the engines. If it failed this time, he'd bail out. Again he primed the fuel pump and went coolly step by step through the start-up procedures. This time, at twelve thousand feet, with just seconds between that height and no height, the engines restarted. He had fallen nearly ten miles but was able to quickly gain control, straighten out the plane, and fly back to the base.

Shepard left the Tiger on the tarmac, turned, and flipped the plane a middle finger. After a meeting with his test chief, he went straight to the Happy Bottom Riding Club, where a couple of drinks eased the taunts and cackles of the Air Force boys.

Shepard wasn't always so fortunate. At the time, the Navy was also having problems with the latest version of its notorious Vought-built F7U Cutlass, an underpowered carrier jet that one test pilot trashed as "an unforgiving, unreliable airplane that took too many lives before it was retired." The glitch du jour occurred when a pilot tried a snap roll—that is, rolled 180 degrees left or right, so the plane was upside down. During a snap roll the F7U would inexplicably slip into an inverted spin, like an upside-down boomerang. Other jets also had a tendency to do that, but ordinarily the pilot could let go of the control stick and the plane usually corrected itself. Not the F7U. Shepard went back out to Edwards, convinced that there was no reason those other pilots should be bailing out and destroying million-dollar airplanes.

He tried a snap roll, and sure enough, the F7U went into an inverted spin and began plummeting. Shepard tried everything he could to save the plane but finally, just a few thousand feet from the ground, bailed out and parachuted to the orange California desert below, where he watched the plane crash and bloom into a fireball on the horizon.

Shepard had almost killed himself twice, but that was in fact the whole point of being a test pilot: to make sure other pilots weren't killed by an imperfect plane. In early 1957 he flew to Edwards once more to wring out another new jet—the F5D-1 Skylancer—as project director of a team of test pilots that would recommend to the Navy whether or not to order more F5Ds. For five days he and Billy Lawrence (his former *Oriskany* mate who had been assigned to Patuxent River, thanks to a recommendation from Shepard) and another test pilot pushed and prodded the F5D. The Navy had high hopes for the bat-winged, supersonic F5D, but Shepard didn't like or trust how it flew, and he said so in a strongly worded report. "This isn't what we want," he wrote.

The manufacturers at Douglas Aircraft were furious. But in subsequent discussions, Shepard held his ground. Only five F5Ds had been built when the Navy canceled production of the plane and instead chose to buy the F8U Crusader. (Two of the five F5Ds would later be donated to the new space agency, NASA). The unsatisfactory report Shepard gave to the Tiger after his harrowing experience prompted the Navy to cancel future orders of that plane as well, after purchasing 199 of them. That plane's maker, Grumman, was also furious. (Ironically, the otherwise agile jet was adopted by the Blue Angels, which flew F11F Tigers for the next decade.)

Shepard's work at Pax River was so highly respected that in 1957 he was asked to become an instructor. It was another indication that, despite his occasional rule breaking, people had begun listening more and more closely to Alan Shepard's opinions. If he said a plane was a bad investment, the Navy believed him, even if millions of dollars were lost in the process. Admirals at the Pentagon had decided that Shepard had become more than a jet jockey. He was now a leader, a mentor, an administrator. He was admiral material.

///

Soon after Alan and Louise had returned to Pax River in 1956, Louise's sister died. The apparent cause of death was a flu-like illness, but there was always something a little mysterious and unexplained about her death, and those closest to the Shepards were never sure what really happened, or where, or why. The Shepards never spoke of it.

In any case, Louise's sister had three children at the time, two boys and a girl. Their father, unable to care for three kids alone, took them to Longwood Gardens to live with their grandparents. When Louise learned that Adele had died, she and her two daughters, Laura and Julie, drove from Patuxent River to Longwood to help her parents. After a few months it became clear that Louise's aging parents couldn't care for Adele's three young children, and the children's father seemed unable or unwilling to try. So the two boys were sent away to boarding school, leaving Louise to care for her niece, Judith.

While Louise tended to this situation, Alan flew up to Longwood on weekends, dropping his jet low and loud over the estate to let the family know he'd arrived (and in the process terrifying some of Longwood's employees). Over the course of long discussions in those days, while walking through Longwood, Alan and Louise decided to bring their orphaned niece into their home.

At first the poor girl was in shock. She didn't know what was happening to her. She was only five years old and was unhappy and confused. Then, to add to the confusion, she received a new name. In order to eliminate the awkwardness of having two girls of the same age with similar names (Julie and Judith) in the same family, the Shepards changed her name from Judith to Alice. "It was a difficult time," said a neighbor, Denni Seibert, whose husband helped manage the Longwood estate and lived in the big stone house beside the Brewers. "People just didn't talk about it," Seibert said. Many years later, they still didn't.

Alice recalled only that Louise "did the best she could with me."

Alan and Alice took a while to find comfortable ground on which to be father and daughter. They were both cautious at first. Except for a few family gatherings at holiday time, they hadn't really known each other. Alice found Alan to be loose and relaxed around the family and surprisingly warm and loving. But he also had a lot of rules and sometimes blew up. Worse was the silent stare. "He'd give that famous stare, and you knew you were in trouble," Alice recalled.

But such moments were infrequent, largely because when Alice first moved in with the Shepards, Alan was often traveling and wasn't around much. Louise and the girls stayed at Longwood nearly a year, and toward the end of that year, Louise finally began to feel like she was making some progress at welcoming Alice into the family. One day Alice and Julie—who were both six—got into an argument over something. Alice burst into tears and ran crying into the kitchen, where she threw her arms around Louise's legs, yelling, "Mommy! Mommy!" At that moment, Louise told a friend, she knew she had done something right, something good for her motherless niece. The Shepards would never officially adopt Alice, but they would continue to raise her as their own.

///

When his tour as Pax River instructor ended in mid-1957, Shepard received word that the Navy wanted him to spend a year at the Naval War College in Newport, Rhode Island. Initially he hated the idea of going back to school and dismissed the stint as merely a chance to "brush up on some academic subjects." But he also knew it was a significant step toward a higher rank. Some of the Navy's elite had attended the college, which was considered an apprenticeship toward an admiral's uniform.

An assignment to the War College meant a chance to study the most sophisticated strata of warfare: philosophies of war, strategies of war, technology, politics, and policy. The college had been created in the late 1800s to prepare midcareer officers to be the next generation of naval leaders. Lectures were given not just by military people but intelligence experts, state department officials, foreign diplomats, politicians, and academics. Though he wasn't thrilled with the assignment, Shepard knew it boded well for his career. "I thought I had a very good chance of becoming the skipper of a carrier squadron in another year or so and going back to sea," he said years later. "And running an aircraft squadron is the big objective of any career pilot in the Navy."

Louise knew the college was just a brief stop before Alan returned to flying. After Rhode Island there would be another move to another city, where Alan would leave them on shore again as he returned to the fleet, to sea—and back to foreign ports of call. But until then they could relish being a family, whole and intact. Alan came home most nights for dinner, getting to know his girls again and getting to know Alice. He played piano some nights after dinner and even bought a pair of bongos to thump on. And on Sundays the family went to church. The liberty hound was nowhere to be seen.

The change of routine was not, however, an easy one. As in many Navy families, Alan's role so far had been that of the oft-absent patriarch. Louise had raised the family according to her own rules, and now Alan would sometimes criticize her methods and try to impose some military-style order on the family. Louise was never much of a disciplinarian nor a housekeeper. She let the girls stay up late and let the dishes pile up. When Alan began laying down new rules, the girls sometimes rebelled. There were times when Louise was relieved that Alan had to leave town again for a meeting or assignment.

Then, in the fall of 1957, just a month into Alan's classes, a startling, disturbing feat of technological mastery would rocket through their world and shock the entire country. Everything would change—for Alan and Louise, for America and the world.

///

Throughout the 1940s and 1950s, while men like Alan Shepard, Chuck Yeager, and John Glenn helped push the Wright brothers' creation to astonishing extremes, another group of men had pursued a parallel obsession. They were the rocket boys.

Instead of model airplane clubs, these boys had belonged to rocket clubs (especially prevalent in Germany through the 1930s), where they learned to build and launch explosive-stuffed tubes and various other self-propelled bullets. During World War II the most significant advances in rocket development had been made by engineers and scientists in Nazi Germany, who created the deadly V-2 liquid-propelled rocket with a bomb attached to the tip that was used to bombard the city of London night after night.

When the war ended, the United States and Russia greedily snatched up the Nazi scientists, with the United States seeming to have won the biggest prize. Wernher von Braun, a brilliant but wildly egotistical engineer who had directed the V-2 program, came to the United States as a technical adviser in 1945; five years later, he was named head of a team of scientists in Huntsville, Alabama, developing a so-called Redstone rocket.

Through the early 1950s, the rocket boys—in the United States and in the Soviet Union, both groups working with modified V-2 rockets—aimed toward a long-term goal of creating rockets that could travel thousands of miles, across entire oceans—so-called intercontinental ballistic missiles, or ICBMs. The Soviets succeeded first, in 1957.

At the same time, some of the rocket boys began to ask: Instead of using such missiles as weapons—essentially delivery systems for bombs—couldn't the ICBM be used to reach space? In the United States, physicist Robert Goddard had explored such theories in the 1920s, and his ideas were used as the platform for discussions in the early 1950s about how to use a rocket to send a satellite into space, where it would circle the earth—a second moon of sorts. America would later learn that Goddard's theories were very similar to those of Russia's rocket pioneer, Konstantin Tsiolkovsky, who had published an article in 1903 called "A Rocket into Cosmic Space," which contained plans for a liquid-propelled spaceship.

Wernher von Braun, who became a U.S. citizen in 1955, began urging his superiors the following year to let him launch a satellite into space atop one of his Redstone rockets. But the cold war that had developed between the United States and the USSR led President Eisenhower to exercise caution. The president was wary of rocket development (thinking it might precipitate nuclear war) and even ordered that no U.S. rockets be allowed to reach space and that no satellites be put into orbit. That edict opened the door for the Russians to strike first, which they did on October 4, 1957, thanks to von Braun's former Nazi colleagues.

The 184-pound, basketball-sized aluminum sphere called Sputnik—Russian for "fellow traveler"—should have come as no surprise. American officials, all the way up to Eisenhower, knew Soviet scientists had been working feverishly to perfect a satellite as well as the powerful rocket needed to boost it into space. Still, as Sputnik arced across the sky that October night, the first man-made object to leave the earth's atmosphere, the effect of its audible *beep-beep* picked up on U.S. shortwave radios below was profound.

Sputnik was the first aircraft to violate U.S. airspace. Not even in World War II had an enemy breached the boundaries of the continental United States. And so, except for the occasional World War II concerns about German submarines lurking offshore, Americans for the first time in their lives imagined being harmed on their own soil. Fears that the Russians were taking overhead pictures and maybe developing plans to drop bombs down from outer space rippled through the country. And every ninety-six minutes that Sputnik soared above, an eighteen-thousand-mile-an-hour reminder of this new age of vulnerability. *Beep-beep, beep-beep*—it was like a message from God, or Satan. And the Soviet Union's mischievous and arrogant leader, Nikita Khrushchev—whom one journalist called "the embodiment of the sheer animal force of the Soviet Union"—celebrated U.S. fears: "People of the whole world are pointing to the satellite saying the U.S. has been beaten."

A month later, Sputnik II reached orbit, carrying a dog named Laika. The space race had begun and all the world knew this: if the Soviets could put a dog into orbit, couldn't they put a nuclear bomb up there? Or maybe a man?

Sputnik was an alarming wake-up call. While the baby boom had boomed and families bought televisions, new cars, and new homes, the threat of communism had stealthily grown, and now here it was, beeping overhead. To make matters worse, the first U.S. response—a Navy-built Vanguard rocket, launched in December of 1957—exploded, and the four-pound grapefruit-sized satellite it had meant to boost into space plopped down amid the wreckage, strewn among the Florida palmettos surrounding the launch pad, intact and still beeping. A newspaper columnist wished aloud that someone would "go out there, find it, and kill it." Foreign newspapers called the United States' failed satellite effort "Kaputnik" and "Flopnik" and "Stayputnik."

More failures followed, usually at a top-secret military base on the Florida coast called Cape Canaveral, where experimental rockets named Thor, Hound Dog, and Matador were launched. Associated Press reporter Howard Benedict, who was sent there to cover missile launches after Sputnik, recalled that at the time they were launching eight or nine rockets a week. "And most blew up," he said.

One rocket—an IRBM, or intermediate-range ballistic missile—veered inexplicably off course one night and splashed into the Banana River, where it exploded and shot a geyser of water into the night sky. Benedict and the few other reporters dubbed it an IBRM—an Into-the-Banana-River Missile. The reporters began running out of ways to describe exploding rockets, and the successes were so infrequent that the engineers would get wildly drunk on the rare night one of their rockets actually flew. It would be another few months before the United States finally launched its own satellite, Explorer I, atop one of Wernher von Braun's rockets, on January 31, 1958.

President Eisenhower, who in his second term had refused to issue a blank check for his nation's increasingly costly satellite program, was by then a crotchety, cynical, and sickly old man. He seemed unable to combat the virulent taunting of Khrushchev, making it clear to the American public that the time had come for young men to replace old, a time for leaders who were born during and shaped by the twentieth century.

Sputnik was not the opening shot of the cold war, but it was a turning point, a catalyst for a new direction for the country. It would lead to the creation the following year of a new space agency and would inspire the post–World War II generation of military men and politicians to direct their talents, the country's money, its defense systems, its best brains, and its deepest emotions to reclaiming the sky.

///

That night in 1957, as Sputnik arched across the sky and as Louise and the girls slept inside, Alan stood in the backyard of his cottage at the Naval War College, smoking a cigarette and looking to the southwest. Earlier in the day he had read in the newspaper that the Russian satellite could be seen on a clear night, so he stayed up late to see it for himself. And for a brief moment, standing there in the backyard, he was the family man he sometimes yearned to be, in the pose of millions of other suburban dads. He could never have guessed what an impact the Soviet satellite would soon have on his life.

Finally he saw the small glow of Sputnik crawl slowly across the night sky. "That little rascal," he said to himself—not amused, but angry.

Alan considered the Soviets to be "technologically inferior" to the United States. He couldn't believe a communist nation that had trouble building washing machines and refrigerators could create this. That fact "gnawed at his insides." Years later, when asked to reflect back on that night, "little rascal" was the term he'd use. But in truth, he had saltier nicknames for the world's first satellite. He wanted to swat the little fucker out of the air—*his* air.

But it was more than just anger that Alan felt that night. Almost as if it seduced him, Sputnik would lure Alan off his admiral-bound career path. Though he had missed his chance to be a combat pilot in World War II or Korea, maybe he could at least fight on the front lines of this strange, high-tech new war. Maybe everything he had accomplished so far had led him perfectly to this moment in history.

Part II

INTO SPACE

///

9

"We made them heroes, the first day they were picked"

One day in January 1959 Shepard was reading the *New York Times* and came across an article about a new space agency that had been created a month earlier.

The political hysteria that had followed Sputnik resulted in the creation of an umbrella organization for the nation's best scientists and engineers: the National Aeronautics and Space Administration (NASA), a government-funded civilian agency whose primary goals would be to regain ground lost in the cold war, prove to the world that Sputnik was a fluke, and beat the Russians into outer space. NASA absorbed a number of scientific agencies, including the National Advisory Committee for Aeronautics, which had been a driving force behind many of the rocket-powered Mach 2 and Mach 3 jet flights of the 1950s. Rocket scientists and their visions of launching missiles into space had been commandeered as soldiers in the cold war, and instead of sending satellites aloft, their new mission would be to send an American man. NASA was unveiled on December 17, 1958—the anniversary of the Wright brothers' first flight.

In the *New York Times*, Shepard read that NASA planned to invite 110 of the military's top test pilots to volunteer for a special mission—to become what NASA chose to call an "astronaut," which is Greek for "space sailor." Shepard read how, after ruling out daredevils and acrobats, race car drivers and mountaineers, NASA had decided it wanted steely, technology-savvy test pilots—who were also optimal choices because they happened to be on the government payroll. The candidates had to be shorter than five foot eleven (so they could fit into the tiny space capsule NASA was designing) and between twenty-five and forty years old—NASA wanted mature pilots who'd been around, been tested, and stuck it out. "Not," said an Air Force doctor who would help choose the astronauts, "those who would be enamored of the project at the outset then lose interest when the luster became worn by very hard work."

Following his year at the Naval War College in Rhode Island, Shepard had been transferred to the Navy's Atlantic Fleet headquarters in Norfolk, Virginia, where the family had relocated and where he now served as aircraft readiness officer, working with the commander of the Navy's Atlantic Fleet. Though he was not currently a test pilot, Shepard figured his name would be near the top of NASA's list. But by Friday of that week, he'd heard through the grapevine and in the halls of his Norfolk office that many of his test pilot colleagues had received invitations to come to the Pentagon for a secret briefing. Where the hell was his invitation? If they were looking for test pilots, he thought, shouldn't they be asking the Navy's best test pilot? He left work that night angry and a little chagrined, the start of what he'd later call a "miserable weekend." He'd joke years later that he went home and "kicked the dog, spanked the children. It was a terrible weekend. It really was."

Louise could tell her husband was in a funk, which was rare for him. So when he asked her what she thought of the whole astronaut thing, she tried to be upbeat. "How would you feel if I *was* one of the hundred and ten?" he asked. "It doesn't really matter because you're not," she said. "But if you were, I'd say, 'Just go right ahead.' I think it sounds wonderful."

Then, first thing Monday morning, a young staffer came up to Shepard and handed him an envelope. Inside was NASA's invitation. It had arrived the previous week. "Somehow it got misplaced," the sheepish young officer said, and Shepard didn't know whether to punch him or promote him.

He rushed home for lunch to tell Louise, who knew before he opened his mouth because Shepard was beaming from ear to ear. That night he and Louise had a long talk about what this meant, for him and for the family. And he asked her what they should do if he actually got selected. "Why are you asking me?" she said. "You know you'll do it anyway."

/ / /

The 110 test pilots were divided into three groups, and the first two groups were told to come to the Pentagon—secretly, and in civilian clothes—for a briefing on their potential role in a top-secret mission; the third group was put on hold. The selection committee was looking for men "who were not only in top physical condition but had demonstrated that they had the capability to stay alive under tough and dangerous assignments." Skeptics—notably the famed test pilot Chuck Yeager, an early and snide critic of the astronauts and their NASA bosses—would snicker that what NASA really wanted were guinea pigs. But Shepard didn't see it that way. He saw aviation at "a crossroads, and space was the new turning point . . . something new and important."

Following the Pentagon briefing, each of the sixty-nine candidates was asked whether or not he wished to volunteer for the astronaut program. A young Navy psychologist, Robert Voas, conducted many of those brief interviews and expected many of the men—especially those who, like Shepard, seemed entrenched in their military careers—to decline. To Voas' surprise, nine out of ten said yes. One man had even recently been offered a four-year scholarship at the Massachusetts Institute of Technology, and after saying no repeatedly, he returned to Voas' office to say, "The hell with MIT—yes."

Shepard also said yes, and was called back a few days later for a more extended interview. At the end of that interview he sat in Voas' office, growing impatient as the psychologist ruffled through some papers. Finally Voas asked Shepard if he'd like to continue on to Albuquerque, New Mexico, for some physical and psychological tests. Voas thought Shepard was going to jump up and kiss him. He then handed Shepard a phone and told him to call his wife, but Shepard said he already knew she was "all for it." Secretly Louise hoped that the odds were too great. When a friend asked Louise if she was worried, she said she wasn't because "he's only one out of a hundred."

NASA had expected a quarter of the 110 to volunteer, but when nearly 90 percent of the first two groups said they were interested, the third group that had been on hold was cut loose. Then the initial sixty-nine volunteers were pared to thirty-two, who proceeded to the next level of testing. Each was assigned a number—no names were to be used, everything was hush-hush—and told to wear civilian clothes when he reported to Albuquerque. There the candidates would experience one of the more ridiculous and, for some, degrading weeks of their lives.

The degradation could be blamed on a few of the doctors who had been appointed to President Eisenhower's scientific advisory committee, men who had started making noisy predictions about the likely effects of space travel and zero gravity on the human body: blindness, brain damage, heart attack, inability to eat or swallow. To shut those critics up, NASA hired Dr. W. Randolph "Randy" Lovelace to conduct some of the most intense medical experiments ever inflicted on a willing human subject. Lovelace's New Mexico clinic was home to the nation's best aerospace doctors, experts in an emerging field who sought answers to such questions as: What happens to a man's body and mind at five thousand miles an hour?

Questions about the medical side effects of flight had been around since 1784, when the first humans left the earth's surface in a balloon. But in the 1950s the rapid evolution of high-speed flight led to the specialized field of aerospace medicine, which studied the physical effects of rapid acceleration and deceleration and whose doctors contributed such advances as pressurized suits worn in high-altitude flights and restraint systems in jets. Lovelace himself was hard-nosed and well respected in his field, but test pilots harbor a built-in enmity for doctors, who have it in their power to ground a flyer for some previously undetected medical defect. The astronaut candidates would ultimately consider Lovelace and his stoic, lab-coated assistants ghouls.

The ghouls didn't deny it: "We were trying to drive them crazy," one doctor said.

For twelve or more hours a day, at all hours of day and night, over the course of one week, Lovelace's team measured and sampled every spot on the thirty-two astronaut candidates' bodies. No muscle, bone, or gland went untouched. Shepard had his throat scraped, gave stool and semen samples, had jolts of electricity zapped into his hand, and had a probe nicknamed the "steel eel" shoved into his rectum. He wasn't alone in feeling like a lab rat beneath the microscope of these all-too-serious doctors with their air of superiority. One frustrated astronaut candidate, who had a difficult time producing big enough stool samples, left an enema bag on a general's desk in protest. Another candidate called the tests "an embarrassment, a degrading experience . . . sick doctors working on well patients." Yet another called the doctors "sadists."

One day Shepard the prankster decided to mess with them. As a bespectacled young doctor slowly inserted the "steel eel" into Shepard's rectum, Shepard began moaning and slowly rocking his hips back and forth. "Oh, yeah," he said in a low whisper.

"Mmmm, that's good. More . . . give me more." Another astronaut candidate who was in the room—John "Mitch" Mitchell, Shepard's former flying partner from the USS *Oriskany*—shook with laughter as the stone-faced young doctor turned cherry red.

At the end of that week, the candidates were sent to another Frankensteinian medical facility, the Wright Aeromedical Laboratory in Dayton, Ohio (named for the Wright brothers), for equally bizarre psychological, psychiatric, and physical tests. There Shepard withstood cold water pumped into his ears, stuck his feet in a bucket of ice water for an hour, and sat for two hours in a 135-degree sauna. He was strapped into the seat of a maniacal machine that jackhammered his body, and then sat for many hours in a darkened, soundproof isolation chamber. He had more probes stuck inside him. They took pictures of his naked body from every conceivable angle; he even had to squat over the camera for what was surely the most humiliating photograph of his career. "Nothing is sacred anymore," one astronaut candidate said. Indeed, the scientists went so far as to wonder if the candidates' interest in flying jets might be related to feelings of sexual inadequacy, and therefore spent a considerable amount of time reviewing what they could of each candidate's adolescence.

Shepard at least understood the point of the physical tests: The doctors wanted to make sure they picked the unbreakable ones. "We looked for real men," a NASA official said at the time. Onto their clipboards, the doctors scribbled notes not only on the results of the specific tests but also about the candidates' reactions to the test. How did they respond when told to stick their feet in ice water? How did they interact with the testers—angrily or with self-control? Those who seemed to exhibit "emotional stability," said psychologist Voas, "came out with a few extra points." In this pursuit of flawless all-around males, candidates lost points for the most minor imperfection; a Navy pilot named Wally Schirra was told to have a lump surgically removed from his throat before he could proceed through the tests. "We wanted perfect physical and emotional and aesthetic specimens," Voas said.

Still, what really perplexed Shepard were the personality questions, such as the analogy tests ("light is to dark as pleasure is to . . . ?") and the annoying true-or-false quizzes. "I often worry about my health—true or false?" or "Sometimes I feel like cursing—true or false?" That day the answer to the latter was clearly true. The psychological tests were excruciating and maddening for him.

Among the 566 personal questions asked of each man were: "What was your true motivation for joining the program? Are you too egocentric to work with a team?" One exercise required him to express his "real feelings" by completing sentences such as "I am sorry that . . ." and "I can never . . ." Finally Shepard was told to submit twenty different answers to the question "Who am I?" Guys like John Glenn—an amateur poet who wrote poems while locked in the isolation chamber—had no trouble. Glenn started scribbling, "I am a man, I am a Marine, I am a flyer, I am a husband, I am an officer, I am a father . . ."

For Shepard, being asked about himself, his emotions, was painful and awkward. "It is always difficult for me to analyze my own feelings or to figure out exactly what is going on in my brain and why," he said at the time. Had he been forced to answer the "Who am I?" question with brutal frankness, he might have included such responses as "I am an egotist, I am a hard-drinking liberty hound, I am an insubordinate flat-hatter, I am a philanderer . . ."

Shepard believed a man's actions, his military record, and his reputation should speak for themselves. He didn't see the relevance of the doctors' questions about who he was and what he wanted. "Al thought it was a bunch of nonsense," John Glenn recalled. Fortunately for Shepard, he kept his complaints to himself and showed only good-natured compliance. The doctors, in turn, came to think of Shepard as "motivated."

In addition to the medical responsibility the doctors felt in administering their tests was a broader sense of the historical responsibility involved—these tests, they reasoned, could ultimately decide who becomes the first man in space. The sense among the doctors was that they were, in effect, choosing the next Lindbergh—or Columbus. "Everyone had in mind that these would probably be famous people," said Voas. "And we wanted those who'd be good representatives."

Of thirty-two candidates sent through the strange battery of tests, thirty-one passed. Of those, the names of eighteen finalists were forwarded to a selection committee, which would choose a final six. Four NASA officials and doctors sifted through their files and selected five they considered to be the best of the bunch, but couldn't decide which of two competing candidates should be the sixth. So they agreed to take them both, for a total of seven.

During the rigorous discussions that led to the selection of those seven, the goal was to choose those with superior flying abilities, but also those with harder-to-measure qualities, strengths of character that could sustain them through the expected media frenzy to come. As the selectors sifted through Shepard's military dossier, they surely came across a few of his less-than-perfect displays—his near arrest after flat-hatting a Maryland beach and his near court-martial after flat-hatting three hundred sailors. But, in the end, his notoriety as an occasional rule-breaking exhibitionist was judged to be a sign of Shepard's boldness and independence, a virtue stitched into the complexity of his overall character.

Shepard had to wait six painfully long weeks to learn whether or not he had been chosen. When he finally heard back from NASA on April 1, the caller simply said: "We'd like you to join us. Are you still willing to volunteer?" Alone in his office, Shepard let out a whoop and then called Louise. When he couldn't reach her, he quit for the day and raced home, amazed that he arrived without mowing down any pedestrians.

That night, he recalled years later, "Louise and I just held each other after I told her—I could see that she was as happy as I was."

///

Two nights later Alan and Louise flew to Boston to attend the wedding of his cousin Anne. Alan's parents and sister met him and Louise at Boston's Logan Airport. During the hour-long drive north to East Derry, Alan broke the news that he'd been keeping bottled up for days.

He told Bart and Renza that NASA had chosen him to be one of its astronauts. He'd been ordered not to discuss the highly classified selection process, but his name was going to be announced at a press conference the following week, so NASA officials told him to quietly prepare family members for the expected onslaught of media attention.

Renza said she was "delighted," but Bart looked as though he'd been rapped in the head with a hammer. The colonel quietly scowled and stewed as Alan explained the events of recent weeks. Finally Bart cleared his throat and spoke up. "I'm not sure you're doing the right thing," he said. "Are you sure you really want to do this?"

"Yeah, I'm sure," Alan said. "What's the matter?"

Bart explained that Alan's "career pattern is developing very, very nicely," and that after serving another few months of administrative duty in Norfolk, Alan could expect another hefty promotion. After that, the Navy would likely give him command of his own fighter squadron, and at that rate he might someday be given command of his own aircraft carrier. "Someday," Bart concluded, "you may be an admiral." More to the point, Bart wanted his son to follow the safe route, the stable, sensible, and predictable course of action.

Alan tried to convince his father that he'd already considered

all those things. He knew he'd be derailed from his military career path. Still, this was a chance to fly faster and go farther, to
look down on the earth from a satellite's view, to become a
human Sputnik. And that, to him, was far more interesting than
wearing an admiral's stars.

It was late when they got home. The conversation ended
and they all went straight to bed. Shepard went to sleep that
night feeling as if he was "splitting up the family."

///

"Ladies and gentlemen, may I have your attention please," the
head of NASA said. "In about sixty seconds we will give you
the announcement you have all been waiting for: the names of the
seven volunteers who will become the Mercury astronaut team."

Shepard and the six others stood backstage in a conference
room of the Dolley Madison House in Washington, D.C. Hands
dug into the pockets of the civilian suits they had been told to
wear, they could hear the crowd murmuring and rustling on the
other side of the curtains. It was clear they were unaccustomed to
"civvies": two of them wore bow ties, two wore plaid jackets. Just
before they were introduced, Shepard told one of his new colleagues, Deke Slayton, he had a splotch of "guck" on his bow tie
that looked like "smeared egg." Slayton would recall thinking
Shepard "seemed kind of cold and standoffish," while another of
the bow-tied men, John Glenn, "was trying to be nice to everyone."

Discreetly the seven men checked each other out, trying not
to appear too curious but instantly aware that the man by his side
was both a colleague and, in the race that had already begun—the
race to be first into space—a competitor.

Each of their names was announced, in alphabetical order:

Malcolm S. Carpenter, a Navy lieutenant who went by his middle
   name, Scott. Carpenter, a Colorado native, was the handsome one, blond and athletic. His wife, Rene, also blond,

was funny and enthusiastic. He sang songs to her while playing guitar. They had four kids, but the relationship would not survive. Of the seven, he had the least amount of experience as a test pilot—and one day that would show.

Leroy G. Cooper Jr., an Air Force captain known as Gordo. Cooper's slow Oklahoma twang sometimes betrayed him; people assumed the rail-thin pilot was less sharp than he really was. In fact, he was a decorated combat pilot with a degree in aeronautical engineering. He had a subtle wit and hoped to have some "real good fun" as an astronaut. He and his wife, Trudy, had two daughters—and a deeply troubled marriage.

John H. Glenn Jr., a colonel and the lone Marine of the group. Glenn, a freckled plumber's son from Ohio, was at thirty-seven the oldest and probably the most accomplished over-all. He had flown fifty-nine combat missions in World War II and over a hundred in Korea. He and his wife, Annie, had a son and a daughter. He liked to sing at parties and played the trumpet for his wife. He believed deeply in God—and in himself.

Virgil I. Grissom, an Air Force captain known as Gus. Grissom, at thirty-two, was the youngest; at five foot seven, he was also the shortest. A reporter once called him "a little bear of a man." He loved to hunt and fish—and fly. He had flown more than a hundred combat missions over Korea, more total combat missions than any of the other seven except Glenn, and was a test pilot instructor at Edwards. He and his wife, Betty, had two sons.

Walter M. Schirra Jr., a Navy lieutenant commander they called Wally. Schirra was the smart-ass of the group. The New Jersey native's father had been a stunt pilot and his mother sometimes performed as a wing walker, walking out on the biplane's lower wing above air shows. Like Shepard, he had attended the Naval Academy. Unlike Shepard, he had flown ninety combat missions over Korea. With his wife, Josephine—the daughter of a top Navy admiral—he had a son and daughter.

Alan B. Shepard Jr., who had more experience as a test pilot than the others but was alone in having zero combat experience. Although NASA gave extra consideration to candidates with combat duty, Shepard's test piloting more than made up for his lack of war making. Still, that glaring gap in his resume would nag at him. He wore a dark suit, white shirt, and narrow tie, slightly loosened. He, along with Slayton and Schirra, fired up a cigarette as soon as the seven were allowed to cross the creaky wood floor and sit at two long tables to await questions.

Donald K. Slayton, an Air Force captain known as Deke. Slayton had as much test pilot experience as Shepard, but he'd flown combat missions in World War II. He had big ears and a ruggedly handsome face. He was shy and taciturn, the no-bullshit one of the group. He'd grown up on a Wisconsin farm and would remember the press conference as "the worst stress test I've ever been through."

The seven men ranged between the ages of thirty-two and thirty-seven, between five foot seven and five foot eleven, between 150 and 180 pounds. Each had a father who had served in the military, although most were also influenced by strong maternal role models. They all had test piloting experience, and all but Shepard had engaged in aerial dogfights against Japanese and/or Korean pilots. All seven were married, with two or three children. The psychiatrists and psychologists noted a few common traits: shades of obsessive-compulsive behavior, an inclination toward action and away from introspection, an off-the-charts exhibition of self-reliance. Together, they were about to soar irretrievably away from their military peers to create their own seven-man fraternity—and a whole new brand of cold war celebrity.

"The nation's Mercury astronauts," the NASA man said after announcing the seven astronauts' names. Those who weren't already standing rose to their feet in ovation. After the applause died down, the NASA guy said, "Take your pictures as you will, gentlemen," and the crowd surged forward, elbowing and nudging each other for position. Shepard muttered to Schirra, "I can't believe this. These people are nuts."

For nearly two hours the reporters grilled them. Each man would lean forward on an elbow and speak into the microphone placed before him. The first question out of the box was among the least expected. What did their "good lady" think? *As if that had ever been a real consideration,* Slayton thought, and his response was just as brusque: "What I do is pretty much my business, profession-wise." Shepard told the questioner, "I have no problems at home."

With that, as with most of the day's questions, the most eloquent of them all was Glenn. In response to the "good lady" question, he said, "I don't think any of us could really go on with something like this if we didn't have pretty good backing at home."

Shepard, his close-cropped hair accentuating his widow's peak, handled most of his responses seriously but briefly. He came across sounding professional and self-assured, well spoken if not very affable. A couple of the others, particularly Grissom and Cooper, fared worse. Cooper, the Oklahoman, confessed in a quiet twang that he felt at a "disadvantage to have to speak loud." And when Grissom was asked about the worst and most stressful part of the candidate selection program, he told reporters, "This is the worst, here."

Glenn, meanwhile, got the highest marks and the biggest laugh of the day when he responded to a question about which of the medical tests he liked least. "They went into every opening on the human body just as far as they could go," he said, alluding to the "steel eel." "Which one do you think you would enjoy the least?" Shepard had to admit Glenn handled that one "pretty well," and must have realized at that moment that he needed to start working on his media relations if he wanted to compete with the likes of the garrulous Glenn.

Cooper, probably the most gung-ho pilot of the group, sat wondering where all the questions about flying and space had gone. Then one of the reporters tossed off another unexpected— and, to them, irrelevant—query: What was their "sustaining faith"? Cooper felt as if Glenn "had been waiting for the religion question all along." The others were amazed at Glenn's un-scripted reply. Whereas the rest offered no more than a dozen or so words about their faith, Glenn spoke with unabashed sincerity and eloquence about heaven, family, and teaching Sunday school, more than four hundred words on destiny, the Wright brothers, and "a power greater than any of us." "We are placed here with certain talents and capabilities," Glenn said. "It is up to each of us to use those talents and capabilities as best you can." Slayton said later that John Glenn "ate this stuff up." "We all looked at him, then at each other," Deke said.

Grissom's response to the religion question made a few of the others cringe. "I am not real active in church, as Mr. Glenn is," Gus said. And Shepard's response wasn't much more pro-found. In military style, he stuck to the facts: "I am not a member of any church. I attend the Christian Science Church regularly."

Later, they'd all realize that the competition among the seven of them—Schirra called it "the seven-sided coin of compe-tition"—began with that afternoon's Q-and-A. And Glenn, with his eloquence and his responses that were ten times longer and more detailed than those of the other six, had taken an early lead. Glenn would say many years later that his exposure to the media prior to that press conference—interviews he faced after a record-breaking supersonic cross-country flight in 1957 and, subsequent to that, a guest appearance on the *Name That Tune* TV show—had given him the confidence to have "a little more to say" than the others. But he also realized that his loquaciousness had cost him points among his new peers.

"Somehow, without intending to, I found myself speaking for the group," he'd write in an autobiography. "I'd probably said too much [and] marked myself among my new colleagues as not being laid back and cool, the way test pilots are supposed to be." Indeed, Cooper recalls thinking: *Who is this Boy Scout?*

The press conference ended, and the reporters scattered to file their stories. Shepard—whom the writers would describe as "imperturbable"—turned to Deke and told him, "There's nothing on your tie, Slayton—gotcha." Slayton laughed, but behind the smiles they all shared with the cameras and each other was a realization that they'd just entered a brand-new game.

One writer would describe them as "square-jawed trim halfbacks recruited from an All-American football team." Another said they bore little "resemblance to humdrum Average Man." Others hailed the "virile" new "space voyagers"—"daring and courageous." Only a few quietly reminded readers that these were "military pilots" and, so far, premature heroes. Even though the public affairs guy had warned the new astronauts about the deep probe of the press, not even Glenn, the savviest of them all, was prepared for what was to come. "Not one of us knew what he was in for," Glenn would recall.

At the time, all they had done was volunteer for some creepy tests and pose for some embarrassing pictures. But in the weeks and months to come, the seven would be praised as heroic cold warriors, the men who would help battle the evil Soviet empire and then claim the sky above for democracy. The aviators must have realized at some point that the instant fame had nothing to do with them directly. A nation of frightened citizens wanted desperately to latch on to some tangible evidence of America's technical determination and superiority. They wanted the astronauts to be supermen.

That hunger for supermen could be seen in the astromania

to come: the astronaut dolls, the rock songs (one California surf band called itself the Astronauts), and television shows and novels about astronauts and space. But there was more than just a cold war need for personified symbols of America's superiority. The nation also sought a new type of male role model. Not the *Father Knows Best* brand, but the Elvis Presley brand. And the astronauts were perfect specimens of what Norman Mailer called "the white Negro." In a 1959 essay of the same name, Mailer praised this new kind of male hipster, the guy who knew how to "follow the rebellious imperative of the self" and, instead of "the single mate, the solid family, and the respectable love life," pursued a life of "Saturday night kicks."

Schirra would later write: "We were seven veteran test pilots but unsophisticated in many ways, not very well prepared for the sudden fame of being America's first astronauts. We were small-town boys . . . only John Glenn had known fame." Equally unprepared were the families.

///

On the day of the press conference Louise had decided to get out of the house. She took the girls to the beach near their house in Virginia Beach, where they had moved after Shepard had completed his year at the Naval War College. It was a chilly, blustery day, but she didn't want to be at home. Actually, she had wanted to be in Washington with Alan, but wives were not invited. As the girls played in the sand, she watched as two men bundled up in coats walked down the beach toward them. "Mrs. Shepard?" they said. "We're from *Life* magazine. We'd like to take some pictures."

Seven crews of photographers had been given orders to track down each of the astronauts' families, to photograph the wives, the kids, the house, the dogs, and so on. Louise agreed to stand for a few awkward pictures, then abruptly turned away and called to the girls. "It's time to go," she said. She was relieved when she pulled away and headed toward home, thinking she'd made an escape. Then she ran smack into the blunt reality of instant fame. The house was surrounded by cameramen, photographers, and journalists wielding notepads and tape recorders. Vans lined the streets.

Louise gasped. "This can't be," she said out loud. One of the girls asked, "Mom, what is all this?" As Louise edged into the driveway, the media parted for her. She told the girls to "stay close to me." The attack was immediate. They lobbed questions like grenades. "How does it feel to be the wife of an astronaut?" "How long have you been married?" "Do you really want him to go?" "Are you worried he'll be killed?"

The last of those questions was repeated a few times, and it bothered Louise, who told the girls to get back in the car while she stood answering questions politely but concisely. She smiled a lot, tried to stay calm, and even let a photographer pose her in front of their mailbox at 109 Brandon Road. That picture ran in newspapers across the country the next day—and hundreds of letters from strangers followed. And, unexpectedly, so did a surprising amount of cash.

///

A few months after that first press conference, Leo D'Orsey, a pudgy, affable, well-dressed Washington tax lawyer who was president of the Washington Redskins football team and who represented sports figures and celebrities such as Arthur Godfrey, tapped on his water glass and cleared his throat, announcing his wish to discuss "our relationship." The astronauts and a few NASA officials had just finished a huge dinner and were sipping coffee and picking at dessert. They'd been invited to a private room at D'Orsey's suburban D.C. country club to discuss D'Orsey's offer to act as the astronauts' lawyer and agent. John Glenn nudged Shepard, and the two joked about whether D'Orsey would ask for a 20 percent or 30 percent cut of their income.

"I insist on only two conditions," D'Orsey finally said. "One, I will accept no fee. Two, I will not be reimbursed for any expenses I incur representing you." The astronauts were dumbstruck. Then D'Orsey hit them with the real bombshell. According to an internal NASA memo that worked its way up to Eisenhower's desk, the Mercury astronauts would be free "to make any agreement they see fit for the sale of their personal stories." Walt Williams, chosen to head the program that NASA was calling Project Mercury, had anticipated the media's love affair with the new spacemen and didn't want them "nibbled to death by ducks." Therefore, while official NASA information would be shared equally with the media, access to the astronauts' personal lives was put up for sale, available to the highest bidder.

Walt Bonney, NASA's public affairs officer, had put out some feelers to news publications, asking them to make an offer on exclusive rights to the astronauts' stories. It wasn't a new idea. The *New York Times* had paid for Lindbergh's story in 1927, and even Eisenhower had been paid to tell about his World War II exploits. But this would be the first of many controversies surrounding the astronauts' unprecedented status.

The starting point for the auction would be $500,000. D'Orsey told the astronauts that night that they'd divide the cash over three years if they decided to sign the contract. D'Orsey finished explaining the offer and then sat down. A quick calculation told the men that they'd each get $24,000 a year over the three years. For most of them, that was double their annual military salary. One by one the astronauts began grinning. Then Leo grinned. And then the whole table busted out laughing. A few weeks later *Life* made the sole bid. *Life*'s offer wouldn't be revealed publicly for another two years, but they agreed to pay the full $500,000.

Time-Life publisher Henry Luce, who had founded and edited *Life*, considered it among his civic duties to promote the masculine heft of his country. Luce had once said that his "mission" for the magazine was "to see life, to see the world, to eyewitness great events . . . to see strange things—machines, armies, multitudes, shadows in the jungle and on the moon." He considered himself the portrayer of what he called the "American century," and for prime ownership of *the* story of the century, $500,000 was a bargain. Alan and Louise would immediately invest their cut, a start toward the life of wealth they'd one day enjoy. Alan would, from that day forth, rely on D'Orsey—"a tremendous guy . . . a very close personal friend"—for financial advice.

Life announced its purchase in a two-page spread on August 24, 1959. Beneath a photograph of the seven, the cut line read: "When one of these men becomes America's first space man, you will read his personal story. And, furthermore: the lives that these seven men—and their wives—will lead between now and the day on which one of them becomes the first American—perhaps the first being—to orbit into outer space will in itself be one of the most absorbing, dramatic, human stories of our time."

Of course, *Life* wouldn't get close to the real story—it probably wasn't interested in the real story. Or when the writers did get close, they were careful not to write all they saw and the photographers would look the other way. Cooper's marriage, for example, was falling apart at the time. He and his wife had been separated, yet Trudy Cooper wrote a story for *Life*—"having my husband become an astronaut hasn't wrought any great change in our lives"—and posed like a pro with the other astronauts' wives. Gordon Cooper admitted years later that he and his wife "would both struggle with the 'happily married' illusion through the years."

Unflattering details of Shepard's life story would also remain unexplored. Not a single word would appear in any publication about his near expulsion from the Naval Academy, his flat-hatting a crowded beach, or his near court-martial at Patuxent River.

Henry Luce believed that the psychological battleground of the cold war was no place for anti-American stories, a belief reflected in the semipropagandistic stories of not only *Life* magazine but other publications in his empire: pro-American *Time*, pro-male *Sports Illustrated*, and pro-money *Fortune*. At a time of rampant national fears about a wily communist foe, reporters considered themselves duty bound to be accommodating and nationalistic. *Life* called its astronaut stories accounts of an "epochal mission" and "man's greatest adventure." A conspiracy of hero making had begun.

The rest of the media spat and hissed about the *Life* deal. Alfred Friendly, managing editor of the *Washington Post*, said the astronauts' story "belongs to the public. It cannot be sold to anyone." Other journalists complained that the astronauts were getting paid extra for a job that Uncle Sam was already paying them to do, and some writers would snarl that *Life* had become "NASA's house organ." A *New York Times* editorial writer would begin asking why the astronauts—basically members of the military—deserved perks that others in the Navy, Air Force, and Marines could only dream of. One critic would one day write, "They were heroes not, like Charles Lindbergh, the first man to fly across the Atlantic, because they had done something, but because they were confident they would."

The astronauts, of course, loved the *Life* deal. They wouldn't have to answer the same questions over and over about childhood and "when did you know you wanted to go to space?" The contract would protect not just their privacy but their families' and would limit the access reporters had to astronauts' homes, wives, and kids. That part of the deal was particularly appealing to Shepard, who right from the start was wary and distrustful of the press. "I rather enjoyed the insulation which they [*Life* reporters] gave us," he told an interviewer years later. What Shepard didn't admit is that he likely had more to hide than the others.

Even the *Life* people knew there was something presumptuous about their role. "We made them heroes, the first day they were picked," said Ralph Morse, a well-respected *Life* photographer who would become the magazine's lead shooter during the early years, and a close friend of the astronauts. "And they hadn't done a damn thing." Nonetheless, most of the nation couldn't read or watch enough about them. And if President Eisenhower and the military men of the Pentagon ever fretted about spending so much money on the space race, the calming effect that the astronaut stories had on a country anxious about the cold war must have eased their concerns at least a bit.

Another benefit of the *Life* deal was that the writers— Loudon Wainwright, Don Schanche, and John Dille—helped ghost-write the astronauts' "first-person" articles. Most of the seven especially liked Wainwright, who "had a way of putting words in our mouths that we wish we'd had sense enough to say," Glenn said years later.

The September 14, 1959, issue contained eighteen pages on the astronauts. Under the headline "Ready to Make History," the stories kicked off a decade of *Life*'s exclusive access to the homogenized, whitewashed versions of the astronauts' home life. "In spite of their extraordinary qualifications, the Astronauts have many of the preoccupations of more ordinary men," the inaugural article said. "They are concerned about the condition of the grass in their yards and proper schooling for their children."

The following week, *Life* dedicated another fifteen pages, this time to the spouses: "Seven Brave Women Behind the Astronauts." Louise, beside a picture of her and the girls playing four-way solitaire on the shag-carpeted living room floor, wrote about Alan's love of a challenge. She mentioned how Alan got his private pilot's license during flight training at Corpus Christi, how he had invited her to his letterman's ball before he had a varsity letter, and how he learned to water ski on two skis, then one, and then barefoot. "But he is not a daredevil about those things," Louise wrote, and Alan's aviator colleagues, leafing through their copy of *Life*, had to wonder whom she was talking about.

10

Eyeballs in, eyeballs out

NASA knew that Washington, D.C., would be a terrible place for the astronauts' base of operations, so it established a new headquarters for the seven men, far from the distractions of politics and politicians. Along with the engineers and supervisors of the newly created Space Task Force, the astronauts were headquartered inside a block-walled World War I–era building at Langley Research Center, a sprawling complex of laboratories, wind tunnels, and airplane hangars near the city of Hampton in eastern Virginia.

Life as an astronaut in training began there, in a large, musty office crammed with seven cockeyed metal desks and one seventeen-year-old secretary among them. To prepare their bodies and minds for the "epochal mission" to come, the astronauts would soon dive into a makeshift and ever-evolving training regimen that NASA had created for them, a sometimes sadistic and punishing routine unlike anything they could have imagined. Once that began, Langley would become simply a place to stop for a quick respite from the many cross-country trips to training facilities.

But at first, the seven spent a few weeks meeting with the engineers at Langley, learning like wide-eyed kids what the rocket boys had been working toward over the past few years. Sitting in classrooms while the engineers scribbled diagrams and equations on blackboards, the astronauts learned some of the basics.

NASA was overseeing a number of rocket-development programs. These programs were being conducted by the military services (Army, Navy, and Air Force), and NASA planned to soon choose one of these programs to provide the booster rocket that would blast the first American into space. Only a year earlier NASA had chosen the type of delivery system to be used: a small cone-shaped capsule bolted atop a booster rocket. The capsule would separate from the rocket as it catapulted from the earth's atmosphere into space. Bolted to the tip of the capsule would be an escape tower, a contraption that looked like a miniature Eiffel Tower and contained small rockets. In the case of an emergency—if the booster rocket was veering off course, for example—the escape tower's rockets would fire and pull the capsule away from the booster rocket. The capsule was designed to reenter the earth's atmosphere backward, and the broad, blunt rear end of the capsule would be covered with a heat shield that could withstand the intense temperatures expected to build up during that reentry. The tip of the capsule would conceal a parachute that would deploy as the capsule fell toward a landing at sea. At first the plan was for the astronaut to simply ride along—according to one early engineer, "he wouldn't have much control over things and he wouldn't even have a window"—but the astronauts learned nothing about that aspect of the plan during their early classroom sessions with the engineers.

The brief lull at Langley afforded the astronauts the opportunity to test and measure one another: Who was funnier? Who was smarter? Who could drink a lot? Who could drive faster? Outlines of their personalities quickly emerged.

Cooper was the quietest and most accommodating; sometimes the others wouldn't even know he was in the room until he let slip some sly commentary that reminded them how witty and bright he could be. Slayton and Grissom were serious and a bit reserved, both men of few words and both shrewdly knowledge-able about the minutiae of flying airplanes. Carpenter and Glenn were thoughtful, more sensitive than the others, and more in-clined to acknowledge the enormousness of what they'd been chosen to accomplish. Schirra was the gregarious class clown, always on the lookout for a practical joke—he called them "gotchas"—that would break the rapidly rising tension.

Carpenter and Glenn quickly became friends; so did Slay-ton, Grissom, and Cooper. Schirra was pals with everyone, always scheming to concoct another "gotcha." Shepard, meanwhile, kind of hovered above them all. He never got so close as to be consid-ered a pal, and the others weren't exactly sure what to think of him at first. Cooper called him "the most complex of the original astronauts."

What lurked behind those big and buggy eyes? the others wondered. Maybe, a couple surmised, a bit of classist elitism. Whereas the other six had folksy manners and speech, Shepard, with his almost haughty New England accent, often spoke down to people. Was it possible he thought he was better than the rest? Was he a coddled rich kid in the company of self-made men? Or was there something else, some deeper darkness or unease be-neath his cool, aloof veneer?

One thing they all learned early on was that when Shepard wanted something, he usually got it. Most of the astronauts played handball, and Gus Grissom, who was short and fast, quickly established himself as the best. The only man to beat him was Shepard, although a *Life* reporter said at the time that the rumor, however "unlikely," was that Grissom might have blown the game on purpose because Shepard was so "anxious to win."

For his part, Shepard decided early on that he liked and trusted Schirra, who was a Navy guy but also a "serious clown." Slayton also seemed like Shepard's kind of guy—"a great test pilot," he called him. He respected Grissom's scrappy persona, too. Shepard thought less of Cooper, whose laid-back personality struck Shepard as a sign of weakness, and Carpenter, who had the least impressive flying credentials of the group.

"There's no doubt about it, we are seven different individuals, seven different personalities," Shepard told a friend one day soon after their selection. "But I think we balance each other out pretty well. . . . Some have stronger personalities. Some have a moderating influence. Nobody pulls any punches when we get together."

And then there was John Glenn. Always smiling and optimistic. Eager to please. Friendly. Chatty. A great pilot, Shepard thought. He spoke his mind, and Shepard liked that. Shepard also decided to take up Glenn's habit of jogging a couple of miles every morning. But there was something between them that didn't exactly click.

They had known each other briefly at Patuxent River, where Glenn worked in the armament division, testing jets and their ability to fire guns and rockets. Glenn had heard Shepard speak at a few meetings about the F8U Crusader—"comments he had made revealed a sharp, analytical mind," Glenn recalled. Shepard, meanwhile, had been impressed by Glenn's record-breaking cross-country flight in a Crusader two years earlier.

But they were tense and awkward around each other at first. *How,* each must have wondered, *could two men at the very top of the same profession be so different?*

Shepard liked to smoke and drink; Glenn did neither. Shepard drove a sports car because he felt "it gave me the right image as a Navy test pilot"; Glenn drove a Studebaker "because," he said, "it was cheap and got good gas mileage." Shepard had dated many women before Louise—and after; Glenn married his high school sweetheart, Annie, whom he had known and apparently remained faithful to since childhood.

And yet despite their differences Shepard and Glenn were the most experienced flyers of the Mercury Seven. Each had fifty-five hundred hours of accumulated military and civilian fly-ing time, the equivalent of nearly eight months in the air, and more than any of the others (Deke Slayton had fifty-two hundred hours; Wally Schirra and Gordo Cooper had five thousand; Scott Carpenter had thirty-five hundred).

Glenn's credentials were amazing. He had flown dozens of missions—in Shepard's beloved Corsair, no less—in World War II, and once met Lindbergh in the South Pacific. He was an in-structor at Corpus Christi and among the first aviators at Patux-ent River. He had flown scores of missions in jets over Korea, where he'd had bits of his planes blown off by antiaircraft fire, where baseball great Ted Williams had flown as his wingman, and where he'd shot down three Korean MiGs during the final days of war.

But, his stunning airborne accomplishments aside, John Glenn was an absolute mystery, unlike any aviator Shepard had known. He was priggish. He could be funny, but in a corny way, not in a foul-mouthed, jet jockey, ready-room kind of way. Glenn wrote poetry, loved music, and was unashamed of his religious beliefs or the Sunday school classes he taught. In Glenn, Shep-ard likely saw reflections of the other mystery man of his life—his father.

Shepard confused Glenn, too. "Al was more of an enigma," he would later write. "One side of him was cool, competent, and utterly dedicated, the other ready to cut up, joke, and have fun. He could defuse a tense situation in an instant with a wisecrack, and he had a way of being able to relax everyone around him and make them perform better. There was a part of him, however, that didn't like the restrictions that came with being a public figure."

Glenn also struggled to find ways to cope with the public recognition and the constant demands of the press. "We were the objects of an insatiable curiosity," Glenn recalled. Still, Glenn fig-ured the public relations stuff came with the job. He accepted it, even embraced it, and tried to use it to his advantage.

Shepard at first shunned the press, focusing solely on becoming the best of the seven, because they all knew that the best would fly first. Despite their different approaches and vastly different personalities, it quickly became clear—to NASA officials, to the reporters, and to the astronauts themselves—that the two to beat were Shepard and Glenn.

In truth, they were more alike than either one may have realized at the time. Despite Glenn's apple pie qualities, he was a fierce competitor who knew how to promote himself to get ahead. That's what he had done in 1957 when he shrewdly devised plans for a nonstop transcontinental flight that would be good PR for the Navy, which he then generously offered to fly himself—right into the record books. Glenn, like Shepard, had also loved flying the tricky Corsair. "Nothing gave me more pleasure," he once said. And just as Shepard had essentially defied his father to become an astronaut, Glenn had turned down his own father's offer to join his plumbing business.

No, Glenn and Shepard weren't opposites. They both aspired to be exemplary men, to perform exemplary feats. They both loved the thrills and glory of flying, the orgasmic self-satisfaction of reaching the extremes of speed, altitude, and distance. They were not opposites. They were more like twins—the bad son and the good son, yin and yang.

And just weeks into their training, each set for himself the ultimate goal of his life: Each wanted nothing more, nothing less, than to be the first man in space.

But first NASA had to learn how to build rockets that actually flew.

///

When NASA engineers began meeting in 1958 to design the rocket-and-capsule system that would carry a man into—and, ideally, back from—space, one official told his crew that their task was simple: "It would be good if you kept him alive." But by

1959 just getting off the ground was a troubling enough task, and the Mercury Seven sometimes had to wonder whether they'd signed on for a suicide mission.

NASA was yet to choose which military branch would provide the booster rocket system. Wernher von Braun, working for the Army, had improved steadily on his Redstone rocket (the progeny of the Nazis' V-2 rocket, a version of which had sent the first U.S. satellite, Explorer, into space in 1958). The Navy, meanwhile, was committed to its unreliable Vanguard rocket (which had exploded during its attempt to launch the Explorer in late 1957). Finally, the Air Force was developing its powerful and promising Atlas rocket. The three services were locked in a contentious and politically charged battle for the job, but each was suffering awful and vexing setbacks. Those failures were especially embarrassing compared to the successes of the Soviets.

By the summer of 1959 the Soviets had already sent a dog into orbit. In a few months' time they would land an unmanned rocket on the surface of the moon. (And during his historic visit to the United States Khrushchev would comment, while downing his first hot dog at a Des Moines factory: "We have beaten you to the moon. But you have beaten us in sausage making.")

In the face of this technological inferiority, on May 18, 1959, after just a few weeks together, the astronauts flew to Cape Canaveral on the eastern coast of Florida to watch their first missile launch. With a dozen other VIPs—congressmen and NASA officials—Shepard and the others donned hard hats and gathered at a viewing stand a quarter mile away. Shepard admired the silver Atlas prototype as it refracted slices of bright orange Florida sunshine. Then the ground shook and white fire screamed out from beneath the beast, which rose slowly above the Atlantic. Shepard cupped his hands around his hard hat's visor as the rocket levitated on its tail of fire. Ice, caused by the insanely cold rocket fuel, rained down from the projectile's nose. Then, just a few hundred yards into its slow ascent, the rocket began to waver. It tipped sideways, its thin skin buckled, and then the Atlas spectacularly exploded. The seven astronauts were so close to the launch pad they all instinctively ducked. Shepard turned to Glenn, who was standing beside him, and broke the stunned silence that followed.

"Well, I'm glad they got that one out of the way," he said. "I sure hope they fix that."

Each of them had to wonder about the parachute that NASA suggested be strapped to the first rocket rider. *What the hell good is a parachute amid such carnage?* Ten days later, however, one of Wernher von Braun's rockets—a modified Redstone, called a Jupiter—successfully launched a capsule containing two monkeys.

In the coming months, NASA would decide not to risk incinerating one of its astronauts on a temperamental Atlas rocket. Instead, the first American space launch would be with one of Von Braun's more reliable Redstones. But because the Redstone lacked the power to send a capsule high enough and fast enough to reach orbit, NASA decided that that first launch would be suborbital, in which the capsule would be sent on an arcing, humpshaped route into space and then right back to earth.

Toward the end of 1959 NASA began making plans for that launch to occur within a year—which left little time for the Mercury Seven to learn to be astronauts.

///

In one of his ghost-written articles for *Life* magazine, Shepard described the astronauts' training regimen—which they were more fully introduced to throughout the latter half of 1959—as a mix of academics, meetings with engineers to discuss the mechanics of the rockets and capsules, and rigorous physical and stamina exercises designed to tone and prepare their bodies for the expected labors of a space flight.

"Some of this was fairly exotic stuff. For we were preparing to penetrate an environment that no one had ever dealt with before," Shepard wrote. "Some of it, however, was just plain down-to-earth hard work." Haunting all the hard work was a constant reminder of why the space race had been launched in the first place: to counter the terrifying power and surge of communism.

Guerillas had overrun Cuba the previous year, allowing Fidel Castro to begin establishing his new socialist, and harshly anti-U.S., government. And Khrushchev, following Sputnik's success, continued to verbally badger America. With a strong foothold in Eastern Europe and Asia, communism seemed poised to take over the world. And the Soviet Union's obvious lead in the space race taunted the United States as apparent proof that communism might actually be a more powerful system. "Communism was on the march," John Glenn recalled. "It was no joke."

The astronauts' training regimen, therefore, was fueled by an almost combatlike mentality and a belief that gaining control of space might just save the world. The men threw themselves into their training exercises, spending extremely long and stressful days at various facilities around the country, strapped inside machines designed to punish their bodies and prove the cynics wrong. And in classrooms they absorbed Ph.D.-level lessons on astrophysics, rocket propulsion, and mechanical engineering.

On top of all that, the astronauts, so recently far removed from the everyday culture of America, so hidden from public view in their cloistered military fraternities, were learning other hard lessons about being famous. The headiness of their newfound fame fueled their competitiveness. In just a few months they had become new symbols of manhood and celebrity. And, as happens in any group of headstrong men, the competitive juices flowed, with each man searching for a way to stand out from the others. Amid such tensions, any tangle of two or more astronauts—from training sessions to card games—could instantly take on the heated energy of a boxing match.

Handball games often escalated into raucous, profanity-laced sessions. Even with the astronauts' vices, the competitive mood dictated that no one let the other guy get a half step ahead.

Shepard, who had been smoking cigarettes on and off for many years, decided to quit. Then so did Slayton, Schirra, and Carpenter. (A reporter at the press conference had asked how they'd find a smoke "when they get up there.") The smokers helped each other—somewhat aggressively—by putting gasoline in the office ashtrays.

During a trip to Dallas, Shepard and Glenn stayed up late one night with an old academy classmate of Shepard's, drinking frozen martinis, called "lead pipes," and playing a confusing card game, similar to bridge, called Huckley Buck. When the other players ganged up on Glenn, who was on the verge of losing the game, he became furious and quit, stomping off to walk around the block.

Each man wanted to be the best at any given exercise, no matter how small. "Jockeying for position became a constant activity," one astronaut said. "The game was to move ahead or—just as effective—move the other guy back."

As they dove into their hectic training schedule, which took them to factories and rural military bases in Ohio, Pennsylvania, New Mexico, Missouri, Florida, and California, it was all about *me*. "It was a competition guaranteed to bring out the worst in a guy," one astronaut said.

And yet it was exactly the kind of competition Shepard thrived on. Just as he had taunted other teams while rowing at the Naval Academy, just as he had taunted the "blue suit boys" at Edwards Air Force Base, he knew how to intimidate his competition while outperforming them. One day, at a NASA research center in Cleveland, Shepard strapped himself for the first time into the cockpit of NASA's weirdest carnival ride, the most challenging exercise in the astronauts' training regimen, a contraption called MASTIF. His attitude was: *If I can land a jet on a carrier, I can whip this thing.* And he was sure he could do it better than the rest.

Trouble was, guys like John Glenn were thinking exactly the same thing.

///

At first, the astronauts had assumed their training program would consist of many hours in the cockpit of a jet-powered airplane. "We didn't know what else to train on," Gordon Cooper once said. "Nobody had trained astronauts before." Instead, training for space flight evolved into an experience unlike anything the astronauts, or any human, had ever been through or, in their wildest dreams, could have imagined. NASA's engineers developed a number of high-tech new machines, scattered at military bases across the nation, that would simulate aspects of what the astronauts would likely confront during space flight. And that became the driving theory behind the astronauts' training regimen: to build machines that re-created the excruciating tremors and pressures of sitting on the nose of a rocket traveling faster than any human had ever traveled; to mimic the weightlessness the astronauts would experience in outer space; to simulate the sensation of tumbling through space in a disabled and out-of-control capsule.

The training program sprang from all the what-ifs that the engineers and scientists had posited. Because, in truth, the experts weren't too sure *what* would happen to a man in space; opinions ranged from "nothing" to "disgusting, painful death." So, to cover all their bases, the engineers decided to explore each what-if and then see if the astronauts could survive an approximate duplication of that scenario. When they weren't in classrooms learning about astrophysics, geophysics, and astronomy, the astronauts were flying from city to city, allowing themselves to be subjected to heat chambers, pressure chambers, a "rotating room," and other of NASA's noisy, dangerous, gut-sloshing experimental training contraptions.

"There was always another what-if," Glenn once remarked, referring to the nervous Nellies in NASA's medical corps who dreamed up many ghastly scenarios. What if the astronauts experienced "separation anxiety" and inexplicably refused to return to earth? What if the astronauts' eyeballs oozed and became mis-shapen in the zero gravity of space? What if the fluids of the inner ear, which control balance, floated out of the astronauts' heads, leaving them permanently dizzy and vertiginous?

And what if the astronauts' orbiting space capsule spun out of control? To prepare for the off chance of such a scenario, the brilliant minds of NASA created MASTIF—the multiple axis space training inertial facility. Similar to a gyroscope, MASTIF was an enormous set of three concentric cages, called gimbals, one inside the other. Each cage was a misshapen, geometric skeletal box that looked as though it'd been assembled from the leftover parts of a set of playground monkey bars. The outer cage was red, and inside that was a smaller green cage, both of them vaguely circular. At the center was a yellow cage, roughly cone-shaped, to represent the as-tronauts' space capsule. And at the center of the yellow cage was a cockpit where the astronaut sat, strapped in tight. Each gimbal was hinged to the next, but they all rotated independently from each other and in different directions, so that the cockpit could be pro-grammed to spin—just like the Mercury capsule might in space—on three axes: pitch (from front to back), roll (from side to side), and yaw (from left to right, in a twisting motion).

The engineers could program the machine to rotate just one of the cages, which would cause the astronaut's capsule to simu-late a side-to-side pitching motion. Then the programmers could rotate two of the cages, causing the astronaut's cockpit to pitch and spin simultaneously. Finally, they could rotate all three cages, sim-ulating a completely out-of-control capsule, tumbling and spin-ning and yawing through space. The astronauts had to learn to use a hand control—similar to the control stick in a jet—that released spurts of gas that acted as a brake against the rotating motion of the gimbals. The goal was to stop the cockpit from tumbling and bring it to a complete stop.

Shepard intended to be the first to master MASTIF. But in a flashback to his downcheck during flight training at Corpus

Christi and the two near-fatal jet crash dives at Edwards Air Force Base, he was immediately, frighteningly humbled.

The practice sessions began slowly, with just one or two of the cages spinning at modest speeds, and Shepard was able to quickly stop the cockpit from tumbling. But when he first gave the thumbs-up for the technicians to spin all three cages, and also to increase the speed—each gimbal was capable of up to thirty revolutions per minute—things got ugly. As the cages spun faster and faster, their breezelike whooshing sound rose into a piercing scream. After just a minute or two, with Shepard's body being tossed front to back and side to side, he reached out and slammed the red "chicken switch" button, which set off a loud klaxon that told the technicians to shut down the machine.

The cages stopped tumbling, and engineers helped a dizzy and nauseated Shepard from the cockpit and led him to the cot they kept nearby—with a mop and bucket beside it, just in case. But Shepard was determined to master the thing. He got back in it that afternoon and performed a little better, but still had to punch the chicken switch, and so he decided to quit for the day. A few of the doctors on hand that first day were surprised at how long it took Shepard to recover from his dizziness and nausea.

The next morning he strapped himself in again. And the next. Within a few days he was able to withstand the full thirty revolutions per minute in each axis. He learned how to quickly and accurately twist and turn the control stick until he stopped one gimbal, then the next and then the next, bringing the cockpit to a standstill. In one of the 35 mm films NASA took of the training sessions, Shepard emerged from a session in MASTIF, then stopped and stared back at the machine, the disgust plain on his face. Then he lifted his head as if to say, *I beat you, you mechanical freak,* turned, and walked out, chin in the air, chest out.

Shepard became the first of the seven to tame the MASTIF, but some of the others had less luck and considered any day with MASTIF a bad day. Schirra, for example, who had been inside his share of tumbling jets, likened a MASTIF session to "a bulldog tearing away at you . . . we'd never felt anything like it."

Another machine—the one Shepard despised most, even more than MASTIF—was the centrifuge outside Philadelphia. It was a small flying-saucer-shaped capsule at the end of a fifty-foot arm that spun in a tight circle, like a tree-sized croquet mallet being swung by a giant. The sadistic purpose of the machine was to expose the astronauts to the type of excessive gravity, or G forces, that they'd experience riding atop a launching rocket. They would be traveling faster than any human had flown, and the doctors had to determine whether their bodies could take the strain.

One G is the equivalent of the earth's gravitational pull. Two Gs is essentially gravity times two. So under two Gs of gravitational pressure, a 175-pound man would feel as if he weighed 350. As the centrifuge rotated faster and faster, the astronauts would be pushed into their couches beneath hundreds of pounds of pressure, pummeled by G loads more excruciating than any fighter pilot had ever felt.

NASA engineers had calculated that during their explosive launch from earth, the astronauts would experience at least five or six Gs—the equivalent of about half a ton of pressure for a 175-pound man. But there were unanswered questions about how many Gs they'd experience during their capsule's plunge from the emptiness of space into the thick, friction-inducing air of the earth's atmosphere. Ten? Fifteen? No one knew for sure, so the doctors decided to give the astronauts a taste of the worst.

At five or six Gs in the centrifuge, it was still possible—but just barely—for the astronauts to lift their arms and flip a few switches on the mock dashboard in front of them. At seven Gs they were slammed into the couch and incapable of movement, as if bags of cement had been stacked on their chest, legs, and arms. They had to tense their muscles to keep the blood from draining out of their head and causing them to black out. With some practice, they reached inhumane G loads of sixteen; the record, achieved (on a dare) by an unassuming Navy lieutenant, was an astonishing 20 Gs. Such spins would smoosh back the skin on their face like Play-Doh. After such sessions, they'd find their backs splotched and red from broken blood vessels.

The technicians called the machine the "County Fair Killer." Shepard called it an "oversize cream separator" that either "whips you or you whip it." And Glenn, after one sixteen-G run, said, "It's something I never want to do again."

Another NASA film shows Shepard in late 1960 riding inside the centrifuge, flipping switches and talking into a microphone to a technician. While watching this film footage, it's easy to tell when the capsule and its occupant have begun spinning faster and the Gs have begun building, because the flesh on Shepard's face smears back from his cheekbones and his already buggy eyes get buggier and buggier.

As if such spinning wasn't bad enough, NASA engineers then devised an even more gruesome exercise with the centrifuge. They had asked themselves: What if the astronaut's capsule lands on its nose, instead of its behind? To test their assumptions, the engineers decided to measure the astronauts' capacity for "reverse Gs."

While the centrifuge arm was spinning and the astronaut was being shoved back into his contour couch, the engineers would rotate the capsule 180 degrees so that the man inside was abruptly thrown into his shoulder straps. They called it the EI/EO test, for "eyeballs in, eyeballs out," which is exactly what happened. Shepard once told a reporter that it was a "real pleasure" to go from spinning forward to backward. But Glenn wasn't the only one who found the test "sadistic." One of NASA's doctors tried the EI/EO and emerged hacking uncontrollably, unable to catch his breath; through some testing the other doctors determined that his heart had slammed into one of his lungs and deflated it.

Much more enjoyable were the exercises that offered a few thrilling moments of weightlessness. The engineers knew at least this much about outer space: A capsule in orbit around earth is in constant "freefall," and its occupants would also be "falling" in such a way that they'd be capable of swimming in air; if an airplane could simulate that free fall, the astronauts would experience weightlessness. The astronauts, wearing crash helmets, would sit in the padded cargo bay of a wide-body C-135 transport plane. The plane would fly in a steep ascent and then arc over into a steep descent. These "parabolic" flights would give the astronauts about fifteen seconds of weightlessness, and they often goofed in front of the on-board cameras like schoolkids, wrestling with each other and doing back flips.

The weightlessness could sometimes come to an abrupt halt, however, and the men would slam into the padded floors and walls of the airplane.

///

As a group or in pairs, the astronauts also regularly visited the various plants where pieces of their spaceships were being built. Development of the capsules and rockets was proceeding more or less in tandem with the results of the astronauts' training exercises, so that the findings of those exercises could be incorporated into design modifications. For example, the EI/EO test led to the development of stronger shoulder harnesses. Shepard and the others treasured their small role in the design of their capsules. The sense of empowerment was similar to what they all had felt as test pilots, informing manufacturers about how to correct defects in their airplanes.

But the astronauts soon discovered that their role in the capsule design was smaller than they had realized. One particularly distressing discovery was made when they all visited the McDonnell Aircraft plant in St. Louis in charge of manufacturing the capsules. The astronauts hadn't realized until that day that there would be no window in the little metal teepee. They were training to go on the greatest journey humans could have imagined, but except for a periscope that offered a blurry view of the outside of the capsule, they wouldn't be able to see a goddamn thing.

Glenn called the oversight "unthinkable," and all of them had to quietly wonder if Chuck Yeager had been right after all; they would just be guinea pigs in a windowless can. Such feelings inspired Shepard and the others to fight harder for design changes that they felt were crucial. Except for the first three capsules, which were too far along, all future capsules would have a window. And, in a battle that the astronauts considered their most important victory, all the capsules would be rigged with a guidance system (including the hand control) that allowed them to manually "fly" the capsule. That victory was the result of their own what-if: What if all this fancy, automated equipment failed while they were in space and they had to bring the capsule back down themselves?

Some days the astronauts called "gee whiz days" because everything was new. They were learning things (about stars, constellations, and planets) and doing things (such as scuba diving in the Gulf of Mexico) that were exciting and challenging.

But the "gee whiz" days were balanced out by plenty of "oh shit" days when they realized, to their shock, how little NASA knew about its task. Sometimes it seemed that NASA and its contractors were making things up as they went along. That wasn't far from the truth. "We were inundated with the newness of everything," Christopher Kraft, NASA's flight director, would later write.

In addition to the rocket boys—men like von Braun, who'd been building rockets their entire life—many of NASA's first engineers came from the same world as Shepard, the aviation world. They were the men who had built and designed the planes and jets that Shepard once flew. But now, as partners with the rocket boys, many of the aviation engineers had to learn the basic theories of rocket propulsion; some engineers learned such lessons sitting in a high school classroom near Langley. "We were airplane people," Kraft recalled. "I wasn't the only engineer who was stunned at how much I didn't know and how much I had to learn."

Trickiest of all was turning ballistic rockets, which had been designed as bomb-carrying man-killers, into man-carriers. But as the hoped-for late 1960 or early 1961 manned launch drew closer, NASA's engineers continued to frighten the astronauts with how much more they apparently still had to learn. Shepard and the others assembled at the Cape one night to watch the test launch of another one of Von Braun's Redstones. As the countdown reached zero, fire and smoke erupted from the rocket's base and quickly engulfed the entire Redstone. A projectile then shot straight up from the smoke and seemed to zip out of view and into the night sky quicker than the eye could follow. "Look at the acceleration on that son of a bitch," Kraft yelled.

But when the smoke cleared, they all saw that it wasn't the booster rocket that had shot from the smoke—the Redstone was still standing on the launch pad. All that had zipped toward space was the rocket-propelled escape tower attached to the top of the capsule. A malfunction had caused it to ignite, but instead of pulling the capsule with it and away from the rocket—its sole purpose—the escape tower blasted away all alone.

A few seconds later, a huge orange parachute popped out of the top of the capsule, which remained bolted atop the failed Redstone. Seconds later, as the huge orange parachute billowed in the breeze, a poof of green stuff spewed out from the capsule's tip—the dye that was supposed to mark the capsule's spot and assist recovery crews when it landed in the ocean. The rocket stood mocking them, and the steady ocean breezes threatened to catch hold of the parachute, fill it with wind, and pull down the entire missile, which was still swollen, ticklike, with highly explosive liquid fuel.

Kraft overheard some other engineers discussing how to release the pressurized fuel. Someone suggested getting a rifleman to shoot a couple of holes in the side of the rocket to bleed off the pressure. Kraft couldn't believe his ears. The slightest spark from a bullet could ignite the volatile mix of liquid oxygen and kerosene. Finally a brave McDonnell Aircraft employee crawled to the base of the rocket and shut down the ignition systems. "That was a hell of a mess," Kraft said afterward.

Later they learned how a few millimeters could mean the difference between life and death for an astronaut. A cord ran from the base of the Redstone, which fed the rocket a steady supply of electricity right up to the moment of launch. When the rocket began to ascend, it would snap the cord and begin supplying its own electricity. But one prong on this rocket's cord had been manufactured a fraction of an inch too short. The rocket lifted four inches off the ground but then the imperfect electrical cord disconnected a few milliseconds too soon, which automatically shut down the engines.

Such failed launches weren't uncommon at a time when the success rate of certain American rockets hovered around an appalling 50 percent. Shepard's response to such failures: *What do you expect from rockets built by the lowest bidder?*

///

By mid-1960, as the astronauts passed their first anniversary as a team and the training and traveling routine reached full speed, the seven were on the road constantly, hundreds of days a year—so much traveling that Gordo Cooper's accountant told him he could pick any state he wanted as his residence for tax purposes.

When the pressure cooker weirdness, the interviews, and instant fame weighed too heavily, or when the ceaseless internal competition became too intense, the men sought out some form of escape. Sometimes that meant playing a crafty practical joke. Sometimes it meant purely physical distraction: water-skiing, handball, fishing, hunting. Or hauling ass in a sports car. Or a few drinks with a female fan. "We were always looking for ways to let off steam," Slayton once said.

One victim of such steam letting was Stanley White, an Air Force doctor who had helped NASA select the astronauts and worked with them at Langley. White was part of the astronauts' medical team. A jovial, balding man with a proud streak of practicality, he had just purchased one of the bulbous new Volkswagen Beetles and bragged annoyingly to the astronauts about its performance and incredible gas mileage. The astronauts, led by Wally Schirra, also a car enthusiast (and the lead practical joker of the group), decided to humble the man. He and Shepard began adding a quart of gas to White's Volkswagen every other day, and White began to rave that his gas mileage was even better than he thought. Then Schirra and Shepard began siphoning off a quart here and there, and loved it as White came into the office bewildered and, day by day, "went berserk." Such "gotchas" would become one of the favorite pastimes of the Mercury Seven, and they would occur more frequently when a man named Shorty entered their lives.

Five-foot-six-inch John A. "Shorty" Powers was a brusque Air Force colonel who took over as NASA's chief of public information. Shorty had been a combat pilot in World War II and Korea before switching to public information jobs with the Air Force. He had an impish grin and a deep, honeyed voice that belied his small physical stature. When he joined the astronauts at their headquarters at Langley, right from the start he felt as if he was a "whippersnapper" whom none of them "respected." "They were leery of me and I was scared to death of them," Shorty admitted a decade later. "I had been a military combat aviator for years, had been to Edwards [Air Force Base], had seen flight tests. But these guys just plain scared me."

The military world exists in a different dimension from the rest of the world. It has its own cities, its own social strata, its own system of governance and law, its own language. A military man could spend his entire career inside that dimension, never crossing over to the "real" world of everyday American life. Shorty Powers controlled the portal between the military world to which the Mercury Seven had become accustomed and the real world, which was now demanding more information about and access to the new astro-heroes. Shorty's job was to train the astronauts to be media darlings. Except for John Glenn, they didn't like it one bit. And they let Shorty know it.

At the time, the astronauts were slowly beginning to get comfortable with *Life* magazine's reporters and photographers, who were given unfettered access to them. Even Deke Slayton, the most rabid press-hater behind Shepard, came to regard some of *Life*'s men as allies rather than adversaries. But Shorty was no ally. "A real pain in the ass," Slayton called him, and complained often of how Shorty pestered the astronauts way too often with "the freedom of the press thing."

Shorty's problem was that he had to answer all the questions from the *other* reporters—those who didn't have *Life*'s exclusive access. To calm them, he tried to set the astronauts up at staged events and occasional press conferences. That made some of the press happy but earned Shorty complaints from NASA and the astronauts that he was exploiting the Mercury Seven. "I think all seven guys really enjoyed the exposure—they are human and they don't mind seeing their names in the papers," Shorty once said. "Yet, as test pilots, they instinctively rebelled at having to spend time with the news media." That continuous problem of being the man in the middle would literally drive Shorty to drink. A lot. And drink would one day cost him his job and, eventually, his life.

In an effort to smooth the feathers that his press policies had ruffled, Shorty one day gathered the seven in a room at Langley and tried to explain that many reporters continued to accuse him, and the astronauts, of giving the *Life* people special access.

A couple of the astronauts said they'd heard such flak at their press conferences, but it wasn't their job to make any of them happy. That was Shorty's job. A compromise was offered: What if they made it harder for the *Life* guys to keep up with the astronauts? Shorty liked the idea and agreed "we would play games with Don Schanche [a *Life* reporter and writer] and Ralph Morse [the lead photographer]."

None of them anticipated the ingenuity of *Life*'s combative, tough-talking, war-hardened shooter, Ralph Morse.

///

The astronauts were scheduled to begin a weeklong desert survival training class in Nevada—an exercise designed to prepare them to live in the desert if their capsule accidentally landed far off course instead of parachuting to a landing at sea. They decided not to tell Morse or Schanche anything, but Morse—not above using juveniles as sources—got to chatting one day with Scott Carpenter's five-year-old son and managed to get the kid to tell him where his astronaut dad was headed. "Daddy is going to Reno," the boy said, and when the astronauts arrived at their Reno hotel, Morse and Schanche were in the hotel lobby waiting for them.

Still, since the training would be run by the U.S. Air Force Survival School, based at nearby Stead Air Force Base, the astronauts figured they could lose the *Life* duo the next day in the off-limits scrub brush of the sprawling air base's inhospitable landscape, full of scorpions, rattlesnakes, and oppressive heat. When Morse urged Shorty to let him tag along, Shorty told him that the training was off-limits. "That's a lot of horseshit," Morse argued in his nasal Brooklyn accent. "The desert isn't owned by the government, it's owned by the people."

A short, scrappy, funny New Yorker, Morse had been a combat photographer in World War II. He had scrambled ashore with the Marines at the bloody Battle of Guadalcanal, joined soldiers storming the death-covered beaches at Normandy, and ridden into Paris beside Patton, snapping photos of the conquering general. When he wasn't chasing war, Morse was snapping photographs of Jackie Robinson stealing home and Ernest Hemingway getting drunk in Paris. He was a resourceful, fearless photographer and the astronauts, despite their decision to elude him, genuinely liked Morse. They'd admired him even more once they saw how tough the man was to shake.

Morse's assignment from *Life* was to "cover space." Since no one was anywhere near space yet, he decided early on that the best way to illustrate the space program with photographs was to shadow the astronauts and see what happened.

Morse learned that the astronauts' desert survival training would be conducted near a base camp of large red-and-white tents. From there, the astronauts were supposed to venture out into the 120-degree heat of the Nevada desert and survive on their own for three days, scrounging up plants to eat and digging to find their own water.

After a morning classroom briefing, the astronauts bumped into Morse and Schanche at their Reno hotel and invited them to go fishing that afternoon, but Morse declined. "I've got to find out where you guys are going tomorrow," Morse said.

Two hours later, Morse and Schanche were flying above the desert in a rented airplane with a dozen one-pound bags of flour at their feet. Morse had learned that the camp was forty to fifty miles southeast of Reno—not at the Air Force base but on public land. He had the pilot fly to a spot near where he suspected the base camp to be, and then fly expanding circles until they found the red-and-white tents. Once he located the camp, Morse told the pilot to fly low and straight until they reached a road. He then opened up a side window and began dropping a bag of flour every few seconds. *Poof . . . poof . . . poof . . .* the bags landed in smoky white eruptions, until the plane reached a dirt road. *Poof . . . poof . . .* Morse dropped a couple of bags on the road, then had the pilot fly to the nearest paved road. *Poof . . . poof . . .* And so on to an intersection near the airport.

Morse and Schanche then tried to rent a car, but the owner of the small car rental office didn't have anything left to give them. When they explained they were with *Life* magazine, the proprietor offered to loan them an old Jeep he had on the lot. Early the next morning Morse and Schanche drove to the intersection by the airport and then followed their pattern of flour bombs toward the training site. They were thankful for the Jeep, which carried them over the dwarf cactus, the tangles of sagebrush, and the sand and right up to the tents of the base camp.

When the astronauts and Shorty arrived by helicopter, Morse and Schanche were waiting beside the red-and-white tents. Morse was wearing a white apron and holding an insulated pot of coffee that he'd borrowed from the hotel. "Okay, guys," he said. "How 'bout a cuppa coffee?"

Shorty was "furious," Morse recalled, but the astronauts had a big laugh. Shorty allowed Morse and Schanche to stay if they promised to get their photographs and interviews quickly and then leave at day's end. But the astronauts weren't about to let Morse get away with such an impressive gotcha.

While Morse was running around taking pictures, Shepard and Schirra rigged one of their smoke flares to his Jeep. They tied a piece of string to a blade on the cooling fan and the other end of the string to the activator cap on the flare. Then Shepard called to him, "Ralph, your Jeep is in the way, you better move it." Morse hit the starter and—*bam!*—was immediately engulfed in a cloud of thick orange smoke, which poured through the vents and into the Jeep's passenger compartment. He drove the rough-running Jeep back the next day to the rental office, but it was closed and he had no choice but to leave the damaged car there and catch a ride back to the airport. For some reason, he says, "I never did get a bill."

For the next three days, the astronauts lolled around during the day amid the sagebrush and cactus and then foraged for food (bugs, the hearts of palm trees) and water (inside cactus) at night, just as they'd been taught in the classroom. They cut up white parachutes to construct tents, makeshift shoes, capes, and hats as protection against the hot desert sun. But mainly they hid beneath their parachutes to escape heat that hovered around 110 degrees and occasionally boiled up to 145.

John Glenn tried an ill-advised experiment to see how long he could go without water. He lasted twenty-four hours, and a doctor found him at the end of the three days lying in a patch of sagebrush, dehydrated and nearly unconscious. "As debilitated as I have ever been," said Glenn, who then drank fifteen pints of water "without passing a drop."

One photograph of the training session shows Shepard standing in long underwear, his unshaven chin stuck out, with a sheet of parachute cloth twirled into a turban on his head. The other six are standing grimly on either side of him looking like malnourished refugees. Glenn is the only one with a trace of a smile.

11

"A harlot of a town"

My name ees José Jiménez."

Every time he heard those words, spoken languidly by a short man in a shiny spacesuit, Shepard busted out laughing. Soon the rest of the nation was laughing, too.

Shepard first heard José's voice when a record album arrived in the mail with a picture of a bug-eyed spaceman on the cover accompanying words that Shepard imagined someday describing himself: "José Jiménez, the astronaut, the first man in space." The record's producer, Mickey Kapp, sent eight copies of the album (one for each astronaut and one for Shorty Powers, who liked to call himself the eighth astronaut) to the astronauts' office at Langley. Kapp never heard back from anyone and assumed his deed had gone unnoticed, the albums landing in the trash with other trinkets from fans.

Not until months later would he learn that the astronauts—especially Shepard—absolutely *loved* the record and listened to it in the office after intense training sessions. Shepard even tape-recorded the album and, during lulls between simulation training exercises or during test launches at the Cape, would play the tapes at full volume over the Mission Control loudspeakers.

Some of the engineers hated the irreverent use of their sound system, but they were powerless to overrule an astronaut.

Shepard's reaction to José could have gone either way. He might have seen it as an insult and gotten pissed off. Instead, he felt that the quivering little Mexican—"Plees, don't let them send me up"—captured exactly what the astronauts sometimes felt.

With all the playing hard and training hard, their lives seemed to exist in a world apart. Shepard and the other six had no idea what movies were popular or what books were best-sellers, and felt very disconnected from the reality of American life. But José brought with him a dose of that other world. "Sometimes we like to have a little fun, too," Shepard once told an interviewer. "It releases the tension."

The album had been recorded at a comedy club in San Francisco. José was the offspring of Bill Dana, a comedy writer on the *Steve Allen Show* who did a routine in 1959 about a Latino Santa Claus ("jo, jo, jo"). After Santa Claus, José became a piano tuner, a rancher, a bobsled racer, a Navy submariner, a lion tamer, a U.S. senator, and a surfer who called himself the "king of the surf." Asked by his straight man how he became king of the surf, José replied, "I had cards printed."

Playwright Neil Simon, Dana's friend since the early 1950s, one day asked if José had ever been an astronaut. A short time later, in early 1960, Dana unveiled José the reluctant astronaut on Gary Moore's TV show. The routine was an immediate smash hit and a turning point in Dana's career. It would lead to a life-long friendship with the astronauts, especially Shepard, and would ultimately—through album sales and television appearances—make Dana a very wealthy man.

The friendship began one night at the Kings Inn, a nightclub in Cocoa Beach, the town just south of Cape Canaveral, where Dana became José before a raucously appreciative crowd of NASA employees. Dana usually performed with a straight man who'd ask such lines as, "Is that your crash helmet?" And

José would respond, in a slightly effeminate Hispanic dialect, "Oh, I hope not."

That night at the Kings Inn, Dana performed without his straight man. But a few minutes into the routine, a guy in the front row began yelling out the straight man's lines.

"Has NASA provided something to break your fall?" the man yelled.

"Oh, jess," Dana/José replied. "The state of Nebada."

The amateur straight man was Shepard, who was sitting with Wally Schirra and Deke Slayton. Dana invited Shepard up onstage and was impressed and flattered that he knew all the lines.

"Mr. Jiménez," Shepard said, "would you tell us a little about your space suit?"

"Yeah, it's very uncomfortable."

"And what's that, your crash helmet?"

"Oh, I hope not."

Shepard wasn't very good at playing the straight man. He kept laughing, so Schirra came up onstage to take over for a few lines. And then Slayton. The club was roaring as the three astronauts took turns. After the show, Dana hurried to a phone to call his producer in New York. "Mickey, you've got to come down here," Dana practically yelled into the receiver. "They *know* us. They know every word. And they love us."

Dana—his real name was Szathmary—was of Hungarian and Jewish descent, from Quincy, Massachusetts. As an infantryman in World War II, he had earned a Bronze Star for bravery, a fact that further endeared him to Shepard and the others. Shepard took to calling him Szathmary, and Schirra called him their "Jungarian Hew" ("Hungarian Jew" in José-speak).

Dana's routine would eventually anger some Hispanic groups who felt the civil rights era was the wrong moment in time for a hapless, milquetoast Hispanic. Under pressure from such complaints, he would one day be forced to retire José. But that was years ahead. In 1960 José the astronaut was the perfect mascot for a group of tightly wound test pilots in need of an occasional dose of escapism.

///

Growing tensions between the press and the astronauts were occasionally reflected in the coverage they received in other publications (*Life* was always laudatory and respectful). One of the papers sought out Chuck Yeager to ask his opinion about the astronaut program. Would he have been interested in joining them? the reporter asked. "No," the gruff aviator said. "It doesn't really require a pilot. And besides," Yeager added, referring to the primates used in test launches, "you'd have to sweep the monkey shit off the seat before you could sit down."

Such comments, from Yeager and other of the astronauts' snide, jet-flying peers, led to occasional quips that the astronauts were nothing more than NASA's guinea pigs, just "Spam in a can." Spam was the molded block of ground-up mystery meat that was a staple of the military man's diet; John Glenn once ate Spam daily for two months during World War II. Comments coming so publicly and from within their own fraternity stung the astronauts. They knew some of their peers were, as Glenn put it, "a little envious," and envy was a common and accepted emotion in the military world.

Still, petty put-downs served as harsh reminders to Shepard and his new colleagues that they were no longer military men, no longer test pilots. And they were astronauts in name only, not in deed. Not yet. Those criticisms also reflected a larger debate within the military about this new and costly emphasis on space travel.

What bothered Shepard and the others even more than the predictable professional jealousies was this thought: *Maybe they're right.* At the time, the astronauts were still struggling to establish their voice in the ongoing design of the capsule they would one day fly.

Shepard occasionally tried to defuse the derisions with a joke about how he was picked to become an astronaut. "They ran out of monkeys," he'd say. But deep down, despite the instant fame, Shepard had to occasionally wonder whether his father had been right. Had he traded an admiral-track career for Spam?

Shorty Powers once arranged to have the seven travel to Los Angeles for a goodwill tour at a few companies in southern California's burgeoning aerospace industry, which at the time was building various pieces of NASA's rocketry. Also, the timing of the West Coast tour coincided with the annual convention of the astronauts' peers, the exclusive Society of Experimental Test Pilots. Maybe, thought Shorty, an appearance there would defuse some of the Spam bullshit.

One of the first stops was a General Dynamics plant in San Diego, where the reticent Gus Grissom was scheduled to give a short speech. Shorty had offered to write the speech for Grissom, but he had declined, which made Shorty nervous. Standing before the eighteen thousand men and women who were building the Air Force's Atlas rockets, Grissom quieted the crowd, stepped to the microphone, took a breath, and said, "Do good work."

That was it. He sat down, and for a few moments everyone was silent. Then the crowd began applauding, and the noise grew to a roar. They loved it, and afterward the workers would adopt Grissom's entire speech as their motto: *Do good work.*

Shepard, meanwhile, had learned—probably from John Glenn's performance in that first press conference—that a few words went a long way. While Grissom was giving his three-word speech in San Diego, Shepard was led on an orientation tour at Inglewood Ballistic Missile Division, a sprawling factory of steam-spewing pipes and rumbling machinery south of Los Angeles. He strutted through the belching factory, the sleeves of his short-sleeved shirt rolled up shorter, a cigarette dangling from his lips, enjoying himself. Later, at an afternoon press conference up at Edwards Air Force Base—where Shepard had twice nearly killed himself—he decided to out-Glenn John Glenn.

Shepard, Scott Carpenter, Shorty Powers, and three NASA officials sat to answer reporters' questions, but the other five could barely squeeze in a sentence. Shepard, relaxed and convivial, pounced on each question. Just as he had learned to speak with authority to younger aviators, he peppered his remarks with definitive and haughty qualifiers. "As a matter of fact," he'd start, or "Qualitatively speaking . . ." One of NASA's public affairs officers later remarked, "You literally couldn't shut him up."

When someone asked if the press would be invited for the first flight, Shepard said they could come—"in the nose cone!" When asked what the other six astronauts would do after one was chosen to fly first, Shepard said they would probably "fall on our swords." He talked about training for zero gravity—"a very comfortable sensation"—and NASA's new astro-food in a tube—"chopped beef . . . very tasty."

Shepard the press-hater was downright garrulous. "I can't help but remember how talkative Shepard was those days," recalled NASA press officer Paul Haney. "He talked his head off at the press conferences." Haney wasn't the only one to notice that while Glenn's star shone brightest at the first press conference, "after that, Al outdistanced John."

///

That weekend, at the Society of Experimental Test Pilots (SETP) convention in L.A., jokes about Spam and monkeys got tossed about at loud and smoky preconvention cocktail parties in the lobby bar of the Beverly Hilton. The astronauts mingled through the testosterone-spiked room, sipped whiskey with the nation's best flyers, laughed, and tried to shrug off the taunts. But it was getting really annoying. Deke Slayton was scheduled to give a speech the next day about the progress of the space program, and that night in the barroom he decided he'd use the podium to defend himself and his new colleagues.

"I've had about all the monkey shit talk I can stand," he said.

In the crowded auditorium, with the smell of cigarettes and last night's booze hanging sickly in the air, Slayton—who hated public speaking—cleared his throat and then announced that he wanted to clear up some "misconceptions" that had been perpetrated by some "military skeptics." He reminded the crowd of his peers that it takes more than a "college-trained chimpanzee" or the "village idiot" to prepare for a space flight, which got the crowd laughing. No, he acknowledged in a pointed rebuttal to Yeager, flying a space capsule isn't like flying a jet. The astronaut role is more important and complex than that. It was the role of the explorer into a dangerous, unknown frontier.

Slayton didn't have to mention what the press had already reported: that some scientists worried deeply that the human body was incapable of adapting to the zero gravity of space, that their eyeballs would ooze, they'd go blind, they'd go insane.

The only person prepared to face such risks, Slayton said, was "a highly trained experimental test pilot." To send anyone of lesser technical ability would be foolish. "If you eliminate the astronaut, you concede that man has no place in space," he said. "I hate to hear anyone contend that present-day pilots have no place in the space age."

At the end of Slayton's stern half-hour speech, his peers rose into a standing ovation, which temporarily doused the Spam comments.

On most such trips in which the seven astronauts traveled together, they had quickly learned to pair up two to a room, and often fought over who'd get the fourth bedroom to themselves— or at least not have to share a room with Schirra or Slayton.

Shepard and the others had discovered that Schirra had a habit of talking in his sleep, which was even more annoying because he never finished his sentences. Glenn once recalled, with frustration, how Schirra would start talking about how "this girl . . . came over to me . . ." but then trail off into mumbles.

Sharing a room with Slayton was to be avoided at all costs. The man's monstrous snores—"major-noise, high-decibel, world-class snoring," Glenn called them—could rattle pictures off the walls.

But on this trip to California they didn't have to worry. Slayton got so drunk after his speech—tossing back Rusty Nails and Salty Dogs—that he flopped into bed and passed out. The others rolled him onto a metal-framed cot and carried the cot out a second-floor access door onto the top of the Beverly Hilton's neon marquee, where Slayton slept until dawn. He woke up early the next morning with the sun shining in his bloodshot eyes, the traffic noise from Wilshire Boulevard pounding in his ears.

They may not have been Spam, but the astronauts still knew—as every hard-drinking flyboy should—how to act like monkeys.

///

In the summer of 1960 the astronaut show moved south. The astronauts and the entire NASA workforce (which was growing fast, fed by an increasingly steady supply of cash from Congress) had emerged from infancy into adolescence, and NASA decided to move everyone closer to where the real work would happen: the launch pads of Cape Canaveral. The engineers went first, then the astronauts, and then, of course, the press.

Just south of the Cape, lazing on either side of the two-lane Highway A1A, sat the raggedy little town of Cocoa Beach. Until the astronauts roared into town, Cocoa Beach was a faded and paint-peeling stepchild to its glitzy Art Deco cousin to the south, Miami Beach. Until the astronauts electrified the place, Cocoa

Beach was roughly six thousand people—just 823 registered voters—patronizing a few tiki bars, three seafood restaurants, several souvenir stands, some neon-encrusted bait shops, and
motels of faded pastel pinks and aquamarines. The narrow strip
of land was bordered by the Atlantic Ocean on the east and the
Banana River on the west; across a thin inlet to the north was the
off-limits elbow of the Cape. It wasn't quite seedy. It had a nice
beach of white-sand dunes. But neither was it a destination for
Mom, Dad, and the kids, what with the mosquito-infested palmetto brush and thick tangles of mangrove. "A stringbean of a
town," one writer called it, "a spit of sand." At low tide, when the
wind was blowing south across the swampy mud flats of Turnaround Basin, Cocoa Beach reeked of dankness and rot.

The arrival of the astronauts, however—and the thousands
of engineers, technicians, electricians, doctors, and nurses, and
then the reporters, cameramen, and photographers—would
transform lazy little Cocoa Beach into a high-tech boom town
and a rocking, rollicking hot spot. The young engineers and their
families built homes, schools, churches. Narrow streets became
choked with commuters, and the smells of cocoa butter, cigarettes, and beer overpowered the stench of Turnaround Basin.

At night the strip came alive. Patrons swarmed to the newly
sprung clubs of A1A, where Caribbean dancers did the limbo,
jugglers juggled, and Tahitian belly dancers traded time onstage
with folk-singing chanteuses in cowgirl garb. A life-sized pink
elephant beckoned from out front of the Carnival Club, and
strippers lured men into back-alley clubs. Top jazz musicians
and comedians began adding Cocoa Beach to their tours—Dave
Brubeck at the Koko, confetti-throwing comedian Rip Taylor at
the Starlight. The Starlight also boasted a sexy, space-themed
dance act called "Girls in Orbit." The Mosquito Coast, for the
moment, became the Platinum Coast, home to the latest American melodrama, an East Coast, space-themed Hollywood.

Over the next few years, surrounding Brevard County

would become the fastest-growing county in the nation—the Silicon Valley of its era. It would also soon claim the highest annual liquor consumption in the nation—$143 worth per person. It was maybe no surprise, then, that Cocoa Beach later gained notoriety as home of America's highest divorce rate. "A harlot of a town," one visiting British journalist sneered.

Foreplay to the Cocoa Beach lovefest actually began a few years earlier, in the late 1950s, when the Cape became the post-Sputnik launch pad for America's imperfect experimental rockets, most of which flopped into the Atlantic or exploded. Howard Benedict, a reporter with the Associated Press, happened to be working the night of October 4, 1957, when Sputnik gut-punched America's psyche. An editor assigned an "interpretive" piece for the weekend, even though Benedict "didn't even know what a satellite was." He wrote a story about Sputnik being the first step toward sending a man to the moon, and was immediately dubbed the news service's space expert. "As sometimes happens in journalism, you write one story about something and all of a sudden you're an expert," Benedict recalled.

But when the astronauts came to town, Benedict's job—and the entire zeitgeist of Cocoa Beach—became less about rockets and more about the new celebrities of the space age. Reporters who were there in the early 1960s would later recall wistfully how there was no better place to be, no better story to cover. At times the boozy swirl of celebrity, technology, and sexuality seemed as surreal as a Technicolor Fellini flick.

When NASA first crashed into town, there wasn't even a church to counter all the debauchery, so a priest began holding makeshift Sunday morning services at a bowling alley. Patrons sat in folding chairs in lanes thirteen and fourteen and those looking toward heaven for inspiration saw instead a neon sign that suggested, DRINK SCHLITZ.

Sand-covered streets turned carnival-like with a kaleidoscope of candy-colored sports cars and skimpy bikinis wrapped around young beauties drawn to the bacchanalia like moths to flame. At night you could stumble half-crocked from Wolfie's and look north toward the reason for it all: the twinkly lights of the launch tower that would propel humans to the skies.

"We knew we were doing the greatest story in history, no question," *Life* photographer Ralph Morse said. Then again, access to the astronauts was a lot easier for Morse than the others. "We couldn't get near them because of that damned *Life* contract," Benedict recalled.

Walter Cronkite, whom CBS sent to the Cape to capture a slice of the drama, recalled how the best place to cozy up to the astronauts was a bar. He ran into Shepard one night and they began talking about two of Shepard's favorite subjects, cars and planes. Cronkite described how, as a cub reporter, he had flown on B-17 bombing runs during World War II and occasionally raced cars. Shepard grew immediately curious and talkative. "Maybe it gave me a little bit of an edge over the other reporters," Cronkite said.

One day Cronkite and Shepard and a few other reporters and astronauts learned about the sea turtles that returned to Cocoa Beach to lay eggs. The females wandered far and wide but always came back to the same exact nesting spot each year. State wildlife officials tried to protect those spots but agreed to take a small group of a dozen astronauts and press out to watch. It was apparently an impressive scene, Shepard had heard, with the females screaming in pain as they laid the eggs.

The group arrived late one evening at a wooden ramp leading down to a secluded section of beach. Minutes after they arrived, they heard strange sounds coming from down the beach—moaning and muted screams that sounded almost human. Everyone wondered if it was an egg-laying turtle, but the wildlife official shook his head. He didn't know what it was, so the group walked toward the sounds to investigate. Parked in the palmetto scrub they found a small convertible. In the backseat was Shorty Powers, tangled up with his secretary. The secretary ducked down behind the seats as Shorty jumped into the driver's seat and began to pull away, hoping no one would see his face. Two photographers in the group began snapping pictures, and Shorty, assuming they were all there waiting for him, started screaming.

"What kind of a trap is this? You people have entrapped me," he yelled.

Cronkite remembers it as "one of the grander evenings" of his time at Cocoa Beach. He and Shepard thought it was so hilarious, they headed straight for the nearest bar and never saw the turtles.

Shepard might have taken Shorty's embarrassing situation as a warning not to get caught with a woman when photographers were near. He did not get that message.

///

Dee O'Hara, a labor and delivery nurse at the Patrick Air Force Base hospital south of Cape Canaveral in Florida, was called into her commanding officer's office one day. Usually such a visit meant one of two things: promotion or punishment. But this day she faced neither. The colonel explained that he and his staff had been watching her for the past few weeks. They needed someone for a special assignment, a woman who was smart, savvy, and assertive, and they believed she had all those qualities. How would she like to be the astronauts' nurse?

O'Hara later learned that her boss, George Knauf, who was part of NASA's vast medical team, had been criticized for suggesting a female nurse for the job. As O'Hara well knew, "It was really a male-dominated world." But Knauf was able to argue that test pilots were trained to distrust doctors. They'd never admit to a doctor of having any ailment, which would put them at risk of being grounded. A female nurse, however—especially an attractive and perky redhead with a trim figure and a cute mole on her cheek—might be able to get closer to the astronauts than any male doctor could hope to get.

"He wanted someone to get to know them so well that she'd know if they were sick or not," O'Hara recalled. "That was the idea behind it. Someone they could trust and someone who'd know when they were ill." But earning their trust was not an easy task—especially with Shepard. When O'Hara had her first meetings with the astronauts, "I was frightened of all of them . . . in awe of them . . . they were good and they knew it."

Her first few encounters with Shepard were especially unnerving. Just as he had always been with people he considered underlings, he was brusque, cocky, and rude to her. O'Hara noticed that, with his razor-sharp intellect, Shepard expected those around him to be razor-sharp as well. He liked to grill her with questions about her job, about the Air Force. She was shocked that he didn't seem to realize how hurtful his scrutiny could be. She came to find that he introduced himself to most people by testing them. "It was a game with him. He enjoyed putting you on the spot—to see if you knew your stuff," O'Hara recalled. "He got great pleasure from putting you through the hoops."

But after a few weeks of that, O'Hara got fed up. She stood up to him and they got into an argument over something. She'd soon forget what they argued about, but she'd never forget the change in their relationship after she raised her voice to Shepard. "I just sort of barked back at him," she said. "And he smiled. And that was the end of it. We became friends right after that. From then on, we never had a problem."

Still, even with those who considered themselves his friends, he could be maddening. O'Hara had many conversations with Shepard that began warm and friendly but ended abruptly, as though a switch had been turned off. "You only got so close to Alan and then he shut you out," O'Hara recalled.

She assumed the technique was a source of power. But she also saw that it reflected a difficulty in making friends, something that didn't come naturally for Shepard. In later years she'd learn he was actually kind, generous, emotional—a big-hearted softie beneath an abrasive exterior. But for some reason, he showed his softer side sparingly. Instead, he showed glowering blue eyes and a sneering flash of those big teeth.

"Alan did not want you to know that he might like you," O'Hara said. "He had a protective mechanism—protection from what, I don't know." O'Hara, like many of Shepard's colleagues and friends, could never figure what lurked beneath his habit of keeping people off balance and at bay. Why didn't he want people to know who he was? And, more to the point, who was he?

"Why don't you want people to like you?" O'Hara once asked him.

"I do," Shepard said. "I just don't know how to do it."

For Shepard, it was all a matter of trust, or lack of it. There were aspects of his personality—secrets, really—that required his small coterie of true friends to practice discretion and restraint. For him to expose the deeper, sometimes darker sides of himself to others meant that they first had to prove they could be trusted. Trust had always been a given in the Navy, a fraternity built upon mutual protection. But NASA and Cocoa Beach and the national press . . . this was more like Hollywood than the Navy.

Figuring out whom to like and whom to trust became a constant and frustrating fact of life at the Cape, where everyone wanted a piece of the astronauts. Shepard would struggle with that balancing act the rest of his life. And all who could call themselves his friend would recall having to first pass the kind of "test" O'Hara faced.

One of the first at the Cape to pass muster with Shepard was Henri Landwirth.

///

Landwirth was thirteen when he and many, many thousands of other Jews were taken from their homes in Poland and sent to Hitler's labor and concentration camps. Landwirth was separated from his parents and later learned that his father, Max, had been shot and buried in a mass grave, while his mother, Fanny, just weeks from war's end, was put to sea with a few hundred other women in an old ship rigged with explosives. After five years in the hellish death camps, Landwirth one day escaped into the woods and, traveling mostly at night, made a terrifying solo journey south to Czechoslovakia and then into Belgium, where he had been born and had spent the first few years of his life. He then said goodbye to his last few relatives—those who hadn't been captured or killed—and fled. He emigrated to the United States in 1947.

In 1957, after working at various Florida hotels over the previous decade, Landwirth was hired to manage the Starlight Motel, which for years was the lone motel on Cocoa Beach. The Starlight, with its fountain of a urinating boy out front—a replica of a famous statue in Brussels—was the social center of Cocoa Beach in the late 1950s. It had a bakery and coffee shop. And when the astronauts came to town, their favorite place for a bourbon was the motel's surreal, space-themed Starlight Lounge, with black lights that illuminated spooky scenes of lunar craters and space capsules painted on the walls.

Landwirth had turned the motel and lounge into a hugely successful enterprise. His method was to treat customers, especially the astronauts, as family. He also hired the most beautiful waitresses and barmaids he could find, threw parties and baked huge cakes for the astronauts, and sent booze and food to the reporters covering missile launches. When the motel became so popular that its ninety-nine rooms were always booked, he began booking two people to a room and earned the nickname "Double-up Henri."

The astronauts worked hard to outsmart Landwirth, concocting various schemes to get a room without a roommate: *My wife is coming tomorrow, Henri, I swear.* But the astronauts were drawn to Landwirth, with his European sophistication, his sad eyes, and his nice suits.

A person had to have some exceptional quality to impress the astronauts—especially Shepard, who didn't place much value on the ordinary. What Shepard and the others all quietly admired in Landwirth was his survivorship, his stoic strength. When they first met Landwirth, the astronauts would be wearing short-sleeved, polyester Ban Lon shirts while Landwirth always seemed to be wearing long-sleeved shirts. One day Glenn asked about it, and Landwirth rolled up his sleeve to expose a tattoo of faded blue ink on the inside of his left forearm: B4343. It was the number Hitler's goons had tattooed into his flesh when he first entered their camps as a terrified young teenager.

Glenn told him, "You should be proud of that. If I had that tattoo, I'd wear it like a dad-gum Congressional Medal of Honor." And in time Landwirth began to wear short sleeves and to regard B4343 not only as a reminder of the horrors he had witnessed and survived but also as "a personal reminder that I live on borrowed time."

Landwirth believed in the heroism and historical value of what his newfound friends had signed on to do. He considered the space program "such an American undertaking that it just pulled you in." And Landwirth was proud to contribute what he could for the sake of his adopted country. He was "awed" by the astronauts and felt obliged to do any little thing they needed, to be their mother—"to make their lives easier." Indeed, he would do anything to protect them.

When the astronauts first began visiting the Cape in 1959 to witness rocket launches, they usually stayed in a building at Cape Canaveral called Hangar S. To Shepard, the three-story, concrete-block building was "austere, nondescript, and totally uncomfortable." Hangar S was a converted airplane hangar with huge sliding bay doors on either end; its insides had been converted to offices, medical labs, and astronaut bedrooms. To reach their rooms, the astronauts often had to make what Shepard called an "unpleasant walk" through a sheet-metal building beside Hangar S that contained cages full of chimpanzees that were used in some of the test launches. Shepard despised those primates—they reminded him of the Chuck Yeager taunts. Plus the screeching chimps had an annoying habit of playing with their own shit. A congressman once toured the Cape and insisted, despite warnings of their inhospitable behavior, on visiting the chimp cages. The lawmaker stood beside the cage talking baby talk to a chimp he called "little spaceman." The chimp, Enos, defecated onto his hands and threw a steaming pile of feces onto the congressman's suit.

To avoid those foul chimps, the astronauts asked NASA for permission to begin staying down in Cocoa Beach at Landwirth's Starlight Inn—that is, until new owners took over, removed the peeing-boy fountain and the black lights, and Landwirth quit in disgust. Landwirth was later hired to manage a new Holiday Inn being built on the beach.

On the day the Holiday Inn opened, the Starlight Lounge coincidentally burst into flames and burned to the ground. The Cocoa Beach police didn't think the fire was such a coincidence and interrogated Landwirth, who professed shock at the implication. The police found no evidence of anything fishy and later blamed faulty wiring.

Late one night, Landwirth found Deke Slayton sitting at his new hotel's Riviera Lounge and asked Slayton if the astronauts would consider moving from the Starlight to his new place. "I don't see any problem," Slayton said. "I'll talk to the boys and let you know." Slayton called the next day and said they'd accept the offer if they could be guaranteed a room whenever they were in town. Landwirth agreed, and even gave them a ridiculously reduced rate—$8 a night.

When the astronauts moved to the Holiday Inn, the reporters all followed, and so did the crowds of attractive women who had previously filled the Starlight Lounge. "Wherever the boys were was where everybody else wanted to be," Landwirth recalled. Soon the Holiday Inn became *the* place to be in Cocoa Beach.

But that success also turned Landwirth's life upside down, adding new duties to his job description. In addition to hotel manager, he became the astronauts' counselor, protector, and enabler. When an astronaut—alone or with company—wanted privacy, Landwirth gave him privacy. When the reporters got too pesky, he shooed them away. If not for Henri Landwirth, the public might have learned that their heroic, Boy Scout–like astronauts were not as all-American as *Life* magazine was portraying them.

"Those first days at the Cape were like a giant fraternity party," Landwirth recalled—although, even decades later, he would keep the details to himself. Even squeaky-clean John Glenn couldn't help noticing and being awed by the near bacchanalia of it all: "The food was lavish and the liquor flowed," he said. "Any one of us who was looking for companionship ... would not have to look very far."

Shepard also considered the escalating party of the Cape to be "like something happening in a movie." For Shepard, it was the perfect place to be an astro-hero, to drink and relax and be admired and adored. With Landwirth willing to run interference, Shepard could enjoy himself while the press sat obediently at a distance. In time Shepard came to consider Landwirth "a real friend to all of us."

But the astronauts didn't always make Landwirth's life easier. He was a frenetic, neurotic man, and Shepard and the others loved to rile him. Gordo Cooper once dumped a bucket of live fish into the Holiday Inn's outdoor pool and sat on the diving board fishing. Landwirth thought it was "the funniest thing I'd ever seen" until the fish began floating to the top, killed by the pool's chlorine.

One night Shepard went hunting for alligators at a wealthy friend's sprawling orange plantation. They wore miners' helmets with lights on top and roamed through the orange groves looking for the red glint of gator eyes; Shepard's friend skinned the alligators to make boots of their hide. This night they caught a four-foot gator that Shepard asked to keep as a pet. He brought it back to the Holiday Inn and dumped it in the pool. A few weeks later Shepard and Leo D'Orsey—the Washington, D.C., agent who had brokered the $500,000 *Life* deal—and a few other astronauts helped a NASA official launch his new boat on the nearby Banana River. But the wind kicked up and the waves got rough— they were spilling their drinks. So they put the boat on a trailer, backed it up to Landwirth's pool, and dropped it in, kicking off a marathon cocktail party.

Landwirth occasionally fought back. John Glenn had once staged a mock scene of noisy outrage at the front desk of the Holiday Inn after he found there were no towels in his room. The next time Glenn came to town, he found his room stocked with thousands of towels, so many that he could barely open the door. Landwirth waited around the corner, giggling.

///

When the relocation to Cocoa Beach occurred, Shepard and the other astronauts all decided not to move their families down there. There would be too much work and training, they argued, and it'd be best for the wives and kids to stay where they were. That, apparently, was fine with Louise, who had settled comfortably in Virginia Beach. She had her church friends and was getting to know some of the other astronauts' wives who lived up at Langley. Louise told a friend that the astronauts' wives understood each other "as no one else could."

A space writer friend of Shepard's once wrote of the "paradox" in an astronaut's relationship with his wife. He might love his wife and his kids, might cherish those weekends at home, smoking a pipe and reading the newspaper in a Barcalounger while the kids played checkers and the wife cooked up a casserole. "But he didn't want his wife with him when he was at the Cape . . . it just didn't work," Martin Caidin, a pilot and space expert, said in his book, *The Cape.*

"If she came along to the Cape, the wife became an irritant."
Why? "There was that élan in being an astronaut . . . that brought
the females panting and eager to his side," Caidin said. "They
were beautiful people and they knew it." Astronauts—even
those who were happily married—didn't want "wives all over the
damn place." Wives and Cocoa Beach were not a good mix. Too
risky. "So, if the astronaut's wife were smart, she stayed at home
when he went to the Cape," Caidin said. "The only wise thing to
do was to arrive just before the launch."

That's exactly what Louise learned to do, she once said,
"rather than stand around and throw in a lot of emotion and
make his job harder for him." "I decided long ago during his
Navy career that it is not good to stand around and complicate
things for him when he has a job to do," she said in a *Life* article.

Just like her dapper husband, Louise was always dressed
perfectly, her hair just right, her demeanor suited to each situation—perfectly *assembled*. And as she approached forty she was
as beautiful as ever. Yet while her sincere smile could make
strangers feel instantly welcome in her presence at parties and in
public, Louise never mingled easily with the other astronauts'
wives. She simply wasn't one of the "gals," wearing cut-off shorts
and flip-flops for an afternoon of drinking martinis and smoking
in the backyard. She preferred needlepoint and games of solitaire. She chose new friends carefully and infrequently.

When Navy wives get together as a group, each tends to assume within that group a position roughly equal to her husband's rank, so that an admiral's wife would figuratively lord it
above a group of commanders' wives. Shepard's rank at the
time—lieutenant commander—was essentially the same as the
other six astronauts, but he sometimes acted as if he outranked
them. And Louise, in turn, often stood out as the classiest, most
sophisticated in a room of astronaut wives.

But what dwelled behind that beatific façade? many ac-
quaintances wondered. Like Alan, Louise maintained an emo-

tional barrier beyond which few people were allowed. Louise's constant smile, her optimistic demeanor and heavy reliance on her church seemed to be covering up some deeper unease. Some friends said it was the media glare that rankled Louise. But other friends knew it wasn't just the media.

Louise saw little of her husband during 1959 and 1960. He'd be gone for weeks at a time—St. Louis, Pensacola, Los Angeles, the Cape—while she stayed home at Virginia Beach with the two younger girls, Julie and Alice. (Laura, the eldest, was sent to Louise's alma mater, Principia.) One summer weekend Alan returned home for a short break, but instead of a quiet night at home, they attended a Navy friend's party, where Alan stunned the guests by water-skiing barefoot, a trick he'd worked hard to perfect. He ended the night by drag-racing in the new Corvette he had purchased, beating the seven other competitors, and then flew off in a jet with an old Navy buddy, leaving a sonic boom in his wake. It wasn't exactly the life Louise had envisioned.

Opinions regarding Shepard's fidelity to Louise varied wildly. At the time, indisputable facts were hard to come by, a testimony to either Shepard's carefulness or the protection offered him by loyal friends and an obliging press. But in time it became clear that Alan and Louise, either tacitly or explicitly, operated under a marital understanding.

Some friends thought Shepard had a "compulsion" to be around other women. "He had a beautiful wife and family. I just never quite understood it," said Al Blackburn, a Naval Academy classmate and fellow test pilot. Others, like Bill Dana, maintain that Shepard may have been "a bit of a rascal" but that "there was a lot of mythology about it." Dana believes that if Alan Shepard did all the fooling around that was attributed to him, "his dick would have fallen off."

NBC reporter Jay Barbree, who covered the Mercury Seven and years later would collaborate with Shepard and Slayton on a book about the space race, recalled the story of a pretty folk singer named Trish who performed regularly at the Cape. Rumors began circulating that Trish had slept with all seven of the astronauts. Barbree said that in truth, she had slept with only one of the seven—and it wasn't Shepard.

Barbree recalled seeing Shepard take Trish home one night and, Shepard told him later, stay for a drink—but nothing more. "It was the appearance they were after," Barbree said. "Shepard wanted his buddies to believe he was seeing Trish."

Not that flings weren't happening. Barbree said the Cape oozed sexuality. An attractive woman once offered him sex in exchange for the sports car he drove. Barbree later learned that the young woman was dating one of the astronauts. "I see you met Diane," Gordo Cooper told Barbree one night in his lazy Oklahoma twang.

Still, like Dana, Barbree thinks that if the astronauts had all the sex they got credit for, "they would have never gone to the moon. They'd have been in bed all the time."

One of Louise's closest friends, Loraine Meyer, with whom she would one day open a needlepoint shop, said Louise never discussed Alan's promiscuity with her. "We were best friends, but that was one thing we didn't discuss," Meyer recalled. She believes Alan and Louise were "very much in love" and that if they did have any marital woes, they worked them out in private.

Whatever deeper truths lay beneath Alan and Louise's complicated marriage, one thing was certain to all who knew them at the time: Alan did not practice fidelity. But he was not the only unfaithful astronaut, and the risks of skirt chasing while the press was watching began to create growing conflict among the Mercury Seven.

12

"I think I got myself in trouble"

Back in 1959, to commemorate his graduation from test pilot to spaceman, Shepard had traded his peppy little oil-spewing green MG ragtop for one of the sexiest American vehicles ever produced. The glossy white Corvette flaunted whitewall tires and a menacing chrome grille that looked like some wild animal's snarling teeth. At first America didn't know what to make of Chevy's new sports cars, and less than ten thousand were sold in the first few years of production. But to Shepard, his secondhand Corvette was worth every bit of the $3,000 price tag. He would drive 'Vettes for the next thirty years, and the car would become an accoutrement for many future astronauts, a jet-shaped and sensual symbol of their coming of age.

Shortly after purchasing his new toy, Shepard invited *Life* photographer Ralph Morse for a ride. He wanted to show Ralph how fast it could fly, with its huge eight-cylinder, 230-horsepower engine. "Goes like a bat out of hell," Shepard promised.

Morse asked how they'd find a straightaway around Langley that was long enough to get up any speed. And, if they did, how would they avoid getting arrested? Despite a nose for a good story, Morse didn't want to be implicated with the first jailed astronaut. Shepard solved both problems by calling the tower at Langley's airfield to get permission to use their runway. Then he roared at a hundred miles an hour down the tarmac, with Morse scrunched in his seat.

When GM officials learned that a famous astronaut was a loyal 'Vette fan, they smelled a publicity opportunity for the struggling model and arranged a meeting between Shepard and the Corvette's chief engineer, Zora Arkus-Duntov. The two men hit it off and Arkus-Duntov convinced a reluctant GM management to donate a brand-new Corvette to Shepard, which was of course even faster.

Mickey Kapp, who produced the José Jiménez albums, recalled that his first encounter with Shepard was an illegally speedy Corvette sprint down Route A1A, weaving through traffic at eighty miles an hour. Kapp was sure Shepard was trying to scare him. It was Shepard's way of checking to see if Kapp had any guts. But Kapp, a car collector, had driven his share of fast cars, and he just sat there smiling and enjoying the ride.

The astronauts' training schedule left Shepard with little spare time to fly, and his velocious Corvette offered a modest substitute for such thrills. Just as he had with jets, Shepard was constantly trying to squeeze a little more horsepower from his car, which one day led him to Jim Rathmann.

Rathmann was a handsome race car driver who, after two second-place finishes in the Indianapolis 500, finally won the race in 1960 in a back-and-forth contest that would go down as one of the most exciting races in Indianapolis history. Rathmann also owned a Chevrolet dealership and an adjacent mechanics' shop near Cocoa Beach. Shepard was always bringing his car into Rathmann's shop, asking him to tweak this or that, trying to get a little extra speed out of the big V-8.

When Rathmann learned of Shepard's love of his Corvette, he called his boss and friend, Ed Cole, Chevrolet's chief engineer (soon to become president of General Motors). Cole had been an early believer in Chevy's first true sports car and agreed to Rathmann's plan to give *all* the astronauts special deals on Corvettes—and, they hoped, boost sales in the process.

Cooper and Grissom accepted GM's offer and began driving brand-new Corvettes. Schirra swapped his Austin Healy for one but later switched back to European cars (and was punished for it by Cooper, who once hid a rotting fish in Schirra's Maserati). Carpenter turned down the Corvette offer, preferring his souped-up Shelby Cobra. Slayton at the time drove a beat-up station wagon that, compared to the sports car crowd, made his family feel like "a bunch of Okies." He was happy to trade the wagon for a 'Vette.

Glenn, on the other hand, turned down the offer. He had recently traded his secondhand Studebaker for an obscure little German thing called an NSU Prinz, which he bought for $1,400 because of its great gas mileage. It got fifty miles to the gallon, and he could drive from his home in Arlington, Virginia, to Langley and back for less than a dollar. Scorning the others' infatuation with race cars, Glenn one day copied on a classroom blackboard a quote he'd found in *Reader's Digest*: "Definition of a sports car: a hedge against male menopause."

In the end, four astronauts—Shepard, Cooper, Grissom, and Slayton—accepted GM's "executive lease" offer. They could lease a new Corvette for $1 a year, then trade it in at year's end for a new model. Rathmann had no problem selling the slightly used astro- 'Vettes.

At the end of a day's training, Shepard, Cooper, and Grissom loved to race each other down some rural stretch of A1A. Sometimes they drove right on the hard-packed beach, and once used one of their Corvettes for water-skiing—they hooked a tow rope to the back and cruised down the beach, pulling the skier through the surf.

The cars had wide tires that sometimes hydroplaned on wet pavement, and a few of the watching reporters cringed as the astronauts sped through Cocoa Beach, swerving and fishtailing. Shepard once spun out on a rain-slicked bridge, narrowly missing an oncoming car. Grissom once let Rathmann drive his 'Vette and, sitting in the passenger seat, dared Rathmann to take a tight corner at eighty miles an hour. He did, but the car spun out and slid two hundred feet off the road into a mud pit, where it had to be yanked free by a tow truck. The reporters couldn't write about all they saw, but privately they expected one of the country's new heroes to slam into a tree. "Some of us were concerned they'd kill themselves—and lose a big investment on the government's part. Or maybe knock off some kid," recalled Bill Hines, a writer with the former *Washington Star* and, later, the *Chicago Sun-Times.*

At first Shepard won many of the three-way races against Cooper and Grissom. But suddenly, after one of his tune-ups at Rathmann's place, Shepard began losing the races, badly. And it drove him crazy.

"What the hell's going on?" he complained one day.

"You lost, Alan," Grissom told him. "Guess you lost your touch."

"My ass. There's something wrong with this car," Shepard insisted.

Often he would get out and kick the car after losing. After a few more lost races, Grissom and Cooper let him in on the joke. Rathmann had adjusted the gear ratios on Shepard's car so that it accelerated more slowly than normal.

"Gotcha," Cooper said, and slapped Shepard on the back. But Shepard had never been much of a sport when he found himself on the losing end of a gotcha, and had to force himself to keep his hands off Cooper's neck.

Such juvenile and combative head-butting rituals reflected the surging intensity of the competition for the first space ride. Working out the many kinks in its troubled rockets had forced NASA to delay its tentative plans for a manned launch in 1960. But things were looking good for early the following year, and the astronauts knew NASA would decide soon who'd ride that historic flight.

///

At times Henri Landwirth felt caught between his two favorite astronauts: Alan Shepard and John Glenn. He knew they were two very different men, but there were qualities in each that, Landwirth felt, strangely complemented the other.

He heard the gripes about Glenn from others. There was the friend of Glenn's who told a *Life* reporter that "John tries to behave as if every impressionable youngster in the country were watching him every moment of the day." And there was the time Schirra gave Glenn a boatload of grief after watching him return to the Holiday Inn from an alleged run on the beach, then splash water on his face so it looked like sweat. But Landwirth generally got along well with Glenn, who could "make me laugh."

Shepard, on the other hand, could infuriate Landwirth with his sarcasm. "I could have choked him at times in the old days," he recalled. And he thought Shepard's pranks could be mean-spirited. One time Shepard and Leo D'Orsey made plans to meet with Landwirth at a hotel in Miami. They told Landwirth the hotel didn't allow Jews, so they would have to sneak him in. Putting a raincoat over Landwirth's head, they scuttled him through the lobby and into a service elevator, where they confessed that they were just messing with him, and both busted out laughing.

Landwirth came to learn, however, that if you put up with Shepard's sharp edges, his antagonism and unpredictable moods, and earned his trust, the payoff was a loyal friend and "a great charmer and a gentleman."

He was always impressed when he'd watch Shepard work a crowd. Though with colleagues or fans, Shepard could so often be icily antisocial, at certain social events he could "charm a whole room by himself—I don't care how many people were there," Landwirth recalled. "Especially the women."

Freed from wearing the required Navy uniform each day, a latent predilection for style also emerged, and Shepard established himself as the best-dressed of the astronauts.

Different as Shepard and Glenn were, Landwirth saw qualities the other astronauts didn't seem to possess. Also, each seemed to be planning far sooner than the others for their life after space. In time, Landwirth would help each of them in different ways. For Shepard, Landwirth would boost him toward riches. Glenn would get a boost toward political power. And one day Shepard and Glenn would repay Landwirth handsomely.

But in 1960, Landwirth's friendship with Shepard and Glenn put him in a tricky spot between the two most aggressive competitors among the Mercury Seven. While Landwirth had the luxury of befriending them both, the other astronauts would have to choose. And deciding between Shepard and Glenn would lead to fissures between the seven, deep and complicated divisions that would break the team apart.

Glenn tried diplomatically to divert the media's attention from the competition for the first flight, claiming to one reporter that the space race was "bigger than one individual." But Shepard, in an interview at the time, made no such pretensions. He told a reporter that he had always been competitive—still was. "I want to be first because I want to be first," he said. "There are lots of ways to answer why I want to be first in space," he continued, "but the short answer would be this: the flight obviously is a challenge, and I feel that the more severe challenge will occur on the first flight and I signed up to accept this challenge. And that's why I want to be first."

///

Among the many small pieces of Shepard's larger game plan was an effort to finally quit smoking. Shepard sometimes dropped his pack of cigarettes on the desk of the pretty new secretary, Lola Morrow, with instructions to give him only one cigarette at a time, and only when it was an emergency. Lola, who herself was trying to quit, soon had a drawer full of cigarette packs from Shepard and the other smokers.

He didn't ease up much on the syrupy thick coffee he loved, or the regular cocktails, but quitting the smokes was a step toward reclaiming the strong and wiry rower's body he'd once doted on back at Annapolis, the one he'd honed as a teen by swimming with a boat in tow behind him. After taking up Glenn's habit of early morning jogging, and in addition to playing feisty games of handball with Grissom and Slayton, Shepard began lifting weights in the gym NASA had built for the astronauts at the Cape.

If NASA wanted a perfect specimen to become the first American in space, he intended to work harder than the other six in every way—in academics, in training exercises, and in matters of fitness and health.

Intense as the competition among the Mercury Seven was, they all knew that their toughest competitors were the Russians. By the summer of 1960, the Russians had launched four more Sputnik satellites and three other satellites. In the three years since the first Sputnik, subsequent Soviet satellites had carried rabbits and mice into orbit. The United States had actually put up many more satellites than the Russians—two dozen between 1958 and 1960—and, by that tally, seemed way ahead of its communist competitors. But the Russians always seemed to find a way to achieve the more impressive "firsts" of the space race—first satellite in space (1957), first dog in space (1957), first man-made object to strike the surface of the moon (1959), first photographs of the unseen far side of the moon (1959).

In August 1960 they did it again. Russia's rocket scientists shocked the world when they announced that two dogs—Belka and Strelka—had been launched into space (crammed inside a capsule along with forty mice and two rats), completed a series of orbits around the earth, and were then returned safe and sound back home. (Strelka later gave birth to six puppies, one of which

Soviet premier Khrushchev obnoxiously sent to the White House.)

After that, no amount of spin would convince the nation that the United States was—at least in terms of the total number of satellites launched into space—ahead of the Soviets in the space race. And even the astronauts began to agree. Slayton acknowledged as much to a reporter, admitting, "There is no doubt in my mind they will be first."

In an effort to gain some psychological leverage in the race with the Soviets, Shepard and the others compiled and signed a confidential letter to NASA officials, proposing what they called a sly "propaganda initiative." Because the American astronauts were clearly in a neck-and-neck contest with the Russian cosmonauts, the Mercury Seven suggested an exchange of visits—the cosmonauts could come to the Cape and the astronauts could visit the Soviet space complex, the massive Baikonur Cosmodrome, on the barren steppes of western Kazakhstan. The idea was to gain some inside information on the secretive Russian space program. And if the Russians refused, it would "reflect unfavorably in the eyes of other countries," the astronauts wrote.

The letter, which was never made public, asserted that "we apparently stand to gain a great deal and could lose little or nothing." But the idea found no takers. Generally, the astronauts and NASA officials tried to keep any us-versus-them sentiments from the public. In one press conference, when asked to compare the U.S. space program to Russia's, Shepard vehemently denied that the American astronauts were in competition with the Soviets. Regardless of the "unfortunate clash of philosophies," Shepard said, "our objective in this program is not to beat the Russians." The same reporter asked if the Mercury Seven's timetable would change to keep pace with the front-running Russians. Shepard's response was terse: "No, sir."

But in a later interview with a *National Geographic* reporter, Shepard acknowledged that they had been "forced into a competitive race with another political philosophy." And he let slip that NASA was "not making decisions based only on our own problems." Meaning: *We're keeping a very close eye on the other side.* NASA officials, who reviewed the story, deleted that quote from the final version.

Another letter penned by the astronauts, which was also never made public, suggested accelerating the first manned launch—now tentatively scheduled for early 1961—by cutting back on unmanned Atlas rocket launches and other test launches with monkeys riding in the capsule, and proceeding more quickly to the one goal that really mattered. The astronauts recommended that NASA "move ahead the entire subsequent Atlas schedule so that it is possible to schedule . . . a manned orbital flight . . . with a tentative launch week of 28 Nov 60." NASA thanked the astronauts for their input but did not change its schedule, and the astronauts felt increasingly frustrated by what they perceived to be NASA's somewhat plodding progress.

///

The space race had become the centerpiece of the tense geopolitical events of the escalating cold war, which had begun to take a few dangerous turns.

When an American U-2 spy plane was shot down by Soviet missiles and crashed into Soviet territory on May 1, 1960, and its pilot—Francis Gary Powers, working for the Central Intelligence Agency—was captured, Khrushchev canceled a long-planned U.S.-Soviet summit meeting in Paris that summer. When Eisenhower refused to officially apologize for the Powers incident, Khrushchev canceled Eisenhower's scheduled visit to Moscow as well. He did, however, keep his scheduled visit to the United Nations' headquarters in New York that September, where he emotionally embraced Fidel Castro, flaunting his support for socialism's new poster boy. Later in the UN session, Khrushchev famously pounded his white shoe on a table during a speech by

British prime minister Harold Macmillan. Americans began asking themselves: Who is this communist wacko, and how dangerous is he?

As the presidential campaign of 1960 heated up, John F. Kennedy shrewdly latched on to the cold war and the space race as themes for his campaign. He promised voters that, if elected, he would usher in a "New Frontier," and his campaign became all about motion, about moving ahead, catching up. With a loud and confident rat-a-tat urgency in his voice, Kennedy bemoaned the "drift in our national course" and a "decline in our vitality."

Kennedy's narrow defeat of Richard Nixon was due, at least in part, to his promise to restore the nation's morale and geopolitical footing by regaining ground lost in the space race. And though Shepard and his family were Republicans, the election of a Democrat from Massachusetts would prove to be a fortunate thing for Shepard.

///

After Kennedy's election focused the spotlight even more intensely on the space program, John Glenn—the self-anointed moralist of the group—began agitating for the astronauts to clean up their behavior. All infidelities had to stop.

"I thought we owed it to people to behave," Glenn would write years later in his memoir. "It was now clear that, rightly or wrongly, we had been placed upon a pedestal."

The Mercury Seven had gotten into the habit of conducting regular closed-door meetings with one another to hash out any conflicts or disagreements. A NASA official called them "séances," and the name stuck. Many of the séances devolved into shouting matches, and a couple of times the arguments teetered toward outright fistfights.

Each man had his own trigger points and pet peeves. Slayton and Cooper once fought vigorously to have rudder pedals installed in the capsule so that it could be flown like an airplane;

Shepard and Glenn, meanwhile, had argued for the hand control stick that was eventually used because it weighed less than the floor pedals. Like brothers, they fought hard, yelled loudly, and then settled on a compromise. "When we came out of the room, we had an astronaut opinion," Cooper recalled—although he added, "some of us were more team players than others."

The two who didn't always play by team rules were Glenn and Shepard. Glenn was a politician about his disagreements; Shepard was a bulldog. As a result, Shepard and Glenn—the two clear front-runners in the race for the first flight—bumped heads more than most.

In fact, they sometimes openly taunted each other. Shepard thought Glenn took the training exercises too seriously. He said Glenn's experiment with dehydration during desert training had been too risky. And he thought it was hilarious when Glenn once waved off a rescue helicopter and tried to ride a raft ashore like a surfboard while practicing escape procedures in rough seas off the Florida coast. He got pummeled by the waves and rolled head over heels to shore. Glenn, meanwhile, thought Shepard was too cavalier, with his occasional partying and Corvette racing.

The personal combat between the two came to a head during one trip to San Diego. When they visited San Diego, the astronauts usually stayed at the waterfront Konakai cottages owned by one of NASA's contractors. Late one night, shortly after midnight, one of the astronauts knocked on the door of Glenn's cottage and said, "I think I got myself in trouble." The astronaut had gone out drinking across the border in nearby Tijuana, Mexico, and had picked up a woman at a bar. Later, when the two were alone, he saw flashes and realized someone was taking pictures.

The next day, a "leading West Coast paper" called Shorty Powers to get a reaction to the story it was planning to run—with "compromising" photographs—the following day. Shorty, who in recent months had been warning Glenn about just such a problem, called Glenn later that night and said, "Well, it's happened."

Glenn immediately called the publisher of the newspaper and begged him to kill the story. He laid it on thick: They were in a race with "godless communists," he said, and the bad guys were ahead. The press had to help in the effort to "get back in the space race." If they didn't, they'd only be hurting the country. Negative press could affect the amount of funding NASA got from Congress, and also the nation's morale.

Until that moment, most of the stories about the astronauts —particularly *Life's* whitewashed version of astronaut life—had been, as Glenn once put it, "bland and upbeat." For the most part, the press had continued to willingly participate in the conspiracy of silence. This story would be an absolute scandal. Glenn wasn't about to get sullied by association, nor was he about to let the entire program be hurt. In the end the newspaper backed down.

"I pulled out all the stops," Glenn later wrote in his memoir. "To this day, and knowing the press much better now, I'm still amazed that it didn't run."

Later that day, at the Konakai cottages, Glenn called for a séance. With the seven men in one room, he angrily announced that they had just "dodged a bullet." "I was mad, and I read the riot act, saying that we had worked too hard to get into this program and that it meant too much to the country to see it jeopardized by anyone who couldn't keep his pants zipped," Glenn said.

Forever after, Glenn would refuse to disclose which astronaut was the subject of that killed story or which newspaper had gotten the photos. But Al Blackburn, Shepard's academy classmate and a test pilot colleague of both Shepard and Glenn's, says that Glenn once told him the culprit was Shepard.

Even though he was the one who had gone to Glenn's cottage asking for help, Shepard became furious at what he later called Glenn's "moralizing." He told Glenn that not only were their personal lives not an issue, they were none of Glenn's business. "Why is this even coming up?" he told Glenn. "Doesn't everyone have the right to do what they want to do?"

Four of the astronauts agreed with Shepard. Only Carpenter sided with Glenn. Cooper said it was a turning point in the group's relationship, and Carpenter felt the same. Until that night, he had thought of them all as "the Seven Musketeers." "The camaraderie was incredible," he said years later. But that séance—and what came after it—would cleave the group into factions, and the wounds would take many years to heal.

Glenn realized immediately that something had changed. "My views were in the minority, but I didn't care," he said. "I had made my point." His one concern, however, was that his firm stance that night would affect his carefully plotted course toward the first space flight.

Indeed, shortly after the Konakai séance, the astronauts were called to a meeting with Robert Gilruth, head of NASA's Space Task Group. Gilruth asked them each to write up a memo including the name of the astronaut—besides themselves—they'd like to see get the first ride. Glenn couldn't believe that nearly two years of training were being reduced to what he later called "a popularity contest." He wrote Scott Carpenter's name atop his memo but had a pretty good idea who the others would pick.

Shepard, on the other hand, was becoming more and more convinced that he was edging ahead, especially after surviving the close call in Tijuana.

He may have been (in a description once used by one of his peers) an "asshole." He may have been a cheating husband, a self-centered speed freak, an arrogant elitist. But Shepard never concerned himself with what other people thought about him. For him, it was always what *he* believed that mattered most, and he believed he was the best man for the job.

Glenn, however, was not ready to give up the game without a fight.

13

"We had 'em by the short hairs, and we gave it away"

On January 19, 1961—the eve of John F. Kennedy's inauguration—Bob Gilruth phoned the astronauts' office at Langley. The seven had been working at Langley in recent weeks, a brief departure from all the travel and training, the long days and nights on the road or at the Cape. Gilruth asked the seven men to stay a little late that afternoon. "I have something important to tell you," he said.

At 5:15 P.M. the seven sat quietly in their cramped office, with its seven metal desks and the walls busy with tacked-up flight plans and technical diagrams. All of them knew what was coming, and they were uncharacteristically silent. Wisecracks eluded even Wally this night. Finally Gus Grissom broke the tension.

"If we wait any longer, I may have to make a speech," he said.

Gilruth entered the room and wasted no time. As soon as the door was shut, he dropped the news, calling it "the most difficult decision I've ever had to make."

"Alan Shepard will make the first suborbital flight," he said.

Gilruth then explained that Grissom would make the second flight, and Glenn would serve as backup pilot to both flights.

Shepard kept his eyes on the ground, fighting back a grin aching to break free. In a competition he had once likened to "seven guys trying to fly the same airplane," he had won. After all those nasty spins in gut-sloshing NASA contraptions, the goal he had pursued ravenously for two uninterrupted years was his. But he knew it was "not a moment to crow," so he kept his head down.

Gilruth asked if there were any questions but was met with silence.

"Thank you very much, and good luck," Gilruth said, and left the room.

Finally, after a few leaden moments, Glenn stepped forward and offered his hand to Shepard, the first of the six to do so. The others came up and congratulated him—some, Shepard noticed, with less enthusiasm than others. And then they left, one by one, as quietly as they had entered. No one offered to buy rounds of drinks to celebrate, and in just a few moments Shepard was left standing in the office, alone.

He sped home to tell Louise, who came bounding down the stairs when she heard him burst through the front door. As soon as she saw his grin-creased face, she knew. "You got it!" She threw her arms around him. "You got the first ride!"

"Lady, you can't tell anyone, but you have your arms around the man who'll be first in space," he told her. Louise pulled back from him and looked around the room. "Who let a Russian in here?" she joked, somewhat presciently.

Shepard wasn't allowed to tell anyone else. Officially, NASA planned to announce in another month that Shepard, Glenn, and Grissom were still vying for the first flight. That meant Glenn and Grissom would have to pretend in public that they still had a chance—a ruse that all the astronauts thought was ridiculous and annoying.

While a couple of the other six were hurt and angered by Gilruth's choice—Wally, for one, felt "really deflated . . . a very traumatic feeling," like he'd been demoted to "the second team"—the decision didn't surprise Scott Carpenter.

"For Al, it was the competition," he said. "He felt for his comrades, but he also had a need to be better than anyone else.... Everything he did was evidence of that. He was single-minded in his pursuit of the first flight." Glenn, on the other hand, seemed during the previous two years to be working equally hard on the public relations side of the pursuit. "John figured he had made all the right moves," Slayton said. "He just figured wrong."

Deke Slayton was "shocked, hurt, and downright humiliated" that he hadn't even been selected among the top three. But, back in December, it had been Shepard's name that he had scribbled on the "peer vote" memo Gilruth had requested. Slayton felt that Shepard not only had the piloting skills but was the smartest and most articulate of them all. And so when Gilruth picked Shepard, Slayton said, "it was all right with me."

Still, something about the decision nagged at him. It wasn't until the next day, Kennedy's inauguration, that "reality walloped me right between the eyes." "Of course! Politics!" Slayton thought. "No way was it an accident that both Shepard and John Kennedy were Navy."

///

Snow began falling after midnight on Friday, January 20, and the next morning was bitterly cold. Kennedy, his breath emerging in puffs of steam, called his inauguration "a celebration of freedom." Alan, Louise, and some of the other astronauts drove up from Langley to join the crowds. Kennedy said a torch had been passed to a new generation—"born of this century, tempered by war, disciplined by a hard and bitter peace, proud of our ancient heritage." He famously asked his people to ask themselves how they could help carry their country toward the freedom of man. And in an auspicious declaration for the space program, he also said, "Together, let us explore the stars."

Later that night Bill Dana performed at Kennedy's inaugural ball, a fête sponsored by Frank Sinatra at the National Guard Armory. With the electricity downed by the continuing snowstorm, generators powered the auditorium's lights. José entered, helmeted and clad in his silvery space suit, escorted by Marine officers. With Milton Berle as his straight man, José complained about his uncomfortable $18,000 space suit, but at least, he conceded, "it has two pairs of pants." Then he told a chuckling Kennedy that the best part about space travel is the blastoff.

"I always take a blast before I take off. . . . Otherwise I wouldn't get in that thing."

Earlier that afternoon, far from the inaugural celebrations, John Glenn sat down and wrote an urgent letter to his superiors, a letter designed to snatch the first space flight from Alan Shepard's grasp.

///

Despite their similar goals, Shepard and Glenn had very different methods.

Glenn loved the spotlight, and it loved him. With his crinkly smile, light blue eyes, and freckled face, he was truly the all-American lad. Despite his aw-shucks demeanor, he worked hard to perfect his boy-next-door image. "Glenn loved an audience on whom he could turn his charm," one top NASA official said. Another NASA official said that Glenn seemed less interested in becoming technically proficient and more interested in "cozying up to top management and thus improving his chances."

It was exactly that image consciousness that led some NASA officials to consider Shepard the better choice for the first flight, not Glenn. "We wanted to put our best foot forward," Walt Williams, director of operations for Project Mercury, said in an unpublished memoir. Williams considered Shepard "the most capable" and said so during discussions about who should fly first.

But in choosing Shepard, NASA knew it was taking a chance

on a mercurial personality. One of the seven anonymously told *Life* magazine, in an article published soon after Shepard's selection: "You might think you'd get to know someone well after working so closely with him for two years. Well, it's not that way with Shepard. He's always holding something back." Shepard admitted it in an interview with the same *Life* reporter: "I have never been my own favorite subject, and I don't think I've found anything new about myself since I've been in this program."

Still, Shepard had shown with his intense focus during sessions in the MASTIF and the centrifuge, with his attention to detail and his curiosity about capsule designs and flight plans, that—despite a sometimes testy personality and a few self-admitted skeletons in his closet and "secrets"—he was the best man to become the first American in space. Shepard wanted to know about all the egghead stuff that some of the other astronauts left in the engineers' hands. He befriended the engineers and learned to speak their language. He was wary but respectful with his superiors, and if he ever disagreed with their decisions on the progress and purpose of the training schematic, he never pouted or whined. Instead he spoke bluntly and openly with his superiors and, in turn, impressed them not with pandering but with a genuine curiosity about space flight and a hunger for information about every detail of the mission he had signed up for.

Shepard was chosen not because he was the most popular, the most likable, or the best person among the seven. He was, in short, the best flyer.

"He was an egotist," said Chris Kraft, who would be the flight director for Shepard's launch, and considered Shepard "a typical New Englander . . . hard, cold." "But he was all business when it came to flying."

Shepard and Kraft began working closely together a few weeks later, in mid-February, beginning with a series of simulated launch exercises at the Cape. The plan for Shepard's upcoming flight was to launch his capsule atop one of von Braun's

Redstone rockets. The Redstone lacked sufficient power to boost the capsule into orbit; an orbital flight would have to travel three times as fast. Still, Shepard's Redstone carried enough thrust to blast him up and through the far side of the earth's atmosphere. Without the necessary speed to reach orbit, though, Shepard's capsule, after reaching speeds of five thousand miles an hour and an altitude of a hundred miles, would arc back down to earth and through the atmosphere for a landing at sea, three hundred miles east of the Florida coast.

That parabolic flight was expected to last just fifteen minutes, and NASA engineers had crammed each of those minutes with many tests and tasks for Shepard to perform. He'd be required to look through his periscope at the coastline below, search for stars above, constantly check the capsule's systems to ensure they were working properly, then briefly take control of the capsule by grabbing the hand control stick and testing the ability of an astronaut to actually fly a spacecraft. To prepare for the densely packed mission, Shepard began to rehearse each second of the flight inside a NASA simulator.

As in a sophisticated arcade game, Shepard would sit in a mockup of a capsule cockpit, facing the same dashboard of buttons, switches, and levers that would be in his own capsule, while he and the NASA engineers practiced launch and landing procedures over and over. Each man rehearsed his role, with Kraft presiding like the choreographer. Shepard would spend so much time in that simulator he'd learn to find and flip switches with his eyes closed.

But during his first simulator session Shepard goofed, and he and Chris Kraft had a showdown. During the computerized launch simulation, the computer program surprised Shepard, as well as the engineers in Mission Control, with a simulated system failure, and Shepard failed to take the obvious and proper action (which was to abort). Afterward, Kraft and his Mission Control team invited Shepard to sit in on their postexercise critique session, which they called their "dog-eat-dog sessions." Kraft was insulted when Shepard shrugged off his mistake, made a joke about it, and then asked for another simulator session.

"Let's go again," Shepard said.

"No," Kraft replied. "It's coffee time."

Kraft took Shepard aside and explained that he and his team took their critique sessions seriously, and suggested that Shepard do the same. He knew Shepard had "quick reflexes and a quicker brain," but he wanted him to admit to his mistake.

"It's how we learn," Kraft said. "I don't want it to happen when you're up there."

Shepard stared at Kraft, and for a few long, silent moments the two men barely moved. Kraft said it seemed as if Shepard was making up his mind about what to do next. And then, slowly, the look on Shepard's face changed, "from one of defensiveness to understanding." He admitted that they used to conduct similar postflight critiques in the ready room of his aircraft carriers, and he also admitted—reluctantly, Kraft felt—that it was probably a good idea.

Kraft would learn that Shepard did not often admit to his faults. But after their face-off, the two men went right back to work and in time became close friends. Kraft felt that he had passed some type of test, had proven himself to Shepard and earned his respect.

///

On February 21, 1961, a month after Shepard had been selected, NASA finally issued a press release announcing that the seven had been narrowed to three. It announced that Shepard, Glenn, and Grissom would begin training for the first manned flight, but that the actual pilot of the first flight "will be named just before the flight." The intent of such obfuscation was to take the pressure off Shepard so that he wouldn't be hounded by the press during his final months of training. But for Glenn, the tactic presented an opening.

Because Shepard's selection wasn't yet public, Glenn figured there was still time to change things. The afternoon of Kennedy's inauguration a month earlier, Glenn had written a letter to Gilruth, criticizing his use of a "peer vote" in deciding who should become the first astronaut, and explaining why he might have lost that vote. In Glenn's mind, he had been punished by his peers for his speech in San Diego back in December about keeping their pants zipped. "I might have been penalized for what I thought was the good of the program," Glenn said in his strongly worded letter. "I didn't think being an astronaut was a popularity contest," he said decades later in his memoir. "I would turn out to be wrong about that."

Glenn wasn't alone in trying to change Gilruth's mind. One or two of the others warned Gilruth of Shepard's "wild antics" and complained that Shepard was "too lighthearted for the job" and didn't have the "perfect image." On the other hand, maybe NASA knew exactly what it was doing. Maybe Shepard was a better fit for NASA's sought-after image. Maybe NASA intentionally overlooked the Boy Scout in favor of the liberty hound.

A few weeks later Gilruth finally intervened. "I want this backbiting stopped right now. Alan Shepard is my choice. That's it."

Glenn grudgingly abandoned his campaign and began training alongside Shepard. But there were days he was withdrawn, even morose. Although he once reprimanded the press for overemphasizing who would be the first American in space—"as though we are out trying to knife each other every night to see who was going to be first"—Glenn had harbored an intense desire for the slot. And now he wouldn't even be second; Grissom had been chosen to fly after Shepard.

"Those were rough days for me," Glenn said a year later. A lingering remorse would addle Glenn for another year, until he got a flight of his own—one that would end up being well worth the wait.

Until that day came, Glenn had to serve as Shepard's backup. The two men began spending long days together, training in the simulators, going over flight plans, and continuing to pretend that they were still competing for the first ride. At a press conference following NASA's announcement that Glenn, Shepard, and Grissom were in the running for the first flight, the normally personable and chatty Glenn was a bit chilly when asked to re-create his wife's reaction when he told her that he had made the cut to the final three. "I would rather not get into places and times, and such things as that," he said.

Shepard, meanwhile, seemed to be having fun with the situation. "If I may be hypothetical: assume that I had the opportunity of going first . . . ," he began, in response to one reporter's question. And when asked how far in advance he'd like to be notified that he had been chosen to fly first, Shepard said, "At least before sunrise on launch day."

At the time he had reason to feel relaxed and confident. NASA was making tentative plans to put Shepard into space the following month, sometime in March. With Glenn's challenge behind, and with all glitches apparently fixed on the rocket, it seemed Shepard was destined to become the first human to leave the earth's atmosphere—the Lindbergh of space.

But then a chimp, a German, and a Russian got in the way.

///

A few weeks earlier, in late January, NASA had launched a chimpanzee named Ham on a flight, using the same type of Redstone rocket that Shepard was scheduled to fly. For two years NASA had been using chimps and pigs in test launches. This time, engineers had designed Ham's flight as a means of testing its system of communicating with the capsule; Ham was trained to pull certain levers during the flight, and if he pulled the correct lever,

As a boy in New Hampshire, Shepard had what his mother called "boundless energy"—so much so that his elementary school teachers advised that he skip ahead two grades, which ever after made him the youngest in his class. *(Courtesy of the Shepard family)*

Shepard attended Pinkerton Academy, the same high school where poet Robert Frost had taught his father. *(Courtesy of Pinkerton Academy)*

Shepard was relentless in his pursuit of the beautiful Louise Brewer, pictured here at his Ring Dance at the Naval Academy. *(Courtesy of the U.S. Naval Academy)*

Shepard (shown here on graduation day with father, Bart, and sister, Polly) claimed he "never really hit my stride" until his final year at the U.S. Naval Academy. *(Courtesy of the Shepard family)*

Wedding day: March 3, 1945, during Shepard's brief hiatus from serving aboard a destroyer in World War II. The marriage would not be a perfect one, but it—and their love for one another—would last more than fifty years. *(Courtesy of NASA)*

More than anything, Shepard loved to fly. And, as one fellow test pilot said, "He could fly anything." Left, at Muroc Airfield (later named Edwards Air Force Base) and, below, in a T-38 NASA jet. *(Courtesy of the Shepard family and NASA)*

Shepard took the illicit practice of "flat-hatting" (flying lower and faster than Navy rules allowed) to new lows; he once flew beneath a bridge, above a crowded beach, and over a parade field of Navy officers—and came dangerously close to a court martial. Above, in an F-106 Air Force jet. *(Courtesy of NASA)*

The Shepard family—Alan, Louise, their two daughters, and the niece they raised as their own daughter—captured by *Life* magazine at home in Virginia Beach. *(Courtesy of the Shepard family)*

The Mercury Seven during desert survival training in Nevada. From left: Gordon Cooper, Scott Carpenter, John Glenn, Shepard, Gus Grissom, Wally Schirra, and Deke Slayton. *(Courtesy of NASA)*

Colleagues learned there were two sides to Shepard. One minute, he was an affable jokester; the next, bitterly competitive, to the point of being a "cutthroat." Above left, goofing at a press conference; above right, after a jog at Cocoa Beach. *(Courtesy of Ralph Morse/Time Life Pictures/Getty Images)*

One journalist called Cocoa Beach—its jazz clubs, dance clubs, and its colorful, carnival-like "strip"— "a harlot of a town." Here, the Starlite Motel in 1959, which was run by Holocaust survivor and astronaut pal Henri Landwirth. *(Courtesy of the Florida State Archives)*

Though he harbored a lifelong disdain for the press, he learned to hone his dealings with reporters, one of whom called him "the cool master of the press conference." Above, flanked by NASA spokesman Colonel John A. "Shorty" Powers. *(Courtesy of Paul Schuster/Time Life Pictures/Getty Images)*

Opposite: Shepard once likened the intense competition among the Mercury Seven to "seven guys trying to fly the same airplane." *(Courtesy of NASA)*

Glenn was furious that Shepard had been chosen ahead of him for America's first manned space launch; each man was like the other's alter ego. *(Courtesy of NASA)*

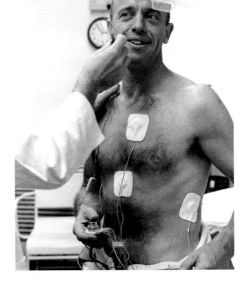

Doctors probed every inch of Shepard's thirty-seven-year-old body before the launch. *(Courtesy of NASA)*

Three weeks earlier, a Russian cosmonaut had orbited the Earth—claiming the title that Shepard had hoped would be his own: first human in space. Shepard had to settle for the title of First American, which occurred on May 5, 1961. Crowds packed Florida's beaches to watch Shepard's historic launch, among them CBS journalist Walter Cronkite, whose crew burst into tears once Freedom 7 was aloft. *(Courtesy of NASA)*

Shepard traveled higher and faster than any other American—"the Lindbergh of space," one newspaper called him. Right, captured by his capsule's onboard camera during his brief taste of weightlessness. *(Courtesy of NASA)*

Louise at home, nervously awaiting word that her husband was safe aboard the recovery ship. *(Courtesy of Leonard McComb/ Time Life Pictures/ Getty Images)*

Shepard being hoisted free of his capsule and into the recovery helicopter. *(Courtesy of NASA)*

"Boy, what a ride," Shepard said, as the helicopter delivered him to the USS *Lake Champlain*, where a cheering crowd of sailors welcomed him back from space. *(Courtesy of NASA)*

At Grand Bahama Island, Shepard spent three days out of public view, undergoing exhaustive postlaunch briefings and invasive medical exams. Doctors reported he was "in the best of shape, in the best of health, in the best of spirits." *(Courtesy of NASA)*

President Kennedy awarding Shepard the Distinguished Service Medal in the Rose Garden. *(Courtesy of Joseph Scherschel/Time Life Pictures/Getty Images)*

Above left: Shepard reading his fan mail, on the cover of *Life* magazine. *(Courtesy of Ralph Morse/Time Life Pictures/Getty Images)* Above right: One of the largest crowds in Washington history clogged Pennsylvania Avenue for a glimpse of the new astronaut-hero and his wife. "Look at these people," Vice President Johnson yelled in Shepard's ear. "They love you." Johnson later advised Shepard, "If you're going to be famous, never pass up the opportunity for a free lunch, or to go to the men's room." Louise, meanwhile, would never become comfortable with the glow of fame that shone upon her husband and his family. *(Courtesy of NASA)*

Shepard's famed love of golf would later inspire him to bring a golf club and two balls to the moon—and earn him many subsequent invitations to golf tournaments. *(Courtesy of Ralph Morse/Time Life Pictures/Getty Images)*

After surgery cured his disease, Shepard fought his way back into the flight rotation and was assigned— along with two men who'd never flown into space before—to a mission to the moon. Some of the other astronauts dubbed the Apollo 14 crew "The Rookies." Others were amazed at Shepard's politicking, which he used to leapfrog ahead of other veteran astronauts who were waiting for a lunar mission. *(Courtesy of NASA)*

Firing up a celebratory cigar after Gemini VI. At the time, Shepard was grounded by a debilitating inner ear disease. *(Courtesy of NASA)*

At forty-seven, he was the oldest of NASA's sixty astronauts, but he trained hard for Apollo 14—that training would come in handy when Apollo 14 experienced problems. *(Courtesy of NASA)*

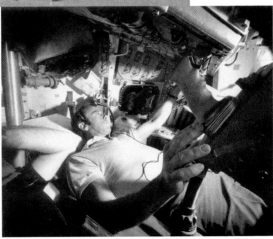

(Courtesy of NASA)

The Saturn V booster rocket beneath Apollo 14 was one hundred times more powerful than the Redstone rocket that had launched Shepard's Freedom 7 capsule ten years earlier. *(Courtesy of NASA)*

Shepard and Ed Mitchell practicing inside their lunar module. *(Courtesy of NASA)*

Just before leaving the moon's surface, Shepard—the fifth man on the moon—whacked two golf balls with a makeshift six-iron (a golf club head attached to a rock-collecting tool handle). *(Courtesy of NASA)*

Playing golf at Pebble Beach in 1995, a year before he was diagnosed with leukemia. *(Courtesy of J. D. Cuban/ Allsport/Getty Images)*

NASA would send a signal to the capsule that would release banana pellets as Ham's reward.

That flight, while considered a success, was riddled with imperfections. A faulty valve caused too much fuel to pump into the engine of the booster rocket, causing Ham to fly too high and too far. Because too much fuel was pumped through the rocket's engines, the tanks ran dry, which triggered Ham's capsule to separate from the spent rocket. The capsule then reentered the atmosphere too fast and at the wrong angle, which increased the friction between the capsule and the atmosphere, causing temperatures inside the capsule to soar. The capsule's electrical system also malfunctioned, so that instead of receiving banana pellets for pulling the appropriate levers, Ham received electrical shocks. Ham's capsule finally splashed into the Atlantic but immediately began filling with seawater. Recovery crews arrived thirty minutes later and pulled Ham from the sinking capsule. The chimp was very pissed off.

Wernher von Braun didn't want Shepard's flight to be similarly marred, and he decided to conduct one more unmanned test launch. But Shepard, despite the life-threatening dangers the chimp had withstood—dangers he now faced himself—was furious at the delays, blaming excessive "German thoroughness" and NASA's willingness to "pacify" von Braun. "We're ready to go. Let's go," he'd tell anyone who would listen. One day he urged von Braun directly, "For God's sake, let's fly now." But von Braun wouldn't budge. And NASA backed him.

Then, to make matters worse, politics intervened. Jerome B. Wiesner, a scientist from the Massachusetts Institute of Technology whom Kennedy had selected to be his technical adviser on science issues, had advised Kennedy a week prior to his inauguration that "the prestige of the United States will in part be determined by the leadership we demonstrate in space activities."

But then, when he became head of the newly appointed President's Science Advisory Committee (PSAC) that spring,

Wiesner got cold feet. His committee—scoffed at by the astronauts as those "pee-sack" people—began warning Kennedy of the damage a dead astronaut could do to his young administration, and advised that NASA first send more chimps into space, possibly two dozen or more. Shepard told Glenn he was ready to have a "chimp barbecue."

Cartoonists had a field day with the chimps. One showed a chimp instructing astronauts how to operate a capsule and get bananas for pushing the right buttons. Another showed Ham explaining to Shepard that at some point during his flight, he'd crave a banana. Shepard's colleagues began teasing him: *first the chimp, then the chump.* Depending on his mood, he either chuckled or sneered.

During one training exercise at the Cape, when Shepard began complaining about some aspect of the simulation run, one of the engineers joked, "Maybe we should get somebody who works for bananas." Shepard grabbed an ashtray and threw it at the man's head, just missing him. At one press conference, Glenn made a joke about the similarities between the astronauts and NASA's chimps. Shepard had finally heard enough about chimps and told Glenn to "scratch" himself.

But he'd soon have bigger worries than chimps.

///

Wiesner continued to advise caution in a memo to the White House: "The effect of TV cameras staring down (astronauts') throats . . . could have a catastrophic effect." The scientist acknowledged that the launch of an American into space would be an event "viewed in the same category as Columbus' discovery of the new world . . . and should be exploited properly by the Administration." But in the interest of safety, he called for a panel of experts to study the situation and prepare a report that would recommend to Kennedy whether or not to go ahead with a manned launch that spring.

Panel members visited all of NASA's training sites, where Shepard and the others were required to perform dog-and-pony shows for the panel, proving all over again that they could handle fifteen Gs in the centrifuge (and, therefore, could withstand the physical forces of a rocket launch), that they could tame MASTIF, and so on. Shepard had to show members how he would exit from his capsule, a replica of which was placed in the pool at Langley. The space program had come so far in the previous two years and was now on the verge of its first major success, but here were these guys in suits, fretting and wringing their hands. Shepard was disgusted and became convinced that the committee consisted of weak men incapable of making a bold decision.

"What the hell can we tell these pee-sack people that we haven't told them ten times?" Shepard complained to a NASA official during the delays to his flight. His overriding fear was that the delays had opened the door for the Russians to reach space first.

A senator who sat on the PSAC committee visited the Cape one day and asked if he could pose for some pictures with Shepard. Shepard was doing simulated launches in the training capsule, and the senator climbed the steps and stuck his head inside the capsule, where Shepard lay on his back, scrunched into a contoured couch. "Well, you seem to be in a rather tight spot there, young man," the lawmaker said. "Yeah, Senator," Shepard said. "But probably not so tight as some of the spots you get into up there in Washington." Shepard laughed loudly at his gibe, and the senator chuckled some, but not much.

The PSAC report was due for release April 12, 1961. Already the original schedule for Shepard's launch—which at one point had been planned for early April—had been pushed back a few weeks. But by the time the PSAC report neared completion, Shepard's window of historic opportunity had closed.

That very day—April 12—Russian cosmonaut Yuri Gagarin

blasted into space, circled the earth, and returned to it. "The stars in the sky look brighter," the blond-haired, blue-eyed cosmonaut reported. His capsule parachuted to safety in a field beside the Volga River; in his bulky orange suit, helmet in hand, he approached a peasant girl and her mother. "Have you come from outer space?" the woman asked.

"I am Soviet," Gagarin said. "I've come from outer space."

At 3 A.M. the next morning a reporter called Shorty Powers, NASA's spokesman, to get a reaction. Shorty, who was groggy and quite possibly drunk, gave a response that would haunt him the rest of his days: "We're all asleep down here." The press ran with it: *U.S. Is Asleep While Soviets Orbit Earth.*

Shepard was in a hotel room at the Cape when he heard the news. A public affairs official from NASA came to his room early on the morning after Gagarin's flight to break the news. They turned on the television and in disbelief watched grainy footage of millions of Russians welcoming their new hero to Moscow's Red Square. Shepard scowled at the coverage and slammed his hand down so hard on a table that the NASA public relations officer feared he might have broken it.

Glenn handled questions from the press later that day and conceded defeat. "They just beat the pants off us, that's all," he said. "There's no use kidding ourselves about that." President Kennedy said much the same that afternoon: "We are behind. And it will be some time before we catch up."

Over the subsequent days, newspaper and magazine headlines reflected America's disgust and, just as Sputnik had four years earlier, chafed at the nation's sense of inferiority. "Russia's Triumph in Space—What Does It Mean?" asked *U.S. News & World Report.* "A Chance That We Missed," said *Life.* Pictures of a jubilant Khrushchev ran alongside pictures of a hangdog Shepard, head down and hands shoved into his pockets, walking away from the camera past John Glenn.

Then, like salt on the wound, Shepard learned of the results of the PSAC committee report that was delivered to President Kennedy that very afternoon. They recommended that NASA proceed with its plans for Shepard's flight, and their report likened his pending mission to "the flights of the Wright Brothers, Lindbergh."

In the days after Gagarin's feat, Glenn tried to keep Shepard focused on their still-busy training schedule, which he hoped would keep Shepard's mind off the disappointment. But Shepard kept saying the same thing, over and over: *We could have, should have, gone sooner.* "We had them," he repeated. "We had them by the short hairs, and we gave it away."

Five days later the nation suffered another cold war blow. A band of fifteen hundred Cuban exiles, trained and financed by the CIA, invaded their homeland with plans to overthrow Fidel Castro. But Castro was waiting for them; many of the rebels were slaughtered and the rest were captured, leaving Kennedy to sheepishly deny that the United States was behind the attack. The Bay of Pigs fueled the determination of Kennedy's young administration to strike back with a victory. In a speech to the nation shortly after the Bay of Pigs, Kennedy acknowledged that he was sick and tired of Russia's successes and of communism's march. And, in the wake of Gagarin's flight, he met with NASA officials and his staff to plead with them to find a way to catch up. A Kennedy aide later called those days "the grimmest I can remember in the White House."

///

In late April, to remind everyone that America was still in this space race, and to give the media a taste of what a real launch would soon look like, NASA conducted a full dress rehearsal of Shepard's mission, which was now scheduled for May 2.

Gordo Cooper, acting as Shepard's stand-in, suited up. He walked from the transport van to the base of the gantry, the skeletal supporting structure that rose alongside the rocket, where an elevator waited to carry him to a platform at the top. With doctors and technicians escorting him and photographers and reporters watching from behind a rope, Cooper suddenly stopped and began backing away from the gantry. "I don't want to go," he bawled in a staged tribute to José Jiménez. "Please don't send me." The crew, who was in on the gag, grabbed Cooper and forced him into the elevator.

But in a reflection of the seriousness of the times, the press didn't appreciate the joke. Stories in the next day's papers excoriated NASA for goofing around at such a tense and important time in the nation's history.

Shepard, meanwhile, was back at Henri Landwirth's Holiday Inn, packing up for a move into the crew quarters in Hangar S up at the Cape, where he'd spend the final week before launch. He'd been staying at the Holiday Inn, wearing dark glasses and disguises to sneak in and out past the press. Henri Landwirth tried to help, telling reporters and intrusive strangers that Shepard wasn't there, spiriting him in and out through the kitchen.

Louise came to visit for a few days, but they saw little of each other. "Strangers and reporters kept barging in on us," he said later. Their longest moment together was the hourlong car ride to the airport at Orlando, during which they shared very few words. They both knew it could be the last time they saw each other.

After dropping Louise off at the airport, Shepard returned to the Holiday Inn, packed his bags, and then drove to Hangar S, where Dee O'Hara, the astronauts' nurse, had decorated the astronauts' air-conditioned second-floor bedroom. O'Hara was always trying to take care of "my boys" and had carefully put together a cozy bedroom, with robin's egg blue walls, champagne-colored drapes, two couches, a recliner, and two sets of bunk beds.

Through the final days of April, Shepard had one set of bunk beds to himself while Glenn and Grissom shared the other. On May 2—just twenty days after Gagarin's flight—the three men woke early, shared a breakfast of filet mignon and eggs, and waited for NASA bosses to unveil to the American public which of them would make history. A heavy rain fell outside, and Shepard felt certain the launch would be scrapped.

NASA had even considered bringing all three men out that morning with Shepard, Grissom, and Glenn wearing *hoods* to keep the secret alive until one man rode the elevator up to the capsule. Shepard thought it was a stupid idea but agreed to the backup plan: to emerge from Hangar S fully suited and wade through a crowd of awaiting reporters and photographers on his way to the launch pad.

But when rain washed out the day's scheduled launch and it was postponed for another three days, NASA decided it was time to unmask the man who had been picked. The press, which had expected all along that John Glenn was going to be America's first spaceman, pestered Shorty Powers for an explanation. Shorty tried to diplomatically explain that Shepard "had what all the others had, with just enough to spare to make him the logical man to go first." Whatever that meant.

That afternoon Shepard soothed his frustration over the scrubbed launch with a big shot of brandy, a long run on the beach, and a brief visit to the top of the gantry to peer inside his capsule, followed by three more simulated practice missions in the procedures trainer and then finally a fifteen-minute nap. (Shorty noted later that the brandy was his idea, that Shepard didn't really need it—"I needed it more than he did.")

Two days later, Shepard and Glenn—who had been insepa-rable for weeks—jogged together out to a deserted, off-limits beach near the launch pad. They chased some crabs along the edge of the surf, just the two of them talking about the flight plans, far from the prelaunch preparations and tensions that began escalating that afternoon.

Shepard and Glenn returned to Hangar S, and Shepard called Louise, his daughter Laura at her school in St. Louis, and his parents in New Hampshire. Then he and Glenn sat down for a roast beef dinner with the other five astronauts and their agent, Leo D'Orsey.

The beef, one of the astronauts was explaining to D'Orsey, was part of NASA's "low-residue" diet. Along with dry toast, skinless potatoes, and white chicken meat, it was designed—with the bathroom-less space capsule in mind—to create very little "output."

"No shit?" D'Orsey asked.

"Exactly," Shepard said, and the table cracked up.

After dinner Shepard thanked Glenn for all his hard work. "John's been most kind," he said, and offered a toast. He still liked teasing Glenn by referring to him as "my backup." And Glenn still considered himself Shepard's superior, both morally and professionally. But it was clear to the others at the dinner table that night that the two men had drawn surprisingly close, that a mutual antagonism had been replaced by something akin to friendship.

Over the previous three months Shepard and Glenn had spent more time together than either had ever spent with another man. "I don't think two people could have worked more closely together than we did," Glenn recalled many years later. As Shepard's backup—"Al's alter ego, his virtual twin"—Glenn often attended meetings and took phone calls that Shepard couldn't handle, and Glenn forced himself to get inside Shepard's head, to try thinking like Shepard so that he could ask the right questions. *What would Al do?* Glenn asked himself.

Shortly after 10 P.M., without bothering to shower or change, the two men lay down in their bunks, and within fifteen minutes both were asleep. During three fitful hours of slumber, Shepard awoke once and walked to the window to check on the weather. Happy to see stars, not clouds, he returned to his bunk, a few feet from where Glenn soundly slept.

1 4

"Light this candle!"

At 1:30 A.M., May 5, 1961, after a quick shower and shave, Shepard and Glenn sat down to another breakfast of filet mignon wrapped in bacon, eggs, juice, and coffee.

"Is there anything else I can do?" Glenn asked after breakfast. Shepard told him no, he was fine, he was ready. The two men parted; Glenn went out to check on Shepard's capsule, and Shepard walked down the hall to the doctor's exam room. Bill Douglas, the astronauts' physician, told Shepard to take off his bathrobe so he could conduct one last checkup, a detailed exam for the record books.

Douglas found a loose nail on the fourth toe of Shepard's left foot—where someone had stepped on him—and clipped it off. Shepard's back was sunburned and peeling in spots from recent afternoons beside the Holiday Inn pool. A blister rose beside one of the four tattoo marks on his chest that the technicians used to mark where their bio-medical sensors attached. Shepard murmured "ninety-nine, ninety-nine" while Douglas listened to his chest. His ear canals were clean, his thyroid was "smooth and symmetrical," and he showed "slight apprehension" about his pending flight, Douglas noted. "I tried to play it cool," Shepard would confess years later. "But there were some butterflies."

At 2 A.M. Alan called Louise once more. She had been waiting to hear from him and told him to wave when he took off. Alan laughed and told Louise that he loved her. Then he squeezed into his tight silver space suit—an exhausting process that took 15 minutes, due to all the zippers and complicated connections on the twenty-pound rubber and aluminum-coated nylon creation. (The suit would surround his body with pressurized oxygen; without such protection, the low-pressure atmosphere of space would cause his bodily fluids to literally boil up through his skin.) Finally, Shepard strapped on his helmet and attached a hose to his suit, the other end of which connected to a portable oxygen and air-conditioning unit that he carried in his hand, like a briefcase.

The adrenaline began pumping—"there were butterflies in my stomach again," Shepard said later—as he and Douglas left Hangar S and climbed into an awaiting transport van. As Shepard rode out to the launch site, leaning back in a reclining chair, he seemed to relax a bit. Adopting his pitiful Spanish accent, he tried a bit of a José Jiménez routine. Gus Grissom sat beside him during the short drive out to his rocket.

"Hey, Gus, you know what it really takes to be an astronaut?"

"No, José, tell me."

"You should have courage and the right blood pressure and four legs."

"Why four legs, José?" Grissom asked, accustomed to the part.

"Because they really wanted to send a dog, but they decided that would be too cruel."

Grissom had intended to tell Shepard to "go blow up"—a gruff old test pilot's line that he hoped would relax his friend. But for some reason, at that moment it didn't feel right. Grissom kept it to himself, and Shepard stepped out of the van.

A waning half moon glowed above, sliding in and out of

some clouds. Batteries of searchlights bathed the Redstone rocket in a bluish haze as liquid oxygen spewed from vents and turned to wisps of steam that rolled down the sides of the rocket. Shepard thought his rocket—"the bird"—looked beautiful.

But the more beautiful sight was Shepard himself, standing at the base of his bird looking dramatically up toward his capsule. Reporters and photographers, technicians and engineers, physicians and psychiatrists . . . everyone who was nearby that morning would recall how profoundly moved they were as they watched America's first spaceman standing self-assuredly beside his spaceship and realized: *We're really going to do it.*

At that moment Shepard had planned to say a few words to the rocket crew and to the reporters standing behind a barrier. But he was unexpectedly overcome with emotion; his throat closed in on itself, and he found himself unable to speak. So he just waved.

Then he rode the elevator seventy feet up to the green-walled room atop the gantry that surrounded the opening to the capsule. Glenn, wearing white coveralls and a white cap like a butcher's, greeted Shepard as he exited the elevator and then helped him squeeze through the two-foot-square opening of the capsule's hatch. Months earlier he had named the capsule *Freedom 7.* The press would give him credit for honoring the Mercury Seven, but it was actually named 7 because it was the seventh capsule produced by the McDonnell Douglas assembly team in St. Louis.

As he settled into the couch, Shepard noticed a sign taped to the instrument panel: No Handball Playing in This Area. Taped beside it was a centerfold ripped from a girlie magazine. Shepard laughed and looked out the hatch into Glenn's grinning face. *I'll be damned,* he thought. *He's becoming a damn prankster.*

Shepard planned to leave the centerfold taped up, but Glenn reached in and grabbed it and the handball sign. Shepard guessed Glenn didn't want the cameras inside the capsule—which would soon begin rolling—to film his joke.

///

For the next hour or so, various heads and hands reached into the capsule, attaching sensors, adjusting straps, shaking his hand. Shepard watched some of the commotion through the screen of the periscope that would be his primary window on the brief journey ahead. Every subsequent capsule would contain windows, but Shepard's had only two small portholes and the fish-eye view transmitted through the lens of the periscope onto a circular screen in front of his face.

Just before they closed the hatch, Glenn reached in and shook Shepard's gloved hand. Shepard thanked him again, then jerked a thumbs-up.

"Happy landings, commander," Glenn said as the crew standing behind him shouted good luck and goodbye. Then they closed and bolted the hatch shortly past 6 A.M., and Shepard was alone. He would learn later that his heartbeat quickened as they shut him inside. The last human face he saw was Glenn's, wide and grinning in the distorted fish-eye image of the periscope's screen.

Finally, after Glenn and the others had descended in the elevator, the gantry rolled back and the Redstone stood alone on the launch pad. Suddenly, without the skeletal framework hugging it, the rocket looked thin and delicate. Scores of NASA engineers would later call it the moment they truly realized there was a *man* up there.

///

"José?" came a voice over the radio into Shepard's headset. "Do you read me, José?"

"I read you loud and clear, Deke," Shepard replied.

Slayton, the capsule communicator or "cap com," would be Shepard's primary contact during the short flight. "Don't cry too much, José," Slayton said.

Shepard had been curled inside the capsule for more than

an hour, and already they were well past the scheduled 7 A.M. launch time. He began to get itchy.

"I tried to pace myself," Shepard reported later, "which is difficult for me to do."

As he communicated by radio to technicians during the first of the delays, Shepard complained about the static in his ear. "I can't hear you on this goddamn phone," he said, and Shorty Powers got on the line to warn, "Watch your language. We're being recorded everyplace."

When clouds rolled across the Florida coast, the countdown stopped—at 7:14 A.M.—to await the expected clearing. During that thirty-minute hold, an electrical inverter failed and had to be replaced. Following that fifty-two-minute delay, the count resumed for another twenty-one minutes, but then engineers discovered an error in the IBM computer in Maryland that would process much of the flight's data. Again the countdown was put on hold.

As the delays mounted, so did Shepard's anxiety. While engineers raced to fix the computer glitch, Shepard had been scrunched inside his capsule for three hours. The flight should have been completed already, but here he still was—adrenaline building, heart palpitating. Shepard told himself, *You're building up too fast. Slow down. Relax.* When he ran out of settings and dials to check, the tension would creep back in, and he'd force himself to look out the periscope at the mass of people and waves on the beach.

"The thought of the consequences of an unsuccessful flight were getting to me too much," he'd admit later.

///

In East Derry, Shepard's mother, Renza, and sister, Polly, had risen early and poked the American flag into the front lawn. Bart slept a little later and finally came downstairs to find his wife and daughter praying at the kitchen table.

In St. Louis, Principia's principal took Shepard's eldest daughter, Laura, into a separate room, where she sat on a wooden chair before a black-and-white television "without any display of emotion."

In Virginia Beach, Louise had been up since 5 A.M., listening to the radio and looking over a copy of the countdown schedule Shepard had given her. It was Alice's tenth birthday, but the family had agreed to wait until the next day to celebrate that.

Louise's parents were staying with her. The family spoke little of Alan in the days before the launch, except for one night at dinner, when Julie—apropos of nothing—announced that her father loved to put salt on radishes and pop them into his mouth.

Alan had called Thursday night, then again at 2 A.M. Friday, sounding confident and relaxed. Louise barely slept after that. She kept hearing footsteps on the front porch, followed by a pause, and then more footsteps. She assumed the steps belonged to newsmen approaching, then leaving the front door, where she'd hung a note: *There are no reporters inside. I will have a statement for the press after the flight.*

After breakfast, the family moved into the living room and gathered around the television, which reported the delays in the flight. Louise sat knitting a sweater when, a little past eight, the phone suddenly rang and she jumped.

It was Shorty Powers. Shepard had radioed from the capsule and asked Shorty to call Louise and tell her that everything was okay and not to worry. "I want her to hear from us," he told Shorty, "that I'm fine and explain that I'm going nowhere fast."

She hadn't seen him for two weeks, not since the day he dropped her off at the airport in Orlando. She had spent a week at the Cape, staying at the Holiday Inn, but saw little of him except early breakfasts and late dinners. On the drive to the airport, they both knew it could be the last time they saw each other, but neither of them had much to say. Shepard tried hard to stay casual, to avoid "any display of emotion."

Louise tried to do the same. She knew it'd be easier for him if she stayed cool, so she said goodbye as if it were "a normal family parting." But as her plane lifted off she began to weep.

Now, as the countdown resumed, Louise sat close to the TV, with a transistor radio in her hand. She felt "the power of good and of God" fill the room.

///

After more than three hours in the capsule, he felt it, and hoped it would go away.

But it didn't, that nagging pressure in his groin. His bladder had filled with the early morning's orange juice and coffee. Finally he had to confront it: He had to urinate. *Bad.*

He radioed to Gordon Cooper, who was stationed in the nearby blockhouse and serving as Shepard's contact until Slayton took over as cap com. "Man, I got to pee," Shepard said. "Check and see if I can get out quickly and relieve myself." Cooper couldn't believe his ears. No one had prepared for anything like this. The flight was supposed to last just fifteen minutes, so no one thought Shepard would be in the capsule long enough to feel the urge.

Shepard said he'd been in there "forever" and if he didn't go to the bathroom, his bladder would burst. He suggested bringing the gantry back and letting him get out. Cooper relayed the message, but Wernher von Braun said no. Shepard had to stay put. Or, as von Braun put it: "Zee astronaut shall stay in zee nose cone."

Finally Shepard began shouting. In a conversation that would be stricken from the transcript NASA would later share with reporters, Shepard said that if they didn't let him get out, he'd have to "go in my suit." Technicians in Mission Control began twittering that the urine would short-circuit the medical wires attached to Shepard's body, including the electrical thermometer inserted in his rectum. So Shepard suggested simply

turning off the power until he'd had time to go. After some frantic discussions, they finally agreed, and Shepard let loose, with a
long "ahhhh," as the warm liquid pooled at the small of his back.

"Weyl," he reported over the radio in his lousy José dialect,
"I'm a wetback now."

Shepard then braced himself for an electrical shock when
they turned the power back on. But the urine was absorbed by
his long cotton underwear and then evaporated in the 100 percent oxygen filling the suit. NASA was spared the embarrassing
task of reporting that America's first spaceman had been electro-
cuted by his own piss.

The PR people did, however, have on hand a scripted response to any potential disaster. The public affairs office had prepared a carefully worded "announcement in certain contingency
situations" that would inform the world of Alan Shepard's death.
There were different announcements for different disasters, such
as death during launch, death in space, death during reentry. If,
for example, Shepard died during the launch itself, Shorty Powers would use the following words: "Rescue units on the scene
report that Astronaut Shepard has perished today in the service
of his country."

Death was not something Shepard liked to discuss or even
think about. A week earlier a reporter had asked him if he ever considered his own demise, and Shepard reluctantly admitted that he'd
made certain "financial arrangements" for Louise. But competing
to fly into space, despite the dangers, had nothing to do with facing
and/or cheating death. Shepard tried to explain to the press that he
considered what he was doing "just a faction of maturity," just taking his flying skills to the next level. "If you don't use your experience, your past is wasted," he said. "You are betraying yourself."

The death of an astronaut, however, was very much on
John Kennedy's mind. The last thing his administration needed
was the publicly televised explosive destruction of Alan Shepard. And in the days before launch, Kennedy became more and

more anxious about the decision to televise the launch live. At one point he called NASA's administrator, James Webb, to ask him to "play down the publicity on this venture."

"He is afraid of the reaction of the public in case there is a mishap in the firing," Kennedy's secretary, Evelyn Lincoln, wrote in her diary early that week.

NASA tried to assure Kennedy that the escape tower atop Shepard's capsule was designed to whisk him away from an exploding rocket. But Kennedy's fears continued right up to the launch. Just minutes before TV stations picked up the countdown, Lincoln called NASA and asked who was in charge. Paul Haney, one of the public affairs officers working with Shorty, picked up the phone and, after looking around and seeing no one who outranked him, said, "I guess I am." "Please hold for the president," Lincoln said, explaining that Kennedy wanted to discuss the details of the live television coverage.

Kennedy's intense interest in Shepard's launch had surprised many. *Time* magazine reporter Hugh Sidey once described the meeting Kennedy held two days after Gagarin's flight, at which he saw a man "awed by the romance of the high frontier" lean back in his chair and scold his staff to offer ideas on catching up with the Russians. "Let's find somebody—anybody," Kennedy said, while picking at the sole of his orthopedic shoe. "I don't care if it's the janitor over there, if he knows how."

After five anxious minutes of holding, Lincoln came back on the line and explained to Haney that Kennedy had had to take a call from an obscure African president, and that Pierre Salinger, Kennedy's press secretary, would speak to Haney instead. Haney told Salinger about the escape tower designed to protect Shepard from any problems with the rocket. Shepard could pull hard on his abort handle if things got ugly, and the rocket-powered escape tower bolted atop the capsule would pull the capsule up and away from the Redstone rocket. Salinger said he'd relay the information to Kennedy.

Other modest protections against accidental death included the parachute Shepard wore strapped to his chest and a small survival kit beside him, carrying items to sustain him in case he landed far off course. He had a knife capable of cutting through metal, a fishing line and hook, a rig that could desalinate a pint of water, a few bites of dehydrated food, and a raft.

But for now, the bigger problem was just getting off the ground.

Shortly after nine, with two minutes before liftoff, the countdown was halted once more. The pressure of the liquid oxygen inside the Redstone was too high. They'd have to either reset the pressure valve—which would require the flight to be canceled—or try to bleed off some of the pressure by remote control. After three hours of sitting (an hour of it in his own urine), Shepard had had enough. They were all acting like spinster aunts, fussing and clucking over a newborn. He was ready to go, his rocket was ready to go—hell, had been ready for months—and he was getting tired of all the fiddling and delays.

"I'm cooler than you are," he finally barked into his microphone. "Why don't you fix your little problem and light this candle."

///

When it seemed as if the last of the glitches was corrected, the countdown resumed—four hours after he'd first climbed into the capsule. But the numbers from ten to one sounded like gibberish to Shepard, whose pulse rose during those last seconds from a rate of 80 beats per minute to 126. In the final seconds, he muttered a prayer to himself, asking "the man upstairs" to watch over him and telling himself, *Don't screw up, Shepard.*

As the count reached zero, Shepard tightened his grip on the abort handle and pushed his feet hard against the floor, bracing himself for a jolt that never came. Despite all the centrifuge training and preparations for an inhuman rush skyward, the ascent felt "extremely smooth—a subtle, gentle, gradual rise off the ground."

"Roger," he said, his first word during the flight, which coincided with his finger punching a button to start the onboard timer. "Liftoff, and the clock is started." Shepard was grateful for Slayton's attempt to ease his tensions: "You're on your way, José."

///

In Newark, New Jersey, Mary Lombardo—one the many ordinary citizens whose reactions were recorded by the nation's journalists—touched a small cross around her neck. "God bless him," she said. In the nation's classrooms, youngsters counted down in time with Cape Canaveral: "Five . . . four . . . three . . . two . . . one." New York City cabdrivers stopped picking up passengers so that they could listen to radio reports. Loudspeakers outside City Hall in lower Manhattan crackled with the live radio broadcast as throngs crowded the park outside. A Philadelphia appeals court judge interrupted a hearing when a clerk handed him a note. Free champagne flowed at a Fort Wayne, Indiana, tavern, and traffic slowed or stopped on southern California freeways as drivers—including two future astronauts—listened on the radio to the blastoff. People danced in the streets at Times Square, hugging each other, thrusting their fists in the air. "He made it!" a woman in Chicago gasped, then burst into tears. "He made it!"

President Kennedy broke up a National Security Council meeting, walked into his secretary's office, and stood before the television. Joined by his wife, brother, and vice president, Kennedy stood silently, hands jammed deep into his pants pockets.

Bart, Renza, and Polly Shepard watched their television, holding hands and silently praying. None of them spoke, each afraid to break the taut silence.

Louise, meanwhile, sat nearest the TV, at one point reaching out to touch the screen. As their father's rocket rose slowly heavenward, the girls shrieked and cheered. But Louise just whispered, "Go, Alan. Go, sweetheart."

///

Shepard had discussed with the operations director, Walt Williams, his plan to talk as much as possible during liftoff, to keep everyone on the ground informed about even the slightest bits of information. So, as the rocket built speed, he began reeling off bits of data: "This is *Freedom Seven*. The fuel is go. One-point-two Gs. Cabin at fourteen PSI. Oxygen is go.... The main bus is twenty-five and the isolated battery is twenty-nine."

Then, two minutes after liftoff, his easy ride turned bumpy. Though the liftoff itself was smoother than Shepard had expected (he experienced only about six Gs during liftoff—less than half what he had trained for in the centrifuge), the turbulent transition from the earth's atmosphere into space was a surprise. The capsule began shuddering violently, with Shepard's head jackhammering so hard against the headrest that he could no longer see the dials and gauges clearly enough to read the data. He decided, instead of alarming those jittery technicians with his garbled voice, to wait to say anything else until the violence passed. Finally his spacecraft rocketed through the riotous and dangerous segment of the launch known as max Q—the point at which the capsule is accelerating beyond the speed of sound and into the thinner air of the upper atmosphere, which exerts enormous dynamic pressure on the spacecraft. The astronauts would come to call this "passing through the gate," and once the rocket reached supersonic speeds, the tremendous buffeting stopped. Only then did Shepard feel comfortable enough to report in to Deke Slayton.

"Okay. It is a lot smoother now," he grunted. "A lot smoother."

"Roger," Slayton replied.

The do-or-die moment came seconds later as Shepard prepared for his capsule to separate from the spent booster rocket. Once the liquid oxygen fueling the Redstone rockets had been expended, it would trigger the ignition of small explosives that would sever the connection between the rocket and the capsule. But if the capsule failed to separate from the rocket, Shepard would have to quickly strap on his parachute, pop open the capsule's hatch, and jump away from the doomed Redstone and capsule—an escape plan with a ludicrously slim chance of success, since Shepard was now traveling at Mach 2. In fact, on future flights, the astronauts wouldn't even bother with the silly parachute.

Shepard's heart rate peaked at 132 beats per minute just before the capsule separation, but then immediately ebbed once the three-inch green "cap sep" indicator showed that the capsule was indeed flying free and clear. "Cap sep is green," Shepard reported.

Shorty Powers, sitting in Mission Control, began describing each moment of the launch to reporters via an audio hookup. He reported that Shepard was acting like "a real test pilot" and that his flight was proceeding "A-okay." He'd use "A-okay" ten times in the subsequent minutes, and it would appear in countless newspaper headlines the next day on its way to entering the country's lexicon. The term—used decades earlier by military radio operators—would be attributed to Shepard, who never once uttered "A-okay."

The closest Shepard came to such a declaration was when speaking to himself. "Okay, buster," he said when the time came for him to manually control the rotation and angle of the free-flying capsule. This was another crucial moment, psychologically and politically. NASA wanted to highlight the primary difference between his suborbital flight and Gagarin's longer global loop, which was that Shepard would actually fly his capsule while Gagarin had been a mere passenger. It was a distinction that the astronauts had fought hard for, and one that Shepard was intensely proud of. As he switched his capsule from automatic to manual control, a mere three minutes into his flight, he felt confident about how smoothly things were proceeding.

Then, using a hand controller identical to the one in the MASTIF trainer, Shepard turned his capsule backward, so the blunt end was flying first. Then he tilted the can up and down, left to right, and side to side. While Gagarin had sat monkeylike in a flight entirely controlled and programmed on the ground, Shepard was now actually piloting his capsule, all the while traveling 5,100 miles an hour—roughly a mile for every beat of his heart.

Until that moment, the fastest American had traveled roughly 1,800 miles an hour, just shy of Mach 3. Shepard was now traveling nearly eight times the speed of sound.

Four minutes into the flight, Shepard and his capsule reached weightlessness, and he felt his body float up from the couch and against his shoulder harnesses. Bits of dust began floating past his face, followed by a single steel washer left behind by workers in the bowels of the capsule. He reached for the washer, but it tumbled slowly out of reach.

At the apex of his arc, Shepard tried to look through the periscope at the world below. His heart sank at the gray blob in the screen. During the lengthy delays back on the launch pad, to block out the intense morning sunlight he had flicked a switch that covered the periscope's lens with a gray filter. He had forgotten to remove the filter before launch. But now, when he tried to reach over and flick off the filter, his wrist banged against the abort handle, and he decided it was best to leave the filter in place.

"What a beautiful view," he declared, trying to make the best of it.

He described being able to identify Lake Okeechobee and the shoals off Bimini and some cloud cover over the Bahamas.

Later, he would tell NASA officials how the view was "remark-able" and "awe-inspiring," and in an article for *Life* he'd describe the "brilliantly clear" colors around Bimini. He'd later confess to friends that the filter "obliterated most of the colors."

As he reached the zenith of his trajectory, 116 miles above the earth, the periscope retracted and Shepard strained to look for stars and planets through two small, awkwardly placed port-holes, one to the upper left and one to the lower right. It always bothered him that there was no "forward-looking window." He often complained to the engineers who'd built the capsule that even Lindbergh had the benefit of seeing where he was flying. He wanted desperately to match Gagarin's claim to have witnessed the stars, but he could find none, no matter which way he twisted and turned the capsule. Suddenly, he realized that his search for the stars had put him a few seconds behind in his tight schedule, in which every second was meticulously assigned a task. With only a few minutes of the flight to actually be spent in outer space, NASA had overloaded Shepard with dozens of small tasks. Falling slightly behind in that schedule was the only time he didn't feel "on top of things."

Still, all the training in simulators had prepared Shepard to play the 127 buttons and switches of the control panel as if he were a "sightless organist." And so, to catch up on the lost sec-onds, he began "running around the cockpit with my hands"— turning the capsule around, firing the retro-rockets that would slow down the capsule, retracting the periscope. All this was preparation for reentering the atmosphere, the dangerous and physically demanding portion of the ride that he knew was "not one most people would want to try in an amusement park." Dur-ing this catch-up period, Shepard reported steadily back to Slay-ton, "Three retros fired . . . periscope is retracting . . . going into reentry attitude."

Shepard then had to align the capsule at the precise angle so that the ablative material on the bottom of the capsule could absorb the intense heat to come. If he was off by just a degree or two, the capsule could be thrown dangerously far off course. As he plunged back into the thicker air close to earth, he was shoved into his couch with a force of 11 Gs—the equivalent of eighteen hundred pounds. Though he tried to keep up a steady stream of talk, Shepard could only grunt as the Gs stomped on his chest.

"Okay . . . okay . . . okay . . . okay," he reported in clenched-mouth growls.

As he rapidly descended from eighty thousand feet to forty thousand, the friction of the capsule's blunt end rubbing against the atmosphere caused the temperature just a foot behind Shepard's back to soar above 1,200 degrees. But inside the can, the temperature peaked at just 102, and inside Shepard's pressurized suit, the temperature hovered at about 82. "At worst it was like being in a closed car on a warm summer day," he said later.

Shepard fretted a few moments waiting for the parachutes to release, and was relieved to see the preliminary drogue chute pop out at twenty-one thousand feet, followed seconds later by the sixty-three-foot orange and white main chute, which caught air and blossomed, snapping his capsule with a sharp but "reassuring kick in the butt." Shepard thought the billowing parachute was "the most beautiful sight of the mission."

"Main chute is coming unreefed and it looks good," Shepard practically yelled.

The parachute slowed the capsule to a descent speed of about thirty feet per second, or twenty miles an hour. Shepard watched his altimeter and prepared for the abrupt slam into the Atlantic, which he would later describe as feeling no worse than the shove in the back he used to get from a catapult launch off an aircraft carrier.

Within seconds of splashing down into the water—302 miles east of the Cape, and about 100 miles north of the Bahamas—Wayne Koons, pilot of the rescue helicopter, was hovering overhead and asking Shepard by radio if he was ready to come out. Shepard was just removing his helmet and the many straps and harnesses, and thought Koons "seemed in a hurry to get me out." He told Koons he wasn't ready. Water lapped against the portholes, and Shepard asked Koons—who'd already snagged the top of the capsule with a hook and cable—to lift the capsule above the waterline. "Okay, you've got two minutes to come out," Koons radioed, apparently eager to get Shepard out of the water and safely into his helicopter.

Finally Shepard popped open the hatch and leaned out to grab the horse's collar, a padded harness that Koons had lowered by cable. NASA officials were nervous about this small piece of the mission. The previous day a Navy balloonist had set a new altitude record by flying 113,000 feet above the Gulf of Mexico in a balloon. When he and his crew landed their balloon in the Gulf, a Navy helicopter lowered a horse collar to pull the crew from the balloon's gondola. One of the balloonists, who was wearing a pressure suit similar to Shepard's, slipped out of the horse collar, fell into the water, and drowned.

Shepard had been given a report on the tragedy earlier that morning. He knew he had to be careful. He pulled the horse collar into the open hatch of his capsule, looped it over his head and under his arm, then gave a thumbs-up. As the winch pulled the cable taut, he was lifted up and away. But Shepard's weight caused the helicopter to drop slightly, and his splayed legs splashed into the water. Finally he was pulled clear. He reached the helicopter's open door, climbed inside, and declared it "a beautiful day."

As they flew toward the aircraft carrier USS *Lake Champlain*, the deck looked like a blanket of white and appeared to be moving. As they neared the ship Shepard realized the deck was covered with sailors, all cheering for him. Until that moment, he'd been focused totally on the specifics of the job, the technical tasks at hand. The crowd of ecstatic sailors below showed him, for the first time, how people perceived his mission. That moment, full circle from his early Navy days, felt "like coming home." He swallowed hard and blinked away the moisture in his eyes. Later, he called it "the most emotional carrier landing I ever made."

The helicopter copilot, George Cox, lowered the capsule onto a stack of mattresses, disconnected it, then landed on deck. Shepard debarked from the helicopter, waved at the cheering sailors, and yelled, "Boy, what a ride!" Captain Ralph Weymouth, the ship's skipper—whose fears the previous night had been that they'd have to "dish him out of the capsule with a spoon"—greeted Shepard aboard. Shepard shook Weymouth's hand and introduced himself.

"Hi, I'm Al Shepard."

///

Back at Mission Control, months of tensions erupted into cheers—and a few tears. Men hugged and slapped each other on the back, then fired up celebratory cigars. "Myself, I damn near cried," said Walt Williams, the operations director.

Guenter Wendt, who oversaw launch pad operations, re-called that he and his crew erupted in jubilation once they re-ceived word of Shepard's safe landing: "I simply cannot put into words the excitement and euphoria that I felt."

On Florida's coastal beaches, the crowds cheered and prayed and drank. John Glenn conducted a brief press confer-ence and told reporters that they should just leave the aircraft carriers out there and set up another rocket for him.

New Hampshire's governor, Wesley Powell, visited East Derry to head up a spontaneous parade through Shepard's home-town, declaring it "the greatest day in the history of the state." Schools closed as children and their families poured into the streets. Army and Air Force planes flew low overhead, dropping pounds of confetti as Bart, Renza, and Polly rode in the rear of a convertible, waving at the crowds. Ever optimistic, Renza told re-porters, "I believe the flight will bring all the world closer together."

And at the Shepard house in Virginia Beach, Louise had

hung on each word of the TV and radio reports, feeling confident as they "never varied in their rightness." As her husband reached his apex, the point of weightlessness, she felt "suddenly staggered to think where I was and where he was." Only when she got a call from NASA, however, telling her that he was safely aboard the aircraft carrier did she relax. And she realized: "I went with him all the way." Then she opened the front door and, looking beautiful and poised in a chocolate brown linen dress and pink cardigan, faced the reporters and their questions. In the sky overhead, a Navy jet spelled S in smoke.

///

NASA doctors had wanted to monitor and record every second of the flight's aftermath—the way Shepard looked, smelled, walked, and talked. But Shepard immediately warned them, "I don't think you're going to have to do too much."

The sailors and crew had been told not to talk to Shepard, let alone cheer. NASA had wanted Shepard to initiate any conversations. The only people who could address him were the doctors, who hovered around him, asking again and again how he felt. They were afraid of some strange delayed reaction, as if he might turn green, float, or explode.

When Shepard reached Captain Weymouth's quarters, after guzzling a glass of orange juice, he was handed a tape recorder and told to record his thoughts. He clicked record and then introduced himself. "My name is José Jiménez. . . ."

For the next half hour Shepard rambled breathlessly about each detail of the flight, at one point praising his overall performance: "I quite frankly did a whole lot better than I thought I was going to be able to do. . . . I felt no apprehension at any time." Psychiatrists later reported that Shepard was "calm and self-possessed," but they also officiously noted the obvious: that Shepard appeared to be exhibiting signs of "excitement and exhilaration." He was absolutely drunk with self-satisfaction.

Then Shepard's whirling monologue was interrupted by a phone call. A sailor handed him a big black phone, and Shepard heard the voice of his old flying buddy Taz Shepard, the drawling Alabaman with whom he'd trained back at Corpus Christi. Taz had been selected by President Kennedy to serve as his naval aide.

"Alan, the president wants to speak to you," Taz said.

"By golly, old boy, you've picked up a New England accent," Alan said.

Taz laughed and told Alan to hold for the president of the United States.

"Hello, Commander," Kennedy said.

"Yes, sir."

"I want to congratulate you very much."

"Thank you very much, Mr. President."

"We watched you on TV, of course," said Kennedy. "And we are awfully pleased and proud of what you did."

"Well, thank you, sir. And as you know by now, everything worked out just perfectly."

Kennedy then said he was looking forward to meeting Alan in three days.

Years later Taz would describe how Kennedy had been "walking on thin ice" in the space between Gagarin's flight and Alan's. During those twenty-three tense days, he would fill his black alligator bag with news clippings and NASA reports to read at night. Kennedy was desperate for success and had been relying heavily on Alan's flight. When an aide had given Kennedy the news that Alan was safely aboard the helicopter, the president broke into a grin and said softly, "It's a success."

"If it had been a failure, no telling what would have happened," Taz recalled.

One of Kennedy's favorite sayings was "Happiness is full use of your powers in pursuit of excellence." In Alan and the other astronauts Kennedy had found exactly the type of men he needed as allies in his pursuit of new frontiers. "President Kennedy had a great admiration for heroes," recalled Taz Shepard, himself a winner of the Navy Cross (for taking command of his ship's guns after the ship's captain and two hundred others were killed at Guadalcanal). "Anybody who excelled at what they did."

That afternoon, an enthusiastic Kennedy told the press that Shepard's day was one for the history books: "All America rejoices in this successful flight of astronaut Shepard. This is an historic milestone in our own exploration into space."

///

Kennedy might have been the most grateful beneficiary of Shepard's success, but he was hardly alone in believing that Shepard had instantly earned a place beside Wilbur Wright and Charles Lindbergh in the history books. In fact, not since Lindbergh's transatlantic flight thirty-four years earlier would the American public react so ecstatically to a feat of aviation. Spontaneous parades, parties, and celebrations erupted across the land.

Walter Cronkite, who would cover many subsequent launches, recalled decades later that none of the launches he witnessed would compare to that first space flight. He recalled that some of his crew members—who'd set up their equipment in the rear of a station wagon parked in mosquito- and snake-filled palmetto scrub a mile from the launch pad—broke down into tears. "There wasn't a cynical enough press man in the gallery to not have a sense of great relief and a certain thrill that we were in space," he said.

For the next few weeks the newspapers and magazines would be stuffed with stories and photographs and commentaries, boasting how "Shep did it!" Headlines in Henry Luce's *Life* magazine trumpeted Shepard's "Thrust into Space" and "Flawless Flight." *National Geographic* would dedicate practically an entire issue to the flight.

And in subsequent years Shepard's flight would continue to resonate as an event that legitimized NASA and propelled the agency throughout the 1960s. "Some countries build cathedrals," said John Pike, director of the space policy project at the Federation of American Scientists. "We have a space program."

With Shepard's help, NASA was now set to grow into the dual-role behemoth it would soon become—a cold war propaganda machine and an agency of brilliant scientists and fearless explorers. NASA would reflect to the world an image of America as a nation of technologically advanced pioneers and risk takers.

"The presumption of the American republic is that we're pioneers, that we explore frontiers, that we use technology in that pursuit, that we are a country with a special sense of our place in history. And, in various guises, I think that's mainly what NASA's been about. It's mainly about making us feel good about being Americans," Pike said.

Furthermore, in legitimizing the still young space program, Shepard's flight gave a boost to the nation's sense of inferiority to the Russians. "Shepard bailed out the ego of the American people," recalled Julian Scheer, a reporter in 1961 who later became NASA's public affairs officer. "As a nation we desperately wanted a success, and we got not only a success, but an instant hero." Even John Glenn would recall his shock at the public's reaction to his colleague's flight. "That took us all by surprise," he recalled.

///

Shepard spent about an hour on board the *Lake Champlain*, which included a medical debriefing—"Were you asleep at any time?" "No." "Did you experience an urge to defecate?" "No." "Were you conscious of any odors?" "Urine." Then Shepard climbed into a dual-engine C1 transport plane that roared off the deck of the *Lake Champlain*, leaving behind the cheering sailors.

Shepard sat up in the cockpit chatting with the pilot. When it looked as if cloud cover would make for a difficult landing at Grand Bahama Island, where Shepard was scheduled for another three days of tests and interrogations, he joked to the pilot that they should divert to Nassau for some liberty.

Shepard drank a cup of coffee on the hundred-mile plane ride and arrived at Grand Bahama giddy and hungry—he'd lost three pounds since breakfast. He was greeted by Gus Grissom, Wally Schirra, and Deke Slayton, who told him, "You pulled it off real good." As Shepard downed a huge shrimp cocktail, a roast beef sandwich, and iced tea, Schirra, knowing that the capsule's periscope was a poor substitute for a window, asked his friend about his breathless report from the heavens.

"So, Alan, what was that 'beautiful view' stuff?"

Shepard laughed. He said he knew that somebody was going to ask him how the earth looked, so he'd had his less-than-poetic one-liner ready from the start. "Shit, I had to say something for the people," he said.

Shepard's $400 million flight had cost "the people"—as in, 180 million Americans—$2.25 apiece. But its success also caused an immediate boost for the stock market, especially among space-age stocks such as IBM and Douglas Aircraft. Wall Street also saw an uptick in distillery and brewery stocks, which the *New York Times* attributed to "the fact that many Americans were toasting the success of the astronaut's feat."

It wasn't even noon yet. But his quarter-hour flight, which took him just 302 miles from the Cape—even Louise called it "just a baby step"—was about to change everything in his life and Louise's.

Doctors reported that despite losing three pounds over the previous ten hours, Shepard was "in the best of shape, in the best health, the best of spirits, and just like he was before he left the Cape—only happier." Then they began probing him, photographing every inch of him, drawing blood, and collecting stool, urine, and semen samples, until Shepard complained of the "unusual number of needles."

"I hope that fewer bodily fluid samples are required in the future," he said.

During another debriefing that afternoon with Walt Williams, an attractive young secretary brought in a tray of coffee, and Williams laughed as he saw "Shepard's brain get up, leave the room, and follow her down the hall."

Thousands of letters and cables from around the world were already on their way. A barrage of reporters were itching for a piece of him. He had always complained about NASA's level of openness with the press and how it sometimes interfered with training. Now reporters would camp out in front of his house and lob questions at his daughters and even their teachers. He thought he had shielded them from the limelight. But he hadn't anticipated becoming a hero.

"This is one of the burdens of a free society," he'd later write.

In time, however, he'd learn how to turn that burden to his advantage.

That night, just past 5 P.M., he called Louise. The connection was full of static, and they had to yell to be heard. He told her about the phone call from "our friend Taz Shepard" and then mentioned his chat with "another friend—Jack Kennedy." Louise laughed, relieved to hear her husband "being himself."

Later the other astronauts and a small group of NASA officials held a small party for Shepard at the base club on Grand Bahama Island. Shepard, Schirra, Shorty Powers, Walt Williams, and a handful of others played darts and drank many glasses of Cuban rum late into the night. Shepard slept soundly that night, with Grissom in the bunk beside him to make sure nothing strange happened to America's spaceman during the night.

The next evening, after another day of tests and interrogations and a brief attempt at fishing for bonefish, Shepard relaxed in a folding chair, sitting beneath the stars while watching a film that was projected against a wall at the base's makeshift outdoor movie theater. He seemed so at ease, happy to be far from the reporters and the politicians he'd soon face. The movie was *The Grass Is Greener,* starring Louise's favorite, Cary Grant.

15

"I believe we should go to the moon"

As they descended toward the White House, a flock of pigeons rose from the ground, an explosion of wing and feather that engulfed the helicopter. Louise gasped and her hand rose to cover her mouth. Shepard just laughed and grabbed her hand. It was a sunny, muggy Washington day. As the Marine pilot guided the helicopter safely through the birds and landed, President Kennedy rushed over to greet Shepard. Jackie Kennedy took Louise by the arm and they walked ahead of the men, looking like sisters.

Joined by his parents and his six astronaut colleagues, Shepard then stood before a small crowd beside the Rose Garden. Kennedy stepped to the dais, thanked Shepard for the "service he has rendered our country," and attempted to award him the Distinguished Service Medal. But the medal slipped and fell to the ground, and the two men nearly bumped heads reaching for it. When Kennedy then handed it to Shepard, he said it "has gone from the ground up," which Shepard thought was a "great line."

After the ceremony, Jackie took Louise, her mother, Shepard's mother, and his sister on a tour of the White House, while

Kennedy took Shepard and the other astronauts into the Oval Office. The president sat in his rocking chair and listened, rapt, to Shepard describe the details of his flight, repeatedly interjecting how "fantastic, just fantastic" he thought it all was.

Shepard pointed out that Kennedy's advisory committee—the "pee-sack" people—had shown a "surprising lack of confidence" in humans' ability to survive weightlessness and that his flight had proved "man can perform effectively in space." Kennedy gushed with questions. His enthusiasm for the space program impressed Shepard, who could tell that Kennedy wasn't nearly as timid as the committee had been. Then Kennedy surprised everyone in the room by hinting at the historic announcement he would soon make.

"We're not about to put you guys on a rocket and send you to the moon," Kennedy said. "We're just thinking about it." The astronauts exchanged looks. They knew a moon launch had been discussed by NASA and that the Russians seemed headed toward the same goal, but they were surprised to learn of Kennedy's interest in the moon. *My God!* Shepard thought, then told Kennedy, "I'm ready."

Then Kennedy had an idea. "Come with me," he said to Shepard. "I want you to meet some friends of mine." He whisked Shepard into his limo for a three-block drive to the convention of the National Association of Broadcasters and introduced "the nation's number one TV performer," which earned Shepard a standing ovation. Shepard felt as if he had become Kennedy's new pet; indeed, Kennedy was blatantly cozying up to the TV people he'd need as allies in the subsequent months of the space race.

In time, Shepard would come to appreciate the good fortune that came with being a personal friend of Jack Kennedy's. And Kennedy, in turn, knew that in 1961 he needed someone exactly like Shepard to teach the nation about courage—someone, as he had written in his book *Profiles in Courage*, willing to "push his skiff from the shore alone."

Later that morning, one of the largest crowds in Washington history jammed Pennsylvania Avenue to get a glimpse of Shepard in the first of many astronaut parades. Alan and Louise rode in a convertible with Vice President Johnson, who was astounded at the parade's turnout. Children had been let out of school and businesses gave workers the day off. "Look at these people," Johnson yelled in Alan's ear. "They love you." Then he offered some avuncular advice: "Shepard, if you're going to be famous, you have to remember two things: Never pass up the opportunity for a free lunch, or to go to the men's room."

Shepard cringed when he saw that they hadn't provided a car for Slayton and Glenn, who tried to hitch a ride in a car full of reporters. The reporters didn't recognize Slayton, didn't believe that he and Glenn were astronauts, and refused to give them a lift until a NASA official intervened.

After the parade Shepard was supposed to attend what he thought would be a quiet reception and luncheon with a few congressmen at the capital. Instead he walked into a "throng-packed, pulsing room of congressional leaders." He tried hard to maintain his nonchalance, but the realization set in quickly that he was now a bona fide celebrity.

New York City began making plans for a ticker tape parade to rival the one given thirty-four years earlier to Shepard's hero, Lindbergh. The *New York Times* had already declared that Shepard's fifteen-minute arc through space "roused the country to one of its highest peaks of exultation since the end of World War II." The Soviet press agency, Tass, belittled the flight as "inferior," and Cuban premier Fidel Castro called it "a desperate effort." But the world knew the communists were now in for a fight. In Chile hundreds had thronged outside newspaper offices awaiting word on his flight. "He's Up There" and "Space Man Friday" blared the headlines in London's papers. An editorial in the *Times* of London exclaimed that Shepard had "exorcised the demon of inferiority that had possessed Americans."

Amid such global hype, the reporters at Shepard's Washington press conference on the afternoon of May 8 were largely respectful of the second man to leave the earth's atmosphere. Early in the hourlong session, a reporter said, "Commander, as a celebrity of whom we are all very proud, no one has yet asked you how you would solve the world's problems." Shepard replied, "I hope they don't."

From that point on, he controlled the reporters like a kindergarten teacher, rewarding them for good questions while chiding or ignoring them for the bad ones. One reporter asked if he had spoken to Louise the night before the flight, and what— "if it's not too personal"—he had said. Shepard responded, "Well . . . it is too personal."

James "Scotty" Reston of the *New York Times* called him a "cool master of the news conference" who "fielded the questions like a pro" and "revived the faith of a sad and disillusioned city." It was an impressive performance for someone who had recently described himself as "neither a statesman nor a politician" but merely "a public servant."

Shepard would never allow his instant fame—or the press—to intrude on his private life. "Becoming a public figure overnight was a little difficult at first," he once said. "I hadn't really expected it, all of a sudden realizing that people wanted autographs, didn't always ask at the right time, they weren't always polite, and they sort of figured we were public property because they were taxpayers." Shepard could occasionally be gracious with strangers seeking his attention or his signature on a napkin. But he could also be acidic and viciously abrupt. One day he and Louise were relaxing on towels draped over the hot Cocoa Beach sand. An autograph seeker approached, and Shepard gave the man such a violent dressing down that a NASA official wrote a letter of apology.

///

Shepard's flight—exactly six months to the day from Kennedy's election—and the nation's euphoric reaction emboldened Kennedy to ask Congress for even more money for the space program. By year's end, the space budget would soar toward $5 billion—ten times more than had been spent during the previous eight years and the equivalent of fifty cents a week for every American. Kennedy acknowledged it was "a staggering sum" but pointed out that it was still less than Americans paid for cigars and cigarettes.

Space, said Kennedy, was "the new ocean," and he was determined that the United States would sail on it "and be in a position second to none." Three weeks after Shepard's flight, he staked his legacy on a promise: to send an American to the moon.

Kennedy gave one of his most historic speeches before a joint session of Congress on May 25. "Now it is time to take longer strides," he urged the country, "time for a great new American enterprise." He acknowledged that space exploration—especially when conducted "in full view of the world"—entailed enormous risks. But, he said, "as shown by the feat of astronaut Shepard, this very risk enhances our stature when we are successful."

Kennedy then asked Congress and the country to commit to sending a man to the moon, "and returning him safely to the Earth," by 1970.

He looked up from his prepared speech and declared, "I believe we should go to the moon," and then asked that "every scientist, every engineer, every serviceman, every technician, contractor, and civil servant give his personal pledge that this nation will move forward, with the full speed of freedom, in the exciting adventure of space."

Kennedy would face harsh criticisms for emphasizing a moon landing ahead of education and other social programs on his priority list. He had admitted in his lengthy speech that he "came to this conclusion with some reluctance" and that all

Americans would have to "bear the burdens" of his costly goal. He knew that committing America's dollars and talents to a moon mission was a risky proposition and among the "most important decisions" of his presidency. But Kennedy believed strongly that a moon program would create jobs (especially in the South and West, which carried the added benefit of yielding political gains and votes), yield technological advances, and—maybe most importantly, in the aftermath of Yuri Gagarin and the Bay of Pigs—boost America's image and morale. As Lyndon Johnson (who headed the National Space Council) had advised him, a successful moon program offered "great propaganda value." Johnson said that, "in the eyes of the world, first in space means first, period. Second in space is second in everything." Kennedy's science adviser, Jerome Wiesner, said years later that Kennedy "became convinced that space was the symbol of the twentieth century. [The moon program] was a decision he made cold-bloodedly."

Kennedy's advisers had told him that because the Soviets had gained the early lead in the space race, one way for the United States to surpass them would be a bold, long-term, and very expensive program aimed at putting a man on the moon. At the current rate of rocket development, it seemed the United States might be able to reach the moon by 1968 or 1969, they told him. But some advisers said the price tag—some $20 to $40 *billion*—would eliminate other space programs in the planning stages, such as the creation of a space station and the exploration of Venus and Mars. Kennedy felt those other programs could wait and that the sole purpose of NASA should be reaching the moon ahead of the Soviets, "to demonstrate that instead of being behind . . . by God, we beat them." Such a brash decision was also consistent with Kennedy's "affinity for heroic causes and the whole spirit of the New Frontier," as one of his biographers put it.

The nation's reaction was at first mixed. A Gallup poll immediately after Kennedy's speech found that just 42 percent of

Americans supported a moon program. Back at Langley, Shepard and the others were thrilled, but wondered aloud, "Is this guy nuts?"

///

Two weeks after Kennedy's historic pledge, Gus Grissom and his *Liberty Bell 7* capsule performed a virtual replica of Shepard's flight—save one near-deadly difference. After Grissom had splashed into the Atlantic, the hatch suddenly blew off the side of his capsule, its explosive bolts sending the door spinning off into the water. With its doorway wide open, the choppy Atlantic began pouring into the capsule, and rather than sink with the can, Grissom dove into the water. A helicopter latched on to the top of *Liberty Bell 7*, but it was quickly filling with water, and the chopper's engines began overheating. Meanwhile, Grissom splashed and waved and yelled to get the attention of a second helicopter's pilot. A valve on the front of his pressure suit, where the oxygen hose had attached, was open and sucking in salt water like a straw. Water began filling the legs of his suit, and he felt himself being pulled under. Frantically he screamed up at the second helicopter, whose pilot was apparently watching the first helicopter release Grissom's capsule, letting it plunge to the ocean floor. Just as Grissom thought his lungs might collapse, he grabbed for the horse collar and was winched up into the helicopter, furious at the pilot—and himself.

Losing a capsule showed the nation what an imperfect science Kennedy had committed them all to, and what a dangerous pairing humans and rockets could be. At the follow-up press conference, Grissom acknowledged that in those waterlogged moments, he had been afraid. In response to a disbelieving reporter, Grissom snapped, "I was scared. All right?" And Grissom would spend the remainder of his life defending himself against claims that he must have blown the hatch himself, by accident. Grissom said no, the damn thing had just blown.

But even in the aftermath of Grissom's tainted flight, Congress agreed to Kennedy's funding requests. Their vote of confidence would be vindicated by the next astronaut flight, but not before a string of troubling delays.

///

For John Glenn, being chosen as number three instead of number one would become a blessing. The unexpected booty of losing his battle to become the first man to blast off from earth was that he'd become the first American to orbit the earth.

Shepard had hoped to gain the first orbital flight for himself. Initially, NASA planned to require each astronaut to complete a suborbital flight like Shepard's before being considered for an orbital flight. That meant Shepard, as the first suborbital astronaut, had also been in line to become the first orbital astronaut. But, ironically, Kennedy's enthusiasm over Shepard's flight inspired NASA to ditch that prerequisite and proceed right from Grissom's flight to the orbit. John Glenn was next in line.

Delay followed delay as Glenn's flight was bumped from December 1961 to January 1962, then February. Some days it was technical, some days it was the weather, but Glenn spent many hours across a half dozen mornings lying anxiously inside his capsule only to have the launch canceled. The delays frustrated Henri Landwirth, too—he had baked a nine-hundred-pound, capsule-shaped cake, and had to rig up an air-conditioned truck so that it wouldn't spoil.

Glenn's luck finally changed the morning of February 20. When he knew there would be no further delays, Glenn called his wife, Annie, who was home with their two kids in Arlington, Virginia. "Don't be scared," Glenn told her. "Remember, I'm just going down to the corner store to get a pack of gum."

Glenn had said in a press conference three years earlier that he wanted to be an astronaut "because it's the nearest to heaven

I'll ever get." But before the day was out, he'd come much closer to heaven than he would have preferred.

"Godspeed," Scott Carpenter radioed his friend as he blasted off from the Cape.

Twelve minutes after liftoff, Glenn and his capsule, *Friendship 7* (named by a Glenn family vote), soared weightlessly above the African coast. He pulled open an equipment pouch, shut tight with a new invention called Velcro, and a little stuffed mouse on a tether floated up toward his face. Glenn knew right away which prankster was responsible. José Jiménez often commiserated with the "leetle mice" NASA sometimes put into test rockets. Stashing one aboard was Shepard's response to the handball sign and centerfold that Glenn had pinned up on the dash of his capsule.

During the first two of the three scheduled orbits around the globe, Glenn transmitted eloquent dispatches as he described beautiful sunsets, brilliant blue bands on the horizon, and mysterious luminescent yellow particles outside his window, which Glenn called "fireflies." (At the time, Glenn withstood some ridicule about his "fireflies"—"What did they say, John?" someone asked—but future flights would determine them to be bits of fuel vapor turned to frost.)

At seventeen thousand miles an hour, Glenn was traveling more than three times faster than Shepard had; he was scheduled to be weightless for more than four hours, compared to Shepard's five minutes. But as Glenn passed behind the earth on his third and final orbit, Shepard got up from his capsule communicator's seat and walked over to flight director Chris Kraft to break some bad news. Another NASA official thought Shepard seemed "numb and in a state of disbelief."

A flashing "segment 51" signal from *Friendship 7* indicated serious trouble ahead. The capsule's blunt end was covered with a thick heat shield capable of withstanding the fiery friction during the capsule's reentry. After reentering the atmosphere, the heat shield would drop a few feet below the base of the capsule, connected by an accordionlike landing bag—a skirt that extended from the capsule's bottom to cushion the impact at sea. A "segment 51" signal meant that the landing bag might already have deployed. Even worse, the signal might mean that the heat shield had come loose.

Shepard told Kraft that he didn't believe the signal. He thought it was a faulty circuit—a mistake. But this wasn't a time to simply hope for the best—he had to be sure. So Shepard radioed one of the engineers and asked the obvious question: "What's going to happen when we cut the retro-pack loose?"

The retro-pack was a canister of small rockets clamped onto the heat shield at the base of the capsule. The purpose of these small rockets was to slow down Glenn's backward-flying capsule, allowing it to drop into the earth's gravitational pull. Once those rockets were fired, the retro-pack was supposed to automatically separate from the capsule and be discarded. If the heat shield wasn't perfectly intact, the engineers feared, the separation of the retro-pack could break the heat shield off completely. However, if the retro-pack was kept against the heat shield during the capsule's reentry instead of being automatically cut loose, it might hold the crucial heat shield in place. Shepard asked question after question—was he *sure?* was he *positive?*—before finally telling the engineer to find the best way to "hold the goddamn thing."

Dozens of engineers and scientists at the Cape, in Houston, and in St. Louis, home of the capsule's maker, McDonnell Aircraft, frantically dove into solving the problem. Shepard and Slayton talked to McDonnell's engineers. NASA's techies pulled out diagrams and blueprints, searching for an explanation. Tension rolled like a sickness across Mission Control—"We were in a state of shock," one top NASA official said later—and within minutes more than a hundred people were working desperately toward a solution. The engineers tossed off their own theories on the cause of the "segment 51." Some agreed with Shepard that it was a faulty signal. But they all agreed that even if the odds were minuscule that Glenn's landing bag had actually deployed and had dislodged the heat shield, it was too risky to allow Glenn to make a normal reentry.

Shepard and Kraft decided not to tell Glenn just yet. There was nothing he could do about it, so why worry him? Instead, they'd try to fix the problem from the ground. Shepard got on the radio and talked to radio operators stationed at various points around the globe, telling them to carefully ask Glenn about his landing bag. Over the Indian Ocean Glenn received the first such message: *Make sure the landing bag switch is in the off position.* He checked. It was. But when Glenn was over Australia they asked again about the landing bag switch, and also if he heard any banging noises. At first Glenn thought they might be concerned about the source of the "fireflies," but as he flew over the South Pacific and they asked once more about the landing bag and whether he'd heard any flapping, a "prickle of suspicion" crawled over him, as he wrote in his memoir.

Meanwhile, Shepard and the crew at Mission Control had settled on a solution, albeit one that was not unanimously supported. Shepard and the others had decided that, if the heat shield was in fact loose, leaving the retro-pack clamped on offered the best chance of keeping the heat shield in place. But it was a dangerous call, because the retro-pack wasn't designed to survive the fiery reentry and was sure to disintegrate once temperatures climbed toward three thousand degrees. And if the heat shield *wasn't* loose, it was possible that burning chunks of the retro-pack could damage the shield or rip it loose.

"We want to be damn sure on this one," Shepard told one NASA technician. "Because if that [landing] bag comes down, it's disastrous, whereas it's not disastrous if we make a reentry with the retros on."

Chris Kraft at one point screamed at an engineer to give

him a straight yes-or-no answer: "Either you give me a decision or I'm going to make one myself."

Finally, while passing over Hawaii, Glenn was told about the "segment 51" signal, and he realized in a split second why they'd been asking about the landing bag. They were afraid the heat shield was loose—and they'd been keeping this information from him for quite some time. As he crossed high above Texas, Glenn began to prepare for reentry, and fired the retro-rockets that began to slow his capsule enough to be pulled down by earth's gravity. Even as Glenn neared the crucial reentry stage, NASA was still arguing about how, exactly, they were going to solve the problem.

After firing the retro-rockets, Glenn prepared for the strapped-on retro-pack to be jettisoned. But now NASA had finally made its decision, and another disturbing message came through Glenn's headset, sent from a radio operator at Corpus Christi, Texas: "We are recommending that you leave the retro package on through the entire reentry.... Do you read?" Now Glenn wanted answers.

"What is the reason for this?" he asked. "Do you have any reason?"

"No," came the response. "Not at this time . . . We are recommending that the retro-package not, I say again, *not* be jettisoned."

Even without an explanation, Glenn knew what was up. He later complained of the "cat-and-mouse game they were playing with the information," but no one needed to tell him he was flying toward a scenario in which he might soon "burn to nothing." With just seconds to reentry, Shepard finally explained what the ground crews had spent the past ninety minutes keeping from Glenn, even though he had figured it out. "We are not sure whether or not your landing bag has deployed," Shepard said. "We feel it is far safer to reenter with the retro-package on. We see no difficulty at this time in that type of reentry. Over."

Out of all the tests on the capsule, leaving on the retro-pack had never been tested. No one had ever envisioned a reason. Leaving it on was, at best, an educated guess. But there was simply no time left to mull it over any longer. Glenn, at the end of three scheduled orbits, was running low on fuel and oxygen. He had to come down.

Flight director Kraft had told Shepard to keep talking, to keep Glenn's mind off his impending doom and focused on smaller tasks within his control. For the next two minutes, Shepard kept up a jargon-filled dialogue, offering small suggestions about how to set the capsule at the best angle for reentry, even giving a weather report. "We recommend that you do the best you can to keep a zero angle during reentry," he said.

Then *Friendship* 7 reached a thick slab of atmosphere and the heat outside the capsule began to rise, which interfered with the radio waves. Glenn would later say that he braced himself for his own incineration. "Every nerve fiber was attuned to the heat along my spine; I kept wondering, 'Is that it? Do I feel it?'" Meanwhile, Scott Carpenter got on the phone to Glenn's wife, Annie, to tell her about the heat shield. He might not make it back, Carpenter warned.

The radio transmissions began to buzz and crackle. Shepard tried to give Glenn one last message, detailing a slight change in the plan: to jettison the retro-pack once the G forces built to 1.5. The engineers had decided that 1.5 Gs of external pressure would hold the heat shield in place, even if it was loose, making it safe to jettison the retro-package.

"We recommend that you . . . ," Shepard began, but that was all Glenn heard; the rest of the message was garbled by static.

"Cape," Glenn said. "You're . . . you are going out. . . ."

An eerie quiet filled Mission Control, where many wondered if they had just heard John Glenn's final words. All they could do now was wait.

Precisely four minutes and twenty-three seconds later—the point at which Glenn should have emerged from the near side of the atmosphere and back into radio transmission range—Shepard began calling him. "*Friendship Seven*, this is Cape. Do you read? *Seven*, this is Cape do you read? Over. *Friendship Seven*, this is Cape. Do you read? Over."

Shepard stared straight ahead, waiting for Glenn's voice. One of the officials behind him—he couldn't tell who—said, "Keep talking, Al." So Shepard tried one more time: "*Seven*, this is Cape. How do you read? Over."

A few seconds later a crackle of static broke through, and a moment later Glenn's voice burst across the airwaves.

"Loud and clear—how me?"

Mission Control erupted in celebration. Shepard's grim face exploded into a grin and he instinctively jerked his arm high to give those standing behind him a thumbs-up. "Reading you loud and clear," he said. "How do you feel?"

"Oh, pretty good," Glenn said.

"What is your general condition? Are you feeling pretty well?"

"My condition is good," said Glenn. "But that was a real fireball, boy. I had great chunks of that retro-pack breaking off all the way through."

Glenn's flight—each moment of which was broadcast live on television—had finally pulled the United States alongside the Russians in the space race. The previous summer, a few weeks after Gus Grissom's flight, the Soviets had sent their second cosmonaut, Gherman Titov, into space for a seventeen-orbit flight. But now, with Glenn's flight, the United States had edged ahead: three astronauts versus two cosmonauts.

///

Glenn became the new astronaut poster boy. But among astronauts themselves, and more widely inside NASA, Shepard still ranked as the elder statesman. And, as was the case during the crucial moments of Glenn's flight, his voice carried weight.

His informal ranking atop the astronaut hierarchy wouldn't last much longer, though. He needed another flight. He was *aching* for another flight. A real flight. *Orbital.* First, though, Scott Carpenter would get his shot. His would be the third of the nail-biting dramas that NASA endured after Shepard's flight.

///

Carpenter's wife, Rene (pronounced "reen"), was making a name for herself as the most outspoken of the seven wives. Unlike Louise, who spoke only of success and trust in her husband and faith in God and NASA, Rene made no pretense about the deadly, imperfect business her husband had joined. She told one reporter that she'd been with seventeen pilots' wives in the first hour after their husbands' death. She also made no illusions about where she stood in her husband's life. His flying and career came first. "It's always been orders first, women and children last," she told reporters.

If Rene broke the mold of the accommodating Navy/astro-wife, Carpenter broke some molds himself. On May 24, 1962, he became the sixth human and the fourth American into space, but immediately became so fascinated by Glenn's "fireflies," the stars above, and the sheer beauty of it all that he started expending too much fuel by twisting his *Aurora 7* capsule this way and that to get a better view.

After the first of Carpenter's three scheduled orbits, NASA communicators began warning him to conserve his three gallons of fuel by switching to automatic pilot. After two orbits, engineers considered cutting the flight short because of how low the fuel had gotten. Shepard, serving as the capsule communicator in California, tried to keep Carpenter focused, telling him that NASA chiefs were getting "somewhat concerned about auto fuel" and advising him calmly to use as little fuel as possible during his final orbit. But Carpenter couldn't help himself. He'd admit later that his mind switched from that of an engineer to that of an awestruck traveler, focused more on his view of the world out-side than the dials and switches on the control board.

The capsule carried two supplies of fuel, one for manual steering and one for the "automatic stabilization and control system," called ASCS. Just prior to reentry, Carpenter switched to ASCS, which normally guides the capsule during reentry. But when he did so, he forgot to turn off the manual control system, and it continued to spew fuel. Then he discovered that the ASCS, which had acted strange earlier in the flight, wasn't working properly. "ASCS is bad," he radioed to Shepard, announcing that he would have to reenter the atmosphere using manual control, whose fuel tanks were almost dry.

Reentering the atmosphere on manual control required precision flying and timing. To help with the timing, Shepard counted backwards from ten, to give Carpenter the exact moment at which to initiate a computer program that would prepare the capsule for reentry. He also made what Carpenter later called "crucial observations"—advising him to retract his periscope, reminding him to check his reentry angle, keeping him apprised of the time—that likely saved Carpenter's life. Shepard also reminded Carpenter that to override the automatic system and use manual control during reentry, he'd have to switch to "attitude bypass and manual override."

"Roger," Carpenter said, but when he fired his retro-rockets above California, he did so three seconds late, and NASA knew the capsule would now be far off course. Then Carpenter told Shepard that his automatic fuel supply was down to about 20 percent, and his manual fuel tank was almost empty, at about 5 percent. Shepard told him to try to quickly align the capsule to the correct angle or "attitude" for reentry before the fuel ran out. But by the time Carpenter tried to adjust his capsule, his manual fuel tank was dry.

"I'm out of manual fuel, Al," he confessed. Not good. If he couldn't get the capsule aligned at the right angle for reentry, at

34 degrees, he'd skip off the atmosphere and back out into space, where he and *Aurora 7* would tumble for eternity. Or burn up.

Shepard adjusted his seat and headset and continued talking Carpenter through the next critical steps. Speaking in a calm voice, not letting any change of pitch betray his concern, he told Carpenter to line up the capsule using what was left of the automatic fuel supply—a procedure called "fly-by-wire," which allows an astronaut to manually control the capsule using fuel from the ASCS tanks.

"Take your time on fly-by-wire to get into reentry attitude," Shepard cautioned. Less than a minute later he checked in again to make sure Carpenter had lined up the capsule properly. "How are you doing on reentry attitude?" Shepard asked.

"Stowing a few things first," Carpenter said. "I don't know yet. Take a while."

Tense as the situation was, Carpenter seemed almost oblivious to the dangers he faced. Landing many miles off course, far from the recovery ships, was dangerous enough; failure to reenter was an astronaut's worst nightmare. Carpenter had to stow a few pieces of equipment that should have already been stowed. Then he even took time to sneak a few more peeks out the window, commenting on the view: "I can make out very, very small farmland, pastureland below. . . . I see individual fields, rivers, lakes, roads." To those on the ground, the failure to focus bordered on the bizarre.

Then, as if snapped back into realization, he reported to Shepard, "I'll get back to reentry attitude." Shepard's final message was firm but calm: "Recommend you get close to reentry attitude, using as little fuel as possible."

Four minutes later Carpenter entered the radio blackout zone, in which the intense heat of the capsule's plunge through the atmosphere blocks out all radio signals. NASA command didn't know whether the capsule had begun reentry at the correct angle or not. At the end of those long and painful minutes,

Carpenter's voice should have come bursting through loud and clear, just as Glenn's had. Instead, for five minutes, then ten, then fifteen, there was only silence. In those horribly long, taut moments, every criticism, every fear, every warning about the dangers of the space game seemed to be coming true.

Gordo Cooper, seated at a Mission Control console, pushed back in his chair and buried his head in his hands. Walter Cronkite, reporting for CBS, also began to choke up. Unsuccessfully fighting back his own tears, he told his audience, "We . . . may have . . . lost an astronaut." Rene Carpenter, watching Cronkite in the company of a *Life* magazine reporter and photographer, smiled bravely, giving away nothing as they snapped her picture. The TV-watching public assumed Scott Carpenter was gone.

It would take forty minutes for a Marine helicopter to finally track down Carpenter's capsule. They found him floating happily in a life raft beside *Aurora*, 250 miles from where he was supposed to have landed. It took another hour for word to reach the Cape—and then Carpenter's wife, and then the nation—that Carpenter had not perished after all.

If he was aware of the many mistakes he'd made and how close he'd come to oblivion, Carpenter never showed it publicly. Some NASA officials were infuriated that he never seemed repentant about his lapses. But for him, flying around the earth had been "a religious experience . . . the chance to see the inner workings of the grand order of things." Years later Carpenter said, "It felt as though I were watching myself, with fascination and curiosity, to see how my great adventure might turn out."

Others had a different take. Cooper said bluntly: "Scott knew he had screwed up." And flight director Kraft was livid. Astronauts weren't supposed to have religious experiences. They were supposed to follow rules and perform with exactitude. Kraft vowed that day that the "son of a bitch" would never fly for him again.

And Carpenter never would.

Kraft had other thoughts about Shepard, whom he credited with saving Scott Carpenter's life. "Anyplace you put Alan Shepard he was going to do a perfect job," Kraft said years later. "He was calm under stressful conditions. . . . If he hadn't been there, I'm not sure Scott would have gotten down."

In his unpublished memoirs, operations director Walt Williams wrote that Shepard "was worth his weight in gold on this flight," adding, "that was typical of Al—to be the father of the situation."

But as well respected as Shepard had become, he was about to be eclipsed by a new generation of astronauts, a younger breed that would fly higher, farther, and faster.

16

"I'm sick . . . should I just
hang it up?"

As NASA continued developing its massive new headquarters in Houston, the space agency was on its way to becoming one of the world's biggest corporations and among the largest government-funded programs in history. Following Wally Schirra's flight, scheduled for the fall of 1962, and Gordo Cooper's flight, scheduled for the following year, Project Mercury was over, and most of NASA's energies and money had already turned toward developing the men, the rockets, and the capsules for Project Gemini and Project Apollo. NASA now employed tens of thousands of people, either directly (at one of half a dozen satellite operations) or through its many subcontractors, with nearly five thousand workers based in Houston alone.

The next step in the space race was Project Gemini. In a series of launches with two-man capsules, astronauts would test feats that would be crucial for a trip to the moon, such as space walks and orbital docking (linking together two orbiting spacecraft).

The candidates for Project Gemini were told to enter the stately Rice Hotel in downtown Houston, passing beneath its ugly, menacing gargoyles, and check in under a false name. In fact, all the candidates were told to use the same fake name, and in late 1962 dozens of nervous men named Max Peck arrived at the Rice Hotel for one of the toughest interviews of their life.

Shepard sat on the interviewing board and quickly let the younger upstarts know he was their superior, that he *owned* them. His eyes drilled into each man. If they tried a joke, he refused to crack a smile. His questions were terse and, at times, combative.

At the end of an otherwise genial interview, Shepard would be the one to pull out a sheet of paper and ask, "In July of 1961 you were reported driving an unregistered car in Massachusetts—can you explain this?" He might have a drink with an astronaut candidate at the hotel barroom, the Old Capital Club. But in the interview room he'd act like a cold, hard stranger. And when he later called to tell a candidate he'd been selected, he wanted a black-and-white response. One of those selected told Shepard he was "99 percent sure" he'd say yes, which Shepard said was an unacceptable answer.

Once they were chosen—men like Neil Armstrong, Pete Conrad, Jim Lovell, and Frank Borman—the next astronauts would come to understand Shepard's attitude. NASA could only build so many rockets and schedule so many flights. Any newcomer was seen as a threat, a competitor. As the number of astronauts grew in subsequent years, so did the intrigue: rooting for your friends to fail, scheming to get ahead, always on guard against some form of political sabotage. Shepard was considered a master of the nasty game called "astro-politics." Many, however, wouldn't realize for years—not until they had finally retired from NASA—how driven they were by the competition with their peers. Shepard, though, never seemed to tire of the competition. He was shrewd, intuitive. Even those who disliked him respected his "sophistication." "His technique was flawless," one astronaut said.

Shepard eased up a fair bit when the first interviews for the Gemini program were completed and the group of candidates had been whittled down to nine potential new astronauts. One day he ushered them into their final physical and psychological tests—similar but less intense versions of the ghoulish testing he had withstood in 1959—and gave them all a piece of advice. "Now, for Pete's sake, don't show any feminine attributes," he said as they gathered outside the doctors' offices. "You've got to be *masculine.*" Some of them heeded the advice and on their inkblot tests told doctors the splashes of ink resembled "a woman's breast" or "a pair of legs."

Shepard couldn't have imagined it at the time, but seven of the "Next Nine" (as they'd call themselves) would soon cumulatively spend hundreds of hours in space. Each of those seven would easily dwarf Shepard's fifteen minutes of space time, and the only two in the group who wouldn't surpass Shepard would instead die a fiery death.

To Shepard, these new guys were now the enemy. At a press conference to introduce the Next Nine, Shorty Powers—in one of his final acts as the astro-spokesman—began by first introducing the Mercury Seven, in reverse chronological order, with a brief description of each of their flights. "And finally," he said, "this is Alan Shepard, the man who's been saying for years, 'But I was first.'" Everyone in the room laughed. Except Shepard, who aimed his hard blue eyes right at Shorty without cracking even a grin.

That same fall of 1962, Kennedy—having recently managed the tense head game of the Cuban missile crisis—turned his attention back to the space race and visited NASA's new Houston digs. Shepard and Slayton gave him a tour of the Manned Spacecraft Center, which was still under construction, letting him sit in the cockpit of a spacecraft simulator and play with the controls. Then, before fifty thousand people at Rice University's football stadium, Kennedy summed up how far he felt the country had traveled in the year and a half since Shepard's *Freedom 7,* delivering one of his more famous speeches. "This country was conquered by those who moved forward—and so will space," he said. Then he quoted one of Shepard's ancestors, William Bradford, who helped found and later governed the Plymouth Bay Colony. Bradford had said that "all great and honorable actions are accompanied with great difficulties." Kennedy put his own stamp on that thought.

"But why, some say, the moon?" he said. "Why choose this as our goal? And they may well ask why climb the highest mountain? Why, thirty-five years ago, fly the Atlantic? We choose to go to the moon. . . . We choose to go to the moon in this decade and do the other things, not because they are easy, but because they are *hard*."

Finally, he highlighted the challenge ahead, cautioning that to make a 240,000-mile trip to the moon in a rocket as long as a football field, traveling at speeds above twenty-five thousand miles an hour, reaching temperatures half that of the sun—"almost as hot as it is here today"—and do it before 1970, "then we must be bold."

The plans were bold indeed. Already in the works was another program that would succeed Gemini, a series of trips to the moon called Project Apollo.

NASA planned to conduct at least ten Gemini flights, which meant that Shepard and his Mercury Seven peers would get the chance to fly again, competing with the Next Nine. Shepard had already begun lobbying for the first Gemini flight, and by the end of 1962 his chances looked strong. But the first Gemini flight was at least two years away, and he started to feel that he couldn't wait that long. The only earlier flight was the final Project Mercury mission, Gordon Cooper's orbital flight, scheduled for mid-1963. *That* was the flight Shepard decided he wanted. And if he couldn't get that flight, he'd try to convince NASA—hell, he'd try to convince Kennedy himself—that America needed one more Mercury flight.

If only he could ignore the terrible ringing in his ears that had started up lately, accompanied by dizziness and nausea.

Some mornings he awoke to find himself disoriented, the room spinning like a jet fighter in a tail spin. He'd reach for the wall, but it would roll out of reach and he'd land on the floor in a heap.

///

The first episode of this strange affliction had actually struck years earlier, just a few months after his selection for the Mercury Seven. Shepard and his father and one of his Navy buddies, Bill Chaires, who had been his roommate on the USS *Franklin D. Roosevelt* back in 1949, were playing golf at a Virginia Beach course. As the threesome warmed up at the first tee, Shepard complained about feeling light-headed. Each time he tried to swing the club, he felt as if he was going to topple over—he was dizzy, and his equilibrium seemed off. They decided to play anyway, but Shepard was shanking and slicing his shots all over the course. After two holes Shepard decided he couldn't play anymore. He told Chaires to keep quiet about the whole thing, which he did—for more than forty years. "I'm sure if NASA had found out, he would not have become an astronaut," said Chaires.

Shepard didn't experience another dizzy spell for a few years after that (or if he did, he kept very quiet about it). But in 1963 the episodes started up again. They usually struck in the morning, when he rose from bed. Perhaps these episodes of intense, debilitating dizziness—which felt as if the earth's gravity had abandoned him, as if he were tumbling through space—spurred Shepard's determination to take over Gordo Cooper's flight. Right up to the final hours, Shepard, who was Cooper's backup pilot, was snapping at Cooper's heels, barking for a chance to ride in his friend's stead. Cooper later said he was reminded then that there were two sides to Alan Shepard: a smiling José Jiménez one day and the next a man "so competitive as to be ruthless."

///

If the list of requisite astronaut traits included braggadocio, excessive competitiveness, hardheadedness, and masculinity with a capital *M*, Gordon Cooper—like Scott Carpenter, in some ways—worked off a different list. Thin, soft-spoken, and gentle, Cooper hailed from Shawnee, Oklahoma—the smallest of the small towns that produced the Mercury Seven. He could be funny and sly and was successful with his share of female astrogroupies. But Cooper was far more laid back than his peers. He trusted NASA to do the right thing and didn't lobby or politick like the others. His trust was such that he named his capsule *Faith 7*, symbolizing, he explained, his faith in NASA, in his rocket, in himself, and in God. NASA cringed at the moniker, envisioning some embarrassing headlines—"NASA Loses *Faith*."

As the days ticked down to the May 1963 launch, Shepard lobbied furiously to take Cooper's place. The story was covered up at the time, and in subsequent decades only a few would know how close Cooper came to losing his flight.

NASA knew Cooper was an excellent pilot, but he had never seemed to train as hard as the others. And despite his love of fast cars and fast planes, his laid-back attitude and laconic Oklahoma twang struck some NASA officials as lazy. As the launch approached, some of them began wondering if Cooper was up to the task. They didn't want another sloppy flight like Scott Carpenter's.

Operations director Walt Williams, NASA's number three guy, a stern and hardworking man, had always considered Cooper "a funny little guy"—meaning he didn't quite understand him. A few months before the flight Williams told Shepard that his faith in Cooper was shaky and there was a strong chance he might ask Shepard to fly instead. Shepard immediately latched on to the idea and began selling himself for the job. Deke Slayton joined the discussions, arguing that it was Cooper's flight. Others piped up, claiming that it would look bad if NASA replaced Cooper so close to the flight.

Finally, on a flight from Houston to Los Angeles, Williams broke the news to Shepard: They'd decided to stick with Cooper. Shepard's eyes bored in on Williams with that intense, unflinching stare of his, but then Shepard broke the tense silence. "Well, you know I could do a better job," was all he said. Williams acknowledged that was "probably the case" but said the decision had been made. And he was counting on Shepard, as Cooper's backup, to work with him and make sure Cooper would be absolutely prepared. "Bring him up to where he would do as good a job as you," Williams said.

Williams tried to temper the situation with a half promise. NASA was fighting to add one last Mercury flight after Cooper's— a test of endurance that might last three or four days. There was "no question" it'd be Shepard's flight if he wanted it, Williams said. "Okay, if that's the answer, I'll do it," Shepard told him. That wasn't the end of it, though. Shepard would get one last chance to snag Cooper's flight for himself. But first Shepard would exact a small slice of revenge on Williams.

One day during a simulation for Cooper's flight, Williams was called away from the Cape to a luncheon and press conference at Cocoa Beach. Williams had gotten a ride to work that morning and didn't have any way to reach the press conference. Shepard tossed him the keys to his Corvette and told him to keep it for the day and return it that night. As Williams sped off the base, Shepard picked up the phone and called security. "This is astronaut Alan Shepard," he said. "Some son of a bitch just stole my Corvette and is heading for the south gate."

According to Williams' unpublished memoirs, the police never stopped him, and he went fishing after lunch and brought the Corvette back late that afternoon. But when he learned that Shepard had tried to have him arrested, he decided to return the gotcha by having an engineer rig a small explosive to the

Corvette's ignition. The explosive didn't detonate, but smoke from the fuse damaged two of the car's eight spark plugs.

"Did the car seem to run rough?" Shepard asked Williams the next day.

"Oh, no," Williams said. "It seemed to be running all right to me."

"Well, it's sure running rough," Shepard said, his eyes spotlighting into Williams'. Shepard later opened the hood and found Williams' failed pyrotechnics.

///

The morning before his launch Cooper learned that a small adjustment had been made to his pressure suit. Technicians had cut into it to insert a new medical probe. He felt that the last-minute alteration had violated an unwritten rule against modifying suits that had been custom-made for each astronaut. "What if the new fitting leaked?" Cooper said later. He was angry that no one had consulted with him and in a very uncharacteristic display of frustration hopped into an F-106 jet and began looping and rolling above the Cape. Then, to be sure NASA really knew what he thought of their suit adjustment, he took the supersonic jet down for an unauthorized and *very* low flyover.

Roaring past *Faith* 7 and down atop Hangar S and the NASA complex, Cooper scared the juice out of a number of NASA officials—Walt Williams among them. He flew so low that Williams, from his second-floor office in the NASA administration building, looked *down* on the passing jet. Williams dropped a stack of papers and grabbed his throat, presumably to keep his heart from leaping out of it. The Cape was restricted airspace, and the switchboard immediately lit up with frantic calls. Cooper had hoped to get away with the stunt, but it didn't take long for NASA to track down who'd recently checked out one of its F-106 jets.

With all the reservations he already had about Cooper, Walt Williams was the wrong guy to scare. When he learned the flat-hatter was Cooper, he screamed that he wanted his "ass on a plate" and immediately called Shepard.

"Is your suit ready?"

"Of course my suit's ready," Shepard said.

Williams said he was pulling Cooper off the flight and that Shepard would replace him the next morning. It would be a day-long mission—the longest to date. Shepard, who was somewhat familiar with low flyovers, told Williams it was the right decision. He felt that Cooper "showed unusually bad judgment" flying so low. (Actually, it wasn't the height Shepard thought was dumb; it was buzzing the administration building.)

A flurry of phone calls followed, with Slayton taking the lead in Cooper's camp. The other five astronauts backed Cooper, too. But Williams spent the entire day refusing to give in. Finally, at 10 P.M.—less than twelve hours before blastoff—he relented and gave Cooper back his flight. Four hours later, after a preflight breakfast with Cooper, Shepard—in response to the emotional turbulence of the countdown to Cooper's flight—indulged in some mischief.

Shorty Powers had arrived with two cameramen who were trying to set up their gear to film some behind-the-scenes footage of Cooper. They found that none of the overhead lights was working and none of the electrical outlets had power. It took Shorty fifteen minutes to discover that someone—apparently someone with too much time and energy on his hands—had cut the wires to the electrical outlets, removed all the overhead light-bulbs, put thick tape into the sockets, and then replaced the bulbs. Shorty also noticed that Shepard seemed to be hovering around, wearing "a grin that is typical of him when he has a mouse under his hat." Shepard never admitted to being the culprit, but Shorty knew one of Shepard's gotchas when he saw one.

He even admitted the gag was a fairly creative "tension reliever," although maybe a little mean-spirited.

///

At dawn Cooper climbed into his capsule. On the seat he found a suction-cup pump called a "plumber's friend." Etched into the metal handle was an inscription: "Remove before launch." It was a small gift from Shepard, a joke about the new urine-collection system they'd placed in Cooper's capsule, a system that would allow him to urinate without having to void into his suit and become a "wetback" the way Shepard had.

Finally Shepard took his seat at Mission Control, and as Cooper blasted off and entered the first of a scheduled twenty-two orbits, Shepard radioed Cooper, telling him "everything looks beautiful." And for the first twenty orbits, the flight was beautiful. At one point, as Cooper passed above Cape Canaveral, he reported to Shepard that he was using very little oxygen (which he'd later attribute to being one of the few nonsmoking astronauts), and Shepard joked that he could "stop holding your breath and use some oxygen if you like." The flight was going so smoothly, Shepard had no instructions for his colleague. "You son of a gun, I haven't got anything to talk about," Shepard said. "We'll let you have some quiet time. Have a good ball."

Cooper then ate a brownie, fruitcake, and some bacon, followed by the first nap in space. He transmitted the first TV images of the earth, pictures so clear that Shepard radioed he could see the fly on Cooper's nose. In a dig at the psychologists who once fretted about astronauts experiencing "separation anxiety"—a psychotic wish to stay in space forever—Cooper reported that he was "thinking very much about returning to earth." He then whispered a touching prayer into his microphone: "Father, we thank you, especially for letting me fly this flight. Thank you for the privilege of being able to be in this position, to be in this wondrous place, seeing all these many startling, wonderful things that you have created."

But despite the prayer, his flight soon devolved into a mess.

During his sixteenth orbit, after a full day in space, a green light on the control panel that measured the earth's gravitational pull blinked on, indicating that Cooper was reentering the earth's atmosphere, which he was not. Mission Control expressed its alarm that Cooper had prematurely begun the reentry procedure. "Like hell," Cooper responded.

While Mission Control searched for an explanation for the light that had blinked on, other systems began malfunctioning, one after the other. First, Mission Control reported that Cooper's telemetry—the data electronically relayed from his capsule back to earth, which showed the position and speed of his capsule on Mission Control computer screens—was blinking on and off their screens. Mission Control sent instructions for Cooper to try flipping switches and resetting the computer system, but then an electrical inverter short-circuited, killing power to the automated control system that would guide him back through the atmosphere. He would now have to steer the capsule home manually, just as Scott Carpenter had, with near-deadly results.

Moments later the cooling system bit the dust, causing temperatures and—more dangerously—carbon dioxide levels to rise. Because the cooling system also filtered out the carbon dioxide of Cooper's exhaled breath, those gases would begin to fill the capsule and in no time could cause Cooper to black out.

Next, the gyroscopes, which helped control the angle of the capsule, went dead. Seconds later his clock stopped—no small matter on a space flight in which every maneuver is timed down to the second. Little by little his capsule was dying, but Cooper remained calm. "Well, things are beginning to stack up a little," he said in his laconic Okie drawl, and then listed all the potentially fatal problems in his wounded capsule, including the fact that the carbon dioxide level had already risen to the maximum. "Other than that, things are fine."

Finally Mission Control determined what was happening: a total power failure. The only thing to do was bring Cooper home as quickly as possible, but no previous astronaut had reentered the atmosphere with such a disabled capsule. Without his automatic control system, he would have to reenter using manual controls. But without his gyroscope and clock, he would have no electronic information telling him whether he was lined up at the correct angle. He would have to use the earth's horizon to align himself, by looking out his window and using a horizontal line etched across it. Once he had the capsule lined up horizontally, he would use a star in the distant sky to align the capsule vertically. It was the spaceman's equivalent of a dead-stick landing on an aircraft carrier, except Cooper was surrounded by poisonous gas, with the temperature in his pressure suit now at 110 degrees, traveling seventeen thousand miles an hour in a dying capsule. Cooper was about to prove the astronauts' argument that the best people for such dangerous missions were steely, highly skilled test pilots.

John Glenn kept Cooper apprised of the exact time, and Cooper used the second hand on his wristwatch to count down to the precise moment for firing his retro-rockets. After the rockets fired, Cooper twitched his hand control slightly, back and forth, front to back, to keep the capsule stable and aligned at the right angle. Glenn, stationed on a ship in the Pacific, asked Cooper about the capsule's attitude, and Cooper reported that it was "right on the old gazoo."

Cooper managed to keep his cool and manually fly the capsule through the atmosphere, keeping it aligned at the required 34-degree angle. Because of the damaged electronics system, he had to reach up and pull the parachute's toggles himself and moments later splashed safely into the ocean. Incredibly, he landed only four miles from the USS *Kearsage*—the closest any astronaut had ever landed to the recovery ship.

The problem, they learned later, had been Cooper's piss. He had taken many sips of water during the flight; Shepard had once asked if he passed any urine, and Cooper responded, "Boy, did I ever!" But at some point late in the flight the urine collection system sprang a leak. Blobs of urine floated up behind the capsule's control panel and little by little short-circuited the electronics.

Walt Williams—"my nemesis," Cooper had called him— was waiting for him when a helicopter delivered Cooper to Hawaii. "Gordo," Williams said as he shook his hand. "You *were* the right guy for the mission." But it would not be the last time NASA would have to decide between Gordon Cooper and Alan Shepard.

///

Following Cooper's flight, the astronauts were invited once again to the White House. It was another morning of ceremony, with Cooper parading through Washington's streets, meeting with congressmen, and receiving a medal from President Kennedy. During the White House ceremony Jackie Kennedy pulled Louise aside and asked if she and the other wives had any plans that night. "Why don't you all drop by for cocktails this evening, since you're in town," the First Lady said.

The president invited the astronauts, too. That night Shepard—drink in hand, man to man—would take his quest for another space flight to the highest authority in the land.

During Cooper's flight, NASA's new administrator, Jim Webb, had announced that Cooper's would be the last of the Mercury flights—even though many NASA engineers were hoping to launch one of the three Atlas rockets they had left. That was Shepard's hope, too, and before going to the White House that night, Shepard stopped by Webb's house in suburban Washington to argue his case.

Shepard's idea was to set a new record, an endurance flight to leap far ahead of the Russians and impress the nation with

NASA's ability to keep an astronaut in space for more than a day. Shepard knew it was blatant politicking, but it might be his last chance for a flight anytime soon. "You know, Mr. Webb, we could put this baby up there in just a matter of weeks. It's all ready to go," Shepard explained in Webb's living room. "Just let me sit up there and see how long it will last. Get another record out of it."

Webb listened but said no. He felt that Project Mercury had run its course. He was anxious to move on. Shepard then told Webb that he'd be seeing his friend the president in a few hours and he'd like to mention his idea for another Mercury flight. Well, Webb said, at least "tell him my side of the story, too." Shepard agreed.

After a few drinks—Shepard called it "getting some of our taxpayers' money back by drinking at the White House"—Shepard saw an opening to corner Kennedy and explain his plan. "Maybe two, maybe three days," he said, adding that it would be one way of jumping ahead of the Russians. Kennedy listened, feigning interest—especially in the beat-the-Russians part.

In recent discussions with advisers Kennedy had revealed his all-out obsession with reaching the moon, even if it came at the expense of other space-related projects. A few months earlier the Russians had launched two spacecraft, two days apart, each carrying two cosmonauts, including the first woman in space. Then the two spacecraft pulled within a few miles of each other—an orbital rendezvous of sorts, a maneuver at least three years away for the United States. The feat clearly gave the Russians the edge. Kennedy, it turned out, had little interest in another puny Mercury flight. His sole concern in the space race was now landing the first man on the moon. "I think everything that we do ought to really be tied to getting onto the moon ahead of the Russians," Kennedy had told Jim Webb in a tense meeting at the White House.

Still, the president listened to Shepard's pitch, finally asking, "What does Mr. Webb think?" Shepard had to confess that

Webb opposed the idea. Kennedy thought a few moments more, then said, "I think we'll have to go along with Mr. Webb." And that was it. The president thanked Shepard for his thoughts and walked away.

///

But there was a consolation prize for not getting another Mercury flight. Deke Slayton had become head of the astronaut office, and among his duties was selecting the flight crews. He had decided—with NASA's blessing—that the best man to kick off Project Gemini was the same man who had kicked off Project Mercury.

In late 1963 Shepard was chosen to command the first Gemini flight, paired with Tom Stafford, who had established himself as one of the leaders of the Next Nine. Their mission, following two unmanned Gemini launches, would be a five-hour flight designed to test the maneuverability of the newer, larger, more sophisticated Gemini capsule. The flight would focus on having the astronauts use the control system to alter the orbit of their capsule—from, say, 100 miles above earth to 140 miles—which would become a crucial part of all future flights. Plans for Project Apollo—still on the drawing board, and often hotly debated—included launching two separate capsules atop a rocket, separating them, and then docking them back together while they orbited the earth, just as the Russians had done. Project Gemini would be a series of warm-up sessions for such tricky maneuvers.

For Shepard, one benefit of being chosen for the first Gemini flight was that it set a precedent and put him—theoretically, at least—in line for the first Apollo flight as well. Furthermore, he was nicely poised for a shot at the moon. NASA had begun indicating a preference to have the crew of the first lunar landing include one of the Mercury Seven, which had now dwindled to four men. Glenn had retired to pursue politics, Slayton was sidelined with a heart murmur, and in 1964 Carpenter broke his arm in a motorcycle accident and was taken off the flight rotation (he would retire in 1967). With that possibility deep in the back of his mind, Shepard threw himself into Gemini training, which included many hours crammed into a training capsule. Shepard loved the two-seater Gemini capsule, which looked and felt like a snug little sports car. He and Stafford—a Naval Academy graduate who had transferred to the Air Force—hit it off well. But not so well that Shepard trusted his new partner with his little secret.

Shepard had been trying—as all Christian Scientists do—to take care of his dizzy spells by himself. But he finally began visiting a private doctor, who prescribed medication (such as diuretics) and vitamins (such as niacin) that he hoped would do the trick. Meanwhile, for Project Apollo, NASA needed more astronauts, and by late 1963 another group of Max Pecks faced Shepard's glaring eyes in the interview room at Houston's Rice Hotel. Many of the candidates assumed that Shepard's sole job on the committee was to be the bulldog, to ask the difficult questions and in so doing to weed out the weak.

Despite the intense efforts of Kennedy's brother, Attorney General Bobby Kennedy, the next group would not include an African-American or a female astronaut, even though the Russians had already launched a woman into space. NASA officials still valued scientific considerations above any social statements they might make. So for now Shepard's colleagues would continue to be all white, all male, and mostly military—just as they had been for twenty years. They were men who had watched on TV in 1961 more than two years earlier as Alan Shepard rose from the launch pad, thinking, *What a lucky son of a bitch.*

Fourteen new astronauts were chosen that fall of 1963, and as with the Next Nine, most were destined for lengthy, complicated space flights that would make Shepard's *Freedom* 7 look like a high school science project. Just like the Next Nine, the only men among the next fourteen who would not shame Shepard's space resume would die horrific deaths.

As the astronaut ranks grew, a hierarchical law emerged: You weren't an astronaut until you flew in space. Until then you were just a "candidate." So while Shepard was technically a legit astronaut, his competitor-peers sometimes reminded him that he'd flown the shortest space flight in history. Slayton once joked that the only astronaut to fly less than Shepard was Slayton, who remained grounded by his heart murmur.

Despite Shepard's limited space time, many of the new astronauts respected him, even feared him. The twenty-two new guys were competitive, headstrong men but not above aspiring to mimic a hero such as Shepard. Some bought Corvettes. Some dressed like Shepard or wore their hair like him. In their eyes, he was everything an astronaut was supposed to be. He didn't have to try hard; he just oozed style and sophistication. One astronaut called it his "oh-so-cool number-one leader shtick," and said Shepard "epitomized cool—the sixties-style 'swinger' then coming into vogue."

///

As NASA continued to build its new headquarters south of Houston, beside Clear Lake (which was neither clear nor a lake), most of the astronaut families settled ten miles further south in a small Quaker-founded village called Friendswood. Texas had welcomed NASA with wide-open arms. A housing developer offered astronauts and their families free homes in his development. Car dealers tripped over each other to sell cars to the astronauts at low interest rates. The Chamber of Commerce held a welcoming parade. Bankers shook their hands. Everyone wanted a piece.

Many of the families built new homes in the east Texas soil known as "gumbo," a mix of mud, clay, sand, and crushed oyster shells. But neither Louise nor Alan had a taste for the muddy, swampy bayfront communities south of Houston, with their cement-hard beaches and brown, frothy waters. Louise preferred the shops, nice restaurants, and rough-edged sophistication of Houston to the astro club down in Friendswood. So they settled in a high-rise luxury apartment building downtown.

It was not an easy transition for Louise. She had grown to love Virginia Beach. And after her distasteful sojourn in Corpus Christi sixteen years earlier, she had vowed never to return to Texas, to its dusty flatness, its punishing heat, and its hard-edged mien. Yet despite her initial concerns she and Alan would settle nicely into Houston's society, more deeply than any other place they'd lived. It would become their home for the next three decades. But in 1963 the life of an astro-wife was never as simple as Louise would have liked, and she often couldn't help being pulled into the vortex of Alan's celebrity.

Louise's handful of selected friends included Carol and Peter Vanderhoef. Peter was a Christian Science teacher and practitioner (similar to a priest, but responsible for the spiritual and physical health of church members), and the Vanderhoefs had two daughters close in age to the younger two Shepard girls. Alan and Louise sometimes left the girls with the Vanderhoefs overnight when they'd travel, and Peter Vanderhoef used to laugh watching Alan pull up with his three daughters—this famous test pilot and astronaut carrying an armload of dolls, tea sets, and dresses.

The Vanderhoefs lived in an upscale section of Houston known as River Oaks, and the backyard of their lengthy rancher adjoined the backyard of George and Barbara Bush. Peter Vanderhoef, who was raised in Connecticut, had once dated Barbara, who grew up in nearby Rye, New York, and he was surprised to discover she was now his neighbor. At the time, in the mid-1960s, George was a successful oilman and aspiring politician—he would lose a run for the Senate in 1964 but win a U.S. congressional seat two years later.

The Bushes had a trampoline in their backyard, and the Vanderhoefs often saw the heads of Bush kids—George, Jeb, and Neil—bouncing in the air above the fence separating the two yards. The Bush boys teased and flirted with the Vanderhoef and Shepard girls. When the Shepards had moved to town, George, the eldest, hosted a party for Laura Shepard, to introduce her to other Houston teens.

Befriending the Bushes would be the first of many tactical steps Shepard would take toward positioning himself alongside Houston's business, political, and social elite—a step toward life after NASA. Quite often, however, he wouldn't have to take such steps—others sought him out.

Among Peter Vanderhoef's list of famous friends was Ginger Rogers, a devout Christian Scientist. When the actress learned that Peter was friends with Shepard, she insisted he host a dinner party so that she could meet the heroic astronaut. Vanderhoef was also friends with actor Gordon MacRae, a former classmate of his. MacRae also wanted to meet the Shepards—it always intrigued Vanderhoef how celebrities wanted to meet other celebrities. A dinner party was scheduled, but history would intervene. President Kennedy was coming to town. It would be his final visit with the astronauts.

On November 18 Kennedy toured Cape Canaveral. Wearing dark sunglasses, he walked around the base of the new Saturn rocket, looking up in awe at the massive booster engine—the strongest ever built, and a predecessor to the one designed to reach the moon.

Then Kennedy flew to Houston to tour the burgeoning Manned Space Center. From there he traveled to a NASA medical facility in San Antonio, where he reminded America that it was still "a time for pathfinders and pioneers." There he told the story of a group of boys walking across the Irish countryside who came to an orchard wall that seemed too high to climb. They tossed their hats over, forcing themselves to find a way to the other side. "This nation has tossed its cap over the wall of space, and we have no choice but to follow it," he said on November 21. "Whatever the difficulties, they will be overcome."

The next morning, as he rode waving through the streets of Dallas, Kennedy was shot dead. Alan and Louise's dinner with Gordon MacRae had been scheduled for that evening at the Vanderhoefs. But Alan called that afternoon to cancel. "They were too shook up," Vanderhoef recalled. Shepard had always considered Kennedy a "space cadet," a genuine fan of their feats, someone who was truly excited about what humankind had done and could do in space. He was shocked and devastated by Kennedy's death—and more than a little worried. *What will this do to the space program?* he thought.

///

About the time of Kennedy's assassination, the frightening, confusing episodes that left Shepard heaped and gasping on the floor were becoming more and more frequent. The worst had occurred one morning only six weeks into his Gemini training.

As he awoke and stepped from the bedroom, the floor tilted like a carnival fun house and he fell to the floor, hanging on to the carpet as if gravity itself had suddenly quit. Then he crawled slowly to the nearest wall and struggled to stand. When he finally reached the bathroom, he felt his stomach roll over and he vomited. And then again.

Jesus, what the hell did I drink last night? he wondered. It was just like the woozy aftermath of a brutal session in the MASTIF trainer—nausea, dizziness, and a momentary loss of the basic ability to stand straight.

In fact, the doctors had wondered about Shepard's slow recovery from one of his MASTIF sessions a few years earlier. Shepard had hit the chicken switch to stop the whirling contraption, then got sick all over the floor and had to lie down awhile on the cot. They didn't feel it was serious enough to keep him from piloting *Freedom 7*. But years later they'd look back and wonder: *Is that where the problem began?*

After vomiting that frightening morning at home, he sat in

his bathroom until the episode passed. Louise offered to drive him to work, but he said he could drive, and made it into the office feeling better, though a bit nervous. The next week it happened again. This time the spinning and vomiting were joined by a loud, metallic ringing in his left ear. In subsequent weeks the episodes continued to come and go. The pills he had been taking seemed to be no help at all. Friends and colleagues would not learn until many years later just how bad these early episodes were and just how hard Shepard had tried to keep them a secret. "He hid that well," Wally Schirra said.

This wasn't an injury that he could just shake off. It was, it seemed, a disease. And in the astronaut world, disease was *unseemly*. Shepard began to worry about keeping up with his Gemini training. He knew that if the ailment was serious, he could be pulled off the flight. But he also knew that if an episode struck during his mission, he—and his partner, Tom Stafford—would be dead.

Finally his secret revealed itself. He was giving a lecture one day, standing on a podium in Houston, when the room began to wobble. He clutched the dais and shut his eyes, blinking back the kaleidoscopic spinning. He had to be helped from the stage and sat in a chair off to the side until the dizziness ceased and he could walk. With his illness so publicly displayed, he had no choice but to walk into Slayton's office and confess. Slayton persuaded Shepard to visit NASA's doctors, which he did later that day. It pained him to tell the astronaut's physician, Dr. Charles Berry, "I'm having a problem. . . . It was a big problem, and it got worse."

Berry and the other NASA doctors did a series of tests and tried various medications, hoping the condition was temporary or at least controllable. During one exam they asked Shepard to stand on one foot. He had survived so many tests up to this point—centrifuge runs, MASTIF sessions, weightlessness training inside nose-diving cargo planes—but now he couldn't even balance on one foot. When the final round of testing was completed, Dr. Berry was out of town, and it fell to a young doctor named Duane Caterson to call America's first spaceman to his office to break the news. "You're medically grounded, *compadre*," Caterson said.

The diagnosis was that fluids were regularly building up in the semicircular canals of Shepard's left inner ear, wreaking havoc with the mechanisms controlling his body's balance. That, in turn, caused vertigo—an extreme form of dizziness—along with nausea, temporary loss of hearing, ringing in the ear, and a constant feeling that his ear needed to pop. The attacks were intermittent, but they were severe and unpredictable. The condition, Ménière's disease, was called an "elusive affliction," meaning doctors had no clue what caused it. In fact, some doctors at the time considered it a self-induced psychosomatic affliction. What they did know was that there was no cure.

Shepard took the news silently—"stoically," Berry recalled. But Shepard said later he was in shock: "total disbelief that they could ground the best pilot they ever had." He took a modicum of comfort in learning that his condition was, as he liked to tell people, "a result of being hyper." It was true—Ménière's was more prevalent in type A people, those who were hyperactive, competitive, and driven. At least, Shepard felt, it was ambition that had hurt him, not weakness. "Maybe it's the price I pay," he told himself at the time. "And if that's the price I have to pay for looking at myself in the mirror, then I'll take it. What the hell."

At first the grounding was temporary. Doctors gave him more medication—diuretics to help drain fluid from his ears and other pills to increase blood circulation—and said there was a 20 percent chance the disease would cure itself. But when it failed to abate or respond to treatment, Berry decided they "couldn't pretend any longer," and the grounding became permanent. Not only did Shepard lose his Gemini flight, but he was also barred from flying NASA's jets unless another pilot was flying with him.

Slayton, thanks to his heart ailment, was not allowed to fly jets alone, either. Two of the Mercury Seven, two of Kennedy's space pioneers, now couldn't even fly a Piper Cub without someone else on board to baby-sit them. That painful truth became apparent one day when Shepard and Slayton requested a NASA jet to ride from Houston to the Cape. "I'm sorry, you can't do that," Berry told them. "I know this sounds horrible, but two half pilots don't make a whole. You have to have another qualified pilot with you."

During the many medical exams that followed, doctors also discovered, to their surprise and his, that Shepard was suffering from a mild case of glaucoma—increased fluid pressure behind the eyes, which can cause nerve damage. That, too, was a symptom of chronic hyperactivity. Doctors felt the pressure from the glaucoma, which may have been with him since birth, was responsible for Shepard's bulging eyes. And that wasn't the last of his medical woes.

In late 1963 Shepard also began complaining of a sore throat and tried hard to convince his doctors it was nothing more than that. When they finally X-rayed his neck they found a small lump on his thyroid, the gland in the neck whose secretions control the body's metabolism. Doctors determined that his thyroid, which they found to be slightly enlarged, was another contributor to his buggy eyes. Shepard joked with NASA officials: "Too bad it didn't cause another part of my anatomy to bulge."

In mid-January of 1964 Shepard underwent surgery to have the lump removed. Surgeons cut just below his Adam's apple and removed 20 percent of his enlarged thyroid. The next day's papers showed Shepard smiling in his bathrobe, reading *Of Spies and Stratagems* (the biography of biochemist and spy Stanley Lovell), and the article said the surgery would "have no effect on his status in the space program." But Shepard's status, unbeknownst to the press, was that he had been grounded for months and was likely to stay there. He had just turned forty the previous November, and it looked as if his astronaut career was over. Plus he was too old to return to the Navy and back onto the admiral-bound career track he had abandoned.

The press had been told none of this. NASA wouldn't announce for another few months that Shepard had lost his Gemini flight, and when the announcement was made, Shepard's condition would at first be described simply as "an ear infection." Meanwhile, John Glenn experienced eerily similar medical problems of his own.

Ever since his wildly successful orbital flight in February 1962, Glenn—just like Shepard—had been pestering NASA officials for another flight. He had continued to train with the new groups of astronauts but felt like he was being "stonewalled" every time he asked about the possibility of a flight. He knew Shepard had been assigned the first Gemini flight and that Grissom had been assigned the second flight, but he could never get a straight answer on when he'd fly next.

At the same time, Bobby Kennedy—who had become one of Glenn's close friends—kept whispering in his ear: *Join us. Run for the Senate. Be a politician.*

Finally, toward the end of 1963, Glenn asked a NASA official straight up whether he'd ever fly again. The answer: not likely. NASA didn't want to risk losing its top star, its prime poster boy. In fact, President Kennedy himself had secretly told NASA officials that Glenn was a national asset whose life couldn't be endangered. Maybe, the NASA official suggested, Glenn would want to become an administrator. Instead, Glenn heeded Bobby Kennedy's call and opted for politics. He resigned from NASA and on January 17, 1964—the same day Shepard entered Hermann Hospital for his thyroid surgery—Glenn announced his candidacy for the U.S. Senate in Ohio.

A few weeks into his campaign Glenn stood looking at himself in the bathroom mirror of an apartment that a campaign patron had rented for him. He was due to meet his advisers for a briefing later that morning, but something about the reflection bothered him. It was the mirror—it wasn't sitting properly in the tracks of the vanity above the sink. As he tried to fix the mirror, it fell toward him. He threw his hands up to block the mirror, but as he ducked, the bath mat beneath his feet slipped. He fell and slammed his head into the metal shower door track on the rim of the bathtub. After a few moments of unconsciousness, he awoke to find himself kneeling in a pool of blood. The mirror had smashed over his head, and the blow from the bathtub caused his head to swell.

Subsequent X rays found a mild concussion, but more serious was some damage to his vestibular system—the canals and delicate structures of the inner ear that serve as the body's balancing mechanism. Swelling and blood in Glenn's inner ear caused the same symptoms as Ménière's disease, but worse. He couldn't walk or even sit in a chair. If he moved his head just an inch, it brought waves of dizziness and nausea. For weeks he was confined to a San Antonio hospital bed, "virtually immobile."

When Shepard's condition became public a few months later, the press pounced on Glenn's nearly identical affliction. The strange twist of coincidence—the fact that the two most famous astronauts had met similar vertiginous fates—created a brief flurry of media speculation about the dangers of space flight. In March Glenn held a news conference in his hospital room and withdrew from the Senate race. His political life seemed to have died before it even began, and as he wondered what road to take next, he had plenty of time to "contemplate the irony" of surviving space "only to be brought down by a slippery bath mat on a tile floor."

Glenn considered returning to NASA, which was anxious to have him back on board—at least in an ambassadorial or administrative role. But Glenn knew his chances of another flight were slim to none, and decided that he didn't want to become the oldest astronaut trainer and "a used astronaut." In much the same way, Shepard contemplated his own future. If he stayed with NASA, he seemed headed toward the exact fate that Glenn feared—a used astronaut. He asked himself, and he asked Louise: "What do I do now? Go back to the Navy? Stick around with the space program?"

Finally he met with Slayton and asked his advice. "Should I just hang it up?"

Slayton told him to stick around. "I've got a job for you," he said.

Shepard stuck around, but many of his peers—the second- and third-generation astronauts who had once considered him one "lucky son of a bitch"—wished he hadn't. Because he would soon become, simply, a son of a bitch.

17

How to succeed in business without really flying—much

While researching a book about space, Italian writer Oriana Fallaci arrived in Houston one hot and sticky day, rented a car, and drove south to the Manned Space Center for a scheduled meeting with Shepard. She had already met Dee O'Hara, Deke Slayton, Wernher von Braun, and others. But she was intensely curious about the man who'd led America into space. What traits distinguished him from the others? Shepard greeted her with a warm smile—a smile that made her wary from the start.

A petite, chain-smoking, mischievous blonde, Fallaci had a reputation for antagonizing interviewees. She once called Norman Mailer "an apologist for violence" and asked Hugh Hefner if he actually liked women, "beyond the sex, I mean." As she sat in Shepard's office, assessing his warm but wary smile, she thought he vaguely resembled a carnivorous plant she once saw in a London botanical garden. He was attractive without being overtly handsome, she thought, but his features were all oversized—protruding lips, large teeth, round eyes that seemed "hungry, and so large."

"Tall and slim, he emanated virility," she'd later write in *If the Sun Dies*, the story of her yearlong quest to understand the purpose and people of the space age. "[But] he reminded me of nobody—that mouth, those teeth, those eyes were unique." Fallaci didn't hesitate. She pounced on him with questions, asking Shepard if he suffered from any psychological "complex" as the first American in space. Shepard kept smiling. "That flight was a personal victory for me, a challenge to the others," he said. But no, he had no complex. Then she asked if he was jealous of Yuri Gagarin. "Of course I was jealous, I'm still jealous," he said. "But the fact remains that I had the satisfaction of being the first American."

Shepard went on to explain that beyond being the first into space, he was also among six Americans to have flown into space alone, since all future flights would now carry two to three astronauts. And he had deserved it, had earned it all. Then he leaned forward, the warm smile cooling a degree or two. "*Now* what are you going to ask?"

Fallaci tried to stare back, to challenge him, "but his eyes swallowed up mine." Shepard told her she was being "too romantic" about space and stars. Then he tried to sell her one of the race horses he had begun raising on his ranch. Or if not a horse, maybe she'd like to buy one of his cows. "You need a cow," he told her.

On days like that, Slayton might have regretted asking Shepard to forgo retirement to become head of the astronaut office. Slayton would find Shepard to be a less than diplomatic administrator and a fairly ineffectual public relations tool.

///

Slayton had known that Shepard, despite his illness, wasn't ready to retire. If there was a sliver of a chance for another flight—and there still was—he'd stay with the program. That's what kept Slayton going, too, willing to work as an astronaut baby-sitter until he'd again become a full-fledged astronaut.

About the time the doctors were giving Shepard doses of bad news and ineffective pills, Slayton had been promoted to chief of flight crew operations. That meant he needed someone to take over his old job running the astronaut office, and he asked Shepard. At first Shepard couldn't picture himself "changing diapers and feeding astronauts." Worse than that, he told Slayton, he'd have to watch all the younger pups fly toward the moon ahead of him.

When he accepted Slayton's offer, Shepard began wearing the job, and his resentment, like a hair shirt. His daily treatment of his new charges was unpredictable and often aggressive. Shepard was never known for being pals with the newer crops of astronauts. Few of them would forget Shepard's attitude toward them during the requisite interview at the Rice Hotel prior to their selection. Gene Cernan, one of the fourteen selected for the third group of astronauts, recalled that Shepard's "cold eyes seemed to look right through me . . . It seemed wise for a rookie like me to steer clear of Alan B. Shepard." Cernan considered Shepard "the best of the bunch" but "a total mystery."

When Shepard took over the astronaut office, his coworkers bestowed a number of monikers on him, with "the Icy Commander" topping the list. Others weren't so complimentary. Some of the NASA contractors called him "the Snake." A *Life* magazine writer called him "a bastard" and "the enforcer." "He didn't make a lot of friends in that period," Walter Cronkite recalled. Nor was he an easy man to live with. Louise once said that being grounded was "the worst thing that can happen to a flyer . . . I mean, the mental anguish."

Some of the newer astronauts would emerge drop-jawed from Shepard's office, having just sat through a withering dressing-down. They'd be baffled that the guy who'd bought them a drink the previous night was now calling them a slacker. Shepard's personal secretary, Gaye Alford, began trying to warn others of Shepard's mood-of-the-day by hanging one of two pictures of her boss on the office door each morning. One picture was of a big-grinned Al Shepard, the other of a stern, scowling Commander Shepard. Some days—particularly after a Ménière's episode, after which Louise would have to drive him to work—he'd walk into the office and slam his briefcase down on his desk. His secretary would know immediately which picture to choose.

Astronauts would turn and walk the other way if they saw Shepard approaching down a hallway, and these were no milquetoasts. They were men who had been fighter pilots and test pilots, who lived to compete and confront. But Shepard wasn't someone to be confronted. "Al could be friendly, outgoing, warm, a good leader and companion," astronaut Mike Collins said. "But he could also be arrogant and put down friends or foe alike, with a searing stare and caustic comment."

When confronted—by Slayton or NASA's brass—Shepard would explain that he was only trying to run a tight ship, treating the guys exactly how he'd expect to be treated. But in calmer moments he'd confess that he was "just mad at the world," taking his frustrations out on those around him—especially those beneath him. He knew what was happening outside his door, that they called him the Icy Commander or worse. Mostly he didn't care. He had little tolerance for "mistakes or frivolity or lack of performance among the astronauts."

One duty as head of the astronauts was hosting biweekly Monday morning pilot's meetings, and if he was feeling good that day, the meeting might devolve into irreverence and jokes and arguments, like the ready room of an aircraft carrier, with pilots exchanging tales of some recent training mission or a jet flight in which they'd almost run out of gas. But if he was having an off day, or if he'd tossed his cookies on the bathroom tiles that morning, he might berate a pilot for the very same out-of-gas exploit.

On such days he'd lecture the astronauts—just as John Glenn had a few years earlier—that they were part of a team, not a group of individuals. And he wanted the team to follow his rules and NASA's. In an echo of his father, Shepard insisted on structure, order, compliance, and no surprises. There was a blatant irony to this, of course. Shepard had always been adept at detouring around the Navy's rules and had become infamous for flouting NASA rules, too, and for playing as if he were a one-person team. Still, Slayton's decision to put Shepard directly in charge of the astronauts—their travel plans, their training schedules, their public appearances—would ultimately pay off in huge benefits, for NASA and the astronauts.

///

Fallaci, who had recently published a book about the historical role of women, called *The Useless Sex*, was fascinated by powerful, conflicted, iconic men. Toward the end of her interview with Shepard that afternoon, she bored in on the question that hovered around Shepard through much of the 1960s: Why was he even there? She knew Shepard was already a wealthy man, having quietly played off his astronaut celebrity status. She knew he owned a plush apartment at the downtown Mayfair building, full of wealthy retirees. She knew he had a beautiful wife there, and a bearded collie named Picasso. And she knew that *he* knew he'd already secured a place in the history books. So she asked him: "Don't you think about life after space?"

"Of course I think about it. I think about it a great deal, but I don't make myself sick over it," he said. "I'll make a success of some other job. I'm a man of many interests."

Indeed, Shepard had become much more than a grounded astronaut/administrator. He even turned down an invitation from a New Hampshire political delegation to run for the U.S. Senate there so that he could devote energy to a new passion: making money.

Since he was no longer throwing his energies into a demanding regimen of space training, Shepard found he could easily run the astronaut office with half his brain while juggling a bunch of moneymaking projects. In addition to continued income from *Life* magazine, he had pocketed a nice profit from his investment in the Cape Colony Inn a few years earlier. When a newspaper reporter had learned that the inn was partly owned by the Mercury Seven, he cried that it was a conflict of interest; Congress agreed, and NASA ordered the astronauts to divest themselves. For their $7,500 shares, each walked away with $49,000. Most of the seven immediately invested that money in some western Florida land with Henri Landwirth, which they later sold for $2 million.

Shepard's growing financial portfolio gave him the luxury of picking and choosing among the business proposals Houston's captains of industry regularly laid at his feet. The first offer he decided to accept was part ownership and a vice president's title at Baytown National Bank; Shepard and two partners bought the bank in 1963. In addition to twice-a-month board meetings, Shepard spent countless hours on the phone in his NASA office overseeing his profitable little bank. He seemed indifferent to, or maybe proud of, any questions about an astronaut who was also a banker—and an occasional oilman and rancher. In a note published in a Naval Academy alumni newsletter he told classmates: "Anticipating more spaceflights soon . . . Banking and wildcatting to a small degree."

Shepard regularly encouraged other astronauts to visit Baytown Bank for loans or to buy its stock shares. Behind his back they whispered yet another nickname, "the Loan Eagle." Luring colleagues into business deals would turn sour one day, resulting in a nasty spat—and a never-made-public threat of a lawsuit—between Shepard and Scott Carpenter. Carpenter claimed that he lost money on devalued bank stocks because Shepard never told him the bank was about to be sold; Carpenter was then unable to repay a $25,000 loan and accused Shepard of "swindling" him.

Often when one venture failed, another opportunity would present itself. Shepard invested in an oil-drilling venture with a

Los Angeles–based petroleum company, but the company would later disappear and blow away, taking Shepard's money with it. He partnered in a ranch in Weatherford, Texas, that raised cattle and race horses. Most were quarter horses, bred to race quarter-mile tracks, and one was worth more than $15,000. But Shepard was losing money on the horses, which might be why he tried to sell one to Oriana Fallaci. "Strong legs, iron fetlocks, excellent teeth," he told her that afternoon in his office, offering a discounted price of $3,000. "Do you want to buy one?" Fallaci suspected he cared more for horses than the moon. She felt that if she didn't leave his office soon, he'd sell her a horse, a cow, and shares in his bank. "He'd have cleaned me out," she said.

She found herself wondering what Shepard's colleagues already wondered: How could he raise cattle, drill for oil, run a bank *and* be an astronaut? The other astronauts never confronted Shepard directly, but it bugged them like crazy that he'd preach to them about not taking gifts from fans, not accepting honorariums for lectures, not getting lured into risky business ventures. Meanwhile, they'd enter his office and hear him conducting bank business by phone. "It struck me as odd that our chief was a bank vice president," wrote astronaut dropout Brian O'Leary in his controversial 1970 book, *The Making of an Ex-Astronaut.* O'Leary said he'd walk past Shepard's office and see him "leaning back and philosophically gazing out the window." There would be nothing on his desk, and O'Leary suspected Shepard's mind was "on airplanes, sports cars, the bank, or the ranch."

Shepard once reprimanded O'Leary for accepting a faculty position at the University of Texas, telling O'Leary that he was an astronaut "24 hours a day . . . and I want to know about these things." O'Leary felt burned by the "strange double standard." He eventually quit the program, claiming that "flying just wasn't my cup of tea."

"I didn't deliberately try to intimidate him," Shepard said later when asked about O'Leary's gripes. "Perhaps I did because I could see that he really wasn't going to work out, he just wasn't our breed of person. But there wasn't any attempt to intimidate him—any more than I do anybody else."

Complaints and rumors eventually wafted toward the top levels of NASA, whose officials carefully questioned Shepard about running his small empire on government time. In a private letter in late 1963 NASA administrator James Webb said he'd been informed of Shepard's growing role at Baytown National, and asked Shepard to "consider it with great care" before sinking deeper roots into the bank. Webb asked him to consider "the image that would be created in Houston" if astronauts began aligning with banks and financiers. Webb also requested that, in the future, Shepard submit an "official request for approval." But it was hardly a letter of reprimand. In fact, Webb closed by offering to "stretch my discretion a long way to help you."

The letter had little effect on Shepard's business activities. He went right on mixing astro-life, business life, and social life. Other astronauts tried to follow the example of the man astronaut Michael Collins called "the shrewdest of the bunch." As astronaut Walt Cunningham learned from Shepard, "The astronaut hero image was directly convertible to dollars if handled right." But none had the same success. Gus Grissom and Gordo Cooper partnered in a boat repair and retail business south of Houston but lost $16,000 each. Scott Carpenter made similarly bad business choices—a wasp-breeding venture among them. "There was Shepard, operating out there with the captains and kings of industry," Cunningham once said. "And here were the rest of us, losing our lunch money."

Such failures eventually bred deep resentment of Shepard's business successes, and the whispers again reached NASA's ears. Two years after his first letter to Shepard in 1963, NASA administrator Webb wrote again after reading in the newspaper that Shepard had agreed to become president of Baytown Bank. Webb was furious that "a person who is doing a full-time job with the government, and particularly one who is in such a prominent position as you are," would think it was acceptable to also be a bank president. Webb urged Shepard to "put the interest of NASA ahead of" his personal interests.

Despite a tiny blurb in a Houston paper on Shepard's promotion to bank president, few national reporters knew of Shepard's business life. And those who did know a few details considered it none of their business and steered clear. But Oriana Fallaci dug in. How could he buy a bank on an astronaut's salary? she asked. "All you need is to be ambitious," he said, without explanation. Fallaci said she suspected he had a "very earthly hunger," and Shepard concurred, locking his eyes on hers, a faint grin on his big lips. "One day I'll be very rich," he told her. And what about the stars? she asked. Didn't he want to reach the stars like the others do? Or was he more interested in banks and cows and horses? "All of it," he said. But shouldn't the stars come first? "You're a very romantic woman—too much so," Shepard said, signaling the end of the interview. "There's nothing romantic about going to the stars, believe me."

Fallaci left Shepard's office feeling a little sorry for him. She had heard he sought out women, money, cars, and "applause." But she liked him anyway. She was confused as she continued researching her book in future months, when she'd meet different versions of Shepard. She'd see him in a bar, at a missile launch, or lying beside a hotel pool at the Cape, sometimes "friendly," other times "standoffish," sometimes "confident," sometimes "shy." She wondered if he'd been burned by the "sickness of celebrity." Burned out, maybe. How else to explain a man who found no romance in the pursuit of the heavens? The truth, however, was not burnout. Not even close.

Shepard knew he had an incurable disease and was often disgusted and demoralized by it. But he was also disciplined and self-confident enough to lie in wait, stalking tigerlike for a chance to cure himself. He may not have considered space exploration a romantic pursuit, but it was an important one and he wouldn't give up. So the real answer to the question "Why are you here?" was that Shepard was absolutely, intractably determined to reach the stars once more.

///

When Shepard's illness sidelined him, NASA gave his Gemini flight to Gus Grissom who, along with John Young, one of the Next Nine, took off in late March of 1965 aboard Gemini 3, ending a two-year hiatus since the final Project Mercury flight. That inaugural Gemini flight was overshadowed, however—as many U.S. flights had been in the early years of the space race—by another Soviet first. Just five days before Grissom's flight, a Soviet cosmonaut crawled through a hatch in his capsule and floated freely in the empty blackness of space, connected to his spaceship by a tether. The first space walk came five months after the Soviets' first three-person space mission, which made Grissom's two-man Gemini flight seem archaic. But the days of Russian dominance in space were about to end. The space walk flight would be the last Soviet space launch for two years. During that lull the United States would send sixteen men into space—four of them twice—and begin racking up many firsts of its own.

Grissom's flight would be quickly followed by another Gemini flight, and then another, turning 1965 into NASA's most productive year. Thirty astronauts were now training for upcoming Gemini and Apollo flights; the number would grow to thirty-five in mid-1965 when NASA selected five more astronauts to join its growing ranks. Shepard's role was helping his astronauts get to training facilities and stick to a tight schedule. To help the men zip back and forth across the land, Shepard and Slayton convinced NASA to replace its older jets with a new fleet that the astronauts could borrow for their many travels. The sleek, two-seater supersonic T-38s could soar to forty thousand feet in ninety seconds.

Flying the T-38 was one of the better perks of astronaut life. The astronauts' training schedule resembled the one Shepard had experienced during Project Mercury: long, dizzy sessions in the MASTIF, body-slamming spins in the centrifuge, many hours of simulated practice sessions, visits to aerospace factories. The jets became trusted companions during the many rootless, grueling days of crisscrossing the nation.

The cockpit of a T-38 offered respite from the public's unrelenting love affair with the astronauts (which was emboldened, in no small part, by the surprising success of a new TV show in which Captain Kirk and the crew of the USS *Enterprise* explored strange new worlds in outer space). Shepard, as their keeper, tried to protect the astronauts from the demands of NASA's public affairs office, which was swamped with fan mail and requests for astronaut appearances. Reaching the moon was still a magical, powerful national goal, and the public wanted access to the men who were right on schedule to achieve Kennedy's commitment to putting men on the moon before 1970.

Shepard had the distasteful task of assigning his underlings to the dreaded "week in the barrel," as he had dubbed the dog-and-pony gigs astronauts served visiting schools and congressmen. The "barrel" referred to one of Shepard's favorite obscene jokes, a story about a weary traveler who staggers into an Alaskan mining camp looking for love and is directed to a back room where there's a large barrel with a hole in the side.

During such weeks, an astronaut might make thirty appearances, giving the same speech to thirty different audiences, in five days. With so much flying, a law of astronaut life evolved: When two or more astronauts are involved in the same activity, it becomes a contest. A race.

Gus Grissom earned notoriety for his "hot refuelings." In an effort to gain a few minutes on the other guy, he'd leave his engine running during a refueling stop and cut the record refueling time of ten minutes in half. That prompted some to try nonstop flights from, say, Los Angeles to Houston. The trick was to reach a safe altitude, catch a tailwind, and fly on just one of the two engines. Wally Schirra once landed in Houston with less than five minutes of fuel left and with his partner, Walt Cunningham, sitting nervously in the back, ready to punch the eject button. Shepard often joined the others on such flights, but some of his colleagues found it painful to watch the former crack test pilot climb into the *rear* seat as a passenger.

"He never talked about it, he never showed it. But you could just tell at times it bothered him," said Chuck Friedlander, who worked as Shepard's assistant at the Cape. "When Al climbed into the back seat of a T-38 and some young guy was flying it, nothing was said, but you could just tell by his face he was feeling the inability to fly." At such times, they all felt his frustration, and that empathy sometimes tempered their reaction to his Icy Commander days.

Jim Lovell flew with Shepard many times through the 1960s, sometimes straight across the country, from the Cape to California. Shepard loved stopping to refuel in El Paso, crossing the border into Mexico to get cut-rate bottles of tequila. In the rear seat, Shepard would often insist on taking the controls and flying the lion's share of each flight.

Still, Shepard operated on the fringes of the astronaut lifestyle he had so recently defined. As the boss of all astronauts, he was their teacher, not their classmate. His job was to corral them, get them places, make sure they didn't take advantage of their easy-access, government-funded jets. Like a camp counselor, he had to make sure no one wandered off into the woods. He was the taskmaster. And he was good at it.

Among Shepard's unique management techniques was the silent treatment. He'd call an astronaut into his office, and the other man would stand in front of his desk while he looked up at them "with those bulging eyes" and "stare right through you," recalled Lovell. "A very cold person," remembered astronaut secretary Lola Morrow. "He knew he could use his eyes as a weapon."

Shepard would then sit there, feet on the desk, and wait for the astronaut to speak first. The new guy would get scared, turn red, look down, look away, speak in mumbles. Finally, after letting him twist, Shepard would get to the point and ream him out. He was especially hard on the younger guys and on the scientists NASA had begun selecting to become astronauts. He was somewhat less harsh with his fellow Navy men. Slayton sometimes intervened as the good cop, but mostly he let Shepard handle things his way. He knew Shepard's intentions were to hone his men into perfect astronauts.

Even so, with so many astronauts—a total of thirty-five by mid-1965—flying and racing across the skies, it was probably inevitable that someone would die. The first was Ted Freeman, who had been selected in 1963 and was training for an early Apollo flight. Freeman's T-38 plowed into a gaggle of snow geese at five thousand feet, which smashed his windshield; shards of Plexiglas were sucked into the engines, which both flamed out. Freeman tried to wrestle the crippled jet back to Ellington. When he realized it was no good, he ejected, but he was too close to the ground. He died six miles from his home. After that, Shepard imposed the "snow goose rule"—no flying during migration season.

A few months later the two-man crew assigned to the Gemini 9 flight—Elliot See and Charlie Bassett—attempted to land one stormy night in St. Louis, where they were scheduled for a few weeks of training in a simulator capsule. See, who was flying the T-38, approached the runway too low and too fast. He tried to pull up and away to attempt another approach but clipped the top of the McDonnell Aircraft plant—the same building where their Gemini 9 capsule was being assembled. More funerals would follow.

///

On the heels of Grissom's one-day launch with John Young in March 1965, Gemini flights began soaring every month or two. From the spring of 1965 to the fall of 1966, ten flights lifted off—sixteen more men flew higher, longer, and faster than Shepard. Four of them flew twice, and five walked in space. Each flight was designed as another technical step toward the moon, and each flight put more and more distance—finally—between the United States and the Soviets.

In December 1965 Gemini 6 and 7, launched eleven days apart, managed to adjust their speed and location and rendezvous with one another. The two capsules flew side by side, a foot apart, traveling at many times the speed of sound. Gemini 7 then shattered all previous endurance records by staying aloft for two weeks. On Gemini 9 Eugene Cernan performed a two-hour space walk. Six months later Buzz Aldrin walked in space for five hours outside his Gemini 12 capsule, the last of the Gemini missions.

The ten flights of Project Gemini provided valuable lessons for the next phase, Project Apollo. Astronauts learned how to rendezvous two fast-traveling spacecraft, to "walk" in space, and to eat, sleep, and live inside a spacecraft for days at a time. For Shepard, all the success was bittersweet. In addition to seven of the Next Nine making a Gemini flight, three of the Mercury Seven flew, too—Cooper, Grissom, and Schirra. Meanwhile, Shepard and Slayton, still sidelined with their illnesses, were considered half-astros, and Glenn, after a lengthy recovery from his head injury and Ménière's-like symptoms, had taken a job with Royal Crown Cola and would soon begin working for Bobby Kennedy's presidential campaign. Carpenter, after recovering from his broken arm in 1964, had returned briefly to NASA but quickly realized he'd not get another flight with Chris Kraft (who was still angry about his sloppy Mercury flight) around. So he went the opposite direction, venturing under the ocean with a Navy deep-sea program, a temporary assignment that would be followed in 1967 by his retirement from NASA.

Shepard, meanwhile, was constantly trying to prove to NASA's doctors that he was getting better, and his condition did seem to be improving slightly in response to the vitamin-and-drug cocktails the doctors had prescribed. In late summer of 1965 Slayton had even suggested that Shepard begin training to command the first Apollo flight, which was scheduled to lift off in 1967. But when doctors conducted a more thorough examination, they found that while Shepard's symptoms were under control, the Ménière's disease itself had not subsided. They decided not to risk putting an imperfect astronaut into space and kept Shepard out of the flight rotation.

Slayton chose Grissom instead to command the Apollo 1 flight, and Shepard sulked back into his conflicted role as administrator—an astronaut who wasn't really an astronaut. He was now forty-one and felt as though he had just lost his last chance to fly.

///

By late 1966 a massive new NASA conglomerate was churning in place of the boutiquelike operation that had helped launch *Freedom 7*. Project Gemini had been a raging success, and NASA was confident that it was on a solid path to Kennedy's moon-by-1970 goal. Congressional funding continued to flow. NASA's payroll now supported an astounding four hundred thousand people, and many more private contractors and subcontractors.

Gone were the quaint early days of Shorty Powers and his deep voice, that made him sound as if he were nine feet tall. Shorty was among many casualties of NASA's mid-'60s explosion. The cocky, skinny, five-foot-six colonel, legendary for his bourbon-drinking abilities, reached for the bottle more and more often.

Shorty had been leaking internal Gemini flight plans to Jay Barbree, a reporter with NBC, who'd stop by Shorty's office and put a fifth of Jim Beam on the table as "payment." When the higher-ups found out, they insisted Shorty release the information to all reporters. When Shorty refused, they asked him to resign. And when he refused to quit, they reassigned him to a small Washington office that ran school fairs.

"In an organization as big as this one, there are people who feel perhaps they've been slighted," Shorty said later. He'd felt trapped in a "three-cornered box" trying to serve the disparate interests of the NASA brass, the astronauts, and the press. After three divorces and many bottles of bourbon, Shorty would one day be found dead in an Arizona cabin. Cause of death: internal bleeding due to chronic alcoholism.

Shorty wasn't the only one burned by the intensity of the new NASA. Schirra, who was mulling his retirement, was no longer the happy prankster he'd been with his Mercury Seven colleagues. He had become a bitchy prima donna. "I have been completely devoured by this business," Schirra confessed at the time. The reason: NASA had become, as he later put it, "a monster." And the turbulent mid-'60s had become a surreal time to be an astronaut.

The world outside—the real world that existed beyond NASA's insular, well-funded, chummy fraternity—seemed to be tearing away at itself, each bit of good news followed by bad. Lyndon Johnson had signed the Civil Rights Act, but then Congress passed the Gulf of Tonkin Resolution, allowing Johnson to send more soldiers to Vietnam, which incited violent antiwar protests on college campuses. Martin Luther King Jr. was awarded the Nobel peace prize, but then his followers were attacked by state troopers during a "walk of freedom" into Selma, which inflamed racial tensions that would soon lead to terrible race riots in Los Angeles, Detroit, and Newark. The voices of some detractors grew louder, questioning the nation's priorities and the billions being spent on space: *What's more important, peace or science fiction?*

A Gallup poll at the time found that two-thirds of Americans felt that funding for space exploration should be decreased; when asked who was ahead in the space race, the United States or the Soviet Union, 29 percent had no opinion on the matter. Pablo Picasso summed up the mood among space critics at the time: "It means nothing to me." But pursuing the moon still meant a lot to Johnson, who continued to promote and protect NASA's mission.

Among the astronauts, meanwhile, broad public support was hardly necessary. Inside the bubble of the astronaut world, contractors continued to throw wild parties and to offer prostitutes. At the opening of Houston's new indoor stadium, the Astrodome, the astronauts were given ten-gallon hats at the giddy opening-night celebration. Airline executives continued to donate penthouse suites and stewardesses, while CEOs offered Acapulco haciendas for astronauts and their girlfriends. But the astronauts would soon learn that everything had grown too big too fast and that workmanship had suffered.

The astro-party was about to crash.

///

A strange theme of Shepard's career was about to be confirmed: Flights he sought ended up being flights that he was lucky to have missed. It had happened with Cooper's jinxed Mercury flight, which Shepard had fought so hard to make his own, and it was about to happen with the Apollo 1 flight that Slayton had briefly assigned to Shepard.

When Shepard's unrelenting medical condition sidelined him—apparently once and for all—Slayton had given Grissom command of the first Apollo flight, the first big leap toward the moon. As commander of the first Gemini flight and now the first Apollo flight, Grissom seemed now to be the front-runner to be the first man on the moon. But as Grissom and his two partners—

Ed White, who performed the first American space walk on Gemini 4, and Roger Chaffee—approached their early 1967 launch, numerous glitches afflicted their complicated Apollo 1 rocket and capsule, requiring costly modifications and delays. Grissom began complaining to NASA and the press about what he considered shoddy workmanship and a sloppy rush not only to meet Kennedy's deadline but also to satisfy President Johnson's desire for a successful space launch to deflect America's attention from the growing war in Vietnam and the internal unrest at home. "This is the worst spacecraft I've ever seen," Grissom once told Shepard. And in a rare display of outspokenness with the press, Grissom said there had been "bushelfuls" of problems and admitted that he had "misgivings" about the flight.

One day in late 1966 Grissom pulled a grapefruit-sized lemon off a tree in his backyard south of Houston, said goodbye to his wife, Betty, and took the lemon nine hundred miles east to the Cape, where he was to begin the final weeks of preflight training. There he hung the lemon from a problematic capsule simulator, built by North American Aviation, which he considered "a piece of crap."

Grissom's concerns aside, the buildup to his launch was a heady time to be part of the NASA family. The stepping-stones of Mercury and Gemini had finally led to the big time, Project Apollo, with its enormous rockets, its three-man capsules, and its powerful "fly me to the moon" ambitions, which had inspired so many songs, poems, and dreams.

Apollo's capsule was easily the most complex piece of machinery the United States had ever constructed. It consisted of two main sections, a bell-shaped "command module" where the astronauts would lie three abreast and, beneath that, a cylindrical "service module." The contractor, North American, despite the $2 billion it was getting from NASA, wrestled with hundreds of problems, large and small, with the command and service modules—welding problems, insulation problems, excessive weight, electrical short circuits, structural imperfections, design modifications, and leaks.

Some NASA engineers called the spacecraft "sloppy and unsafe"—"a bucket of bolts." Nonetheless, NASA's top officials defended their contractor and stuck to their tight schedule. Following Apollo 1, a fast-paced series of subsequent Apollo flights was scheduled to take longer and longer strides toward the moon, and some NASA officials were already predicting that a man would walk on the moon as early as 1968. But then the construction woes, the frantic schedule, and Grissom's nagging fears all converged on January 27, 1967, at the end of a long, frustrating Friday of training.

North American had corrected many of Apollo 1's problems—at least to NASA's satisfaction—and the capsule was bolted atop a massive new Saturn IB booster rocket. For the purposes of the test, the rocket wasn't filled with fuel, but the capsule was fully powered and the astronauts sat inside, fully suited, as the hatch was shut tight and pure oxygen filled the cramped space, where Grissom, White, and Chaffee lay on their backs for a daylong dress rehearsal called a "plugs out" test. NASA had decided against a system that would fill the cockpit with a mix of oxygen and nitrogen (which makes up the air on earth); to cut the extra space and weight, NASA chose a simpler system that supplied 100 percent oxygen.

Throughout that Friday afternoon, it became clear that North American had not fixed all of its glitches. One of the first things Grissom noticed was a foul smell in the oxygen supply. That was followed by malfunctions in the communications system, which caused radio transmissions between the astronauts and Mission Control to fill with crackling static. At one point Grissom barked, "Christ, how are we going to get to the moon if we can't even talk between two or three buildings?" Later he found he couldn't shut off his microphone—"Damn it!" he yelled. As tempers flared, an engineer suggested calling it quits for the night, fixing the problems, and resuming the test the next day—it was already past 6 P.M., and the astronauts had been in the capsule for five hours. The engineer was overruled, and NASA's bosses decided to keep working for another hour.

Thirty miles of wiring snaked beneath, over, and around Grissom and his two colleagues. One of those wires, overlooked by North American's engineers, was frayed and exposed—a bad thing in a capsule full of pure, flammable oxygen—and at 6:31 P.M. a spark or two leaped off that frayed wire and ignited Apollo 1. Grissom yelled, "Hey!"

Engineers at the Cape and at Mission Control in Houston then listened in horrified, helpless silence as three astronauts screamed their final words.

"We've got a fire . . . fire in the cockpit."

"Get us out of here!"

"We're burning up!"

Finally there was a scream . . . and then silence.

The hatch on the spacecraft had been designed to be opened manually by an astronaut from the inside. Unlike the Mercury hatches, whose explosive mechanism allowed them to be popped off in an emergency, the Apollo hatch was a complicated, double-hulled door that took at least ninety seconds to open. Everyone knew that if there was a fire inside the cockpit, it would be impossible for the astronauts to get out in time.

Shepard, at that very moment, was in Dallas about to make a speech at a dinner event. Someone rushed to his side and whispered in his ear. He walked slowly to the podium and in a quiet, choked voice said, "I have just been informed of the loss . . . the loss of my comrades." He stood there for a long, silent moment, then walked away.

Shepard went home and told Louise, who left immediately to visit Grissom's wife, Betty. Shepard then phoned his assistant, Chuck Friedlander, who was stationed at the Cape. "Chuck, did we have an accident?" he asked, already aware of the answer but needing to hear it directly and from someone he trusted. "Did we lose anybody?"

"All three."

"I'll be right there," Shepard said quietly.

Shepard's secretary, Lola Morrow, made arrangements for Shepard to travel to the Cape. "I'll never forget the pain in Al Shepard's eyes, in his face," she said.

Betty Grissom was at home with her two children when Wally Schirra's wife, Jo, her next-door neighbor, knocked on the door. A black NASA car pulled up a few minutes later, and she knew she had been widowed. Louise came by that night to offer comfort.

Grissom was buried at Arlington National Cemetery, with Shepard and the other surviving Mercury Seven carrying his dark-wood, flag-draped casket. Lyndon Johnson sat in the front row, trying to catch Betty Grissom's eye, but she stared straight ahead.

Suddenly four jets roared into view, flying low and fast, wingtip to wingtip. As the foursome approached the cemetery one of the planes pulled up and away from the others—the traditional missing-man formation, which left an empty slot where the fourth plane should be. As the jets disappeared, a volley of rifle shots cracked, followed by the painful notes of taps played by a lone bugler.

Shepard, Slayton, Schirra, and public information director Paul Haney drove into Georgetown and sipped scotch and water at the Georgetown Inn. They stood near the windows, staring out at the chilly day, its sunny skies. Haney looked over and was amazed, flat-out floored, to see tears streaming down Shepard's cheeks.

"I hate those empty-slot flyovers," Shepard said, and swallowed another scotch.

///

Just weeks before his death Grissom had told an interviewer that "the conquest of space is worth the risk of life." Still, many of the astronauts felt that a fire in the cockpit—the result of sloppy construction, no less—was no way for a test pilot to die. Better to have perished in a midair explosion than on the launch pad during a test.

A lengthy follow-up report determined that the fire had started beneath Grissom's couch, spread quickly along nylon webbing beneath the seats, and then crawled up the walls, igniting everything in its path—especially the many straps made of a new invention called Velcro, which had been installed to hold tools and equipment in the zero gravity of space but, in an atmosphere of pure oxygen, had burned like gasoline.

Investigators said that the three astronauts died of asphyxiation in less than a minute. It was clear from the position of the bodies that Grissom and Ed White had been frantically trying to open the hatch when they died.

Once the public sorrow had abated, Congress and the media began painfully and publicly exploring all the possible reasons for the first casualties of the space program. Some newspapers blamed NASA for trying to accomplish too much too fast, and one went so far as to call it "downright criminal." Ironically, when a Soviet cosmonaut on the first Russian mission in two years died during a fiery reentry just three months later, many in the United States were reminded that the space race was indeed a complicated, imperfect, and dangerous venture.

The U.S. space program would be grounded for more than a year, during which time all the people involved in the race for the moon reassessed their life, their goals. "I was miserable," Slayton said of that period. "But Al was worse. And he took it out on everybody."

In the weeks after the fire, Shepard became insufferable. He felt in some small way responsible for what had happened to Grissom and his crew, for not doing more to prevent it. He knew of Grissom's complaints about the equipment; he'd heard them daily. But everyone wallowed delusionally in a "sense of false security . . . a sense of complacency—including myself," Shepard said. A congressional report would later use almost exactly the same words in blaming NASA's "overconfidence" and "complacency." Everyone in Houston had thought, after the huge success of Gemini and the absence of any Soviet flights between 1965 and mid-1967, *We're winning. We're beating the Russians.* But by not taking Grissom's complaints seriously enough, Shepard felt, "Deke and I insidiously became part of the problem." Shepard got even tougher on the other astronauts after Apollo 1, determined not to "let those guys get away with anything."

"He was mad at the world and he let everybody know it," astronaut Gene Cernan recalled.

One day Slayton had asked Shepard to stay behind after a meeting. "Don't you think you're being a little tough on the guys?" he asked. "I suppose I've been taking it out on them," Shepard admitted. At the end of a long talk, Slayton asked that he at least consider easing up a bit.

Meanwhile, the public affairs office was trying to find a way to restore the public confidence and its own morale—or at least offer a brief diversion. The solution was a party held May 6, 1967, at the Escape Velocity Press Club. The dual purpose was to celebrate the sixth anniversary of Shepard's *Freedom 7* launch and, to a lesser extent, to memorialize Gus Grissom, Ed White, and Roger Chaffee. Proceeds from the banquet would go to the Ed White Memorial Scholarship Fund.

It was an emotional night for Shepard—and a turning point.

/ / /

The lights dimmed and the flicker of a movie projector lit up the screen. More than five hundred pairs of eyes—aerospace executives, NASA officials, politicians, editors, photographers, and reporters—watched as a Redstone rocket lurched into space.

Shepard and his *Freedom 7* capsule then filled the screen. In his silver space suit, aboard the USS *Lake Champlain,* just moments after his fifteen-minute flight, Shepard looked like the perfect astro-stud as the James Bond theme pumped through the speaker system and the film's title flashed onto the screen, one word at a time.

Astronaut Hero . . . or . . . How to Succeed in Business Without Really Flying—Much.

Laughter filled the hotel banquet room as Wally Schirra's voice narrated the pseudo biographical documentary. After several scenes of spectacular airplane and jet crashes, intended to imply that Shepard had been at the controls, Schirra's voice explained that, "in the interest of national security, the Navy requested that Shepard be assigned to NASA." Then Shepard's despised chimpanzees, Enos and Ham, filled the screen, and Schirra's narration explained how Shepard "had studied their methods." Shots of Shepard were then interspersed with shots of Einstein, Washington, and Lincoln.

The narration ended with Schirra thanking "the fabulous Wally Schirra" for the five-minute film. It appeared the film was over, but then a shot of Shepard at his desk flickered onscreen. Unbeknownst to Schirra, the filmmakers had given Shepard the last word. Shepard, looking stern in a self-deprecating rendition of his own Icy Commander, said, "Wally, I expect to see you in my office at oh-eight-hundred Monday morning."

After the film, the roasting continued with a few gag songs, most of them written by Shepard's record producer friend Mickey Kapp. Schirra and a few other astronauts joined Kapp to sing of Shepard's smile—"like the hiss of a cobra before lunch"—and how Shepard had sold them on some business scheme and "we lost our shirts." "It's okay, we'll borrow money to pay the rent," they sang. In a knockoff of "King of the Road," they sang, "I always win and my partners lose." Then Shepard joined the group and sang a rendition of "I Believe in You," from the Broadway show *How to Succeed in Business Without Really Trying.* But that night's version of the song was "I Believe in Me."

After dinner they invited Shepard to come to the podium and say a few words. The gags continued as two huge bodyguards kept shoving Shepard back into his seat. When they finally allowed him to reach the dais, a tableful of NASA officials stood and made for the door. They returned laughing, but then when Shepard tried to speak, he found that Schirra (the mastermind behind the evening's gotchas) had turned off his microphone.

The laughter finally settled down, and it was Shepard's turn to speak. As he stood there that night, a decade after Sputnik had started it all, he looked out into a crowd full of peers, bosses, politicians, journalists—a cross-section of everyone who'd played a role in the first ten years of the space race. He'd spent eight years as an astronaut but only fifteen minutes in space. At that moment it seemed unlikely that he'd ever fly again. In fact, he was considering a possible return to the Navy if his ear continued to sideline him. So he decided to use his evening in the spotlight to clear his plate, to say things he'd stored up, but carefully, with a smile and a bit of classy, soft-edged sarcasm. One by one he addressed his adversaries, critics, and colleagues.

To the press: "I know we've tried your patience, and certainly you've tried ours on a number of occasions."

To Shorty (who'd been invited back for the occasion) regarding his infamous 3 A.M. "We're all asleep" quote on the morning of Gagarin's flight: "The truth of the matter is, that's the earliest he'd gone to bed in weeks."

To Bill Hines, the dogged reporter who broke the Cape Colony story: "The truth of the matter was, we refused to serve him a corned beef sandwich."

To the men who'd given him the opportunity to make history six years earlier, he elaborated. When the Russians reached space in April of 1961, "it was discouraging to us all." The United States could have beaten them if they'd flown a few weeks earlier, "and the temporary flush of victory would have been ours," he said. He admitted that he had been "heartsick" over getting "so close to an event that the country needed." But, he continued— and at this point he looked out toward Wernher von Braun, whose caution had led to the delays that allowed the Russians to beat America into space—a rash decision could have easily resulted in failure. Waiting until everything was ready, he now realized, had been the right decision, the "mature" judgment call. "It exonerates the careful judgment of you men who placed success over temporary propaganda advantage," he said.

For someone as proud as Shepard, it was an extraordinary concession. He'd been so angry back then. But losing Grissom to shoddy workmanship had taught him something. He still wanted "every chance for this country to be first in everything it does," but not at the expense of lives. He wanted von Braun and the others to know that he now realized "that we will be remembered in fact for *how* we did it, and not *when* we did it." The applause was loud and sustained, and a few of the men in the room bowed their heads to hide their tears. Shepard held up his hands and asked for quiet. He wasn't finished. He wanted to "close with a few words about the recent accident."

The room felt silent.

"All of us here tonight jointly share the responsibilities for the human frailties which are now so apparent and for the insidious combination of materials and equipment which was so devastating in their behavior. [And] we jointly share the responsibility for future prevention of similar circumstances."

But, having said that, it was also time to put Apollo 1 in the past, to stop pointing fingers and casting blame and asking "what if" and hanging heads. "The time for recrimination is over," he said, taking a cue from his wife's life view. "There is much to be done. Morale is high. Vision is still clear. Let's get on with the job."

Amid the thunderous ovation that followed, one might have detected in Shepard's words a clue that he wasn't talking just about NASA. Indeed, a cure for the Icy Commander was nigh.

18

"Captain Shepard?
I'm Charles Lindbergh"

On wintry East Derry evenings, he'd sit at the big wooden table in Nanzie's kitchen while she cooked dinner at the wood-fired stove and told him this family story:

It's 1750 and twenty-one-year-old Josiah Bartlett has just finished his schooling and moved to Kingston, New Hampshire, to practice medicine. He has seen only a few patients when he himself becomes a patient. One day he feels a damp chill crawl across his body, up his spine. The next day he is sweating, dizzy, nauseated. As his fever continues to rise, another doctor friend tells him, "Shut tight all the windows in your room, and refrain from drinking liquids." But the fever rises higher still. The young man grows weak and delirious. After many such days, his doctor declares that all has been done that can be done. Bartlett's condition is hopeless. He is dying. Bartlett lies in his bed, waiting for darkness to claim him. But one night the young man rebounds slightly, breaking briefly through the haze of his delirium, and opens his eyes. He is parched from the doctor's orders to avoid liquids. His lips, dry and cracked, ache for something cool and wet. To a friend attending his bedside, he says: "Bring me a jug of cider." With his friend's help, he sips cider through the night. The cool, rich apple nectar moistens his sear, sapless body, infuses it, and by morning he is finally able to break a sweat. The perspiration cools him, the fever subsides, and in only a few days more he is back on his feet. And Josiah Bartlett vows never again to trust another person's judgment above his own.

When Bartlett returns to his medical practice, he begins experimenting with nontraditional treatments. Patients are drawn to him, his friendliness, and his intelligence. Success with such treatments—like using tree bark to relieve sore throats—earns him a large and faithful clientele. The popular doctor, tall and handsome with curly red hair, is elected justice of the peace, then appointed by the king of England to command the local militia. In 1765 he becomes a representative in the New Hampshire state legislature. Nine years later he and other representatives begin complaining about Britain's restrictive rules for the colonies. Bartlett is fired from his job as justice of the peace and commander of the militia, and the legislature is ordered to disband, which it does—only to meet elsewhere in secret. As colonial resistance and aggression grows, Bartlett travels to Philadelphia to help the colonies' other activists create a Continental Congress. On the evening of July 4, 1776, Josiah Bartlett is the first delegate of the new Congress to stand and vote "yea" in favor of a document declaring freedom from Great Britain and the creation of "free and independent states." An old bellman in the tower of Independence Hall clangs the Liberty Bell, signifying the birth of a nation.

///

In the months following Shepard's sixth-anniversary dinner and into 1968, the effects of the Ménière's disease, after occasionally subsiding over the previous few years, suddenly became worse than ever. His balance was shaky, and he lost most of the hearing in his left ear. His fate seemed confirmed: He'd never fly again.

One day in the summer of 1968, Tom Stafford—Shepard's partner during his short-lived courtship with the first Gemini flight—stopped by the office. Stafford knew how hard the illness had been on Shepard and often kept his eyes open for possible solutions. That morning he had some news. He'd heard through friends about an ear, nose, and throat specialist in Los Angeles who had been experimenting with surgery to cure Ménière's. Shepard flew to L.A. and met with the doctor, William House, who made no promises. The surgery had been performed only a handful of times, and it carried no guarantee of success. There was even a slim chance the symptoms could worsen as a result of the surgery and that Shepard might lose all hearing in that ear.

But Shepard felt this was his last chance. If it didn't work, he would leave NASA.

As a Christian Scientist, Shepard had been raised to believe that God would make things right if he was right with God. He respected his mother's devotion, which was also Louise's, but he never fully accepted the idea that a deity controlled life's ups and downs. He was more inclined toward self-reliance, believing in his own abilities—and that, like Josiah Bartlett, he could cure himself. But with Ménière's disease, he had met his match. He had tried exercise, medication, optimism, and even patience. "I convinced myself it would eventually work itself out," he said years later. "But it didn't."

Now, despite Louise's lifelong aversion to medical treatment and her deep-seated belief in healing oneself through positive thinking and prayer, a doctor's knife was the only possible answer, and she had no choice but to support him. Do it, she said. Go for it. Shepard called Dr. House and scheduled the operation.

Shepard consulted briefly with NASA doctors, but he didn't want the entire NASA machine involved in the decision, so he told very few people about the upcoming surgery and asked NASA to keep it quiet. He checked into St. Vincent's Hospital in L.A. under an assumed name suggested by House's Greek nurse: Victor Poulos. "If this thing doesn't work, I don't want a lot of people feeling sorry for me," he said.

The procedure was to cut through the mastoid bone, behind the ear, and into the part of the inner ear called the sacculus, which is where endolymph fluid resides. In Shepard's case, excessive pressure in the sacculus was causing the endolymph fluid to inflame the sacculus, disrupting the inner ear's delicate balance of bone, fluid, and tissue. With tiny instruments and a delicate touch, House cut a small hole in the sacculus, releasing a spurt of blood-and-pus-filled fluid.

House then inserted an inch-long rubber tube, as thin as pencil lead, into the sacculus. He connected the other end of the tube to a space behind the sacculus that is filled with cerebrospinal fluid, the fluid that surrounds the brain. If it worked, the tube would drain excessive endolymph fluid from the sacculus into the spinal column.

But it would take months to see results. Shepard returned home wearing a big bandage behind his ear, which he then had to explain to his fellow astronauts. While recovering from his surgery, Shepard returned to his job as head of the astronaut office. But first he stopped in Deke Slayton's office one day to tell him about the surgery—and to begin lobbying for one of the upcoming Apollo flights. The Icy Commander was so confident that the operation would be a success, his mood turned noticeably upbeat in the following weeks.

Walter Cronkite had seen Shepard occasionally in the years since he had first met him in 1961. He considered Shepard "aloof" but respected him for sticking with NASA and heading up the astronaut office while his teammates flew. One day shortly after the operation Cronkite saw Shepard sitting by the pool of the Cocoa Beach Holiday Inn, where Shepard often stayed while visiting the Cape. As they shared a drink and reminisced about the early days of the maturing space program, Cronkite tried to get Shepard to confess to feeling at least a twinge of fear while sitting inside his capsule six years earlier. Shepard insisted, as he had in previous conversations, that riding the Redstone rocket was "duck soup" compared to his previous test piloting and nighttime landings on storm-tossed aircraft carriers. But Cronkite wouldn't let up.

"C'mon, Al," he said. "There you were, lying flat on your back at the top of that rocket, and you're about to be blasted off. What were your thoughts? C'mon, I won't print it. I promise. I won't even tell anyone. But I want to know." Shepard thought about it a minute, then looked at Cronkite. "Well, you know," he said, "I looked at those toggle switches I had to turn on cue, I looked at the dials I had to turn on cue, and I thought to myself: *My God, just think, this thing was built by the lowest bidder.*" The two men cracked up, and Cronkite realized he hadn't seen that toothy, big-lipped smile in ages.

About six months after Victor Poulos emerged from surgery, the symptoms that had dogged Shepard for more than five years disappeared. House's surgery was a great success, and Shepard returned to Slayton's office and told him that he was ready to fly again. "Get me a flight to the moon," he said.

///

The soul-searching, investigations, shake-ups, and restructuring that had occurred throughout NASA after the Apollo 1 disaster resulted in a completely redesigned Apollo capsule—and a ridiculously huge new rocket. Except for the Apollo 7, the new flights scheduled to begin in October of 1968 would be boosted from earth atop a Saturn 5 rocket, which Wernher von Braun had spent nearly a decade creating. The 363-foot rocket (actually three separate rockets, or "stages," containing a total of eleven booster engines) would pack 7.5 million pounds of thrust—a hundred times more powerful than the Redstone rocket that had propelled Shepard's *Freedom* 7 capsule.

Unlike the bell-shaped Mercury and Gemini capsules, the Apollo spacecraft consisted of a bell-shaped command module and a cylindrical service module beneath that. Beneath the service module was the Saturn rocket's "third stage"—an engine that would boost the spaceship away from the earth's gravity on its 250,000-mile journey to the moon. Tucked in a compartment beneath the service module rode another capsule of sorts—the bug-shaped lunar module, the vehicle that would take the astronauts to the moon's surface.

The new system was finally tested in October when Wally Schirra, with crewmates Donn Eisele and Walt Cunningham, spent eleven days orbiting the earth and testing all of Apollo's systems on Apollo 7. Two months later NASA made one of the boldest decisions of its history. Instead of a repeat of Schirra's test, NASA decided to send Apollo 8 all the way to the moon. NASA administrators asked Shepard to discuss the idea with the astronauts in his charge, and Shepard reported back that he felt it was "a stroke of genius." He then pushed the three-man crew of Apollo 8—Frank Borman, Jim Lovell, and Bill Anders—into a relentless training schedule. He didn't want any astronaut errors to taint the flight.

Three days after liftoff Apollo 8 reached the moon, and while orbiting it on Christmas eve the astronauts sent home vivid, moving reports on the gray, dead beauty of the land just sixty miles outside their windows. "A vast, lonely, and forbidding place, an expanse of nothing," they called it, "a grand oasis." The three astronauts took turns reading from the Bible—"In the beginning, God created the heaven and the earth"—before wishing the world a merry Christmas. Then Frank Borman looked out the window in time to see the blue and white earth "rise" like the sun above the flat gray of the moon. "This is the most beautiful, heart-catching sight of my life," he whispered.

The public fell in love again with the space program. The glorious photographs taken by Apollo 8 all but erased the terrible memories of Apollo 1.

///

In March 1969 the crew of Apollo 9 orbited the earth while conducting crucial tests, such as releasing the lunar module from its garage beneath the service module and docking it nose to nose with the command module. Two months later Apollo 10 performed a dress rehearsal of the moon landing that was planned for mid-July. During Apollo 10's flight to and around the moon, astronauts Tom Stafford and Gene Cernan flew their lunar module down to within nine miles of the moon's surface. The final step would be taken later that summer by Apollo 11.

By mid-1969 Slayton—with Shepard's help—had adopted a fairly consistent method of choosing astronaut crews for the Apollo flights. First a three-man crew would serve as another crew's backup. Three flights later that backup crew would become the prime crew. The three men who backed up Apollo 7, for example—Tom Stafford, Gene Cernan, and John Young—became the prime crew for Apollo 10. Apollo 10's backup crew included Gordon Cooper, who therefore fully expected to take command of Apollo 13. But Shepard's desires would again intrude on Cooper's fate.

In a masterly—some said devious—stroke of what some astronauts dubbed "astro-politics," once Shepard had proved to NASA doctors that his surgery had been a success, he convinced Slayton to give him the flight that Cooper has assumed was solidly his. Actually, as Slayton's partner in crew selections, Shepard essentially assigned himself to Apollo 13, which made

Cooper "furious" that Shepard seemed to be placing "his own interests" ahead of the good of the space program.

As the excitement of the upcoming Apollo 11 lunar landing grew, Shepard began sitting in on classroom sessions, reading up on Apollo flight systems, training in simulators, hanging out with the flight operations crews, and working out at the gym. He was back in the game, and the whispers swept across Houston. The astronaut corps knew something was up long before word leaked out of Shepard's assignment.

When Cooper learned that Shepard had been given command of a flight—even though the Navy hadn't yet cleared him to fly jets—he went to see Slayton to complain, and found Shepard in Slayton's office. "Deke and I are making crew assignments now," Shepard said, as if to imply: *You're out of your league, Gordo— what's done is done.*

Some were amazed, some were pissed, but few were really surprised. Shepard had less space experience than most of his peers. He'd never served on an Apollo backup crew, and now he was leapfrogging more than a dozen veteran astronauts. But no one was in a position to tell the first American spaceman he had to wait in line.

Actually, one person did: Shepard's choice for his Apollo 13 copilot, Jim McDivitt, who complained that Shepard wasn't ready to fly to the moon. McDivitt was subsequently replaced and lost his chance at the moon—he'd never fly again. However, when word of Shepard's assignment to Apollo 13 reached NASA's headquarters in Washington, Slayton and Shepard were overruled. NASA administrators in Washington agreed with McDivitt that Shepard needed more time to train.

The Apollo spacecraft was a hundred times more complicated than the Mercury capsule Shepard had flown in 1961, and the training regimen for Apollo astronauts was complex, time-consuming, and exacting. Apollo astronauts were required to know how to fly both the command and lunar modules and had to spend 180 hours and 140 hours, respectively, in the training simulators for each vehicle. They had to know how to navigate their spacecraft using only the stars and moon, in case the computerized guidance systems ever failed. They had to spend a minimum of 240 hours in the classroom, absorbing Ph.D.-level lessons on meteorology, physics, rocket propulsion, flight mechanics, and computers. To withstand the punishing demands of spending a week inside a metal can, they had to be perfectly fit. And they had to quickly become geology experts, training in deserts and canyons to learn how to identify rocks and minerals, which they'd have to collect on the moon, and to practice walking in their bulky space suits across rocky, sandy moonlike terrain.

There simply wasn't enough time for Shepard to catch up and be unambiguously prepared to command Apollo 13, which was scheduled for an early 1970 launch, less than a year away. Slayton had no choice but to pull Shepard off Apollo 13.

But instead of giving the flight to Cooper, Slayton asked Jim Lovell—currently assigned to Apollo 14—if he could take Apollo 13. "Sure, why not?" Lovell said. "What could possibly be the difference between Apollo 13 and Apollo 14?" Shepard also saw little difference between the flights. His notorious impatience aside, he was thrilled to have gotten any flight to the moon. And despite some rolling of eyes and bruised feelings, most astronauts and administrators grudgingly admitted that he deserved the flight, regardless of how he had achieved it. Said flight director Chris Kraft: "He stayed with the program. He paid his dues."

Wally Schirra, who had retired after his Apollo 7 flight, wondered, "How the hell did he pull that one off? Unreal." But deeper down, Schirra respected his colleague for sticking it out. "Al was probably bitter at times, watching us all fly. It was probably tough watching his buddies make all these flights," he said. "I can't believe he stuck around." There was one astronaut who was less than magnanimous: Gordon Cooper, the big loser in all the politicking.

Slayton argued later that it wasn't just Shepard's maneuvering that cost Cooper his flight. Cooper had always rubbed NASA management the wrong way, which was why he'd almost lost his Mercury flight six years earlier. He had also been reprimanded in 1968 for attempting to race a car at Daytona Beach and then bitching to a reporter afterward that NASA wanted "tiddlywinks players" for astronauts. Also, Cooper never seemed to train as hard as the others, especially during the more complicated Apollo training sessions, and so Slayton felt it was just "time for him to move on."

Cooper knew he "had little recourse," but he vented one day to a *New York Times* reporter. "I'm considerably younger than Shepard. I'm still in good physical condition," Cooper said, but declined to say why he was planning to leave the space program, other than to say "the politics" got too complicated. "I would rather not speak too much about Captain Shepard. I have my own feelings about him." Cooper felt Shepard had flat-out stabbed him in the back. "He had to have what he wanted to have," Cooper said ruefully years later. Though Cooper claimed to love him like a brother, "it took me years to forgive Al." In Cooper's mind, Shepard had snatched something that had been his.

"I lost the moon," he would write later.

///

Shepard was officially restored to flight status on May 7, 1969, just eleven days before Apollo 10's launch. NASA wouldn't announce publicly for another few months that not only was Shepard an astronaut once more, but he had been chosen to command Apollo 14.

First NASA wanted to run Shepard through the wringer, looking for any residual signs of the Ménière's disease. They spun him in the centrifuge and dunked him underwater and whipped him about in the MASTIF. These were all efforts to shake loose Dr. House's tube, but they all failed—the flesh around the tube in his ear had healed and now held the tube tightly in place.

On July 16 Alan and Louise joined the crowds at the Cape to watch Neil Armstrong, Mike Collins, and Buzz Aldrin make history in Apollo 11. In a roped-off VIP section of the viewing stands, Shepard stood off by himself, looking out at the enormous skyscraper of a rocket, the same Saturn 5 booster that would soon deliver him above. He stood looking dreamily out at the rocket standing three miles away, "aloft in my own thoughts," when an old man wearing rumpled clothes and an upside-down sailor cap approached and introduced himself. "Captain Shepard?" he said. "I'm Charles Lindbergh." Shepard knew who he was before he'd opened his mouth. The two men had briefly met a few years earlier at a White House dinner. Shepard called his daughters over and introduced them, and then Louise, to Colonel Lindbergh. Then the two men walked off along the sand, to talk alone as the countdown to Apollo 11's blastoff continued.

Shepard told Lindbergh how his 1927 flight had inspired him as a three-year-old boy, had planted the seeds of his future and boosted him toward a career as a Navy pilot. Lindbergh told Shepard that his 1961 space flight had been pretty heroic, too. They talked about the similarities between the early days of aviation and the genesis of the space race—the danger, the media crush, the politics. The two men talked for thirty minutes and then watched as a river of fire trailed behind Apollo 11 as it began its 250,000-mile journey.

Lindbergh later described the awe he felt as he witnessed the launch by Shepard's side: "My chest was beaten and the ground shook as though bombs were falling nearby. Then a flame arose, left the ground behind—higher—faster—a meteor streaking through the sky. It seemed impossible for life to exist while carrying that ball of fire."

///

Ten years earlier, when Shepard began attending his first meetings with engineers at Langley, he quickly learned—from the arguments, the dissension, and the naiveté—that NASA's best and brightest didn't yet have a clue how to get to the moon. They were brilliant men, no doubt about it; NASA's half-decent pay scale and noble mission attracted some of the sharpest minds in the nation. Still, just as there had been many competing theories over how to fly like the birds in the late 1800s, no one knew for sure how best to travel the quarter of a million miles to the moon.

The tricky part was the thrust. How, the engineers argued, can a rocket carry enough fuel to not only blast off from the earth but then also travel to the moon and back? Such discussions had intensified during the summer of 1961, in the wake of Shepard's *Freedom 7* launch and Kennedy's historic vow to reach the moon within eight years.

Among the ideas on the table in the early 1960s was to build the largest rocket yet known, cram it with enough fuel to blast it all the way to the lunar surface, and at the last minute turn it around and bring it in backward—like backing a car into a garage. The same rocket would blast off again and fly back to earth. When that "direct ascent" theory proved to be unrealistic, another plan emerged and was soon adopted by Wernher von Braun as the best plan. The "earth-orbit rendezvous" theory called for launching two rockets, one carrying the astronauts' capsule and another carrying an extra engine full of fuel; that engine would be attached to the astronauts' capsule while they orbited the earth, and then used to propel them to the moon. But there was one "voice in the wilderness," as NASA engineer John Houbolt called himself, who had a completely different plan.

Houbolt called his theory "lunar-orbit rendezvous." It called for a two-piece mothership—the bell-shaped command module and the cylindrical service module beneath that—to reach and then leave earth orbit, at which point a spidery lunar excursion module, or LEM (whose acronym was later shortened to LM, but was still pronounced "lem"), would be released from a "garage" of sorts (actually, the Saturn rocket's third stage) beneath the service module; the command module would then turn 180 degrees so that it could attach to the nose of the lunar module. The Saturn's third-stage engine, still attached beneath the LM, would then boost the linked-up spaceship—command, service, and lunar modules—toward the moon. Once the spacecraft reached orbit around the moon, the LM (having already shed the Saturn's third-stage engine) would detach from the command module's nose and descend to the moon's surface, carrying two astronauts, while the third stayed with the command module as it continued orbiting the moon. The lunar module would carry enough fuel to blast off from the moon's surface and rendezvous with the orbiting command module. The astronauts would crawl out of the LM into the command module and then discard the LM and fly back to earth in the conjoined command and service modules. Just before reentering the earth's atmosphere the command module would separate from the service module and parachute to a landing at sea. At the time the concept seemed so bizarre that Houbolt suffered the ridicule of his peers and was dismissed by supervisors. Mission Control's flight director, Chris Kraft, considered Houbolt "a madman with a mission."

But at a tense and historic meeting with von Braun in 1963 Houbolt was able to finally sell his method to the proud, stubborn German, and NASA officially selected lunar-orbit rendezvous as the wisest means of reaching the moon. NASA officials look back with wonder at those heady days and the powerful collusion of politics, technology, imagination, and youthful determination. "If Jack Kennedy had been older and wiser, he would never have committed us to the moon. The same was true for all of us," Kraft said years later. "If we'd been older and wiser, we would have known that we couldn't get it all done. But we weren't. So we did it."

Not, however, without various terrifying imperfections. Three days after leaving the Cape, Apollo 11 reached the moon and began to circle it. Neil Armstrong and Buzz Aldrin climbed through a hatch into their lunar module, called *Eagle*, and separated from the nose of the command module, called *Columbia*, piloted by Mike Collins. Standing side by side inside the backward-flying LM, Armstrong and Aldrin fired the thruster engines that slowed *Eagle*'s orbit and allowed it to be pulled by the moon's mild gravity down toward the lunar surface.

But just six thousand feet above the surface, a yellow warning light began to flash, indicating an overload of data pouring into *Eagle*'s onboard computer. Mission Control staff turned anxiously for advice from the twenty-six-year-old whiz responsible for the LM's computer. Steven Bales knew the computer well enough to believe that the landing could proceed, even with the overload signal. For that bold decision, Bales would later stand alongside the three astronauts to receive a Medal of Freedom from President Nixon.

Moments later Armstrong gently brought the LM down onto a flat expanse called the Sea of Tranquillity and famously reported, "The *Eagle* has landed." Mission Control reported back that its engineers had begun breathing again. During the six-hour rest period that followed, Aldrin silently celebrated the Christian rite of communion—he sipped wine from a chalice, ate a wafer, and prayed—while Armstrong ate a snack and described the gray land he saw outside his window. Finally Armstrong climbed backward out the hatch.

It was four minutes before 11 P.M., Eastern Daylight Saving Time, and the world below watched and listened to the scratchy television transmissions as Armstrong backed down the ladder, landed softly with a *poof* in the powdery grit, and said, "That's one small step for man . . . ah . . . one giant leap for mankind."

Fifteen minutes later Aldrin stepped down onto the surface—and immediately gave in to an uncontrollable urge to pee. He later called it a "unique feeling" to know "the whole world was watching" as he silently wet his space pants.

"Magnificent desolation," Aldrin said as he took his first look around. After three busy hours, during which the two astronauts set up equipment for solar wind experiments, collected rock and soil samples, and spoke briefly with Nixon, they climbed back into the *Eagle*, threw out their garbage—food containers, urine collection bags—and closed the hatch for a seven-hour rest period before lifting off.

Neither man slept. They were elated, cold, and distracted—Armstrong looked through a telescope at the bright beauty of the earth. They finally launched and rejoined Collins, and on the three-day trip home, as a gag for Houston, listened to a tape of earthly sound effects, including diesel locomotives and dogs barking.

The Apollo 11 crew embarked on a boastful, celebratory around-the-world tour—Bonn, London, Rome, Belgrade, Ankara, Kinshasa, Tehran, Bombay, Sydney, Tokyo—as if the world needed to be reminded that the Americans had won the space race. Aldrin, meanwhile, began experiencing the emotional letdown that would afflict most future moonwalkers—and which would lead him to a nervous breakdown. Walking on the moon, it turned out, carried a hidden risk, in the form of a question: *What next?*

///

When Gene Cernan learned he'd been named Alan Shepard's backup for the upcoming Apollo 14 flight, he knew he'd never get a chance to go on that flight. No way would Shepard, after nearly ten years of waiting, let a backup pilot take his place. Still, Cernan thought he should let Shepard know that he was no rookie and wasn't about to play the lackey's role. After being selected as an astronaut in 1963, Cernan had flown twice—he walked in space on Gemini 9 and orbited the moon on Apollo 10. He strode into Shepard's office one day, congratulated him on getting Apollo 14, then promised to do everything he could to get his backup crew ready. If necessary, said Cernan, who was ten years younger and a couple of notches lower in rank, he'd be ready to replace Shepard if something should happen.

Shepard was leaning back in his chair, arms folded, feet on the desk, giving a look that Cernan called his "big fucking deal" look. For the longest time Shepard said nothing, and Cernan didn't know if he was angry or indifferent or what. He had come to like Shepard but knew the other man could "turn the ice water on in a second." Finally Shepard stood up, grinned, and stuck out his hand. "Geeno," he said, "we're going to have a ball."

Cernan felt like a thick wall—"not a veil, it was a wall"— had crumbled. Behind the wall was a door that Shepard rarely opened to others. But once Shepard let Cernan cross that threshold, "he let me realize what a tremendous man he really was." He would recall later, "It's almost like he was waiting for someone to crash through that barrier, someone who had enough guts to face off with him. But I don't know how many people got into that inner sanctum."

///

Two weeks after Neil Armstrong and his crew returned home, on August 6, 1969, NASA told the press that Alan Shepard was back in the game. It was already well known that Shepard was rich, his net worth somewhere between $1 million and $5 million (he'd never volunteer exactly how much, except to say, "I was storing a few nuts away for the winter"). When asked why a comfortably wealthy forty-seven-year-old would risk his neck for the moon, Shepard told the *New York Times:* "Because space is about the only business I know. It's something I believe in." Besides, he'd been trained his entire adult life to be an aviator, and what aviator wouldn't aspire to make the biggest flight of all?

As his Apollo 14 crewmates, Shepard had chosen Ed Mitchell, known as "the Brain," a studious, serious Navy commander with a Ph.D., and Stu Roosa, an Air Force major and former smoke jumper from Oklahoma with a sweep of red hair and a sly humor that Shepard liked. Neither had yet reached space, and their peers—and then the press—began calling the three-man crew "the rookies." Cernan loved to tease Shepard about that.

Mitchell, the studious one, and Roosa, the beer drinker, were shocked at how Shepard—now the oldest of NASA's sixty-plus astronauts—trained for Apollo 14 like a kid. He jogged a few miles each day ("although it's rather distasteful to me," he once admitted) and lifted weights ("not anything really heavy," he said) at the astronaut gym.

Part of the crew's training scheme took them to a remote part of the Bavarian region of Germany, where they sifted through ancient rocks and silt as part of an exercise to acquaint them with the rocks they'd have to identify and collect on the moon. Shepard's crew and their three-man backup collected rocks and practiced "moonwalking" across the rocky terrain in their space suits. Each night they went out to throw back foot-tall steins of beer. They once climbed to the top of an old bell tower outside Munich, beer bottles in tow, and late that night had to bang on the door of their dormitory, which the proprietor locked at 10 P.M. Another time, during geology training in an Arizona canyon, at the end of a long day of hiking, Shepard nudged a public affairs guy along for the trip. "Let's race," he said, then sprinted the last quarter mile.

Shepard practiced for many hours on an ugly, ingenious contraption called the Lunar Landing Training Vehicle (LLTV), which NASA designed to simulate the up-and-down flying that astronauts would do in the lunar module. Nicknamed the "flying bedstead," the LLTV was a set of rocket thrusters bolted beneath a structure that looked like it belonged on a kid's playground. Balancing the LLTV atop the downward thrust of its rockets and taking it up to five hundred feet or so was a delicate and danger-ous endeavor. Neil Armstrong had almost killed himself a year earlier when a prototype of the LLTV began rocking out of con-trol, forcing Armstrong to bail out in his rocket-propelled ejection seat; Armstrong parachuted to safety as his flying bedstead spun, flipped, and exploded.

Colleagues were amazed at how many times Shepard took the dangerous LLTV up for a spin. Then, after a lifetime of airplanes and jets, Shepard learned to fly helicopters, too—also to help him prepare for flying his LEM down to the moon's surface. Mitchell, Roosa, Cernan, and the others all found themselves asking, "This is the Icy Commander?" The ice man, it turns out, was having the time of his life.

During another trip to southern Arizona, for more geology training, a friend of Cernan's invited him, Shepard, Mitchell, and Joe Engle (part of Cernan's backup crew) to cross into Mexico and dine at his restaurant. The four astronauts were supposed to meet Cernan's friend at a car dealership just across the border, but instead of Cernan's friend, two chauffeur-driven cars picked up the astronauts. The cars stopped in front of a large, brightly lit complex with a motel, restaurant, and dance hall.

They were led into a motel room. On the dresser sat four square glass bottles of Ballantine scotch, with a room key sitting next to each one. The four astronauts tried to ask the chauffeurs what was happening, but they left without a word. A man wearing a huge sombrero finally showed up, wearing an impressive six-shooter on his hip. He spoke broken English, and none of the four astronauts spoke Spanish, but with some gesticulating they were finally able to discern that he was the local sheriff. "I thought we were going to dinner," Shepard told Cernan. "What happens now?"

Just then, as the sheriff stood by the door smiling, four young women entered the room and sat on the bed, side by side, across the room from the four astronauts. They weren't the most attractive of Mexico's women; one had a wide gap between her front teeth, another was hefty. They all started giggling and fluttering their eyelashes. "Okay, Cernan, I think I know what's supposed to happen," Shepard finally said.

For the next forty-five minutes, in a mélange of tortured Spanish and charades, the spacemen tried to explain why they couldn't stay. They each tried what little Spanish they knew: *el presidente . . . no es possible . . . we can't stay out late . . . we can't drink . . . have to train for mission in the morning . . . going to moon . . . la luna . . .* Finally the women realized they were not going to sleep with an American astronaut that night. The sheriff beckoned to the chauffeurs. During the ride back, the astronauts joked that they didn't even get dinner, nor did they think to grab the bottles of scotch.

"I think they just wanted to show us Mexican hospitality," Cernan recalled.

///

Apollo 11 was followed by a near-perfect Apollo 12 mission, during which Pete Conrad and Alan Bean bounced, danced, and sang on the moon like awestruck schoolboys. Suddenly America was making lunar travel look easy, and Apollo 13—the mission that had briefly been Shepard's—was up next, scheduled to explore the exotic and hilly lowlands of the moon, a rugged and geologically intriguing region called Fra Mauro.

Apollo 13 began uneventfully, but two days and two hundred thousand miles from earth—on April 13, 1970—one of the ship's two oxygen tanks was ignited by a damaged wire and exploded, smashing a hole in the side of the service module (attached beneath the command module) and wrecking everything nearby. The blast violently rocked the spacecraft, and Jack Swigert's message to Mission Control—"Okay, Houston, we've had a problem here"—was followed by a more urgent confirmation from Jim Lovell: "Ah, Houston, we have a problem."

Lovell peered out the window and saw fumes spewing from the jagged hole in the side of his ship: the second oxygen tank, damaged by the unexplained blast, was rapidly venting the crew's precious oxygen into space. The news kept getting worse:

The oxygen supplied power to fuel cells that energized the electrical system, which was now dying; without electricity, there would be no lights and no access to the water supply. Nor would the crew be able to ignite the engines that would slow the ship and bring it into orbit around the moon. Apollo 13 seemed headed for oblivion.

The crew quickly powered down the command module, called *Odyssey,* to preserve what little electricity remained. Then Houston confirmed what the crew already knew: The three couldn't survive in *Odyssey,* which would run out of oxygen in an hour. They'd have to use the lunar module as a "lifeboat." The LEM, named *Aquarius,* which Fred Haise had already docked to the nose of *Odyssey,* carried only enough oxygen to sustain two men for two days. Now it would have to keep three men alive for four days—that is, if the crew could figure a way to whip around the moon and fly back to earth.

Lovell and Haise crawled through a hatch into the cramped space of the LEM while Swigert stayed in *Odyssey,* using a flashlight to shut down *Odyssey's* systems; Lovell and Haise ran a hose from Haise's now obsolete moonwalking suit through to the command module, to give Swigert enough oxygen to breathe. The next four days were among the most terrifying and ingenious in NASA's history. Shepard, at Mission Control, assigned astronauts to climb into simulators to test theories on how to get the ship home.

Instead of turning Apollo 13 around and using the last bits of *Odyssey's* fuel to propel the ship back to earth, Mission Control decided to let Apollo 13 continue coasting to the moon, to use small boosts from the LEM's fuel supply to adjust its course, and then whip around the moon, using the momentum from that U-turn to swing it back to earth.

Other engineers, meanwhile, devised a makeshift canister that would filter carbon dioxide from the air inside *Aquarius,* and the crew used hoses, batteries, tape, plastic, and cardboard to rig a purifying system. Then they settled back to live in *Aquarius*, shivering at near-freezing temperatures, sharing little more than a pint of water among them per day. Deke Slayton tried to encourage the men: "Just wanted to let you know we're gonna get you back. Everything's looking good. Why don't you quit worrying and get some sleep." Finally, with a billion people around the world glued to radios and televisions, Apollo 13's haggard crew crawled back into the cold, clammy command module, which Lovell felt looked "forlorn and pitiful," and separated from *Aquarius*. "She was a good ship," Lovell reported with a catch in his voice. Sixty tension-filled minutes later, Apollo 13 was bobbing safely in the Pacific. Incredibly, they had landed within three miles of the recovery ship, USS *Iwo Jima*, the most accurate landing of the entire space program.

///

Weeks later Shepard met with Jim Lovell back in Houston, and Lovell asked Shepard how he felt now about losing Apollo 13. It would become a persistent joke between Shepard and Lovell. Every time the two astronauts bumped into each other, Lovell would joke, "Anytime you want Apollo 13 back, Al, you can have it."

Apollo 14 was delayed for four months to allow crews to modify Shepard's spacecraft and, they hoped, prevent a similar disaster. Those delays only prolonged the anxious agony Louise began to experience during the long countdown to her husband's launch. If Shepard was a fair-weather Christian Scientist, Louise was a perfect specimen, everything a Christian Scientist was raised to be: self-reliant but not arrogant, confident but not confrontational, friendly but wary, uncomplicated and unopinionated but unyieldingly true to her beliefs. It was not always an easy balancing act.

At Principia she had been quiet, shy, and sometimes sickly. She avoided public speaking and crowds, and she rarely spoke her mind. Even with her children, she was a halfhearted disciplinarian, preferring not to get tangled in battles of will with her girls. Across their years of marriage, however, friends watched Louise blossom as Alan's partner. Despite his infidelities and the long absences, he complemented her somehow. He gave her confidence, and she sometimes felt he had enough for the two of them. She learned to handle herself in the most demanding social situations: cocktails with Jack Kennedy and Cary Grant, dinner with kings and queens.

But as the launch of Apollo 14 neared, Louise was a wreck. She couldn't sleep at night, and she couldn't keep her food down. It wasn't just that she feared his death. That fear had long since been accepted as just another one of the accommodations in a Navy wife's life. What seemed to be bothering Louise was a culmination of all those years of waiting, of dealing with the brutal mornings of Alan's illness, of watching him teeter on the edge of quitting NASA, only to rise and go to the office each frustrating day.

Louise thrived on evenness, and the ups and downs of Alan's life took a toll on her delicate physiology. The first weeks of 1971 were a repeat of 1961, with reporters calling at all hours, showing up at the door, talking to neighbors, asking her all those questions about death and fear. Contributing to Louise's unease in the days before Apollo 14 was the resurfacing of the occasional questions about Alan's rumored infidelities. As newspaper stories about Alan proliferated, a bold young reporter from a Houston newspaper asked Louise how she handled those rumors. She gave the reporter a taut smile and said, "What do you expect from a sailor?"

Some of the other NASA wives considered Louise "our Jackie O" (who also, for the sake of history, put up with her husband's wanderings). "People wondered, 'How did an asshole like that get a queen like her?' " Gene Cernan said of Alan and Louise. "But no one had the balls to question him publicly." Alan complicated the matter by forever refusing to deny anything. "It's almost like he didn't feel he had to," Cernan recalled.

It's possible Louise simply didn't know the truth because she didn't want to know. She had a "don't confuse me with the facts" attitude toward such rumors, recalled Louise's lifelong friend and former Principia classmate Dorel Abbot. "Some things you want to know, some things you don't need to know," Abbot said. Whatever combination of factors were nagging at her, the effects became more profound as the days counted down to Alan's blastoff. He had been away from home many weeks at a time during his preflight training. And in the final two weeks before liftoff, he and his crew were held in quarantine—a new NASA prelaunch precaution.

Louise had seen very little of him. He still called at 5 P.M. on most nights he wasn't home for dinner. But now he was headed someplace where he couldn't call. She was tossing and turning at night, throwing up during the day. The launch date—January 31, 1971—couldn't come and go soon enough.

///

To prevent Shepard and his crewmates from catching a bug or virus in the weeks before their mission, which might seriously sicken them in space, NASA created a strict preflight quarantine procedure that limited the astronauts' exposure to other humans.

For three weeks the men were limited to the astronaut crew quarters in Hangar S or a nearby beach house on the Cape. They were occasionally allowed to climb into a T-38 to let loose with some spins and rolls, which NASA figured would help acclimate their bodies to the tumblings and gyrations of their upcoming mission. But whenever they were with other people, they had to wear protective surgical masks over their face.

During the final week the restrictions grew even tighter, and the crew of Apollo 14 was required to begin sleeping inside an aluminum-sided recreational vehicle that NASA had converted into a quarantine room. The crew would also live in that room for two weeks after their return; NASA was afraid that some alien lunar microbe—a fungus, a spore, or a bacterium—might hitch a ride back to earth on an astronaut.

Not that Shepard exactly abided by all the restrictions. He felt cooped up inside the small quarantine room and had a hard time sleeping—he was too geared up. His crewmates would settle down at night and watch TV, but Shepard got dressed, left his surgical mask behind, and sneaked out for a few hours of who knew what. One night, with just eighteen hours before the launch, Shepard grabbed his backup commander, Cernan, and took him along for a drive out to the launchpad, where his skyscraper-tall rocket awaited.

Cernan had kept his promise to train as hard as Shepard, calling him "the old man" and threatening to steal Apollo 14 from him. A week before the launch, though, Cernan had dumped a helicopter into the Indian River and was lucky to escape the flaming wreckage alive. When he returned to the crew quarters that morning, burned and bleeding, he saw Shepard at breakfast and said, "Okay, Al, you win. It's your flight."

In the aftermath of Apollo 13, NASA canceled three of its future lunar missions—Apollo 18, 19, and 20. They even discussed canceling Apollo 15, 16, and 17, which would have put Shepard in line to become the last man to walk on the moon (a title Cernan would later earn on Apollo 17). That night, standing beneath his rocket with Cernan by his side, Shepard was destined to soon become the fifth human to step onto the gritty lunar ground—the oldest, and the only one of the Mercury Seven astronauts to do so.

A decade had passed since Bob Gilruth had picked Shepard to be the first American spaceman. Public interest in space had waned some in the months after Neil Armstrong touched the moon's surface, but the near-fatal flight of Apollo 13 reminded the nation once more of the dangers and drama of space exploration. NASA was now hoping that Apollo 14 would prove to the world that Apollo 13 had been a fluke, that America's space program could execute a perfect lunar mission.

Launchpad 39-A was alive with engineers twittering around the rocket, pumping it full of fuel. The rocket's thin walls groaned as the pressurized liquid surged inside. A symphony of hisses and spurts, hums and clacks filled the Florida air. Shepard and Cernan drove through a security checkpoint and walked out to the launchpad. Wordlessly the two men approached the enormous Saturn 5 booster rocket, then stood beneath holes that would soon expel enough pressurized fire to shake the earth.

Shepard had to realize, at some point, how lucky he was to have come so far. If not for the Ménière's disease, he might have been sitting in Gus Grissom's seat four Januaries earlier and been consumed by flames. Or, if not for NASA's caution, he might have flown the ill-fated Apollo 13. It was about 9 P.M. He and Cernan looked like ants beneath the rocket engines' gaping maw. The capsule Shepard would soon ride sat four hundred feet above them, atop a rocket nearly five times taller than the old Redstone that had given Shepard his first space ride. They spoke very little, but Cernan felt he was standing beside a man who had "redefined the meaning of the word *commitment.*"

He was even afraid to look at Shepard, for fear of seeing his hero in tears. "It may have been the first and only time I'd seen Alan humble," he said. Finally Shepard put his arm around Cernan's shoulder and said, "Okay, let's go."

19

"What's wrong with this ship?"

In the VIP launch viewing area, as menacing clouds tumbled overhead and a light drizzle began soaking the crowds on the beach, Louise stood beside a white Chevy convertible with the women closest to her in life. There was her mother; her two daughters and her niece Alice; her friend and embroidering partner, Loraine Meyer; her best friend, Dorel Abbot; and two other astronauts' wives, Marge Slayton and Jo Schirra.

As the Sunday afternoon launch neared, the drizzle became a downpour, and the launch was put on hold for forty minutes. The delay was almost too much for Louise to take, so Dorel led her away from the others to a quieter spot. Huddled beneath Dorel's umbrella, they stood beside a hurricane fence, and Louise confessed that she was a lot more nervous than she'd been pretending. She looked beautiful, as always, in a navy blue pantsuit, a white blouse, and blue boots. But her stomach was doing acrobatics.

The day before, she'd visited Alan for the last time. She and Ed Mitchell's and Stu Roosa's wives, but no other family members, were briefly allowed into the quarantine room for a quiet dinner. After dinner Louise left the quarantine room and turned for one last goodbye. Standing on opposite sides of a thick window, Louise and Alan pressed their lips to the glass. Then Alan told her he wouldn't be making his customary 5 P.M. phone call the next evening. "I'm going to be leaving town," he said.

That night Louise attended a reception held by Alan's friend John King, the millionaire oilman and rancher from Colorado (for whom Wally Schirra had recently gone to work). As soon as she arrived, she saw Cary Grant standing by the bar getting a cocktail. Louise's friends dragged her over to meet her favorite actor, and in no time they were all laughing about that day more than twenty-five years ago when Alan and Louise, bound for Corpus Christi and a new life together, had seen Grant outside a southern California realtor's office, and Louise had insisted that Alan pull over. Grant asked her about the next day's flight, and Louise told him what she'd been telling the newspapers in recent weeks. "I'm constantly aware of the moon these days," she said. "It takes on a whole new look when you know your husband is going up there for a visit."

The next day Louise declined NASA's offer to watch Alan, fully suited, emerge from his crew quarters and ride a bus out to his rocket. Instead she stood in the rain with Dorel, three miles away from Apollo 14.

///

"I plan to cry a lot." That had been Shepard's response when asked what he planned to do on the trip to the moon. An extra oxygen tank and a backup battery had been added to his capsule, among other modifications, to prevent a repeat of Apollo 13's woes. Still, Shepard almost had reason to cry before he got anywhere near the moon.

Following the forty-minute delay due to a thunderstorm—during which Shepard impatiently snapped, "Let's get on with it"—Apollo 14 lifted off from the Cape on the afternoon of January 31, 1971, ten years after Shepard had become the first

American spaceman. Shepard was surprised at how much gentler the eighteen-thousand-mile-an-hour ascent was than his five-thousand-mile-an-hour *Freedom 7* launch had been. When Apollo 14's spacecraft separated from its booster rockets, passed through the atmosphere, and settled into orbit around the earth, Shepard and his two colleagues unhooked their harnesses and floated giddily around the cabin. Compared to the brief taste of weightlessness *Freedom 7* had offered, floating freely inside the more spacious Apollo command module was a thrilling moment—"very smooth and strangely quiet," Shepard said later—and was alone worth the trip.

After the Saturn rocket's third-stage engine had boosted them out of earth's orbit and toward the moon, Shepard and Stu Roosa then swapped seats so that Roosa could take the controls and perform the mission's first crucial task: docking with the lunar module. The LM rode in a "garage" beneath the conjoined command and service modules. Roosa's job was to detach the LM (and its garage, the now used up third-stage engine), then turn the command module around and guide the tip of the module into the nose of the buglike LM, the vehicle Shepard and Ed Mitchell would later ride down to the moon's surface. Once the command and lunar modules were docked together, nose to nose, the two ships would continue coasting toward the moon, and the LM would shed the spent third-stage engine from its behind. Docking was a delicate maneuver, since both ships were traveling at nearly five miles per second, but the docking mechanism itself was one of the simplest on the entire spacecraft, and the procedure had been perfected on previous Apollo flights, none of which experienced any significant problems with docking.

Roosa turned around the command module, which he'd named *Kitty Hawk*, so that it was coasting backward. Shepard peered through a side window and coached Roosa as they neared the LM. Roosa lined up his capsule and tapped the thrusters so that it eased forward and hit the LM's nose dead center. Shepard and the other two astronauts then waited to hear the satisfying clacks of the command module's arrowlike probe jamming into and then locking onto a port on the LM. No clacks. Or as Shepard reported to Houston in the sexually tinged language of the fighter pilot, "No joy."

Roosa backed up *Kitty Hawk* and tried to dock a second time. Again he guided *Kitty Hawk*'s probe precisely into the center of the LM's port and even held the thrusters on for a few seconds, trying to jam the two spacecraft into a "hard dock." But when he eased up on the thrusters, the two ships again drifted apart. Now Houston was worried, and so was Shepard. If they couldn't dock, their moon shot was over. In the next hour Roosa tried three more times. He was using too much fuel, and Houston was running out of hope. Shepard then suggested a never-before-tried spacewalk, in which he'd exit *Kitty Hawk*, float out to its nose, and pull the two ships together by hand. He knew it was risky and not likely to get an okay from the cautious flight directors. But he wasn't going to give up without trying everything.

Mission Control overruled Shepard's idea as too dangerous and began discussing whether to cancel the mission, which would have been devastating not only to Shepard but also to the entire space program, coming on the heels of the disastrous Apollo 13 mission. But first NASA advised one last high-speed stab at docking. This time, however, Gene Cernan—the capsule communicator stationed at the Cape—suggested that, a split second before the two craft touched, Shepard hit the retract switch that pulled the command module's probe out of the way to allow the latches to slap closed and draw the two ships together. Shepard told Roosa to "juice it," and as the command module again nudged against the LM, Shepard punched the retract switch and waited for the *clack clack clack* of the latches. For four long seconds nothing happened. "It's not working," Shepard said. A second later the cabin filled with the metallic *clack clack clack* of the twelve latches pulling the ships tightly together. "We have a hard dock," Shepard reported to the cheers of Mission Control.

NASA remained concerned, however, that the problem with the docking mechanism could recur after Shepard's moon landing and might prevent the LM from docking again with the command module, which would spell disaster. They allowed Apollo 14 to continue toward the moon while engineers debated whether or not to allow the lunar landing to proceed. For the next three days, Shepard and his crew slept fitfully in their hammocks, listened to Roosa's Johnny Cash tapes, ate food from cans, brushed and flossed, excreted in plastic bags ("a messy operation," Shepard said, and a good time for the other two to put on their oxygen masks), chatted with Houston, floated from floor to ceiling with just the push of a finger, and swiped at a few washers and screws floating in midair, left behind by sloppy workers. They watched the earth shrink away, becoming a small and lonely little ball, as the gray blur of the moon grew bigger and rounder.

Day and night became one. At one point, when he thought his two partners were asleep, Roosa saw a flashlight flickering inside Mitchell's sleeping bag. He was too tired to ask, and never thought to mention it to Shepard, who wouldn't learn about the secret behind Mitchell's flashlight until they were all safely back on earth.

///

She thought it was "a beautiful launch" with a "Fourth of July" feel to it, but she wasn't ready to go home yet. At the Cape, Louise felt closer to Alan, even though he was so far away. So Louise stayed an extra night at her Cocoa Beach motel, ate an omelet, watched TV reports on the docking woes, and flipped through a copy of the flight manual he'd given her, trying to absorb all the details of what he was doing each moment.

The next day she flew home to their eleven-room manse with the big white pillars in the Houston enclave that was home to oilmen, celebrities, and politicians. Louise's parents and in-laws were already there. Louise's mother, seeing how fragile her daughter seemed, invited her friend Dorel—pleaded with her, actually—to help around the house.

With all the bedrooms filled with family members and the Shepards' daughters, Dorel slept in Alan's spot, right beside Louise. That first night Louise was up most of the night. She finally fell asleep near dawn, but at 6 A.M. there was a loud knock at the front door and then the shrill ringing of the doorbell.

Louise sat bolt upright in bed and gasped. An early morning visitor could only mean bad news. She pictured a dark NASA sedan out front, a chaplain inside carrying a message of sadness and condolences. Dorel told Louise to wait upstairs while she answered the door. It wasn't NASA. It was only the press—the jackals. They wanted a statement. Dorel was furious and kicked them all off the property, scolding them never to touch that doorbell again, especially not at six in the morning. She "really gave them hell," then said that Louise would come outside with a statement when she was ready.

Later that day Louise pulled herself together, fixed her hair, put on a nice outfit, and went out to face the hungry press. She tried to exude confidence and gave a defiantly curt statement. "There are lots of other occupations that are demanding of men. I think you have to build a good mental attitude toward your husband's occupation," she told them, then turned and went back inside.

///

Meanwhile, inside the command module, Shepard was tense, and everyone on the ground at Mission Control felt it. Two days into the mission he abruptly canceled a scheduled television broadcast—they were "too busy" and the broadcast was "not important," he said. His replies to questions from communicators in Houston were curt, sometimes rude, and the ground crew thought he was being "uptight" and "snappish."

Shepard acknowledged later that he "found it difficult to relax" and was "very tired." He tried to eat and drink a lot and to do some isometric exercises, but his body felt tense the first two days—especially his legs, which he kept braced against the wall to keep him from floating around—and he could only sleep a few hours at a time. Maybe it was the weight of taking center stage after a failed mission. Or maybe the earlier docking problem had spooked him. Whatever the reason, Shepard spoke very little en route to the moon, reporting back to Houston only what he felt was absolutely necessary. He didn't try to describe the dark vastness of the universe around him, nor the dead little planet ahead. He kept his thoughts and his words to himself.

Finally NASA reported that after studying the problem with the docking mechanism, they had decided to allow the lunar landing to proceed as planned. "You are go for Fra Mauro," came the message from Mission Control, followed by Shepard's response: "Hot damn."

The blueprint for Apollo 14's mission was essentially a duplicate of what Apollo 13 had planned: to land in and explore the rocky hills of Fra Mauro, which scientists believed contained some of the oldest rocks in the universe. Three days after leaving the earth's orbit, the linked-together ships of Apollo 14—the combined command-service module and, docked to that, the lunar module—reached the moon and fell smoothly into orbit. On the far side of the moon, the cabin grew dark and eerie, followed by the sudden burst of sunlight as they swung around the other side.

After a few such loops Shepard and Mitchell exited the command module, *Kitty Hawk*, through the yard-wide port in its nose and entered the LM, which Mitchell had named *Antares*, the brightest of the stars in the constellation Scorpio (which happened to be Shepard's astrological sign).

Mitchell stood at the controls, Shepard beside him. To conserve weight, the LM, with its paper-thin aluminum walls and spidery legs, had been designed without seats. Then they separated from Roosa and *Kitty Hawk* and prepared to descend toward a land of deep craters, undulating gray deserts, and house-sized boulders. "This is really a wild place," Shepard said as he looked out his window down onto the brown and gray surface, finally breaking out of his tense silence. Mitchell called it "the most stark and desolate-looking piece of country I've ever seen."

But then another glitch reared up and threatened to keep them off the moon. A signal on the LM's dash lit up, indicating that its abort program had been triggered. Mitchell immediately assumed that the signal was erroneous, and when he tapped on the control panel the light blinked off. It came on again a few minutes later but disappeared once more when Mitchell tapped it with his pen. He and Shepard assumed a loose ball of solder was floating back there, but they had no way to fix it. "Houston!" Shepard radioed. "What's wrong with this ship?"

The LM's automated abort procedure was designed to kick in during an emergency. If Shepard experienced a sudden problem just prior to landing, the abort program would automatically ignite the engines beneath the LM and blast it away from the moon and back into orbit, where it could join again with the command module. Fortunately for Shepard and Mitchell, the abort program worked only when the LM was in the final stages of its descent to the surface; *Antares* was still in orbit and ninety minutes away from that descent. But if the problem wasn't fixed and the signal was triggered again during their descent, they'd be irrevocably blasted away from the moon.

A similar glitch had threatened to abort Apollo 11's lunar landing, but twenty-six-year-old NASA engineer Steve Bales made his split-second decision that it was safe to ignore the beeping computer overload signal and allow the historic landing to proceed. But Shepard's problem was more complicated; it could not be ignored, nor could it be fixed by Shepard or Mitchell. So NASA turned to another twenty-something engineer at MIT's Draper Labs, who had helped design *Antares'* computer software.

While Shepard continued to orbit the moon, an Air Force officer screeched to a stop in front of Donald Eyles' Massachusetts apartment and pounded on the engineer's door—at 2 A.M.—to tell him that he had ninety minutes to create a new program that would override the faulty abort switch. Eyles threw a coat over his pajamas, and the Air Force officer drove him to his nearby computer lab at MIT. Eyles sat before his computer terminal and tapped away on his keyboard, struggling to create from scratch a substitute software program that would eliminate the erroneous abort signal.

Most of the LM's computer program was locked inside the computer's memory and couldn't be altered. So Eyles had to devise a patch that advised the computer program to essentially ignore the abort signal. Eyles had only ninety minutes because that was the window Shepard had in which to land on the moon. If Eyles missed that deadline, Shepard would have to return to the command module and fly home. The astronaut's life's goal now rested in the hands of a computer geek.

Sixty minutes later the engineer looked up from his computer. "Done," he said. The ingenious little program was transmitted by radio to Houston, which ran it through a simulator, to make sure it worked, and then transmitted the instructions by radio to *Antares*. While Shepard continued to fly *Antares,* Mitchell entered sixty new codes into the computer, using a keyboard on the control panel. Shepard watched in helpless, anxious silence.

By now the window for a lunar landing was down to about twenty minutes. One of the reasons Shepard had chosen Mitchell—"the Brain"—was for his computer expertise and his knowledge of the LM. But one wrong computer entry, one slip of the finger, could cause the whole computer system to crash, so Shepard tried hard not to rush his partner. Mitchell finished in about five minutes, which left a fifteen-minute window to start the landing procedures. Shepard reported back to Mission Control that they were ready to land. "Houston, we've got it. We're commencing with the descent program."

But Mission Control ordered Shepard to wait while it checked to make sure the new software program was working, and Shepard gritted his teeth through ten more long minutes of delay. Finally, with just sixty seconds to spare, capsule communicator Fred Haise gave the okay to land: "You are go for Fra Mauro." "Thank you," Shepard replied sarcastically. "You troops do a nice job down there."

Shepard quickly fired the engine that slowed *Antares'* orbit, and the LM immediately began dropping toward the moon's surface. "All righty. It's a beautiful day to land at Fra Mauro," Shepard reported back to Houston, relieved that his mission was back on track. All the training he had done in the LLTV had prepared him to carefully keep the LM at just the right angle. The LM was still traveling at thirty-seven hundred miles an hour, but because it was angled with the bottom flying first, the thrusters slowed its speed and helped it drop lower. Flying backward and at an angle meant Shepard was flying blind, lying on his back and facing up into space, relying on his instruments to tell him where he was in relation to the surface. It was just like instrument flying in an airplane.

But as *Antares* reached thirty-two thousand feet, the landing radar failed to accurately lock onto the moon's surface. Instead of displaying *Antares'* exact position, the radar instruments in front of Shepard's face were blank. If the screens didn't light up with solid landing radar readings before they reached ten thousand feet, the rules required Shepard to abort the landing. "Houston, our landing radar is out," Shepard reported. "Come on, radar!" Mitchell barked as they dropped to twenty-five thousand feet. "Come on."

At fifteen thousand feet, as Shepard flicked his wrist left, right, forward, and back, each flick sending spurts of gas hissing from the small thruster valves, finessing the LM downward, Houston broke through to remind Shepard of the abort plan, which he would have to implement if the radar failed to lock onto the moon. That plan called for Shepard to stop his descent at ten thousand feet, ignite his main thruster engine, and blast away from the moon. Just the thought of it was sickening. *"Antares,"* said Haise, "we should go over the procedures to abort."

"We're aware of the ground rules, Houston," Shepard snapped. But that didn't mean Houston could stop him from violating those rules. Just three miles above the surface, Shepard wasn't about to turn back now, and he told Mitchell about his plan: "If the radar doesn't kick in, we're going to fly her down." A few minutes later, as *Antares* reached fourteen thousand feet, Houston suggested a laughably simple solution. They told Shepard to try resetting the radar's circuit breaker. Just like in an ordinary earthly basement, he pulled out the breaker and stuck it back in. Still no radar. "Negative," Shepard reluctantly told Houston.

But a second later the radar system flickered to life, locked onto the moon, and gave Shepard a full view on his control panel of all the information he needed to land. "Houston, we have a radar lock," Shepard practically yelled. The radar information was immediately relayed back to Houston, which gave the go-ahead for a landing. "You better believe, Houston," Shepard said.

"Great," said Mitchell. "Whew, that was close."

Shepard quickly dropped below eight thousand feet and then slowly coasted lower toward his destination, a deep lunar divot called Cone Crater, which appeared "fat as a goose" beneath him. He descended very slowly—at less than five miles an hour—while still moving forward between craggy lunar ridges and hillsides. When a rough patch of craters and rocks loomed below him, he'd veer right or left, keeping Houston informed of each move—"shifting course," he once said, then dodged another rocky plateau. Finally he found the smooth, flat space that they'd chosen two years earlier as the ideal landing zone, and

420 / LIGHT THIS CANDLE

brought *Antares* down within fifty feet of the spot—closer to his target than the previous two moon missions. The only imperfection in the landing was that he touched down on a small slope that caused the LM to tilt a few degrees to one side.

"Right on the money," Shepard said, practically giggling at this point.

"Not bad for an old man," Fred Haise reported from Houston.

"Okay, Fredo," Shepard replied. "That was a real fine job. Thank you, buddy."

///

Neil Armstrong had never revealed whether or how he'd scripted his famous first sentence on the moon: "That's one small step for man . . . one giant leap for mankind." But they seemed the perfect words to immortalize the occasion.

Pete Conrad, the five-foot-six-inch commander of Apollo 12, was somewhat less elegant with his first words: "Whoopie! Man, that may have been a small one for Neil, but it's a long one for me." (With those words, Conrad won $500 from Oriana Fallaci, the Italian writer Shepard had antagonized, who during an afternoon of poolside drinks bet Conrad he wouldn't dare attempt a glib remark at such a serious moment.)

Shepard clearly didn't give much advance thought to his first words. But for those who knew the rough route he'd taken to reach Fra Mauro, what he said seemed appropriate enough: "Al is on the surface. And it's been a long way. But we're here."

Shepard had about three minutes on the surface alone, waiting for Mitchell to finish his checklist and descend the ladder himself. Shepard tried to describe what he saw—"very impressive sight . . . boulders near the rim . . . Cone ridge going along to the north"—but nothing could accurately convey the lifeless gray-brown world splayed before him.

Shepard then looked up and found the earth, two-thirds of it illuminated by the sun, a quarter of a million miles away and so tiny, just a crescent of blue and white suspended in a black sky. He was exhausted. There'd been so many close calls and near misses the past few days. And there was much work ahead. But the hardest part of the journey was over, and for those few solo moments before the mission would again consume him, Shepard was suddenly overcome by the silence, the stark beauty, the loneliness of it all. His distant and delicate home planet was "very finite . . . so incredibly fragile," he reflected—just a tiny ball in space containing everyone he knew. He told himself, "Hey, not too long ago, I was grounded. Now I'm on the moon."

As the moment came to an end, a private moment he'd never forget, Shepard was surprised to feel tears welling up into his eyes. But he had no time to savor or consider his emotions, and the tears quickly dried inside his air-conditioned suit.

///

With almost every second of their time on the moon accounted for, Shepard and Mitchell quickly set about performing the hundreds of tasks they'd been assigned. After punching a flag into the dust, they set up solar experiments and radar equipment, then rigged their TV cameras so the audience back home could watch their adventures. Each astronaut took scores of pictures—of each other, of the earth, of the LM, of space. Slayton broke in to relay a message from President Nixon; he wanted them to visit the White House when they returned. Great, they said. Then back to the schedule. Apollo 14 was the first mission to be equipped with a two-wheeled cart called a modularized equipment transporter, or MET. After yanking the MET out from its storage space beneath the LM, the two men quickly stocked it with rock-collecting tools, picks and shovels, hammers and tongs. No time to muse or gawk—there were many jobs to do. Shepard had had his personal moment, and now it was all about the work. As Buzz Aldrin, the second man on the moon, would put it years later: "We weren't trained to smell the roses . . . we had a job to do."

Fra Mauro had been chosen because lunar scientists had studied it for years and decided it likely contained some of the moon's older rocks. The bulk of Shepard's next thirty-three hours would be consumed with scientific experiments—primarily gathering weird rocks. Abiding by NASA's tight schedule was difficult, and trudging along the powdery surface, Shepard and Mitchell felt like they were falling behind.

Walking, they found, was easier if they kept up a one-two, one-two, one-two pace that was more like a horse's trot than the left-right-left-right gait of a jogger. Also, they learned to lean forward to keep their balance. Fra Mauro turned out to be far more undulating than the photographs they had studied. The two previous lunar landings were in wide, flat areas known as "mare." Apollo 14 was the first to land amid the moon's jagged foothills, which made walking more difficult. The land bucked and buckled, but the harsh glare of the sun hammered the landscape flat, casting unreliable shadows. With no points of reference, craters seemed to appear suddenly beneath their feet. Boulders that seemed a mile away were suddenly within spitting distance. "As tough as trying to find your way around the Sahara Desert," Shepard said.

At the end of their five-hour first moonwalk, dusty and tired, they crawled back into the LM, took off their dirty boots, sipped water from a tube, emptied their urine bags, and crawled into their crisscrossed hammocks, Shepard on top, Mitchell beneath. But sleep was almost impossible. Shepard felt like he had no place to rest his head. Air hissed from the air conditioner. Mitchell kept raising the window shades to look outside. So, like two kids camping out, they kept whispering to each other.

"Ed. Are you awake?"

"Hell, yes, I'm awake."

"Do you feel like we're tipping over?"

"Yeah."

Because they'd landed at an 8-degree angle (which rankled Mitchell a bit), both men felt as if the LM was leaning too far, maybe even sliding down the slope. In the light gravity—with a pull one-sixth that of the earth's—they feared that one false move would topple their only means of returning home. During their first fitful night Shepard awoke once when he thought he felt the LM slipping. As he scrambled to get out of his hammock and look out the window, he fell on top of Mitchell, who was bunked below.

Through the "night" (actually a Friday afternoon back on earth), each time they drifted toward sleep they were awakened by the slightest sounds: the rustling of the paper-thin walls, the metallic pings of tiny particles hitting the LM, the slight change in pitch of the small on-board engine as an air-conditioning pump kicked in. Mitchell felt the weight of being "the only two living creatures on this dead world."

"Ed, did you hear that?" Shepard asked in an urgent whisper.

"Hell, yes, I heard that."

"What the hell was that?"

"I don't know."

"Ed?"

"What?"

"Why the hell are we whispering?"

Unable to sleep, they radioed Houston two hours early, saying they were ready for Cone Crater. The majority of the second day's moonwalk would be dedicated to reaching the rim of this wide, deep geological gold mine, which scientists guessed was actually the remains of an ancient volcano. The goal was to find rocks that had been ejected from the volcano billions of years ago—ancient slag that might harbor clues to the mysteries of the moon's origins. With their hand-pulled golf cart full of rock-collecting tools and bags, the two men set off just before 3 A.M.

Saturday for the mile-long hike—the longest, most difficult lunar trek two astronauts would ever make.

More than an hour into the hike, Shepard stated—mistakenly, it would turn out—that Cone Crater "looks a lot farther than it is." Mitchell and Shepard had studied maps and photographs of the terrain, had memorized all the landmarks—various boulders and smaller craters, each of which they'd named. But the more they walked, the farther away the lip of the crater seemed to be, as if it was taunting them. Finally the ground began to slope upward, and they sensed that Cone Crater might be just over the next rise. It wasn't, and pulling the MET cart up the slope became more and more difficult. Mitchell suggested leaving the MET where it was and hiking up without it, but Shepard wasn't about to lose a case of scotch. He'd bet a skeptical Gene Cernan that he'd be able to pull the MET all the way to the top of Cone Crater. "Okay, we're really going up a steep slope here," Shepard told Houston, where doctors listened to his heavy breathing and watched his rising heart rate. "It's hard."

As the slope became even steeper, Shepard lifted the rear of the MET as Mitchell pulled the front handle. Shepard called out, "Left, right, left, right," and they marched in sync. Tensions between the moonwalkers rose, and they began arguing about where the hell they were headed. When Shepard's breathing became more labored and his heart rate reached a danger zone of more than 140 beats per minute, NASA's doctors—already slightly edgy about a forty-seven-year-old man, recently recovered from a debilitating medical condition, trekking around on the moon—suggested a rest. While catching his breath, Shepard hinted that maybe it wasn't their day to reach Cone Crater.

But Mitchell wasn't about to give up. "We've lost everything if we don't get there," he said. "Why don't we lose our bet, Al, and leave the MET and get on up there? We could make it a lot faster." Shepard finally agreed to "press on a little farther," and Slayton got on the radio back at Mission Control and offered to cover the bet—he'd buy Cernan his case of scotch if Shepard and Mitchell decided to leave the MET behind.

"We'll get there," Shepard said, and a few minutes later, at the top of a small rise, said he expected to "be approaching the rim here very shortly." But one rise led to another, and another. They were already a mile away from the LM and should have reached Cone Crater by then. But their time was running out, and they were still a little unsure of their bearings. If they continued too far in the wrong direction, they risked depleting the oxygen supply strapped to their backpacks. Most of the time Shepard took the lead, but Mitchell kept stopping to warn Shepard that he was leading them in the wrong direction. At one point Mitchell pulled out a map and began gesturing at it as if they were just two travelers lost somewhere in Arizona. "Al? Head left. It's right up there," Mitchell said, pointing. "We're down here. We've got to go *there*."

But it seemed as if there was no *there* there. A few minutes later Houston made the decision for them: time to collect a few samples and return to the lunar module. A frustrated Ed Mitchell told Houston they were "finks." Later Shepard would learn they had been within seventy-five feet of the crater.

The downhill walk back to the LM was faster, but both men were tired and more than a little disappointed. "Damn," "hell," and a terse "son of a bitch" littered their radio transmissions as they loped past Turtle Rock and Weird Rock toward *Antares*. "We're going to have to mush, Ed," Shepard said.

His mood picked up a bit, though, once they reached the LM. "It's fantastic up here," he said. He and Mitchell now had just a few minutes to stow all their collected rocks into compartments in the LM and say goodbye to Fra Mauro before blasting off and reconnecting with Roosa's orbiting *Kitty Hawk*.

But first Shepard had a little surprise, which he had promised Slayton he would unveil only if the mission was proceeding on schedule and there were no unexpected glitches. Shepard moved quickly to set up the little performance he'd long planned, with hopes of distinguishing himself from all other moonwalkers.

He adjusted the television camera, making sure it was aimed at him. Then he trotted over into the camera's view, reached into his thigh pocket, and pulled out "a genuine six-iron" club head, which he attached to the end of the telescoping arm of a rock-collecting tool. He reached into another pocket and withdrew what he described to the camera as "a little white pellet that's familiar to millions of Americans."

Louise had watched him practice this surprise many times in their backyard. But, except for Slayton, he'd kept it a secret. He didn't tell his backup, Gene Cernan, or even Ed Mitchell or Stu Roosa. During the preflight quarantine he'd sneak out after hours, put on a space suit, and practice swinging without falling over.

Now he dropped the ball to the moon and told Houston he was "going to try a little sand-trap shot." He bent his knees, twisted back, and swung awkwardly at the ball, missing it completely. Fred Haise, commenting from Mission Control, said it "looked like a slice to me, Al," and Shepard admitted that he "got more dirt than ball." On his second swing Shepard caught a piece of the ball and sent it dribbling just a few dozen yards away. Then he pulled out a second ball, made "beautiful" contact, and watched it fly "straight as a die . . . miles and miles and miles."

Later he'd admit it went about two hundred yards. But he had done it—something no one else had done or ever would do again, something that put his personal stamp on Apollo 14. He'd golfed on the moon, a gesture that would forever endear him to golfers back on earth.

As Shepard and Mitchell launched away from the moon, Roosa looked down at the stunning sight of the little bug spewing fire as it rose above the gray moon. He asked Shepard if he had anything profound or prophetic to say at that historic moment. "Stu, you know me better than that," Shepard said.

Minutes later *Antares* docked nose to nose again with *Kitty Hawk*, and Shepard knocked on the hatch between the two spaceships. "Who's there?" Roosa replied. The two moonwalkers entered *Kitty Hawk*, vacuumed moon dust off their boots, and wrenched off their sweat-soaked suits. The ride home was unusually quiet, each of them contemplating what had just happened to them and what it meant. Then exhaustion struck and they slept.

Except for Mitchell, that is. Halfway home Mitchell curled up inside his sleeping bag and again pulled out the flashlight Roosa had noticed a week earlier.

///

Watching Shepard's lunar landing on television, with a crowd of family and friends around her, Louise had burst out laughing, and then immediately broke into tears. "Good, good, they made it," she said.

Louise had long nursed an "I told you so" attitude toward those who'd hinted that her husband might be too old for the space game. There had been many references to his age in the press that had miffed her, and she tried to defend him at every opportunity. "It takes a pretty remarkable person to do it, as far as I'm concerned," she told the *Washington Star*. "He won't take second best," she told the *Washington Post*.

During the three days of Shepard's tension-filled, problematic traverse to the moon, his thirty-three hours on the surface, and his three-day return, Louise had visited Mission Control a few times to listen to radio transmissions from her faraway husband. Once she ran into William House, the doctor who had performed the surgery on Shepard's ear, whom Shepard had invited to the launch and to Mission Control. NASA flight controllers gave House a headset so he could speak to Shepard. "I'm talking to you through the ear that you operated on," Shepard had told House.

Questions, jokes, insinuations, and insults about his ear and his age had dogged Shepard in the months leading up to his launch. A New Hampshire politician wrote to Richard Nixon complaining that Shepard's Ménière's disease, regardless of the surgery, should have prevented him from taking other, healthier astronauts' spots in space. At a press conference Shepard had even been asked about being the "granddaddy of space." But he insisted he didn't feel any historical significance. "Either you cut the mustard or you don't," he said.

Still, the reminders had continued until moments before the launch. Guenter Wendt, who ran the flight pad and was the man who closed Apollo 14's hatch, had presented Shepard with a white walking cane labeled "Lunar Explorer Support Equipment." At forty-seven, Shepard was by far the oldest lunar explorer. Six other men would walk the moon in the next two years (in Apollo 15, 16, and 17), for a total of a dozen men between 1969 and 1972. Among the eleven others, the average age would be thirty-nine. Shepard would later admit he sometimes felt he had to work harder to prove an older man could hack it. "Nobody said to me, 'Look, you're too old. You've been away from it too long. Forget it.' Nobody said that to me directly," he told *Life* magazine a few weeks after his return to earth. "But indirectly I've sensed that there are certain people who felt that maybe the old guy shouldn't be given a chance."

He was the only active astronaut left from the Mercury 7. Slayton was still with the program but grounded. Grissom was dead. Schirra, Carpenter, and Cooper had retired. Glenn had suffered another political defeat, losing his second campaign for the U.S. Senate in Ohio in the primary, and then almost killed himself when he lost control of the pace car at the Indianapolis 500 and slammed into a flatbed trailer crowded with journalists.

Other colleagues, like Bill Lawrence, his old flying buddy from the USS *Oriskany* and Patuxent River—who, like Slayton, had a slight heart murmur, which had kept him from becoming an astronaut—had been shot down and captured in North Vietnam. That war was born of the same communist threat that had inspired the space race, but Shepard's race had existed on an entirely different plane, allowing Shepard to emerge unscathed from an era that damaged so many colleagues.

Through luck, hard work, and arrogant persistence, through timing and shrewd political maneuvering, he had survived, and had now achieved what he called "the most personally satisfying thing I've ever done." As he once put it: "Given a disciplined self, all things are possible."

Louise knew all this, too. Though she threw up again and again during the long night before her husband's splashdown, she was elated after watching on TV as Shepard boarded a Navy ship bound for Houston, where he would be safe behind the glass windows of the postflight quarantine room. She was relieved, exhausted, and proud—proud of her "old man Moses . . . because he made his promised land."

///

Back at Houston they brought overflowing breakfast trays into the quarantine room, where Shepard and his two crewmates sat reading the newspapers and drinking coffee, still isolated from the rest of the world, still in a world of their own. Shepard had always been a good eater. During his nine days in space he "ate just about everything there was to eat." He popped open cans of beans, squirted water into bowls of dehydrated soup, peeled the wrappers off granola bars.

In fact, after nine days in space, despite the strenuous and sweaty two-mile round-trip hike to Cone Crater, Shepard returned to earth one pound heavier than when he'd left. Every other astronaut before him had lost weight—sometimes a lot. Jim Lovell, during his terrifying Apollo 13 mission, had lost an amazing fourteen pounds. John Glenn had lost four pounds during his tension-filled, four-hour flight back in 1962—a pound an hour. Even Shepard's crewmate Stu Roosa lost ten pounds over the course of Apollo 14.

The fact that Shepard was, as the *New York Times* put it, "the first man to gain weight while in space" fascinated NASA scientists and made for a curious story in that day's *Times*. Another headline caught Shepard's eye that morning, too: "Astronaut Conducts ESP Experiment on Moon Flight." Shepard had read enough inaccuracies in the press to immediately distrust the story. He shook his head, then looked up from his breakfast. "Hey, Ed. Did you see this? Isn't it amazing the things that people make up?"

Mitchell had always kept his deeper feelings about space flight to himself. He regarded outer space more philosophically than most of the other astronauts, who were strongly tech-minded. Though he had enviable scientific credentials, Mitchell had always considered the cosmos "something larger than myself . . . something incomprehensibly big." And in traveling to the moon, he intended not only to collect rocks but also to conduct his own personal experiment that might lend a clue to "the origins of our existence." Years later, he'd admit that a trip to the moon was more than a science experiment for him, more than an aeronautic adventure; it was "a mystical experience." He had no choice but to tell Shepard the truth. "I did it, boss."

En route to the moon, that night Roosa had seen him with his flashlight, Mitchell had pulled a small pad from his pocket. On the pad were symbols—circles, squares, wavy lines, stars— with a number assigned to each symbol. He concentrated for fifteen seconds on each symbol. Back on earth, at the prescribed time, friends of Mitchell's tried to telepathically pick up his thoughts and to write down the numbers they "heard." He did this twice on the way to the moon and twice on the way home, with the earth sliding in and out of his window as the capsule slowly spun like a pig on a spit to disperse the sun's rays.

During those quiet moments, while his two crewmates slept, Mitchell had experienced a feeling of "being swaddled by the cosmos." Much later he'd elaborate about his feelings of "joy," energized by the "divine presence" he felt electrifying the universe around him. But at breakfast back on earth that day, Mitchell made no apologies or explanations, and Shepard just stared at him a few moments; he said later that he had had no idea about Mitchell's experiments, that he was "surprised" and might have even nixed the plan if he'd learned about it in advance. But that morning, still buzzing from a successful mission, Shepard just nodded and smiled a bit, then returned to his newspaper, eggs, and bacon. Mitchell later compared his ESP tests to Shepard's golf shot: "He did his thing, I did my thing."

///

Once freed from their quarantine, the three astronauts surfed a tidal wave of parades, galas, ceremonies, and television appearances, capped off by the invitation to Nixon's White House for dinner. Although Shepard was a fairly consistent Republican, he was not a big fan of Nixon, who he felt "didn't know anything about space," was far less interested in NASA than his Democratic predecessors, and was guilty of letting Washington's support for the space program lag.

That night at the White House Nixon kept up the tradition of promoting astronauts. Mitchell became a Navy captain, and Roosa became an Air Force lieutenant colonel. But Navy rules prevented him from promoting Shepard from captain to admiral. In place of a promotion, Nixon commended Shepard—and the "first celestial hole-in-one"—by inducting him into the "distinguished order of lunar duffers," despite the fact that "Shepard's first two swings were embarrassing failures." But Nixon promised to "find a way to make you an admiral eventually."

A month later he made good on his promise. In late April 1971, from a list of two thousand Navy captains, Nixon approved the promotion of forty-nine of those captains to the exalted rank of rear admiral. Among the names was Shepard's, the only astronaut to make admiral and among the few Navy admirals who had never commanded a ship.

Shepard's father, Bart, was thrilled to learn that his son had reached the pinnacle of the Navy's hierarchy. From then on, just as his father had insisted on being addressed as "Colonel," Shepard asked to be called "Admiral," even by his children.

Shepard's celebrity also led to an invitation from George H. W. Bush, then the U.S. ambassador to the United Nations, to serve as a delegate. The friendship between Shepard and Bush dated back to when they had been neighbors in Houston's wealthiest suburb. They'd recently met again at a UN meeting in San Francisco, where they talked about how great it would be to take the UN's Security Council into space and ask each member to point to his country. "He wouldn't be able to find it because there are no political boundaries," Shepard told Bush. "As a planet, we are so small and unified."

Across two months with the UN delegation in New York, Shepard took part in an eight-hour session that led to mainland China being voted into the UN. In the halls and at cocktail parties, he signed autographs and tried to tell UN members "what a fragile, beautiful place" the earth was when viewed from space. "It's too bad there are so many people on earth who can't get along," he said.

///

When all the accolades and public appearances had settled down—the appearance with Bob Hope before troops in Vietnam, the invitations to prizefights, the Broadway plays, the drunken night in New York with Lauren Bacall, and the overtures from politicians trying to lure him into politics—Alan, Louise, and their daughters traveled to New Hampshire for a much-needed respite. There Alan attended a retirement ceremony for his favorite high school teacher and hosted a fiftieth wedding anniversary for his parents at a nearby country club.

One night during their stay in New Hampshire Louise,

Renza, and the girls worked in the kitchen, cleaning up after dinner, while Alan and his father—the admiral and the colonel—sat in the living room sipping snifters of brandy. In the corner stood the pipe organ that Bart still played each day, a reminder of the Saturday afternoons so long ago when Alan trundled along with his father to the church and helped him tune the six hundred pipes of the huge church organ. Over the years Bart had continued running his small-town insurance agency, driving a half mile to work in the same office, lunching at the same restaurant, day after day, year after year.

His son, meanwhile, sailed aboard Navy ships to all corners of the globe, flew jets at supersonic speeds and superhuman heights, drove Corvettes, rocketed to space, and golfed on the moon—arguably one of the most eloquently traveled men alive.

And yet Alan had developed an admiring respect for his father's consistently homespun and simplified lifestyle. "My father's example was he led a good life," Shepard would one day admit.

That evening after dinner, father and son talked about Shepard's promotion to admiral, about his plans for the future, and about the moon. At one point Bart turned to his son and said, "Do you remember when you first told us back in 1959 that you were going to become an astronaut?"

"Yes, sir," Alan said.

"Do you remember what I said?"

"Yes, sir, I certainly do," Alan said. In fact, Alan would never be able to forget Bart's admonitions against veering off his Navy career path, and how he'd felt as though he was tearing the family apart with his risky enrollment in NASA. "You were not in favor of it."

"Well," Bart said, his voice a little shaky as he raised his glass of brandy in a toast, "I was wrong."

///

Fifteen months later, the colonel died at the age of eighty-two.

AFTER SPACE

///

20

"When you've been to the moon,
where else are you going to go?"

Some astronauts, upon retiring from NASA, had no clue where to go next. They'd seen things, experienced things, and visited places that set them apart. NASA employees said they could often tell which astronauts had been to space and which hadn't—a legit spaceman's face carried a look of contentment, his gait had bounce, he was patient and dreamy and mysterious. Such men were special, different, and they knew it. But how to transfer the gift of space into a fulfilling life on earth? Some astronauts, unable to answer that question, dove into misery.

Shepard's moonwalking partner, Ed Mitchell, returned to earth convinced that his ESP experiments had been a success. In his ongoing search for deeper meaning after the "epiphany" of Apollo 14, he became obsessed with parapsychology and founded an institute for aspiring psychics. Meanwhile, his marriage collapsed and he was named in a paternity suit by a Playboy bunny who later became his third wife. "My personal life has been somewhat in turbulence ever since," he said thirty years later.

On the moon, Apollo 15's LM pilot Jim Irwin had "felt the power of God as I'd never felt it before" and subsequently dedicated years of his life to finding Noah's ark in the rugged mountains of Turkey. Buzz Aldrin often bristled at his second billing behind Neil Armstrong, arguing that they were *both* the first men on the moon ("we landed at the *same time,*" he'd say); he later fell apart, weeping and drinking on his way to a nervous breakdown from which he later recovered. Gene Cernan, who as commander of Apollo 17 became the last man to walk on the moon in 1972—a moment he called "the climax of my life"— spent many years afterward trying to top his lunar experience. "The search goes on, and sooner or later you come to grips with the fact that you're going to have to live within the confines of what's left," Cernan said.

Cernan and other lunar explorers found they had neglected everything else in their life—wife, kids, friends, finances. Some astronauts retired from NASA and discovered they had become complete strangers to their children—after Aldrin returned from the moon and reunited with his family, he asked his son how school was going, only to be told that it was summer vacation and school was out. Aldrin wasn't alone in feeling that life had progressed in his absence. Astronauts found that their wives had created their own lives—their husbands were now expendable. An epidemic of divorces swept through NASA in the early 1970s as the astronaut wives' club begat an offspring, the ex-wives' club.

Many astronauts—especially the twelve who walked on the moon—also suffered from severe shock upon learning that, despite their wild expeditions, they were regular, flawed humans. A common conceit was *If I can go to the moon, I can do anything.* But many returned to their regular lives to find they could not do everything—they failed at business, parenthood, love, and life. The reality of life after NASA was also devoid of the astro-perks many were accustomed to: mingling with world leaders and celebrities, dining at the White House, sleeping with groupies, and having NASA jets at their disposal.

Years after bouncing across the lunar surface on his Apollo 12 mission, Alan Bean said that, having achieved his life's goal of reaching the moon, he felt fortunate to have found another mission to sustain his life: painting gray-toned lunar landscapes and portraits of space-suited astronauts. "Some unfortunate ones didn't have a dream to replace the dream of going to the moon," Bean said years later.

///

For Shepard, returning to real life was neither a shock nor a disappointment. He did not return from the moon to find his earthly life in a shambles. In his hyperkinetic way, he had never allowed himself to slow down, even during his lengthy battle with Ménière's disease, and had therefore paid careful attention to all matters of his life, big and small.

He had always tried to carve out father-daughter moments. Julie, Laura, and Alice were often among the only astronauts' children at NASA events. He took them skiing in Colorado and taught them and their friends to water-ski at the lake house he and Louise had purchased near Austin, Texas. He once rented a small plane to fly his daughters and their girlfriends from Texas to Maine for summer camp—although the friends later complained that they would have preferred a more comfortable commercial flight. When Laura, Julie, and Alice began having children of their own, he doted on his six grandchildren, too. He'd visit their classrooms and teach them to ski. He once told a friend he didn't realize how much fun kids were until he became a grandfather. After leaving NASA, he tried to incorporate the girls—and their kids—even more into his life.

In the years after Apollo 14, Shepard began spending more time with Louise, too. As he watched colleagues' lives fall apart, he realized how valuable she had been to him. "He knew he had a good one," recalled NASA secretary Lola Morrow. Alan and Louise began to travel together: biennial trips to the Paris Air

Show and a long tour of the Orient, ski trips to Colorado and golf trips to Pebble Beach, where they were thinking of retiring. "Louise never thought of leaving him, never," said Louise's friend Dorel. "And I don't think he ever thought of leaving her. It was a strong marriage that grew stronger."

///

For Shepard, an Apollo 14 medallion hanging around his neck was the only outward sign of the moon's effect on his life. He considered his moonwalks something to cherish but chose not to dwell on the experience; rather, he decided "to put it in a box, and on a shelf, look at it once in a while, put it back on the shelf, and try something totally different."

Unlike some peers, the question of what to do next was full of possibility and promise, not dread. As he'd told Oriana Fallaci years earlier when she'd asked about life after space: "I'll make a success of some other job—I'm a man of many interests."

He could have been anything he wanted to be—a celebrity, a politician, a TV announcer. But he turned all of it down, preferring not to remain in the public eye. "I've gone to great lengths to maintain my privacy," he once said after turning down a request to appear in an American Express television ad. "I don't want to give it up for the lure of commercial endorsements."

Not that he didn't wrestle some with the issue of how to spend the rest of his days. He once acknowledged the significant weight of the question: "I've been the world's greatest test pilot. I've been to the moon. I mean, what else is there? When you've been to the moon, where else are you going to go?"

One thing Shepard knew for sure was that after announcing his decision to retire from NASA in 1974, he did not want to return to the Navy. He loved his admiral's rank, but he had little interest in actually *being* an admiral—which infuriated the U.S. Navy. When Nixon had promoted Shepard to rear admiral, the expectation was that he'd stay with the Navy and serve in some

high-profile position. Instead he took his rank and retired. Some called him a "tombstone admiral"—someone who sticks it out just long enough to earn a rank to have etched into their tombstone. "The Navy was really pissed off," said astronaut Jim Lovell. "He knew he wasn't going to go back to the Navy."

What Shepard chose instead was the world of business. By the time he'd left NASA, at age fifty-one, Shepard had already sold his shares in Baytown Bank and Fidelity Bank and Trust Co., earning $581,000 and $50,000, respectively. He'd sold his rural Texas oil wells—"about broke even on that," he once said—and conceded defeat and sold his money-losing quarter horse business. "So," he once said, "I've made some good business deals and I've made some bad ones."

In the early days of post-NASA life he sifted through many offers from private contractors doing business with NASA who would have loved to employ a high-profile ex-astronaut. But Shepard claimed to feel strongly that he shouldn't use "the visibility" of his ex-astronaut status "for my own personal gain." The truth was, he wanted some distance from the astronaut world, and turned down lucrative offers to lecture and requests to seek public office for the same reason: He didn't want to be in any spotlight.

But sorting through all the offers could be a full-time, complicated job in itself. Gordo Cooper sometimes saw Shepard at NASA functions, and they'd talk about how businessmen flocked to them "like ducks to water." Once they stood in a parking lot outside a conference swapping business cards and stories about this one and that one.

"Did you meet this guy?" Shepard would ask, then slap a business card down on his car hood. "How about this one? Is this guy for real?"

Wally Schirra and Scott Carpenter suffered through their share of business deals gone bad, too, but Gordo Cooper slogged through some of the worst investments among the astronauts. He lost his shirt on his boat dealer business south of Houston and had to testify in court a few times against accused swindlers, including some guys who tried to drag him into a helicopter manufacturing scam in South America. The FBI once stepped in to warn him about a certain bad apple he was considering as a partner.

Cooper recalled that Shepard also experienced "his share of close calls." But in time Shepard came to realize that, despite his intent "not to use my position as an astronaut" to win favor with businessmen, that was easier said than done. "I tried to separate the two," he told one reporter. "But to say that I do not use my [astronaut] position in business is really fallacious, because it's not black and white."

The solution—selling beer, oil, and buildings in the Lone Star State—seemed the perfect challenge for a hyperactive test pilot/astronaut. But Shepard would learn a few hard lessons in a world that Texas newspaper columnist Molly Ivins once described as the "land of wretched excess," a land of whiskey and women-loving "sumbitches" where doing "bidness" often involved taking kickbacks or stealing public funds, a land of cattle rustlers, pornographers, racist Bible-thumpers, and sexist good ol' boys—and that's just among the politicians. "For virtue," Ivins once suggested, "try Minnesota."

///

Every five years, Howard Benedict—the Associated Press reporter who had been at the Cape with Shepard in the early days—would come to Houston to interview Shepard for another of his *Freedom 7* anniversary stories. One year Benedict met Shepard at his office in Deer Park, a rough Houston suburb surrounded by factories and oil refineries. In a rented pickup truck, Benedict followed the directions Shepard had given him to Winward Beverage Co., the beer distributorship Shepard had bought with an old Navy buddy. After a few beers in the English-style pub Shepard had built beside the warehouse, he grabbed the keys to one of his delivery trucks and gave Benedict a tour of his new world. Suburban Houston was full of grungy little bars where oilmen and ranchers drank the local brews: Lonestar and Rattlesnake. Shepard called it "Rattlesnake country," the bars full of posters with a half-nude woman petting a snake, saying, "I love my Rattlesnake." (Shepard's beer was Coors.) His partner, a handsome Navy test pilot named Duke Windsor whom Shepard had befriended at Patuxent River, had been married to a Coors heiress. Duke's wife died in the mid-1970s, but he stayed in touch with the Coors family, and he and Shepard flew to Denver one year to meet with Bill Coors, whose father, Adolph, had founded the massive Colorado-based brewery.

Coors had been trying to break into new markets and agreed to let Shepard and Windsor open the first Coors distributorship in southeast Texas. But it was no easy task to introduce a beer made in the snowy Rocky Mountains to dusty "Rattlesnake country." Shepard marketed his brew by paying regular visits to the gritty oilman bars. That afternoon he gave Benedict a glimpse of his beer-selling skills.

He blew through the barroom doors—"Hey, fellas!"—and everyone recognized the famous astronaut. He bought the house a round of Coors, chatted up the bartender, and then strutted out—"See you fellas next time!"—with Benedict traipsing after him, taking notes. "He was quite a salesman," Benedict recalled.

Before Benedict left that day, Shepard tossed a six-pack of Coors into the passenger seat of his pickup. "Now all you need is a rifle," he said. "Then you'll be a real Texan." But selling Coors was just the beginning of Shepard's life as a moneymaking Texan. At the time he told friends, "The business world has smiled upon us."

///

Despite once buying a piece of a Los Angeles brokerage firm, Shepard was "never really a fan" of the stock market. He just didn't trust it—"I can't figure the psychology of it and I never found a relative as a broker whom I trusted," he once said. What he trusted were solid, tangible investments, like beer, land, and buildings. *Solid* also described his partner Jack "Moose" Coogan, a bear of a man who had played pro football for the Los Angeles Rams and helped introduce Shepard to the sometimes shady and illegal workings of the Texas real estate development world.

Moose Coogan and a colleague, Roland Walters, had honed a specialty: building shopping centers, particularly those with a Kmart department store attached. Shepard became partner and chairman of a Coogan and Walters subsidiary called Marathon Construction, which bought parcels of land in Texas, Oregon, Kansas, and Nebraska as future Kmart sites. His first successful development was a Kmart shopping center in Oregon, but it was also his first Kmart mistake, albeit a minor one.

Shepard offered to appear at the ribbon cutting, but the new store's manager got "a little overzealous" and ran his picture in newspaper ads. The following day's newspapers accused Shepard of using his ex-astronaut status to promote the store. Astronauts hawking products was nothing new; Wally Schirra, who caught a severe cold on his Apollo 7 flight, became a spokesman for Actifed cold medicine. But Shepard didn't need the attention, and after that he made sure his name was never publicly associated with his Kmarts. He also had the overzealous store manager "moved to another area."

The deal with the Detroit-based Kresge Company (which put the *K* in Kmart), was that Shepard's firm would buy the land, develop the store, and then enter into a long-term lease with the Kresge Company. Shepard called it "a relatively good investment" and would go on to develop fifteen Kmarts during his decade with the firm. His real estate successes would lead to membership on corporate boards of directors and a seat on Houston's Port Commission. Such positions, and the income from his distributorship and Marathon Construction, were enough to support the mansion in River Oaks and the lakefront cottage near Austin with a ski condo in Breckenridge, Colorado. "I like being my own boss. I enjoy being in business for myself," he once said. "The pay is a lot better than going to the moon, I can tell you that."

///

In the late 1970s Shepard began thinking bigger than Kmart. He and Jack Coogan partnered with ex-Houston mayor Louie Welch and began buying some lowland property south of NASA (now named Johnson Space Center), with plans to create a huge housing development with a waterfront marina and golf course. The name would be Shepard's Landing.

The idea seemed solid: buy up many acres of scrubland, subdivide it into lots, sell the lots off at a reasonable price—say, $4,000 to $5,000 an acre—then bring a builder in to construct the houses, the golf course, the clubhouse, and the marina. Some of it worked out as planned, and houses began rising along the streets of Shepard's Landing, golf- and space-themed streets that Shepard had named himself: Admiral Road, Fra Mauro Drive, Masters Drive, Pebble Beach Road. Some buyers were sold on the idea of having astronauts like Deke Slayton and Alan Shepard as neighbors; Deke and Bobbie Slayton built a home on Masters Drive, while Alan and Louise began building a huge new home beside the undulating golf course, near the banks of the murky San Jacinto River.

There was just one problem: No one on Shepard's team got permission to develop land that had essentially been designated a swamp. When Shepard and his partners sought approval for the subdivision in 1978, the Montgomery County commissioners said no. The land was too low, too close to the San Jacinto River, and too likely to flood, they said. Two years later Shepard's team went ahead with the project anyway.

Shepard began trying to lure old Navy and NASA friends into the project. He asked his old Navy boss and flying mentor, Doc Abbot, to run the marina, but Abbot declined. Then

Shepard asked former NASA flight director Chris Kraft if he wanted to buy into the project. Kraft agreed to put $10,000 down on a condominium, but when he stopped by the work site one day to check on the progress, he didn't like what he saw—shoddy, sloppy construction—and asked for his money back. A while later Kraft saw Shepard at a space shuttle launch at Mission Control and, referring to the real estate firm hired to develop the land, warned, "Al, I don't trust this guy and I think he's going to get you in trouble."

Other unsuspecting buyers had no idea they were building dream homes on swampland—until they sought building permits from the county and in some cases, were told they'd have to build homes twenty-one feet off the ground to be above the flood-prone zone. Others on slightly higher ground got permission to build homes but then watched as rainstorms filled the neighborhood with ponds that lured poisonous water snakes.

Finally the complaints of more than a dozen property owners reached the county attorney's office, which brought charges of false real estate filings against Shepard, Coogan, and Welch. The misdemeanor charges carried a ninety-day jail sentence. Coogan blamed the real estate firm they'd hired to develop the property—the one Chris Kraft had warned Shepard about—and told Houston's newspapers that he'd invested $200,000 "and I haven't seen a dollar of profit yet." Ex-mayor Welch said he didn't expect a profit "until I'm pushing up daisies." Shepard refused to talk to the papers, and with good reason.

A Polish immigrant named Steve Szladewski paid $4,000 for an acre of Shepard's Landing, thrilled to have Alan Shepard as a neighbor. Instead he "got taken." "They promise to fix the roads. They say they build a nice entrance to [the] subdivision, something beautiful," Szladewski said. "We have nothing." Szladewski was among those who were not allowed to build houses because county engineers found that their land was, essentially, part of the riverbed. Even Shepard's own house beside the San Jacinto River was flattened by Hurricane Alicia in 1983.

In the end, Shepard and his partners agreed to fix some of the problems and return some of the money, and the charges were dropped. After that, Shepard sold his 25 percent stake and put as much distance as possible between himself and Shepard's Landing. "He was lucky he didn't go to jail," Kraft said.

///

Despite his brush with the law, Shepard's otherwise successful business career opened wide the doors to Houston's high society, an oil-rich club of kings and queens, barons and dukes, ex-presidents, movie stars, golf pros, and other celebrities. In her "Big City Beat" column, the *Houston Chronicle*'s society columnist regularly mentioned where and with whom Alan and Louise had dined, and began referring to his house—as she did with many of her wealthy Houstonian pals—as a "swankienda."

When Frank Sinatra came to town for a performance, he'd set up a bar in his dressing room and invite Alan and Louise back for drinks. Alan and Louise attended galas with former Texas governors, dined with Donald Trump, and played golf with the king of Morocco, as columnist Maxine Messinger breathlessly told readers. Sometimes Shepard was spotted at a star-studded dinner at Tony's, a famous Houston restaurant. Other times it was a cheeseburger with famed heart surgeon Denton Cooley at the lunch counter of Avalon Drugstore, a messy-but-chic old pharmacy and convenience store on the edge of Shepard's River Oaks neighborhood, where Shepard kept a running tab.

Alan and Louise befriended Joan Schnitzer and her sister, the civic patroness Bernice Weingartner, both heiresses to a family of real estate and department store developers. Schnitzer's ex-husband, Kenneth, one of Houston's biggest developers (later convicted of bank fraud stemming from the 1980s savings and loan debacle), had owned Houston's old Cork Club nightclub and got to know many of the stars who performed there. After their divorce, Joan Schnitzer stayed close with many of her husband's celebrity friends, and Alan and Louise mingled at many a Schnitzer shindig with the likes of Jack Lemmon, Judy Garland, Shirley MacLaine, and Mitzi Gaynor.

But Shepard didn't want to become a flabby society poof. He had his other reputation to consider—that of a rambunctious, large-living test pilot—and he worked hard to stay young-looking, fit, and adventurous. On weekends he water-skied at his lake house, carving sharp turns on his single slalom ski, skiing barefoot, or flying off jumps on his wide jumping skis. He drove a maroon Corvette that, he once bragged, "goes at least 143 miles per hour on Texas highways." He sailed a yacht and flew his own airplane. Shepard also took up boat racing and once collided with another boat at the Thunderbolt World Championship races at Clear Lake, near NASA. Shepard was knocked from his boat, which was flying at sixty miles an hour, and received some relatively minor cuts on his arm. But in an interview afterward he made a point of telling the reporter, "I was leading the race at the time of the accident."

His favorite hobby, though—besides making money—was still a good round of golf, which took him to some of the more beautiful corners of America.

///

It sometimes irked Shepard to realize, as he once put it, that he was "a hell of a lot more famous for being the guy who hit the golf ball on the moon than the first guy in space." Still, that lunar golf shot earned him many friends in the celebrity-filled world of golf. In addition to his Texas business domain, Shepard showered much of his post-astronaut attention on the game of golf.

Shepard hadn't gotten serious about golf until he was in his forties, living in Houston and working (more or less part time) as head of the astronaut office. His astronaut fame exposed him to such golf greats as Masters winner Jackie Burke, who founded the Champions Club at Houston and would give Shepard pointers. But Shepard never quite found his swing and constantly struggled with his game.

To Shepard's disgust, *Sports Illustrated* would one day list him among the hundred worst athletes of the century. The reason: Although his golf shot on the moon had made him one of the world's famous golfers, he was a fairly mediocre duffer. A Florida newspaper also put him on its worst-athletes list, ranking him forty-fifth out of fifty, right before Sallie Blue, a racehorse that lost seventy straight races.

Still, Shepard was invited each year to the Bing Crosby Pro-Am, one of his favorite events of the year and a chance to have a cocktail with Frank Sinatra, Clint Eastwood, Arnold Palmer, and Jack Nicklaus.

But, despite many pointers from the world's best golfers, Shepard never got better. He was especially erratic off the first tee, where crowds of twenty thousand made him more nervous than any jet or rocket ever had. "Having been a test pilot," he said at one tournament, "I've metabolized a lot of adrenaline in my life. But on that first tee, on that first day, the old heart is really pumping." Bob Murphy, a West Coast sports announcer who often met and played with Shepard at the Crosby Pro-Am at Pebble Beach (later named the AT&T Pro-Am), said Shepard took his golf seriously, "but his ability didn't always match his competitiveness."

Shepard's famous love of golf also subjected him to questions over the years about the frivolity of golfing on his costly, taxpayer-funded moon mission. Sometimes he'd argue there was scientific and educational value to the golf shot, which showed how objects travel in one-sixth gravity. Other times he'd joke that his golf balls—whose weight reportedly added $11,000 in fuel costs—were "chicken feed" compared to the bowling ball, dumbbells, and billiard table Ed Mitchell had smuggled aboard Apollo 14.

///

"**H**it it like you did on the moon, Al!" someone in the gallery would yell at almost every tournament in which he played. Such heckling bugged him almost as much as the nagging question raised at most of his golf outings: What brand of golf ball did he hit on the moon? At one tournament in Houston he told hecklers, "I won't say. But one thing I will say is that the ball went a lot farther on the moon than it did today."

Shepard didn't mind retelling the story of how he noticed that his friend Bob Hope carried a golf club with him wherever he went, even during a mid-1960s tour at the Cape, and how the comedian's love of golf had inspired him to find a way to bring a golf club to the moon. But as for the moon balls, he forever insisted that the name printed on those balls would "remain the world's best kept secret."

"I've never told anybody. I've never told my wife," he once said, and even sued a ball manufacturer that had claimed to have made the balls he used on the moon.

(Shepard's moon balls were, in fact, driving range balls made by Spalding.)

And yet despite the heckling—about his mediocre abilities, about the ball manufacturer—Shepard's loyalty to the game of golf, his love of a sport at which he never quite excelled, was always tied to a fierce pride in having golfed on the moon. One night, after the welcome party that kicked off the Crosby Pro-Am at Pebble Beach, Shepard and his friend Bob Murphy, the sports announcer, walked out of the clubhouse into the crisp, clear night and stood looking up at a full moon. Murphy had to ask the question many had asked before: "What do you think about when you look up there?"

"You know, Murph," Shepard finally said, "I wonder where my golf ball is."

21

"I saw a different Alan Shepard, completely different"

The idea started when *Rolling Stone* magazine assigned Tom Wolfe to cover astronaut Gene Cernan's Apollo 17 flight, the last launch to the moon.

Until that time—late 1972—Wolfe had paid little attention to astronauts or space. But as he immersed himself in the assignment, he quickly became fascinated with "the psychology of the test pilot . . . and the question of what bravery is." The result was a four-part series of stories for *Rolling Stone*, which Wolfe then planned to expand into a book. He thought it would take a few months. But at the time NASA was just beginning to declassify many of its previously off-limits internal documents, such as postflight briefings. Wolfe was able to gain access to information that no previous writer had gotten near. And he became both mired in and awed by what he learned.

Wolfe initially planned to tell a book-length story of the entire space race, but he realized after writing hundreds of pages that he would instead focus only on the remarkable early years of the program, particularly the story of the Mercury Seven.

In 1979 *The Right Stuff* was published to rave reviews, selling millions on its way to becoming Wolfe's most successful book. *The Right Stuff* (which became a movie four years later) reminded the world of the exploits of seven exceptional men who volunteered to ride rockets into the sky. The book—and the 1983 film of the same name—resurrected all the glory and drama of the cold war era of the astronaut and reintroduced America to the astronauts' antagonist, Chuck Yeager, whom Wolfe portrayed as the overlooked hero. Far more than a story of the space race, *The Right Stuff* was viewed by many as the first book to deeply explore the rich brotherhood of the jet jockey and the only-in-America culture of the celebrity astronaut.

Wolfe's unique voice brought to life an era that no previous writer had managed to capture so fully. Maybe it required distance and perspective, and maybe that's why previous attempts to scratch deeper than the sanitized *Life* magazine version of the space race—by such notable writers as Norman Mailer, no less—had failed. But *The Right Stuff*'s huge success was due in part to its telling of the dark and sexy side of the astronaut story—the less-than-heroic stuff that all other journalists and authors of the 1960s obediently stayed away from, or never got near.

Freed from the limits of being an obligatory hagiographer, Wolfe let loose with sensual references to "young juicy girls with stand-up jugs and full-sprung thighs" lurking around the astronauts. Astronauts probably wondered what the hell Wolfe was talking about when he wrote of astro-groupies with "conformations so taut and silky that the very sight of them practically pulled a man into the delta of priapic delirium." Astronaut wives didn't exactly appreciate the exposition.

Louise's friend Dorel Abbot had just finished reading the book and, shocked at the portrayal of Shepard and the others—but especially Shepard—immediately phoned Louise. "Did you read it?" Dorel asked.

"Nope," Louise said.

Dorel asked again six months later. "Did you read it?"

"Nope," Louise said.

Finally, a year later, she asked once more, and Louise said, "Yup."

"Well, are you going to do anything?" Dorel asked. "Say anything?"

"Nope."

Louise said she had decided not to confront Alan. It wasn't worth rocking the boat. Not this late in their marriage, which in nearly every other way was an ideal union. Besides, even if she did confront him, she felt he'd probably not admit it anyway. "I have nothing to gain and everything to lose," Louise said.

///

The surviving Mercury Seven reacted with varying degrees of distaste to *The Right Stuff,* although they uniformly resented its portrayal of their dead friend Gus as a bumbling goat who panicked, blew the hatch off his Mercury capsule, and let it sink. Slayton said "none of it was all that accurate, but it was well done" and "captured the spirit of the times." Schirra said Wolfe took a lot of "poetic license"; Cooper called it "literary license." When the film was later released, Carpenter called it "a great movie."

Glenn, whom Wolfe portrayed as the "prig" of the group, came across as a moralizing prude, but admirably so. And while it's impossible to prove a connection, when Glenn ran for his second Senate term in 1980, a year after the book came out, he won by a landslide. Emboldened by that victory, he soon launched his presidential campaign. Glenn liked the book but said it was "not exactly our favorite movie."

Shepard, on the other hand, more than any of the others, hated the book, calling it "just fiction." He never hid his distaste for the movie, either. "What movie?" he'd say. In lighter moments he'd joke that the actor who portrayed him—Scott Glenn—"was nowhere near as tough as I was, and nowhere near as good-looking." It infuriated Shepard that Wolfe re-created the lives of the Mercury Seven without interviewing any of "the original guys," he once said. Also, without coming out and specifically saying it, Wolfe insinuates that Shepard was the king of the Mercury Seven womanizers. At one point Wolfe describes how Shepard acted when he was away from home: "A great goomba-goomba grin would take over his face. You halfway expected to see him start snapping his fingers, because everything about him seemed to be asking the question: 'Where's the action?' " It's no wonder Shepard detested *The Right Stuff*.

And yet no one had ever pulled the curtain back so far on the astronauts' lives as did Tom Wolfe. The public's reaction was one of awed rediscovery. Those who had lived through it were reminded of the heady days of Sputnik, Kennedy, Armstrong. Those who hadn't lived through it got a history lesson on the thrills and spills of the space race. Suddenly astronauts were heroes again. People wanted autographs again. Organizations wanted the Mercury Seven to attend their fund-raisers and their banquets.

Shepard and the others were celebrities once more.

///

Through the 1970s and early '80s, Shepard and the other five surviving space pioneers had quietly drifted apart, each pursuing his own postspace life. Carpenter, Cooper, Schirra, and Glenn hadn't been astronauts since the 1960s. Shepard had left NASA in 1974. Slayton stuck around longer than any of them and, after conquering the heart murmur that had gotten him grounded back in 1962, finally reached space aboard the final Apollo mission, a joint 1975 U.S.-Soviet mission called the Apollo-Soyuz Test Project.

But in the aftermath of *The Right Stuff* fever, the Mercury Seven began appearing together at regular events. "Thanks to the book and the later movie," Slayton said, "we were all lumped back together in people's minds again, whether we wanted it or not." After years of nursing old grudges over business deals, astro-politics, and hurt feelings, the original astronauts became friends again. They began calling each other on the phone, swapping dirty jokes. As Slayton put it, "old disagreements didn't seem so important anymore."

Shepard and Glenn still sometimes bristled against each other, however, and their strained and rusty friendship took a while to loosen up. At one commemorative banquet in Houston Shepard spoke to the crowd about the glow of fame that had shone on him after *Freedom 7*, how people called him a hero and stoked his admittedly large ego, which at the time made him wonder how many living Americans were truly great. "One less than you think," Glenn interjected.

Prompted by *The Right Stuff* hype, the astronauts' old innkeeper friend from the Cape, Henri Landwirth—who had maintained his delicately balanced friendship with both Shepard and Glenn—began floating an idea for the astronauts to use their newfound exposure to raise money for charity, which could also serve to keep the Mercury Seven team together. After successfully managing the Cocoa Beach Holiday Inn in the early 1960s, Landwirth had gone on to greater successes with the Holiday Inn corporation, and even partnered in a few hotels with Glenn. Landwirth the Holocaust survivor had become a rich man and was now dedicating his life to charitable ventures. His idea was for the six surviving Mercury Seven astronauts—along with Gus Grissom's widow, Betty—to create a scholarship program for needy students interested in science and engineering.

Shepard liked the idea from the start and agreed to serve as the foundation's chair and president. But he was still running his Texas business enterprises and didn't have time to spare. "We like the idea; there's only one catch. You'll have to make it happen," he told Landwirth. "Your idea, you do it." Landwirth, who was living in Orlando, agreed to handle all the paperwork, found an office, and hired a part-time director.

But the Mercury Seven Foundation got off to a very slow start, raising less than $100,000 in its first two years, and often teetered on the brink of collapse. Neither Shepard nor the other astronauts at first served as anything more than halfhearted philanthropists. Then an unexpected source of inspiration occurred in 1986, two years after the foundation began, and coinciding with the twenty-fifth anniversary of Shepard's *Freedom* 7 mission.

On January 28 Shepard joined other celebrities, such as Clint Eastwood and George C. Scott, and golf pros like Jack Nicklaus and Tom Watson at the AT&T Pebble Beach National Pro-Am golf tournament (formerly the Crosby Pro-Am, the celebrity-filled tournament started by Bing Crosby in the 1950s). While playing a practice round on the spectacular beachfront Pebble Beach course, Shepard learned that the space shuttle *Challenger* had just exploded. Clutching a drink in the clubhouse after his round, Shepard watched televised accounts of the tragedy, and those around him winced as they watched Shepard's face contort with each replay of the shuttle's destruction. Killed in the disaster were six astronauts and Christa McAuliffe, a schoolteacher from Shepard's home state of New Hampshire, who just prior to her flight had told reporters how "thrilled" and "envious" she'd been watching Shepard's flight twenty-five years earlier. Shepard was disgusted by the *Challenger* tragedy, which was caused by a faulty "O"-ring seal and which he blamed on the same "insidious" factors that had caused the Apollo 1 fire—"a sense of overconfidence, a sense of complacency."

Three months later, on May 5, the Mercury Seven Foundation held a black-tie, $150-a-plate banquet in Los Angeles to commemorate the twenty-fifth anniversary of *Freedom* 7. Shepard had asked his friend Bob Hope to serve as the foundation's honorary chairman—a first step toward rejuvenating the foundering scholarship program. "We thought, as a group, we'd collectively have a lot of credibility still, and maybe we should use that to help inspire young people to become involved in space," Shepard told a newspaper reporter in a rare interview.

After two years during which the foundation had struggled to survive, Shepard decided to step in and help revive it. More financial support for science and engineering, he reasoned, might contribute to the prevention of deadly explosions such as happened to the *Challenger,* and might prevent the demise of the Gus Grissoms of the future.

///

Somewhere around this same time Shepard began to explore what he now considered an even greater challenge than making money: giving money away. In addition to rededicating himself to the Mercury Seven Foundation, he began working with friends in Houston to raise money for a school for deaf children. He helped raise money for the Houston-based Charles A. Lindbergh Fund and secretly gave money to help a child in Seabrook, Texas, suffering from leukemia. He also agreed to chair a golf tournament sponsored by the Loctite Corp. in Detroit (on whose board of directors he sat), which raised money for scholarships to send underprivileged kids to a weeklong space camp at Kennedy Space Center.

On top of that, he regularly gave money to friends—including a few astronauts—to help them out of a bind or help them get started in business. He helped his Apollo 14 colleague Stu Roosa establish his own Coors distributorship and gave one of his secondhand cars to a former NASA colleague. When his parents' longtime housekeeper's well water dried up, he called and arranged for a new well to be drilled, on his tab; later, when the housekeeper's husband died, he sent her $5,000.

Shepard was especially dogged in his efforts to collect donations for the Mercury Seven Foundation. He gave a few thousand of his own money here and there. Anything he earned from one of his golf tournaments or the rare speaking engagement, he donated to the foundation. "He didn't take one penny for himself," Landwirth recalled.

At first the foundation had been run by a part-time, $18,000-a-year employee. But Shepard decided it needed a full-time manager and cajoled his friend, the AP reporter Howard Benedict, who was about to retire, into taking over as the foundation's manager. Benedict found he couldn't turn Shepard down and agreed to work twenty-five hours a week for the foundation. But as Shepard began touring the country, hosting fund-raisers and asking friends and corporations for money, Benedict's part-time job became a seriously full-time commitment. After giving just seven $1,000 scholarships in 1986, the foundation was handing out ten $7,500 scholarships annually by 1990, and across its first fifteen years would dole out more than $1 million. "He became passionate about it," Benedict recalled. "I think it was a legacy he wanted to leave. It was his baby."

The foundation was renamed the Astronaut Scholarship Foundation and in 1990 moved to Titusville, a small town beside Kennedy Space Center on Florida's coast. The foundation inspired the creation of another charitable group, the Space Camp Foundation, and an increasing flow of donations helped fund the construction of an Astronaut Hall of Fame and gift shop, whose profits would go back into the scholarship foundation. The other surviving Mercury Seven were amazed that Shepard, a man known for occasional self-indulgence and conceit, was now throwing himself at philanthropy. "He was very generous," Schirra said. "But he kept it to himself." Said Glenn: "Al was the one who really persisted and got that thing going."

///

Glenn and others noticed that something had considerably mellowed in the formerly hyper and combative Icy Commander. The raw whiskey of Shepard's younger self had aged and matured into a smooth and smoky bourbon. And yet, like a teenager with a new car, he became famous among his circle of friends for popping up in their cities—Dallas, Denver, Los Angeles, Las Vegas, Cocoa Beach—and calling unannounced in search of some fun, a few drinks, dinner, or a round of golf. "Hey, what're you doing?" he'd say, without ever identifying himself on the phone. "Let's do something."

One of the other twelve moonwalkers once said: "I think almost everyone who went to the moon became more like they really were down deep inside." Said another: "You really end up caring for this planet." Shepard never opened up publicly about such things, but those close to him felt that being among a handful of humans to have seen the delicate blue marble of the earth floating 250,000 miles off in the black sea of the universe did *something* to him.

Henri Landwirth certainly felt that Shepard had become a better man. In 1986, after helping create the Mercury Seven Foundation, Landwirth had started his own charitable organization, Give Kids the World. On a fifty-one acre plot of central Florida on the outskirts of Disney World, Landwirth created a wonderland where terminally ill children and their families could have ice cream sundaes for breakfast, play all day on carousels, and watch movies every night. A place of joy, but also sorrow. Landwirth's dream was to give dying children a last chance at giddy, all-expenses-paid happiness—a fairy tale come true. Money raised for Give Kids the World offered children and their families a week in Landwirth's fantasy village, a break from the hospitals and doctors, a last chance to be a family before the blackness of death. Shepard began raising money for Landwirth's project as well as his own foundation.

He would wrestle a $100,000 donation from Coca-Cola for the astronaut foundation one week. The next week he'd pressure his friends at Kmart (whose stores he had helped develop) to donate to Landwirth's Give Kids the World. In future years, at

Shepard's encouraging, Kmart would become one of Give Kids the World's biggest supporters, donating millions of dollars year after year. "I saw a different Alan Shepard," Landwirth said, "completely different from the man I'd known in the old days."

Shepard's friend Allen H. Neuharth, the founder of *USA Today*, also saw a "gradual softening" in Shepard's once-icy demeanor, and invited Shepard to sit on the boards of two Washington-based foundations endowed by the Gannett newspaper chain, the Freedom Forum and the First Amendment Center. Freedom Forum board members were each given an allotment of up to $100,000 a year to donate to the charity of their choosing. Shepard chose the Astronaut Scholarship Foundation and Give Kids the World. "He had money and time, and he did what his instincts told him: to spend his time spending his money on others," Neuharth recalled.

Another sign of the kinder, gentler Alan Shepard was his commitment to a book project with Slayton. In 1992 Slayton began working on a book with Neil Armstrong, Howard Benedict, and NBC reporter Jay Barbree. When Armstrong backed out, Benedict asked Shepard to help out. Until then Shepard had never considered writing a book. Other astronauts had published their autobiographies or had books written about them. But whenever the idea was broached with Shepard, he shooed prospective biographers away. There was nothing he needed to share with the public that hadn't been shared already. But when he learned that Slayton had been diagnosed with a brain tumor and that his prospects did not look good, Shepard agreed: "If this will help Deke, I'll do it."

In 1993 Slayton died at the age of sixty-nine, and Shepard immediately flew to Houston to help Deke's wife, Bobbie, make funeral arrangements. *Moonshot* came out a year later—the *New York Times* called it a "swashbuckling" version of the space race—and Shepard vigorously promoted the book, with appearances at bookstores across the country. He knew that Slayton, who'd spent twenty-three years with NASA, did not leave millions behind for his family. Shepard figured strong book sales could help Bobbie and her family. "He didn't do all that for himself," Bobbie recalled. "He did that for Deke and me."

///

One night, about a year after *Moonshot* was released, Shepard met in Cocoa Beach with his Mercury Seven friends, now down to five. He, Glenn, Cooper, Carpenter, and Schirra, each of them in their late sixties or early seventies and easing toward retirement, sat at a restaurant table talking about Gus, Deke, and what they'd all do next in life.

Shepard had sold off his Texas business ventures and his Coors distributorship and consolidated his assets beneath the umbrella of Seven-Fourteen Enterprises, Inc., named for his two space flights. Then, in 1989, he and Louise exchanged their Houston apartment for the perfect semiretirement retreat, a cliff-side house at 1512 Bonaficio Drive in the exclusive, privately owned Pebble Beach community. He and Louise had fallen in love with California's central coast in the 1950s, when they were stationed nearby—those distant days of earning $12,000 a year. Now their back deck loomed above the sixth, seventh, and eighth holes of the Cypress Point golf course, three of the most spectacular holes in all of golf.

He seemed perfectly content with the simple life he now lived, a life grounded by golf and charity events and Louise. He and Louise celebrated fifty years of marriage in 1995. On their back deck they could sip coffee each morning and wait for the thick Pacific fog to lift and expose the rocky shores below, the seals and the seabirds, the wind-gnarled cypress trees, the wildflowers, and all the deer and millionaires mingling on the fairways of Pebble Beach.

A round at one of Pebble Beach's courses costs at least $350. Nonmembers often waited months for a tee time, and fanatics had been known to arrive at 2 A.M. to wait in front of the pro shop in hopes that one of the day's players had canceled. Shepard could play there anytime he wanted. The Pebble Beach pro shop would call Shepard late in the day if they had an opening, and Shepard would drive down—in the sky-blue Camaro convertible he'd swapped for his Corvette—for a twilight round. Or he'd impress an old Navy buddy by getting a morning tee time ten minutes before the place officially opened.

When he wasn't playing in his backyard he'd fly to Phoenix, Hawaii, or Palm Springs to play with friends or at a charity tournament. He and Louise often traveled to Morocco, where they'd play in King Hassan II's annual tournament. He'd take friends or, one time, his daughter to Frank Sinatra's house outside Palm Springs after a tournament. He once canceled plans with another friend so he could play a round with Tiger Woods.

At seventy-one, he was in perfect health, living high above the glory of Pebble Beach, flush with money, fame, and fortune, enjoying the type of retirement most men dream of. But the days of idyllic retirement would end all too soon.

In 1996 Shepard was diagnosed with leukemia.

22

"This is the toughest man
I've ever met"

Shepard's illness wasn't apparent immediately. He was a proud man who tried to hide it, and at first he succeeded. But to those who looked closely, there were signs.

In October 1996 the Naval Academy's athletic director, Jack Lengyl, called to tell Shepard the rowing team had purchased a new racing shell and planned to name it after him. At the christening ceremony for the *Alan B. Shepard Jr.*, Shepard stood at the podium on a dock beside College Creek and spoke for forty passionate minutes about what the Naval Academy meant to him. He placed flowers on the boat and, per tradition, poured water over the bow. The crew climbed into the boat, shoved off from the dock, and rowed off a few hundred yards. They turned around, and as they glided back past the dock the crew lifted their oars into the sideways "stiff-oar" salute position. Shepard walked to the edge of the water and saluted back.

Midshipmen on the dock stood gape-mouthed as tears sprang to the eyes of the steely American hero. There was hardly a dry eye in the crowd. Afterward Shepard climbed into his limousine and told the driver to turn right instead of left toward the exit. Lengyl would learn later that Shepard already knew he was sick. He wanted to tour "the Yard"—the launching pad of his Navy career—one last time. Indeed, it would be the last time he would set foot on the Naval Academy grounds.

That same year Shepard and three of his old Naval Academy classmates—including his roommate, Bob Williams—got together for two days of golf. Shepard's swing had never been great, but this weekend it was particularly weak. No power, no distance, no "miles and miles." Williams knew something was wrong. Shepard and his old roommate shared a cart, but Shepard spent very little time in it. Instead of riding in the cart from one shot to the next, he *ran*. It was a very strange round of golf, with Shepard swinging like an old man, then jogging a hundred yards up to his ball. Later, over drinks, Shepard confessed that he was sick. "But I'm going to beat this," he said.

///

Also in 1996 Shepard played so poorly in his favorite golf tournament—the AT&T Pebble Beach Pro-Am, played annually in his backyard—that the tournament's organizers decided not to invite the perennial competitor back again. The tournament, which began in the 1950s as "Bing Crosby's Clam Bake," was notorious for being marred by torrential rains and fierce winds, and for the wildly erratic play of some celebrity amateurs; Gerald Ford famously sprayed balls into the crowds, where many fans wore hard hats. One year Shepard watched in amazement as actor James Garner punched out a drunken heckler. It was one of his favorite weeks of the year.

The 1996 tournament coincided with the twenty-fifth anniversary of Shepard's six-iron shot on the moon, and Shepard allowed the TV reporters to interview him about that after playing a five-hole Celebrity Challenge charity event with Bill Murray, Clint Eastwood, John Denver, and Kevin Costner, who won the event. But Shepard, as usual, played poorly. The AT&T accepted only golfers with a handicap of eighteen or less. Shepard was listed at the limit, eighteen, and across three decades at the Crosby/AT&T would annually end up with some of the worst scores of the tournament. After his lousy performance that year, tournament officials finally decided that enough was enough. He was crushed, hurt, and humiliated. The blow was especially painful because in 1997 he also learned that he wasn't just sick. He was, indeed, dying.

///

At first, after some intense drug treatments and blood transfusions, the leukemia had seemed headed toward remission. Just as he had beaten back his Ménière's disease, it had seemed for a while as if he might also beat his cancer. But the leukemia returned in full force in 1997. His confidence remained high, but the doctors' reports told a different story. So he finally began telling his friends the truth.

One night Shepard and his record producer friend Mickey Kapp were having drinks at the Pebble Beach country club, and Kapp asked, innocently enough, how Shepard was feeling. "Well," he said, "the docs tell me I have a touch of leukemia. But I'll beat it." Kapp had no words. He thought, *This is the toughest man I've ever met.*

Because of his age, Shepard was not a candidate for a bone marrow transplant. The best he could do was visit the local hospital, Community Hospital of the Monterey Peninsula, for blood transfusions. He'd check in under an assumed name and have his diseased blood drained and replaced with donor blood. Then he'd walk out feeling better—he called it his twice-monthly "pinking up." But two weeks later he'd be pale and weak again. If anyone asked, he'd say, "I've lived a good life, I have no regrets, I'm not afraid. Nor am I ready to stop fighting." Instead, he traveled the country looking for a cure. His almost desperate travels took him one day to the home of his old competitor, John Glenn.

///

In 1996 NASA had announced that Glenn would be granted his long-simmering wish to return to space. Unlike Shepard, Glenn was still flying planes, was in perfect health, and had convinced NASA to exploit the scientific value of sending an octogenarian into the heavens. Shepard's record of being, at age forty-seven, the oldest spaceman had already been shattered many times over. Prior to Glenn's return to space, the oldest astronaut had been sixty-one. But Glenn was scheduled to surpass all records. If his late 1998 space shuttle launch was a success, he would be the first seventy-eight-year-old in space.

As part of his training, Glenn became involved with scientists at the National Institute on Aging, part of the National Institutes of Health (NIH) in Bethesda, Maryland. When Shepard asked for his help, Glenn made some calls to leukemia experts there. He found to his dismay that there wasn't much the NIH experts could offer. Shepard's disease, they'd determined, was indeed incurable; it was just a matter of time before his body surrendered. Glenn did convince NIH doctors to contact Shepard's doctors in Monterey, and they suggested tweaks in Shepard's treatment.

In the early summer of 1998, as Glenn continued training for his space flight, Shepard agreed to a television interview to discuss Glenn's impending return to orbit. Shepard reminisced about his own two space flights and told the CNN reporter that traveling to the moon "wasn't that exciting." But standing on the surface, looking down on the earth ... that had profoundly changed his life. He had always lacked the eloquence to explain who he was, how he felt, what the earth looked like from space, and especially what the moon meant to him. Usually he didn't see the point in explaining or exposing himself. But now, with the end of life looming ahead, he offered a rare public description of how he'd stood beside his lunar module, *Antares,* waiting for Ed Mitchell to join him on the surface and "thinking about the millions and millions of people that are down there . . . trying to get along, desperately trying to get along." The reporter seemed taken aback: "Terrific . . . That was great."

Shepard added that he was happy his friend Glenn was getting a chance to be up there again looking down. But when the reporter asked if Shepard would like to go back up, he said, "I think I'm through," adding, "given a good solid physical condition, I would probably say, 'Hell, yes, I want to go again.' But I think I've . . . I'm finished."

The reporter tried a joke, encouraging Shepard to "never say never." Shepard's response was "Go talk to my doctor."

///

A few months before that CNN interview, in late 1997, Shepard had been roasted at a celebratory dinner in the ballroom of the Peabody Hotel in Orlando, where Henri Landwirth threw an annual black-and-white gala to thank the benefactors of his Give Kids the World foundation. Landwirth always timed the event to coincide with the annual Astronaut Scholarship Foundation meeting, and Shepard and the others looked forward to the yearly reunion. In 1997 the dinner commemorated the end of Shepard's tenure as head of the Astronaut Scholarship Foundation. He had realized he was too sick to carry on and had decided to hand the reins over to Jim Lovell. The roasters knew he was sick, but they put on a good face, digging up funny old Shepard stories from the good old days. Louise sat by his side, still lovely at seventy-four, laughing heartily and whispering now and then in his ear, asking how he felt. He'd had a blood transfusion the previous day, but a nurse stood backstage just in case.

At evening's end, Don Engen, a former Navy test pilot and flying buddy of Shepard's who had become head of the National Air and Space Museum, stepped to the podium. After a few jokes he announced that he had a surprise. "You've been bugging me about this for years, Al," he said. "Well, I give up ... Apollo 14 is all yours."

What he meant was this: The capsule that in 1971 had been Shepard's cocoon for nine days, to and from the moon, across half a million miles, at speeds up to twenty-four thousand miles an hour, which had been on display at the Smithsonian in Washington, would finally be his. Shepard had been asking Engen for years to donate it to the scholarship foundation so that it could be displayed among the space suits, rockets, and memorabilia at its Astronaut Hall of Fame and Museum on the outskirts of Cape Kennedy. Clearly unprepared, Shepard was speechless. Tears suddenly filled his eyes, and his large lips trembled. "Oh, honey," Louise said, and took his hand in hers. Glenn called it "a very emotional evening."

"People knew Al was sick," he said. "But we didn't know how long he had left."

The next day the ceremony continued at the Astronaut Hall of Fame, where Engen pulled a white sheet off the Apollo 14 command module, *Kitty Hawk*. Shepard stood at the foot of the space capsule, frail and full of drugs and disease, his hair thinned and his skin a bluish hue from the chemotherapy, looking so fragile. He reached out and touched *Kitty Hawk*'s cool metal skin. Then, surrounded by his closest friends, the Icy Commander wept. His thin body shook, and he put his tear-streaked face in his hands. It would be the last time most of his friends saw him.

///

On July 4, 1998, at a waterfront concert and picnic in Monterey, Shepard brought a couple of bottles of his favorite California chardonnay. He and Louise sat on a blanket. He waved and acknowledged the applause when the bandleader introduced him.

On July 7 Mickey Kapp met Shepard for a drink at the Pebble Beach golf lodge. Shepard seemed in good spirits, reporting that his blood test results were good. People stopped by to ask how he was feeling, and he gave them all a thumbs-up.

On July 20 Louise took him to the hospital in Monterey. He was having stomach pains. It didn't seem serious. It didn't seem like the end. But he slipped into sleep, and the next night, at about nine-thirty, at age seventy-four, he died.

"Only battle I ever saw him lose," Mickey Kapp said.

///

Shepard would have been happy with the words in the newspapers. "One Cool Moonwalker," "America's Lindbergh of Space," and "Rocket Man," the press called him. He had once despised them—and the feeling was often mutual. But now they were kind, laudatory, and proud. They wrote how Shepard's 1961 venture into space had given a troubled Kennedy administration a boost, how it had been a brave salvo in the cold war, how it had emboldened Kennedy to make his famous promise to reach the moon.

And above all, the papers stressed that he was first. That, to him, had been paramount. Reaching the moon in 1971 was different. He talked less about that. That was, somehow, a personal thing. He'd fought back from the Ménière's disease to get there. But ten years before that, being picked to be first into space— that was the thing.

A man who as a boy was smaller, weaker, slower than most. A boy who pushed himself to be better than the others had become the man, the flyboy, he had always wanted to be. And so it was never the fifteen-minute *Freedom* 7 flight itself that symbolized his life. He'd had more thrilling adventures as a test pilot and fighter jock. But being chosen, that was the thing. Because for Shepard, life had been one big competition. "That was competition at its best," Shepard had said just a few years earlier.

///

A week later Louise flew to Houston for an August 1 memorial service at NASA. She seemed quiet but strong. Theirs had not been a perfect union, but they had survived many pitfalls, and

Shepard's name had not been lumped in with those of Scott Carpenter, Deke Slayton, Gordon Cooper, Ed Mitchell, Buzz Aldrin, Neil Armstrong, and others, astronauts whose marriages ended in divorce. Or, in some cases, two or three divorces. One astronaut had seven wives in sixteen years. Partly it was Louise's willingness to overlook things, to accept things. The payoffs were nights when she'd hear him tinkling at the keys of their piano, playing "Danny Boy" as she got dressed for a dinner date.

And now here she was at his memorial service, listening to the piercing alto of a Navy choral singer singing their song, "Danny Boy," to a crowd of NASA dignitaries.

Glenn rose before the crowd and talked at length about Shepard the patriot, Shepard the leader, Shepard the friend, hero, and competitor—"a fierce competitor," he called him—and then read a poem, a favorite for generations of aviators, called "High Flight."

> Oh I have skipped the surly bonds of Earth
> And danced the skies on laughter-silvered wings
> Sunward I've climbed and joined the tumbling mirth
> Of sunlit clouds and done a hundred things you have not
>   dreamed of . . .

Wally Schirra took the podium to claim how "the brotherhood we had will last forever." But he couldn't finish. He began sobbing, apologized, and walked back to his seat. Gordo Cooper spoke next. He looked to the sky and told Shepard, "We'll be there before long."

As the crowd shuffled outside for a tree-planting ceremony, all heads looked up in response to the roar of four Navy jets. Just before crossing above Johnson Space Center, one jet peeled off from the rest—the missing-man formation Shepard so hated. Then they heard the painful first notes of the bugler blowing taps.

///

That night Louise had dinner with her friends the Vanderhoefs, who back in the 1960s had introduced her and Alan to George and Barbara Bush and their kids. The Vanderhoefs were surprised at how composed Louise seemed. But the next day Louise spent all morning in her Houston hotel room. Another friend arrived to take Louise to lunch and found her sitting on the couch, looking terrible. The friend went to sit beside her, and like a deflated balloon Louise just folded, bursting into tears. They talked for an hour, missing lunch entirely, as Louise spoke of how much she missed him, how much she loved him, how she didn't know what she would do now without him.

She knew his illness had been terminal but never let herself believe it. Just like his "incurable" ear disease, she believed that he—they—would get through it somehow. She had prayed for him, was optimistic and hopeful like a good Christian Scientist. But this time it hadn't worked. And now she dreaded the thought of returning to the house on the hill alone. Louise's friends feared she might not be cut out for widowhood.

Indeed, without her husband, Louise's heart wasn't right.

Earlier that year she had begun experiencing a mild heart flutter, caused by an extra heartbeat. Despite her Christian Science instincts, Alan had convinced her to see a heart specialist, who had prescribed medicine for the occasional fibrillations. Some friends now wondered: With Alan gone, would she continue to take her heart medicine?

After Shepard's memorial service, Louise flew to Colorado to visit her daughter Laura. A month later she seemed ready to tackle the Pebble Beach house alone. She took a Tuesday morning flight to San Francisco, where she had to wait three hours to catch her connecting flight back to Monterey. The small propeller-driven commuter plane took off that afternoon, August 25, 1998, and Louise sat quietly by herself, looking out at the Pacific.

It was just a small plane, a short hop. There was no defibrillator aboard. When her heart stopped, there was nothing the flight attendants could do, and she died high above the Monterey Peninsula and the Pacific. The crew found a tag with Laura's phone number on it and called to break the news.

In the span of five weeks, they were both gone. The only minuscule sliver of consolation to the family was the timing of Louise's death. She died at exactly 5 P.M.—the precise time Alan used to telephone her, year after year, when he was out of town. As their daughter Laura told a family friend, "Daddy called Mommy at about five o'clock in the afternoon, just one last time."

///

Louise hadn't wanted to bury Alan. In the days after his death she'd begun making plans to have his body cremated and have the ashes scattered above a special place: the rocky cove visible from their back deck. When Louise died, the family decided to have both of them cremated and to have their ashes scattered together.

On the afternoon of November 18, 1998, a handpicked crowd of Alan and Louise's closest friends stood on the seventeenth green of Pebble Beach's Cypress Point course. The helicopters seemed to explode from thin air, fluttering from over the hills, over the house on Bonaficio Drive, and out over the water. The two craft stopped suddenly above a rocky inlet called Stillwater Cove and turned slowly toward each other as ropes snaked out from their bellies. Tied to the end of each rope was an urn— one carried Alan's ashes and some dried flowers, the other Louise's ashes and dried flowers.

On cue, both urns tilted forward and the ashes and flowers came spilling out, got caught by an ocean breeze, and swirled and swished together before slowly sprinkling down onto the rocks below. Then, almost as if it was choreographed, two seals swam at each other from opposite directions, slid up onto a rock, and touched noses.

NOTES

Prologue

page xv, **John Glenn was furious:** John Glenn, *John Glenn: A Memoir* (New York: Bantam Books, 1999), pp. 232–233; Fred Bruning, "Glenn's Return to Space: A 2nd Launch Into History," *Newsweek* (October 11, 1998); John Glenn, "A Detailed Plan," *We Seven* (New York: Simon and Schuster, 1962), p. 304.

page xv, **[Gilruth:] stop "backbiting":** Jay Barbree et al., *Moonshot* (Atlanta: Turner Publishing, 1994), p. 81.

pages xv–xvi, **Shorty—"[Shepard] had what all the others had . . .":** Jewel Spangler Smaus and Charles Spangler, *America's First Spaceman* (New York: Doubleday & Co., 1962), p. 147.

page xvi, **Shepard was the most capable . . . :** Walt Williams, *Go* (unpublished manuscript).

page xvi, **"[W]anted to put our best foot forward":** Ibid.

page xvi, **"Come on, Al . . ." [entire conversation with Douglas]:** Oriana Fallaci, *If the Sun Dies* (New York: Antheum House Inc., 1966), pp. 85–88.

pages xvi–xvii, **Glenn's "maudlin sentimentality":** Alan Shepard, "The Astronaut's Story," *Life* (May 19, 1961), p. 26.

page xvii, **"I was hoping it was you":** Barbree et al., *Moonshot*, p. 103.

page xviii, **"I love you" [entire conversation]:** Ibid.

page xix, **"that little rascal":** Alan Shepard, interview, Academy of Achievement (1991).

page xix, **stopped to symbolically kick:** Alan Shepard, "The First American," *We Seven*, p. 241.

page xix, *She's got an air of expectancy:* Ibid.

page xix, his throat choked up and he just waved: Barbree et al., *Moonshot*, p. 105.

page xix, **Douglas' crayons:** Ibid.

page xx, **"I want to be first because I want to be first":** Martin Caidin, *Man Into Space* (New York: Pyramid Books, 1961), p. 37.

page xxi, **"I need your help":** Author interview with Al Blackburn.

page xxi, keeping their pants zipped: Glenn, *A Memoir,* p. 221.

page xxii, **Shepard was suddenly moved:** Robert Godwin, ed., *Freedom 7: The NASA Mission Reports* (Ontario: Apogee Books, 2001), p. 72.

page xxii, his heartbeat quickened a bit: Ibid.

page xxii, *Okay, buster...don't screw up:* Barbree et al., *Moonshot,* p. 108; Shepard, *Life* (May 19, 1961), p. 27.

page xxiv, the face . . . "close and friendly": Shepard, *Life* (May 19, 1961), p. 27.

PART I /// BEFORE SPACE

1: "Alan was really kind of a loner"

page 3, **Carpenter: "better than anyone else":** Christopher Cheney, "The First Astronaut," OpenUniverse.com (May 5, 2001).

page 3, **"you'd better get out of town":** Author interview with Henri Land-wirth.

page 4, **"infamous stare":** Author interview with Alice Wackermann.

page 4, **"the world's greatest test pilot":** Jim Watson, "Shepard Sky High on NASA," *Washington Times* (August 6, 1986).

page 4, **"He could fly anything":** Author interview with Bob Baldwin.

page 4, **"the best aviator I've ever known":** Author interview with William Lawrence.

page 4, **"flamboyant" and "indulgent":** Author interview with Robert Elder.

page 5, **"bitterly competitive, to the point of being cutthroat":** Author interview with Gordon Cooper.

page 5, **accused Shepard of "swindling" him:** Scott Carpenter, quoted in "Subject: Alan Shepard," *Federal Bureau of Investigation* (1971).

page 5, **Shepard "really didn't want to have anything to do with the rest of us":** Author interview with Betty Grissom.

page 5, **"the biggest flirt in the country":** Author interview with Don Gregory.

page 6, **"[T]his was his compulsion":** Author interview with Al Blackburn.

page 6, **"She was the rock":** Author e-mail exchange with Robert Windsor.

page 6, **"real men . . . perfect physical and emotional and aesthetic specimens":** Author interview with Robert Voas.

page 6, an "asshole" or a "son of a bitch": Author interviews with Gene Cernan, James Schefter, and others.

page 8, "the terrain of my poetry": Louis Mertins, *Robert Frost, Life and Talks-walking* (Univ. Oklahoma, 1965).

page 8, Frost was also rebuffed . . . : Kathleen Morrison. *Robert Frost, A Pictorial Chronicle* (Holt, 1974).

page 10, thirty-cent cheese sandwich: Cheney, OpenUniverse.com.

page 11, "a small pond": Shepard, Academy of Achievement interview.

page 11, "He appreciated a chuckle once in a while": Mel R. Allen, "The Disciplined Life," *Yankee* (October, 1991), pp. 74–77, 134–139.

page 11, "two popular and prominent young society people": Hattie Durgin interview and scrapbook.

page 12, "A people person," Alan called her: Allen, *Yankee.*

page 13, "pizzazz": Author interview with Dudley Shepard.

page 13, Glenn called Shepard "an enigma . . .": Glenn, *A Memoir,* p. 232.

page 13, "If he wanted to talk to you . . .": Author interview with George Sheldon.

page 14, Shepard's personal best was thirty-five feet: Smaus and Spangler, *America's First Spaceman,* p. 58.

page 15, When the cider ripened . . . : Author interview with Dick True and Sherman Brickett.

page 16, "not awed by authority": Author interview with Dudley Shepard.

page 16, "keep a teenager with boundless energy out of mischief": Smaus, *America's First Spaceman;* author interview with Charles Spangler.

page 17, "Mrs. Wiggins was tough," Shepard recalled: Allen, "The Disciplined Life," *Yankee.*

page 19, two hundred thousand copies [of We] had been sold: A. Scott Berg, *Lindbergh* (New York: Berkley Books, 1998), p. 167.

page 19, *A Literary Digest* survey found . . . : Susan Faludi, *Stiffed: The Betrayal of the American Man* (New York: William Morrow and Co., 1999).

page 19, "He was always my hero": Alan Shepard, interview with Pam Platt, "Shepard Detailed 'Real Stuff' in Florida Today Interview," *Florida Today* (July 22, 1998).

page 19, "I was just fascinated by planes": Allen, *Yankee.*

page 20, "a locomotive that has left the track . . .": Dave English, *Slipping the Surly Bonds—Great Quotations on Flight* (New York: McGraw Hill, 1998).

page 20, "man is more than man": Ibid.

page 21, "matchsticks": Author interviews with Al Deal and Harold Moynihan.

page 22, "inventor's dream" . . . "everyday actuality": "Amelia Earhart," *Microsoft Encarta Encyclopedia* (2002).

page 22, he thought dreamily of a poem: Smaus and Spangler, *America's First Spaceman*, p. 53.

page 23, "a wine of the gods of which they": Charles Lindbergh, *We*.

page 24, had already traveled a hundred miles [entire DC-3 scene]: Smaus and Spangler, *America's First Spaceman*, pp. 53–66.

page 24, On Sunday, February 19: Ibid.

page 25, Park sensed ... "a good kid": John Clayton, "Carl S. Park Sr. Made His Living in the Skies," *The Union Leader* (September 14, 1998).

page 25, Instructors tell their students ... "has no similes in our life on the ground": Wolfgang Langewiesche. *Stick and Rudder: An Explanation of the Art of Flying* (New York: McGraw-Hill, 1944).

page 26, "a natural": Geoff Dougherty. "Instructor Recalls Hero's First Flight," *St. Petersburg Times* (August 8, 1998).

page 26, he knew he was hooked: Allen, "The Disciplined Life," *Yankee*.

page 26, New Hampshire produced a few ... of note: Jean Batchelder, *History & Heroes of New Hampshire Aviation* (Spring Hill, Florida: Arrow Publishing Co., 1995).

page 28, "Appreciate you putting more pressure on him ..": Shirley Thomas, *Men of Space*, Vol. 3 (Philadelphia and New York: Chilton Co. Book Division, 1961), p. 189.

2: "I think I love you"

page 30, The U.S. Navy had first attempted to create ... : Jack Sweetman, *The U.S. Naval Academy: An Illustrated History* (Annapolis, Maryland: Naval Institute Press, 1995).

page 32, There was no escape from the small cruelties of plebe life: Author interview with Robert Williams.

page 33, Shepard was forced to dive under the table: Author interview with Dick Sewall.

page 33, "As an Army brat ..": Letter from Bob Kirk to U.S. Naval Academy.

page 34, One classmate called Shepard "ratey": Author interview with Paul Havenstein.

page 34, One morning Shepard organized a small rebellion: Author interview with Dick Sewall.

page 35, "There's a bigger game, a bigger battle": William Wallace, "Pushing Aside Games for a World War," *The New York Times* (December 7, 1991).

page 35, "Gentlemen, we are at war": Ibid.

page 36, "Hey, that's why we were all there": Darrell Fry, "Army-Navy '41: On the brink; New meaning for an old rivalry eight days before Pearl Harbor," *The Washington Times* (December 7, 1941).

page 38, **poor grades made Shepard eligible for "reassignment"**: Shepard's academic records, obtained from the U.S. Naval Academy archives.

page 39, **Shepard made a habit of it:** Author interview with Dick Sewall.

page 40, **Shepard "appreciated the better things in life"**: Letter from Bob Kirk to U.S. Naval Academy.

page 40, **"he processed a lot of women"**: Author interview with Robert Williams.

page 41, **stood side by side singing carols [entire scene]:** Smaus and Spangler, *America's First Spaceman*, pp. 88–89.

page 41, **made many men worship her from afar:** Author interview with Tamie Watters.

page 43, **"VIP girls"**: Juliana Brewer, oral history, Longwood Gardens' archives.

page 43, **Each year they received gifts of fine china:** Ibid.

page 43, **"being a girl and knowing . . ."**: Louise letter to Alan (May 3, 1943).

page 43, **cold and standoffish:** Author interview with Ike Evans.

page 44, **"Frosty" and . . . "Miss Westinghouse"**: Louise letter to Alan (October 7, 1943).

page 44, **It was ruled an accident, although . . . :** Author interview with Dudley Shepard.

page 44, **could sometimes lead to early, unexpected death:** Caroline Fraser, *God's Perfect Child: Living and Dying in the Christian Science Church* (New York: Henry Holt and Company, 1999).

page 45, **"I hope I can really accomplish something"**: Smaus and Spangler, *America's First Spaceman*, p. 82.

pages 45–47, **[Crew team details]:** Author interviews with Robert Williams, H. Y. Davidson, William McLaughlin.

pages 46–47, **Her shrieks filled the academy's hospital ward:** Author interview with William McLaughlin.

page 47, *Nyah . . . what's up, doc?*: Author interview with H. Y. Davidson.

page 48, **"Spectacularly beautiful"**: Author interview with J. T. Cockrill.

page 49, *Thanks seems like such an inadequate word*: Louise letter to Alan, June 14, 1943.

page 51, **"tip of my tongue"**: Phone call to Louise (July 30, 1943).

page 51, **"Maybe," Louise suggested:** Louise letter to Alan (September 25, 1943).

page 51, **"pugilistic" features:** Author interview with Tamie Watters.

page 52, **"the most wonderful, handsome, loveable, bad boy"**: Fran letter to Alan.

page 53, **"But Alan, I was *wrong*"**: Louise letter to Alan (October 7, 1943).

page 54, **Fran felt "struck by lightning":** Fran letter to Alan (January 24, 1944).

page 54, **"heartbreaks . . . are a part of life":** Fran letter to Alan (February 15, 1944).

page 54, **George was crushed:** Author interview with Don Hawes.

page 55, **"I could never have been happier . . .":** Smaus and Spangler, *America's First Spaceman*, p. 96.

page 55, **"never really hit my stride":** Alan B. Shepard, unpublished interview with author Robert Sherrod.

page 56, **"I was only twenty . . .":** Ibid.

3: "The kamikazes raised hell last night"

page 58, **"my fiancée":** Alan Shepard letter to Robert Williams (July 28, 1944).

page 61, **[Lindbergh at Biak]:** Berg, *Lindbergh*, pp. 447–455.

page 61, **"he could really put it away":** Author interview with Andrew Atwell.

page 61, **One day the crew of a B-25 bomber . . . :** Smaus and Spangler, *America's First Spaceman*, p. 101; author interview with Robert Williams.

page 63, **"a promising prospect" and "get my own bunk":** Shepard to Williams, Nov. 18, 1944.

page 63, **"Have been running into all kinds of people":** Ibid.

page 64, **"a brilliant and courageous piece of fighting":** Author interview with Howard Johnson; Howard Johnson's personal diary.

page 64, **opposition came from unexpected fronts:** Ibid.

page 65, **"the worst storm we have been in":** Personal diary of John F. Huber III.

page 65, **"Several men have been lost over the side":** Personal diary of Howard Johnson.

page 66, **"You have started me on my way as a Shepard":** Smaus and Spangler, *America's First Spaceman*, p. 101.

page 69, **"The old 'rump' certainly gets around":** Shepard to Williams, Aug. 22, 1945.

page 69, **"Wholesale debauchery!":** Ibid.

page 70, **Perley's mustachioed lips:** Author interview with Tom Spargo.

page 70, **More than once Perley sent Shepard . . . :** Author interview with Andrew Atwell.

page 71, **"One of these days—if I don't get killed . . .":** Ibid.

page 72, **"We have lost a lot of classmates":** Shepard letter to Williams (August 22, 1945).

page 72, **The *Cogswell's* first picket duty:** Personal diary of John F. Huber III; personal diary of Howard Johnson.

page 72, "If we last that long": Personal diary of John F. Huber III.

page 72, "We have a slim chance . . . I am a little bit nervous": Personal diary of Howard Johnson.

page 73, "The smell of burned flesh and cries of pain": Oral history of Jack Gebhart, "Oral History—War in the Pacific," Naval Historical Center.

page 74, "The war's not over yet!": Author interview with John Huber.

page 74, One night . . . the throat of an officer on a ship directly behind *Cogswell*: Personal diary of John Huber; personal diary of Howard Johnson.

page 75, "The kamikazes raised hell last night": Author interview with John Huber.

pages 75–76, one sailor scrambled aboard . . . crying like a baby: Author interview with Andrew Atwell.

page 76, "I heard screams as she slipped under the water": Oral history of Jack Gebhart.

page 76, "A bottle of whisky was passed around": Ibid.

page 76, "The burial of the dead was terrible": Oral history of Samuel Robert Sherman, "Oral History—War in the Pacific," Naval Historical Center.

page 77, "Much evidence of bloodshed and violence": Author interviews with Howard Johnson and Ray Bates.

page 77, "[Much] sooner than was expected": Shepard letter to Williams (August 22, 1945).

page 78, "turn on your lights and let them know": Author interview with Howard Johnson.

page 78, thirty-four Navy ships were sunk off Okinawa . . . Ernie Pyle: William Manchester, *The Glory and the Dream: A Narrative History of America* (Boston: Little, Brown and Co., 1973), pp. 417–424.

4: "UNSAFE FOR SOLO" in Zoom Town

page 82, "They were kind of falling all over the place": *An Oral History of the Corpus Christi Naval Air Station During World War II* (Del Mar College, 1995).

page 82, . . . at the urging of a young congressman named Lyndon Johnson: Ibid.

page 83, burned, peeling faces: Donald D. Engen, *Wings and Warriors: My Life as a Naval Aviator* (Washington, D.C.: Smithsonian Institute Press, 1997), p. 25.

page 83, "Man, I have arrived at heaven": *An Oral History of the Corpus Christi Naval Air Station.*

page 84, thousands of dead frogs: Ibid.

page 85, "exuded confidence the way a lamp gives off light": Antoine de Saint-Exupéry, *Wind, Sand and Stars* (Harcourt, 1992).

page 85, "tasted the proud intoxication of renunciation": Ibid.

page 85, Of twenty-seven men aboard the two planes, only five survived: *An Oral History of the Corpus Christi Naval Air Station.*

pages 85–86, "were dropping down, just like rain": Ibid.

page 87, After mastering the Stearman [all training scenes]: Author interviews with Tazewell Shepard and John Glenn.

page 88, "skill, composure, enthusiasm, judgment . . .": *An Oral History of the Corpus Christi Naval Air Station.*

page 88, "It was wonderful . . . I loved it": Paul Gillcrist, *Feet Wet: Reflections of a Carrier Pilot* (Pocket Books, 1990), p. 21.

page 89, he approached with his nose too high: Shepard's flight training records, obtained from Chief of Naval Air Training in Corpus Christi.

page 90, his grades plummeted: Ibid.

page 90, "Cadet Brownstein is of quiet, meek disposition": *An Oral History of the Corpus Christi Naval Air Station.*

page 91, "eager to learn . . . above average": Shepard's flight training records.

page 91, "Student was confused": Ibid.

page 92, Going "to the lakes": *An Oral History of the Corpus Christi Naval Air Station.*

page 93, "Barran . . . you fly like shit": Author interview with Jack Barran.

page 93, "IN THE WRONG DIRECTION": Shepard's flight training records.

page 94, "UNSAFE FOR SOLO": Ibid.

page 94, "If you are looking for perfect safety . . .": William Langewiesche, *Inside the Sky: A Meditation on Flight* (New York: Vintage Books, 1999), p. 14.

page 95, hemorrhaging of grease monkeys: Author interview with Tazewell Shepard; Faludi, *Stiffed.*

page 96, Then it was Renza's turn: Smaus and Spangler, *America's First Spaceman,* p. 109.

page 96, "You goofed off a little bit": Allen, *Yankee.*

page 97, "That kind of complacency is so insidious": Ibid.

page 97, "Naval aviators were not angels": Gillcrist, *Feet Wet,* p. xvii.

page 97, "escorting a fervor as tender": Saint-Exupéry, *Wind, Sand and Stars.*

page 98, Pilots would swoop down low for a look: *An Oral History of the Corpus Christi Naval Air Station.*

page 98, One famous Corpus Christi story involves the trainee: Ibid.

page 99, "She captivated everyone she ran into": Author interview with Robert Williams.

page 100, "the best-trained men in the world": *An Oral History of the Corpus Christi Naval Air Station.*

page 100, "it was difficult to walk without swaggering.": Gillcrist, *Feet Wet*, p. 17.

page 100, **The crazy notion of using ships as floating runways:** Roy Grossnick and William J. Armstrong. *United States Naval Aviation: 1910–1995* (Washington, D.C.: Naval Historical Center, 1997).

page 101, **The first LSO was . . . Kenneth Whiting:** Alfred M. Pride, oral history interview, U.S. Naval Institute.

page 103, "Absolutely perfect . . . right in the center.": Allen, "The Disciplined Life," *Yankee.*

page 103, "one of the best moments" Ibid.

5: A perfectly charming son of a bitch

page 105, **"I earnestly desire to fly fighter-bombers":** Shepard's flight training records.

page 106, **"The air, not the runway, was the Corsair's element":** Glenn, *A Memoir,* p. 79; author interview with John Glenn.

page 106, **[Lindbergh, World War II, Corsair]:** Berg, *Lindbergh,* p. 448.

page 106, **"whistling death":** Glenn, *A Memoir,* p. 94.

page 107, **"for real men only":** Author interview with Robert Williams.

page 107, **He was killed in a fireball:** Author interview with Dick Hardy.

page 107, **Another peer failed to adjust the mixture control:** Author interview with Bill Botts.

page 107, **"the bent-wing widowmaker":** Ibid.

page 108, **her fragile constitution . . . :** Author interview with Dorel Alco Abbot.

page 110, **"A rivet or two could pop":** Al Blackburn, *Aces Wild: The Race for Mach 1* (Scholarly Resources, 1998), p. 2.

page 111, **proceeded to handpick each of his pilots:** Author interview with Dick Hardy.

page 111, **Abbot chose Shepard to be his wingman:** Author interview with James L. "Doc" Abbot.

page 111, **Abbot . . . took them down to the naval air station at Pensacola:** Author interview with Dick Hardy.

page 112, **Abbot . . . explained how his men had accidentally missed the turn:** Author interview with Doc Abbot.

page 112, **The *FDR* sailed first to Guantánamo Bay:** Ibid.

page 113, **Abbot's boss—had been killed:** Author interview with Robert Baldwin.

page 114, **One dark, calm night in the Caribbean . . . :** Author interview with Doc Abbot.

page 114, **Why hang around with the other wives to watch the ship:** Louise

Shepard, "Just Go Right Ahead," *Life*, Vol. 47, No. 12 (September 21, 1959), p. 150.

page 115, **Enormous swells lifted and dropped the *FDR*:** Harry D. Felt, oral history interview, U.S. Naval Institute.

page 115, **Most of the *FDR*'s airplanes were tied down [entire scene]:** Author interview with Doc Abbot.

page 117, **continued military spending cuts . . . :** Author interviews with Dick Hardy and Robert Baldwin.

page 117, **"If they lay off too long, you're asking for trouble":** Felt, oral history.

page 118, **Abbot decided to give Shepard command:** Author interview with Doc Abbot.

pages 118–119, **"bodacious" . . . and it turned some colleagues off:** Author interview with Bill Botts.

page 120, **"Baldwin, with you sucking on one end of this ship . . .":** Author interviews with Robert Baldwin and Warren O'Neil.

page 121, **Many Navy marriages were battered:** Felt, oral history.

page 121, **"Why not?" Shepard said:** Author interview with Bill Chaires.

page 123, **Caldwell often walked down from his office:** Author interview with DickHardy.

page 124, **ironically, his successor was killed in a Corsair:** Author interview with Robert Baldwin.

6: Shepard should be court-martialed

page 125, **"aviation plan 65" . . . "outstanding flying proficiency":** *United States Naval Test Pilot School: Historical Narrative and Class Date, 1945–1983,* (Annapolis, Maryland: Fishergate Publishing, 1984), p. 7.

page 126, **"may not have extra talent":** Shepard, Academy of Achievement interview.

page 127, **"drank cheap booze . . . and almost ended up in jail":** Steve Vogel, "In Patuxent, Past Flies Home to Roost: Naval Pilots Return to Celebrate the Glory Days," *The Washington Post* (April 19, 1998).

page 127, **"There wasn't much to do":** Author interview with Robert Elder

page 128, **"Training was very informal, to put it politely":** Matt Bortz, "Memories of WWII Training," unpublished memoir.

page 128, **they raised the requirements for new test pilots:** *United States Naval Test Pilot School.*

page 128, **Just barely avoiding slamming into the tail [entire scene]:** John Hyland, oral history, U.S. Naval Institute.

page 129, **"He could fly anything":** Author interview with Robert Baldwin.

page 129, **One of Shepard's projects was to fly . . . :** Author interview with Bill Chaires.

page 130, "If it sucked, he'd say so": Author interview with Robert Elder.

page 130, "some of the best reports we had": Hyland, oral history.

page 131, could "roll a plane a little better": Shepard, Academy of Achievement.

page 131, "fly the best test flight that anybody had ever flown": Ibid.

page 132, he couldn't condone such flights or every yahoo: Author interview with Robert Baldwin.

page 132, He gave Shepard a stern lecture: John Lacouture, "You Can Be Good and Be Colorful," *Naval History* (June, 2001).

page 132, He flew down low and screamed across the beach: Ibid.

page 133, As Shepard took off, he radioed the air traffic: Author interview with George Whisler.

pages 133, "Get that pilot's name": Ibid.

page 133–134, thought his career was over: Hyland, oral history.

page 134, "Were you just over Chincoteague?": Entire scene based on author interviews with Robert Elder, H. Y. Davidson, George Whisler; Hyland, oral history.

page 134, Shepard should be court-martialed: Lacouture, *Naval History;* Hyland, oral history.

page 134, "I want to straighten this kid out": Hyland, oral history.

page 135, "He [Pride] was furious": Author interview with Robert Elder.

page 136, He also grounded Shepard for two weeks: Lacouture, *Naval History.*

page 136, "Now look, Shep, if you want to fly low . . .": Hyland, oral history.

page 136, "I thought he was a little indulgent": Author interview with Robert Elder.

page 136, when Shepard was allowed to fly again . . . [entire scene]: Author interview with Doc Abbot.

page 137, "It was a remarkable piece of work . . .": Ibid.

page 138, Miss America's impressive cleavage: Lacouture, *Naval History.*

page 138, "Let's show them how to do it": Author interview with Robert Elder.

page 138, He painted pubic hair: Author interview with Robert Williams.

page 139, " . . . it was blowing the airplane apart" [entire scene]: Author interviews with Robert Elder; Mike Machat, "Bob Elder: Naval Aviator," *Wings,* Vol. 31, No. 6 (December, 2001).

page 140, "I don't know what a genius IQ is, but he had it": Hyland oral history.

page 141, Shepard compiled an extensive report . . . : Ibid.

page 141, friends . . . "are going to run right over you on the way to the same target": Shepard, Academy of Achievement.

page 142, "Maybe you are a little bit better": Ibid.

page 142, "I was the best graduate . . .": Allen, "The Disciplined Life," *Yankee.*

7: "Do you wish to declare an emergency?"

page 144, waiters thought they were all drunk: Author interview with Charles Spangler.

page 144, "Mommy, how come Daddy is so rich . . . ?": Shepard, Academy of Achievement.

page 145, "a pretty good return on the investment": "Two Aces in Korean Air War," *Naval Aviation News* (September, 1953).

page 145, a two-foot hole in Glenn's tail: Glenn, *A Memoir*, p. 134.

page 146, Shepard . . . "slow-roll": Author interview with Jig Dog Ramage.

page 146, "I was lying, cheating, and stealing": Ramage, oral history, *U.S. Naval Institute*.

page 146, "At that time, friendships were strong": Author interview with Jig Dog Ramage.

page 148, "Stop damaging the flight deck": Ibid; Ramage, oral history.

page 148, That decision would ultimately save Jig Dog's life: Ibid.

page 149, "there are no old, bold test pilots": Pam Platt, "Shepard Detailed 'Real Stuff' in Florida Today Interview," *Florida Today* (July 22, 1998).

page 150, Captain Griffin later summoned . . . Lawrence: Author interview with William Lawrence.

page 152, Frank Repp came up a few inches short: Author interviews Frank Repp and Jig Dog Ramage; Ramage, oral history.

page 153, "Pretty colorful, wasn't I?": Ibid.

page 153, Shepard's colleague John Mitchell once . . . : Author interview with John Mitchell.

page 154, "MiG Mad Marine": Glenn, *A Memoir*, p. 141.

page 154, "irrepressible spirit": Author interview with William Lawrence.

page 155, Shepard was put in hack: Ibid.

page 155, "LT Shepard is a very fine Naval Aviator, but . . .": William Lawrence, "Reminiscences of Alan Shepard," *Foundation*, journal of the National Museum of Naval Aviation (Spring, 1990).

page 155, "You are not aiding the individual or the Navy": Ramage, oral history.

page 156, Once, during a change-of-command ceremony . . . : Author interview with Jig Dog Ramage.

page 156, "He always had a lot of protection": Ibid.

page 157, A winter night over the Sea of Japan: Barbree et al., *Moonshot*, p. 57.

page 157, *I might be in real trouble* [entire scene]: Ibid; *We Seven*, p. 84.

page 158, "the vast tribunal of the tempestuous sky": Antoine de Saint-Exupéry, *Wind, Sand and Stars*.

page 158, **burning fuel at a horrendous rate:** Barbree et al., *Moonshot*, p. 57–60.

page 159, **He roared to himself:** Ibid.

page 159, **"normal carrier landing":** Ibid.

page 159, **"separates the men from the boys":** Ted Wilbur, "Once a Fighter Pilot," *Naval Aviation News* (1970).

page 160, **"He always wanted to be one of them":** Author interview with Frank Repp.

page 161, **"we took a few liberties":** Author interview with Robert Elder.

page 161, **They'd fly straight at each other:** Author interviews with Robert Elder and William Lawrence.

page 161, **"The star of the show was Alan Shepard":** Charles D. Griffin, oral history interview, U.S. Naval Institute.

page 161, **the Mangy Angels made plans to get a photograph:** Author interview with William Lawrence.

page 162, **"Guys would go there like flies":** Walt Radosevich, oral history interview with Thomas Saylor, *Oral History Project of the World War II Years*.

page 163, **"short-arm" inspection:** Author interview with Jig Dog Ramage.

page 163, **Friends called him a . . . "liberty hound":** Author interview with Ralph Stell.

page 163, **"Shep never revealed . . . who he screwed":** Author interview with John Mitchell.

page 164, **nearly a million men subscribed to** *Playboy* David Halberstam, *The Fifties* (New York: Fawcett Columbine, 1994), p. 573.

page 164, **wondered why she stayed with him:** Author interview with Betty Whisler.

page 165, **still managed to reach Mach .93:** Author interview with John Mitchell.

page 166, **Rooney . . . "a little stinker first class":** Griffin, oral history.

page 167, **unauthorized happy hour:** Author interview with Bill Geiger.

page 167, **"Shake the hand that held the tit of Ava Gardner":** Ibid.

page 167, **attack on the battleship USS** *Iowa:* Author interview with Jig Dog Ramage; Ramage, oral history.

page 169, **"Shep, I owe you one" [entire scene]:** Ibid.

8: "That little rascal"

page 170, **"He didn't like to be needled":** Author interview with John Mitchell.

page 175, **four planes flying in the same direction:** Barbree et al., *Moonshot*, p. 56.

page 175, falling "like a Steinway piano": Ibid.

page 176, aviators . . . killed as a result of . . . : Gillcrist, *Feet Wet*, p. 69.

page 176, "using up the sky in a terrible hurry": Barbree et al., *Moonshot*, p. 55.

page 176, Shepard left the Tiger on the tarmac [entire scene]: Ibid.

page 176, "an unforgiving, unreliable airplane": Test pilot John Moore, written for the National Museum of Naval Aviation's Web site (www.naval-air.org/AircraftCollection).

page 177, watched the plane . . . bloom into a fireball: Author interview with Larry Richardson.

page 177, "This isn't what we want": Author interview with John Mitchell.

page 178, At first the poor girl was in shock . . . : Author interviews with Denni Seibert, Betty Whisler, and Alice Wackermann.

page 179, Louise . . . knew she had done something right: Author interview with Betty Whisler.

page 179, "brush up on some academic subjects": *We Seven*, p. 84.

page 180, "I thought I had a very good chance": Ibid.

page 180, The change of routine was not, however, an easy one: Author interview with Dorel Alco Abbot.

page 183, "the embodiment of the sheer animal force of the Soviet Union": Halberstam, *The Fifties*, p. 702.

page 183, "Kaputnik . . . Flopnik . . . Stayputnik": Ibid, p. 627.

page 185, "That little rascal": Barbree et al., *Moonshot*, p. 43.

page 185, "gnawed at his insides": Ibid.

PART II /// INTO SPACE

9: "We made them heroes, the first day they were picked"

page 190, "Not . . . those who would be enamored": Thomas, *Men of Space*, p. 185.

page 190, a "miserable weekend": Shepard, Academy of Achievement interview.

page 190, "kicked the dog, spanked the children": Platt, *Florida Today*.

page 190, " 'Just go right ahead' ": Louise Shepard, "Just Go Right Ahead," *Life*, Vol. 47, No. 12 (September 21, 1959), p. 150.

page 191, "Why are you asking me?": *We Seven*, p. 85.

page 191, "stay alive under tough and dangerous assignments": Thomas, *Men of Space*, p. 185.

page 191, "space was the new turning point . . . something new and important": *We Seven*, p. 85.

page 191, **To Voas' surprise . . . :** Author interview with Robert Voas.

page 192, **he already knew she was "all for it":** Shepard, Academy of Achievement.

page 192, **Secretly Louise hoped . . . "he's only one out of a hundred":** Smaus and Spangler, *America's First Spaceman*, p. 123.

page 193, **"We were trying to drive them crazy":** Caidin, *Man into Space*, p. 132.

page 193, **"sick doctors working on well patients":** Walter M. Schirra, *Schirra's Space* (Annapolis, Maryland: Naval Institute Press/Bluejacket Books, 1995), p. 60.

page 193, **"sadists":** Gordon Cooper, *Leap of Faith: An Astronaut's Journey into the Unknown* (New York: HarperCollins, 2000), p. 13.

page 194, **he even had to squat over the camera:** James Schefter, *The Race: The Uncensored Story of How America Beat Russia to the Moon* (New York: Doubleday/Random House, 1999), p. 57.

page 194, **"Nothing is sacred anymore":** Loyd S. Swenson Jr. et al., *This New Ocean: A History of Project Mercury* (Houston: NASA History Series, 1989).

page 194, **reviewing . . . each candidate's adolescence:** Caidin, *Man into Space*. p. 134.

page 194, **"We looked for real men":** Swenson et al., *This New Ocean*.

page 194, **Those who seemed to exhibit "emotional stability":** Author interview with Robert Voas.

page 195, **"We wanted perfect . . . specimens":** Ibid.

page 195, **Glenn started scribbling . . . :** Glenn, *A Memoir*, p. 189.

page 195, **"difficult for me to analyze my own feelings":** Shepard, *We Seven*, p. 86.

page 195, **"Al thought it was a bunch of nonsense":** Author interview with John Glenn.

page 196, **"motivated":** Author interview with Robert Voas.

page 196, **"these would probably be famous people":** Ibid.

page 196, **couldn't decide which of two competing candidates should be the sixth:** Charles Berry, oral history interview, NASA archives, University of Houston, Clear Lake.

page 196, **Shepard let out a whoop:** *We Seven*, p. 86.

page 197, **"Louise and I just held each other":** Ibid, p. 87.

page 197, **Renza said she was "delighted":** Jim Watson, "Shepard Sky High on NASA," *The Washington Times* (August 6, 1986).

page 197, **"Someday . . . you may be an admiral":** Allen, *Yankee*.

page 198, **"splitting up the family":** Watson, *The Washington Times*.

page 198, **a splotch of "guck" on his bow tie:** Barbree et al., *Moonshot*, pg. 62.

page 198, **"cold and standoffish" . . . "trying to be nice":** Donald K. "Deke"

Slayton, Michael Cassut, *DEKE! U.S. Manned Space: From Mercury to the Shuttle* (New York: Forge Books/A Tom Doherty Associates Book, 1994), p. 73.

page 200, "the worst stress test I've ever been through": *We Seven*, p. 17.

page 201, "These people are nuts": Barbree et al., *Moonshot*, p. 63.

page 201, "I have no problems at home": James M. Grimwood, ed., *Project Mercury: A Chronology* (press conference transcript, NASA, 1963).

page 201, "disadvantage to have to speak loud": Ibid.

page 201, "This is the worst, here": Ibid.

page 202, "waiting for the religion question all along": Cooper, *Leap of Faith*, p. 18.

page 202, Glenn "ate this stuff up": Slayton and Cassut, *DEKE!* p. 74.

page 202, Grissom's response . . . made a few of the others cringe: Ibid.

page 202, "the seven-sided coin of competition": Swenson et al., *This New Ocean*.

page 203, his loquaciousness had cost him points: Glenn, *A Memoir*, p. 197.

page 203, *Who is this Boy Scout?*: Cooper, *Leap of Faith*, p. 18.

page 203, "There's nothing on your tie, Slayton": Barbree et al., *Moonshot*, p. 64.

page 203, "square-jawed trim halfbacks": John W. Finney, "7 Named as Pilots for Space Flights," *The New York Times* (April 10, 1959).

page 203, "virile": Norman Mailer, *Of a Fire on the Moon* (Boston: Little, Brown and Co., 1969); Faludi, *Stiffed*, p. 455.

page 203, "daring and courageous": *We Seven*, p. 4.

page 203, these were "military pilots": *The New York Times* (April 10, 1959).

page 203, "Not one of us knew what he was in for": Glenn, *A Memoir*, pp. 198–201.

page 204, "unsophisticated in many ways": Schirra, *Schirra's Space*, p. 63.

page 204, "Mrs. Shepard? . . . We're from *Life* magazine": Barbree et al., *Moonshot*, p. 67.

page 204, orders to track down each of the astronauts' families: Schefter, *The Race*, p. 60.

page 205, "Mom, what is all this?": Barbree et al., *Moonshot*, p. 68.

page 205, "our relationship": Author interview with John Glenn.

page 206, According to an internal NASA memo . . . : Robert Sherrod, unpublished manuscript, NASA archives.

page 206, "nibbled to death by ducks": Glenn, *A Memoir*, p. 200.

page 206, the whole table busted out laughing: Author interview with John Glenn; Glenn, *A Memoir*, p. 201.

page 207, "a tremendous guy . . . a very close personal friend": Alan Shepard, interview transcript (James Burke, BBC TV, 1979).

page 207, "the 'happily married' illusion": Cooper, *Leap of Faith*; Author interview with Gordon Cooper.

page 208, *Life* . . . "NASA's house organ": Faludi, *Stiffed*, p. 455.

page 208, "They were heroes not, like Charles Lindbergh . . .": Ibid, p. 454.

page 208, "I rather enjoyed the insulation": Shepard, interview with Burke.

page 208, "We made them heroes, the first day they were picked": Matt Schudel, "Rocket Town," *Sunshine* magazine (October 18, 1998).

page 209, "a way of putting words in our mouths": Author interview with John Glenn.

10: Eyeballs in, eyeballs out

page 211, "he wouldn't even have a window": Chris Kraft, *Flight: My Life in Mission Control* (New York: E. P. Dutton, 2001), p. 64.

page 212, "the most complex of the original astronauts": Cooper, *Leap of Faith*, p. 21.

page 212, Shepard was so "anxious to win": *We Seven*, p. 11.

page 212, "serious clown": Platt, *Florida Today*.

page 212, "a great test pilot": Ibid.

page 213, Shepard thought less of Cooper and Carpenter: Ibid.

page 213, "we are seven different individuals": *We Seven*, p. 9.

page 213, "comments . . . revealed a sharp, analytical mind": Glenn, *A Memoir*, p. 194.

page 213, "it gave me the right image as a Navy test pilot": David W. Temple, "The Car with the Right Stuff," *Car Collector* (August, 2001).

page 213, "it was cheap and got good gas mileage": Glenn, *A Memoir*, p. 202.

page 214, "Al was more of an enigma": Ibid., p. 204.

page 214, "objects of an insatiable curiosity": Ibid., p. 198.

page 215, "Nothing gave me more pleasure": Ibid.

page 215, "It would be good if you kept him alive": Kraft, *Flight*, pp. 65–68.

page 217, "glad they got that one out of the way": Glenn, *A Memoir*, p. 207.

page 217, "I sure hope they fix that": Guenter Wendt, with Russell Still, *The Unbroken Chain* (Ontario: Apogee Books, 2001), p. 14.

page 217, "Some of this was fairly exotic stuff": *We Seven*, p. 203.

page 218, "Communism was on the march": Author interview with John Glenn.

page 219, During a trip to Dallas: Author interview with Larry Richardson.

page 219, "Jockeying for position became a constant activity": Walter Cunningham, *The All-American Boys* (New York: Macmillan Publishing Co., 1977), p. 82.

page 219, "It was a competition guaranteed to bring out the worst": Ibid.

page 220, "There was always another what-if": Author interview with John Glenn.

page 222, A few of the doctors . . . were surprised: Author interview with Robert Voas.

page 222, the first of the seven to tame the MASTIF: Swenson et al., *This New Ocean*.

page 223, "a bulldog tearing away at you": Mickey Kapp (producer), *To the Moon*, 6-CD audio book.

page 224, the record . . . was an astonishing 20 Gs: Glenn, *A Memoir*, p. 209.

page 224, "County Fair Killer": Barbree et al., *Moonshot*, p. 73.

page 224, "oversize cream separator": Press conference (December 15, 1959).

page 224, "It's something I never want to do again": Ibid.

page 224, "sadistic": Ibid.

page 226, "unthinkable": Ibid.

page 226, "inundated with the newness of everything": Kraft, *Flight*, p. 116.

page 227, Shepard and the others assembled at the Cape: Ibid.

page 228, "That was a hell of a mess": Barbree et al., *Moonshot*, p. 72.

page 228, Cooper's accountant told him he could pick any state: Cooper, *Leap of Faith*.

page 229, "We were always looking for ways to let off steam": Slayton and Cassut, *DEKE!*, p. 88.

page 229, "went berserk": Schirra, *Schirra's Space*, p. 65.

page 229, a "whippersnapper" whom none of them "respected": Shorty Powers, oral history, NASA Historical Center.

page 229, "They were leery of me": Ibid.

page 230, "A real pain in the ass": Slayton and Cassut, *DEKE!* p. 80.

page 230, "they instinctively rebelled": Powers, oral history.

page 231, "we would play games . . .": Ibid.

page 231, "Daddy is going to Reno": Ibid.

page 231, "That's a lot of horseshit": Author interview with Ralph Morse.

page 232, "cover space": Ibid.

page 233, "How 'bout a cuppa coffee?" [entire scene]: Author interview with Morse.

page 234, "As debilitated as I have ever been": Glenn, *A Memoir*, p. 225.

11: "A harlot of a town"

page 236, "Sometimes we like to have a little fun, too": Fallaci, *If the Sun Dies*, p. 93.

page 238, "sweep the monkey shit off the seat": Slayton and Cassut, *DEKE!*, p. 82.

page 239, "They ran out of monkeys": Al Neuharth, "Soft Side of Shepard: 'Ran Out of Monkeys,'" *USA Today* (July 24, 1998).

page 239, He strutted through the belching factory: NASA film footage, National Archives and Records Administration.

page 240, "You literally couldn't shut him up": Paul Haney, oral history interview, NASA Historical Center.

page 240, "He talked his head off": Author interview with Paul Haney.

page 240, "after that, Al outdistanced John": Haney, oral history.

page 241, "I've had about all the monkey shit talk I can stand": Slayton and Cassut, *DEKE!*, p. 82.

page 241, Deke's speech and "Spam" comments [entire scene]: Slayton and Cassut, *DEKE!*, p. 82; Swenson et al, *This New Ocean*; Kraft, *Flight*, pp. 91–94.

page 242, "this girl . . . came over to me . . .": John Glenn, speaking at Deke Slayton's memorial service (1994).

page 242, Sharing a room with Slayton . . . : Slayton and Cassut, *DEKE!*, p. 88; John Glenn's speech at Deke Slayton's memorial service.

page 242, He woke up early the next morning . . . : Kraft, *Flight*, pp. 91–94; Schefter, *The Race*, p. 88.

page 243, just 823 registered voters: Henri Landwirth, *Gift of Life* (self-published, 1996), p. 96.

page 243, "A stringbean of a town": Lew Scarr, "The Space Age Had a Bright Beginning," *The San Diego Union-Tribune* (September 1, 1985), p. 1.

page 244, the fastest-growing county in the nation: Matt Schudel, "Rocket Town," *Sunshine* magazine (October 18, 1998).

page 244, $143 worth per person: Martin Caidin, *The Cape*, p. 41.

page 244, America's highest divorce rate: Schudel, *Sunshine* magazine.

page 244, "A harlot of a town": Caidin, *The Cape*, p. 62.

page 244, "As sometimes happens in journalism . . .": Author interview with Howard Benedict.

page 244, DRINK SCHLITZ: Scarr, *The San Diego Union-Tribune*.

page 245, "the greatest story in history, no question": Schudel, *Sunshine* magazine.

page 245, "We couldn't get near them": Author interview with Howard Benedict.

page 245, "Maybe it gave me a little bit of an edge": Author interview with Walter Cronkite.

page 246, "What kind of a trap is this?" [entire scene]: Ibid.

page 246, "really a male-dominated world": Author interview with Dee O'Hara.

page 247, "they were good and they knew it": Ibid.

page 247, "It was a game with him": Ibid.

page 247, "You only got so close to Alan": Ibid.

page 250, "You should be proud of that": Landwirth, *Gift of Life*, p. 138.

page 250, "awed" by the astronauts: Author interview with Henri Landwirth.

page 250, "austere, nondescript and totally uncomfortable": Barbree et al., *Moonshot*, p. 86.

page 250, "unpleasant walk": Ibid.

page 251, The chimp . . . defecated onto his hands: Wendt, Still, *The Unbroken Chain*, p. 18.

page 251, The police found no evidence: Landwirth, *Gift of Life*, p. 118.

page 251, "Wherever the boys were . . .": Author interview with Henri Landwirth.

page 252, "like a giant fraternity party": Ibid.

page 252, "Any one of us . . . would not have to look very far": Glenn, *A Memoir*, p. 220.

page 252, "like something happening in a movie": Landwirth, *Gift of Life*, p. 113.

page 252, "a real friend to all of us": Ibid., p. 106.

page 252, "the funniest thing I'd ever seen": Ibid., p. 122.

page 253, dumped it in the pool: Ibid.

page 253, wives understood each other "as no one else could": Smaus and Spangler, *America's First Spaceman*, p. 137.

page 254, "They were beautiful people": Caidin, *The Cape*, p. 90.

page 254, "rather than stand around": Louise Shepard, "Just Go Right Ahead," *Life*, Vol. 47, No. 12 (September 21, 1959), p. 150.

page 255, ended the night by drag-racing in the new Corvette: Bishop Schuyler, "Finding Out About the Right Stuff from America's First Man in Space," *Sports Illustrated* (October 8, 1984).

page 255, "his dick would have fallen off": Author interview with Bill Dana.

page 256, "Shepard wanted his buddies to believe he was seeing Trish": Author interview with Jay Barbree.

page 256, "that was one thing we didn't discuss": Author interview with Loraine Meyer.

12: "I think I got myself in trouble"

page 257, "Goes like a bat out of hell": Author interview with Ralph Morse.

page 258, convinced a reluctant GM management to donate a brand-new Corvette: Temple, *Car Collector*.

page 259, "a bunch of Okies": Slayton and Cassut, *DEKE!*, p. 75.

page 260, Shepard once spun out on a rain-slicked bridge: Author interview with James Lovell.

page 260, the car spun out and slid two hundred feet: Temple, *Car Collector.*

page 260, "concerned they'd kill themselves": Author interview with Bill Hines.

page 260, "There's something wrong with this car": Barbree et al., *Moonshot,* p. 84.

page 260, Often he would get out and kick the car after losing: Author interview with John Fasolino.

page 260, "Gotcha," Cooper said: Barbree et al., *Moonshot,* p. 84.

page 261, "John tries to behave as if . . .": *We Seven,* p. 13.

page 261, "make me laugh": Landwirth, *Gift of Life,* p. 120.

page 261, "I could have choked him": Author interview with Henri Landwirth.

page 261, confessed that they were just messing with him: Landwirth, *Gift of Life,* p. 105.

page 261, "charm a whole room by himself": Author interview with Henri Landwirth.

page 262, "I want to be first because I want to be first": Caidin, *Man into Space,* p. 37.

page 264, "There is no doubt in my mind they will be first": Allan C. Fisher Jr., "Exploring Tomorrow with the Space Agency,": *National Geographic* (prepublication version of article, March 14, 1960).

page 264, "our objective in this program is not to beat the Russians": Press conference, San Diego (September 25, 1959).

pages 264–265, "forced into a competitive race": Fisher, *National Geographic.*

page 265, NASA officials . . . deleted that quote: Ibid.

page 267, "When we came out of the room . . .": Author interview with Gordon Cooper.

page 267, "some of us were more team players than others": Ibid.

page 267, "I think I got myself in trouble": Author interview with Al Blackburn.

page 267, "compromising" photographs: Shorty Powers, oral history, NASA.

page 267, Shorty . . . called Glenn . . . "it's happened": Author interview with John Glenn.

page 268, "godless communists . . . get back in the space race": Author interview with John Glenn; Glenn, *A Memoir,* p. 221.

page 268, "bland and upbeat": Glenn, *A Memoir,* p. 230.

page 268, "keep his pants zipped": Ibid.

page 268, Shepard became furious at . . . Glenn's "moralizing": Barbree et al., *Moonshot,* p. 78.

page 268, "Doesn't everyone have the right to do what they want to do?": *Moonshot: The Inside Story of the Apollo Project* (Turner Home Video, 1995).

page 269, "The camaraderie was incredible": Cheney, OpenUniverse.com.

page 269, "My views were in the minority . . . I had made my point": Glenn, *A Memoir*, p. 221; author interview with John Glenn.

page 269, "a popularity contest": Glenn, *A Memoir*, p. 221.

13: "We had 'em by the short hairs, and we gave it away"

page 270, "If we wait any longer . . .": Barbree et al., *Moonshot*, pp. 77–81.

page 270, "the most difficult decision": Ibid.

page 270, "Alan Shepard will make the first suborbital flight": Ibid.

page 271, it was "not a moment to crow": *We Seven*, p. 229.

page 271, "Thank you very much, and good luck": Alan B. Shepard, oral history interview with Roy Neal (Johnson Space Center Oral History Project, February 20, 1998).

page 271, "Lady, you can't tell anyone . . .": Barbree et al., *Moonshot*, p. 81.

page 271, "Who let a Russian in here?": Ibid.

pages 271–272, "really deflated . . . a very traumatic feeling . . . the second team": *Moonshot* (Turner Home Video, 1995).

page 272, "For Al, it was the competition": Cheney, OpenUniverse.com.

page 272, "John figured he had made all the right moves": Slayton and Cassut, *DEKE!*, p. 93.

page 272, when Gilruth picked Shepard . . . : Slayton and Cassut, *DEKE!*, p. 93; Barbree et al., *Moonshot*, p. 78.

page 272, "Of course! Politics!" Slayton thought: Barbree et al., *Moonshot*, p. 79.

page 273, "Glenn loved an audience . . .": Williams, *Go*.

page 273, "cozying up to top management": Kraft, *Flight*, pp. 80–87.

page 273, "We wanted to put our best foot forward": Williams, *Go*.

page 274, "it's not that way with Shepard": Loudon S. Wainwright, "Shepard: A Cool Customer and a Hot Pilot with an Eye for the Big Picture," *Life* (March 3, 1961), p. 30.

page 274, Shepard . . . "secrets": Michael Collins, *Carrying the Fire: An Astronaut's Journey* (New York: Cooper Square Press, 1974), p. 24.

page 274, "He was an egotist": Author interview with Chris Kraft.

page 276, "It's how we learn": Kraft, *Flight*, p. 136; author interview with Chris Kraft.

page 277, "I might have been penalized . . .": Glenn, *A Memoir*, p. 233.

page 277, "I didn't think being an astronaut was a popularity contest": Ibid.

page 277, "too lighthearted for the job": Barbree et al., *Moonshot*, p. 81.

page 277, "trying to knife each other": Caidin, *Man into Space*, p. 39.

page 277, "Those were rough days for me": *We Seven*, p. 304.

page 277, **A lingering remorse . . .**: Fred Bruning, "Glenn's Return to Space: A 2nd Launch into History," *Newsweek* (October 11, 1998).

page 278, **"If I may be hypothetical . . ."**: Press conference, San Diego (September 25, 1959).

page 279, **excessive "German thoroughness"**: Swenson et al., *This New Ocean*.

page 279, **"We're ready to go. Let's go"**: Barbree et al., *Moonshot*, p. 91.

page 279, **"the prestige of the United States"**: Swenson et al., *This New Ocean*.

page 280, **"chimp barbecue"**: Glenn, *A Memoir*, p. 235.

page 282, **"I've come from outer space"**: Schefter, *The Race*, p. 135.

page 283, **"We had them by the short hairs"**: Barbree et al., *Moonshot*, p. 91.

page 283, **"the grimmest I can remember in the White House"**: Sherrod, unpublished manuscript, NASA archives.

page 284, **"I don't want to go . . . Please don't send me"**: Williams, *Go*.

page 285, **"the logical man to go first"**: Smaus and Spangler, *America's First Spaceman*, p. 147.

page 285, **"I needed it more than he did"**: *We Seven*, p. 238.

page 286, **"I don't think two people could have worked more closely"**: Author interview with John Glenn.

page 286, **"Al's alter ego, his virtual twin"**: Glenn, *A Memoir*, p. 237.

14: "Light this candle!"

page 287, **Douglas found a loose nail on the fourth toe**: *We Seven*, p. 234.

page 288, **"Hey, Gus . . ."**: Ibid.

page 291, **"I tried to pace myself . . ."**: Ibid.

page 291, **"Watch your language"**: *Moonshot*, Turner Home Video.

page 291, *You're building up too fast. Slow down*: *We Seven*, p. 247.

page 291, **"the consequences of an unsuccessful flight"**: Shepard, *Life* (May 19, 1961), p. 26.

page 292, **"without any display of emotion"**: TK, "Mrs. Shepard Sees Shot on TV," *The New York Times* (AP) (May 6, 1961).

page 292, *There are no reporters inside*: Barbree et al., *Moonshot*, p. 110.

page 292, **"I want her to hear from us"**: Ibid.

page 292, **"any display of emotion"**: Shepard, *Life* (May 19, 1961), p. 26.

page 293, **"the power of good and of God"**: Ibid.

page 293, **"Man, I got to pee"**: Barbree et al., *Moonshot*, p. 107; Shepard, oral history interview with Roy Neal (Johnson Space Center Oral History Project).

page 293, **"Zee astronaut shall stay in zee nose cone"**: Shepard, oral history interview with Roy Neal.

page 294, **"If you don't use your experience, your past is wasted"**: Wainwright, "Shepard: A Cool Customer and a Hot Pilot with an Eye for the Big Picture," *Life* (March 3, 1961), p. 30.

page 295, "He is afraid of the reaction": "Kennedy Apprehension About Shepard's Flight Comes to Light," Associated Press (July 23, 1998).

page 295, "Please hold for the president": Swenson et al., *This New Ocean;* Kapp, *To the Moon,* audio book.

page 295, "awed by the romance of the high frontier": Hugh Sidey, "Why We Went to the Moon," *Time* (July 25, 1994).

page 295, "Let's find somebody—anybody": Ibid.

page 296, *Don't screw up, Shepard:* Barbree et al., *Moonshot,* p. 111.

page 297, "extremely smooth—a subtle, gentle, gradual rise": *We Seven,* p. 250.

page 297, "You're on your way, José": Ibid.

page 298, "Go, Alan. Go, sweetheart": Barbree et al., *Moonshot,* p. 115.

page 299, "Okay, buster": Ibid.

page 301, "obliterated most of the colors": Robert Godwin, ed., *Freedom 7: The NASA Mission Reports* (Ontario: Apogee Books, 2001); author interview with Wally Schirra.

page 301, didn't feel "on top of things": Godwin, *Freedom 7.*

page 301, as if he were a "sightless organist": Alan Shepard, untitled radio report for Voice of America (May 23, 1961).

page 301, "not one most people would want to try": *We Seven,* p. 259.

page 302, "the most beautiful sight of the mission": Barbree et al., *Moonshot,* p. 124.

page 303, "a beautiful day": Caidin, *Man into Space.* p. 34.

page 303, [Entire *Freedom 7* scene]: *We Seven;* Swenson et al., *This New Ocean; Results of the First U.S. Manned Suborbital Space Flight,* NASA Special Publications; Barbree et al., *Moonshot;* Caidin, *Man Into Space.*

page 303, felt "like coming home": Shepard, Academy of Achievement.

page 304, "the most emotional carrier landing": Barbree et al., *Moonshot,* p. 125.

page 304, "Myself, I damn near cried": Williams, *Go.*

page 304, "I simply cannot put into words the excitement": Wendt, Still, *The Unbroken Chain,* p. 35.

page 305, "I went with him all the way": Louise Shepard, "The Spaceman's Wife: 'Alan Was in His Right Place,' " *Life,* Vol. 50, No. 19 (May 12, 1961).

page 305, "I felt no apprehension at any time": Godwin, *Freedom 7.*

page 305, "excitement and exhilaration": *We Seven,* p. 263.

page 306, "It's a success": Sidey, *Time.*

page 306, "If it had been a failure": Author interview with Tazewell Shepard.

page 307, "a certain thrill that we were in space": Author interview with Walter Cronkite.

page 308, "Some countries build cathedrals": Peter Carlson, "Has NASA Lost Its Way?," *Washington Post Magazine* (May 30, 1993), p. 10.

page 308, "The presumption of the American republic is": Ibid.

page 308, "Shepard bailed out the ego of the American people": Ibid.

page 308, "That took us all by surprise": Author interview with John Glenn.

page 309, divert to Nassau for some liberty: Ted Wilbur, "Once a Fighter Pilot," *Naval Aviation News* (1970).

page 309, lost three pounds since breakfast: *Results of the First U.S. Manned Suborbital Space Flight*, NASA Special Publications.

page 309, "You pulled it off real good": Caidin, *Man into Space*, p. 36.

page 309, "I had to say something for the people": Author interview with Wally Schirra.

page 309, "just a baby step": "Mrs. Shepard Sees Shot on TV," *The New York Times* (AP) (May 6, 1961).

page 310, "unusual number of needles": Shepard, *We Seven*, p. 265.

page 310, "I hope that fewer bodily fluid samples are required": "Transcript of Shepard's News Conference," *The New York Times* (May 9, 1961).

page 310, "Shepard's brain get up, leave the room": Schefter, *The Race*, p. 143.

page 310, "This is one of the burdens of a free society": Shepard, untitled radio report for Voice of America (May 23, 1961).

page 310, "our friend Taz Shepard" and . . . "Jack Kennedy": Louise Shepard, "The Spaceman's Wife: 'Alan Was in His Right Place,' " *Life*, Vol. 50, No. 19 (May 12, 1961).

15: "I believe we should go to the moon"

page 312, As they descended toward the White House . . . : Barbree et al., *Moonshot*, p. 127.

page 313, "man can perform effectively in space": Alan Shepard, oral history interview with Walter Sohier (for the John F. Kennedy memorial Library, 1964).

page 313, "We're just thinking about it": Barbree et al., *Moonshot*, p. 129.

page 313, *My God!*: Ibid.

page 313, "Come with me": Shepard, interview with Burke.

page 313, a standing ovation: Shepard, oral history interview with Walter Sohier.

page 314, "Shepard, if you're going to be famous": Shepard, interview with Burke.

page 314, "throng-packed, pulsing room of congressional leaders": Shepard, oral history interview with Walter Sohier.

page 315, "neither a statesman nor a politician": Shepard, untitled radio report for Voice of America (May 23, 1961).

page 315, "Becoming a public figure overnight": Shepard, Academy of Achievement.

page 316, "the new ocean" Sidey, *Time*.

page 317, "great propaganda value": Robert Dalek, *An Unfinished Life: John F. Kennedy, 1917–1963* (Boston: Little Brown & Company, 2003), pp. 392–395.

page 317, "in the eyes of the world . . .": Ibid.

page 317, "a decision he made coldbloodedly": William E. Burrows, *This New Ocean: The Story of the First Space Age* (New York: Random House, 1998), p. 324.

page 317, "by God, we beat them": Dalek, *An Unfinished Life*, p. 652.

page 317, Kennedy's "affinity for heroic causes": Ibid., pp. 392–395.

page 317, Gallup poll: Burrows, *This New Ocean*, p. 336.

page 318, "Is this guy nuts?": Author interview with Allen Neuharth.

page 319, "Don't be scared": Glenn, *A Memoir*, p. 258.

page 320, "What did they say, John?": *Moonshot*, Turner Home Video; *We Seven*, p. 401.

page 320, "numb and in a state of disbelief": Williams, *Go*.

page 321, He thought it was faulty circuit: Ibid.

page 321, "What's going to happen when we cut the retro-pack loose?": Mickey Kapp (producer), *To the Moon*, 6-CD audio book.

page 321, "hold the goddamn thing": Ibid.

page 322, "We want to be damn sure on this one": Ibid.

page 323, "Either you give me a decision or . . . : Williams, *Go*.

page 323, ". . . leave the retro package on": Glenn, *A Memoir*, p. 271.

page 323, "cat-and-mouse game": Ibid., p. 272.

page 323, "We are not sure whether or not . . .": Williams, *Go*.

page 324, "Every nerve fiber was attuned to the heat": Glenn, *A Memoir*, p. 273.

page 325, "Keep talking, Al": *We Seven*, p. 427.

page 325, {Entire *Friendship* 7 scene]: Glenn, *A Memoir*, pp. 256–274; author interview with John Glenn; Williams, *Go*; *Results of the First United States Manned Orbital Space Flight* (NASA Special Publications, 1962); author interview with Henri Landwirth; *Moonshot*, Turner Home Video.

page 326, "It's always been orders first": Kapp, *To the Moon*, audio book.

page 326, Carpenter couldn't help himself: *Moonshot*, Turner Home Video.

page 327, "crucial observations": Scott Carpenter, *For Spacious Skies: The Un-*

common Journey of a Mercury Astronaut (New York: Harcourt Inc., 2002), p. 284.

page 328, "I'll get back to reentry attitude": Ibid.

page 329, Gordo Cooper . . . pushed back in his chair: Williams, *Go.*

page 329, "as though I were watching myself . . .": Carpenter, *For Spacious Skies*, p. 285.

page 329, "Scott knew he had screwed up": Cooper, *Leap of Faith,* p. 35.

pages 326–329, [*Aurora* 7 scene]: Carpenter, *For Spacious Skies,* pp. 284–293.

page 330, "He was calm under stressful conditions": Author interview with Chris Kraft.

page 330, "that was typical of Al": Williams, *Go.*

16: "I'm sick . . . should I just hang it up?"

page 332, "you were reported driving an unregistered car": Brian O'Leary, *The Making of an Ex-Astronaut* (Boston: Houghton Mifflin Co., 1970), p. 54.

page 332, "99 percent sure": Ibid, p. 73.

page 332, "His technique was flawless": Cunningham, *The All-American Boys,* p. 80.

page 333, "You've got to be *masculine*": Author interview with James Lovell.

page 335, "so competitive as to be ruthless": Cooper, *Leap of Faith,* p. 21.

page 337, "Well, you know I could do a better job": Williams, *Go.*

page 337, "Okay, if that's the answer, I'll do it": Ibid.

page 337, "This is astronaut Alan Shepard": Wendt, Still, *The Unbroken Chain,* p. 16.

page 338, "What if the new fitting leaked?": Cooper, *Leap of Faith,* p. 37.

page 338, Williams . . . grabbed his throat: Ibid.

page 339, "ass on a plate": Kraft, *Flight,* pp. 180–183.

page 339, "Is your suit ready?": *Moonshot,* Turner Home Video.

page 339, "a grin that is typical of him": Shorty Powers, oral history (NASA Historical Center).

page 340, "Father, we thank you": Cooper, *Leap of Faith,* p. 68.

page 343, Blobs of urine: Kraft, *Flight,* pp. 180–183; Cooper, *Leap of Faith.*

page 343, "Why don't you all drop by for cocktails . . .": Williams, *Go.*

page 344, "Just let me sit up there and see how long it will last": Shepard, oral history interview, Roy Neal (Johnson Space Center Oral History Project).

page 344, "tell him my side of the story, too": Ibid.

page 344, "Maybe two, maybe three days": Alan Shepard, oral history interview, Walter Sohier.

page 344, "everything that we do ought to really be tied": Dalek, *An Unfinished Life,* pp. 392–395.

page 345, "I think we'll have to go along with Mr. Webb": Shepard, oral history interview, Walter Sohier.

page 345, Shepard was chosen to command the first Gemini flight: Williams, *Go*.

page 347, "oh-so-cool number-one leader shtick": Carpenter, *For Spacious Skies*, p. 229.

page 348, The Bushes had a trampoline: Author interview with Peter Vanderhoef.

page 350, *Jesus, what the hell did I drink last night?*: Barbree et al., *Moonshot*, p. 168.

page 350, *Is that where the problem began?*: Author interview with Robert Voas.

page 351, Finally his secret revealed itself: Author interview with Dr. William House.

page 351, "I'm having a problem . . .": Berry, oral history interview (NASA); Barbree et al., *Moonshot*, p. 168.

page 352, "You're medically grounded, *compadre*": Berry, oral history interview (NASA).

page 352, Shepard took the news silently: Ibid.

page 352, "total disbelief . . .": *Moonshot*, Turner Home Video.

page 352, "a result of being hyper": Barbree et al., *Moonshot*, p. 168; Platt, *Florida Today*.

page 352, "Maybe it's the price I pay": Allen, *Yankee*.

page 353, began complaining of a sore throat: Author e-mail interview with Paul Haney.

page 353, "Too bad it didn't cause another part of my anatomy to bulge": Ibid.

page 354, "an ear infection": Ibid.

page 354, "stonewalled": Glenn, *A Memoir*, p. 298.

page 354, President Kennedy . . . secretly told NASA officials: Author interview with John Glenn; Glenn, *A Memoir*, p. 298.

page 355, "virtually immobile": Glenn, *A Memoir*, p. 304.

page 355, "brought down by a slippery bath mat": Ibid., p. 305.

page 356, "What do I do now?": Shepard, oral history interview, Roy Neal.

page 356, "I've got a job for you": Barbree et al., *Moonshot*, p. 169.

17: *How to succeed in business without really flying—much*

page 357, Norman Mailer . . . Hugh Hefner: Oriana Fallaci, *The Egotists* (Chicago: Henry Regnery Company, 1963), pp. 1–18, 113–124.

page 358, "You need a cow": Fallaci, *If the Sun Dies*, p. 94.

page 359, "changing diapers and feeding astronauts": Barbree et al., *Moonshot*, pp. 169– 170.

page 359, "cold eyes seemed to look right through me": Eugene Cernan, with Don Davis, *Last Man on the Moon* (New York: St. Martin's Press, 1999), p. 58.

page 359, "a bastard" and "the enforcer": Robert Sherrod, unpublished manuscript (NASA archives).

page 359, "He didn't make a lot of friends": Author interview with Walter Cronkite.

page 359, "the mental anguish": "Alan Shepard: Oldest, Richest of Astronauts," *Washington Post* (January 3, 1971).

page 360, "Al could be friendly": Barbree et al., *Moonshot*, p. 178.

page 360, "just mad at the world": *Moonshot*, Turner Home Video.

page 360, He had little tolerance: Ibid.

page 361, turned down an invitation: "Subject: Alan Shepard," Federal Bureau of Investigation (1971).

page 362, [Cape Colony sale]: Landwirth, *Gift of Life*, p. 147.

page 362, "the Loan Eagle": Author interview with James Lovell.

page 362, "swindling" him: "Subject: Alan Shepard," FBI.

page 362, [Oil-drilling venture and cattle ranch]: Ibid.

page 363, Shepard once reprimanded: O'Leary, *The Making of an Ex-Astronaut*, p. 165.

page 363, "I didn't deliberately try to intimidate him": Shepard, unpublished interview with author Robert Sherrod.

page 364, "the shrewdest of the bunch": Collins, *Carrying the Fire*, p. 59.

page 364, Cunningham . . . "dollars": Cunningham, *The All-American Boys*, pp. 170–171.

page 364, "losing our lunch money": Ibid., p. 173.

page 367, A typical astronaut day . . . : Ibid.

page 367, "week in the barrel": Collins, *Carrying the Fire*, p. 93.

page 368, "He never talked about it": Author interview with Chuck Friedlander.

page 368, "bulging eyes" and "stare right through you": Author interview with James Lovell.

page 369, "A very cold person": Author interview with Lola Morrow.

page 371, [Shorty's drinking and reassignment]: Author interviews with Jay Barbree and Paul Haney; Shorty Powers, oral history (NASA).

page 372, "a monster": Author interview with Wally Schirra.

page 373, [Gallup polls and Picasso]: Burrows, *This New Ocean*, p. 380.

page 374, "This is the worst spacecraft I've ever seen": Shepard, oral history interview, Roy Neal.

page 374, "misgivings": Barbree et al., *Moonshot*, p. 193.

page 374, lemon . . . "a piece of crap": Ibid; Betty Grissom and Henry Still, *Starfall* (New York: Ty Crowell Co., 1974).

page 374, [North American's problems]: Richard S. Lewis, *Appointment on the Moon* (New York: The Viking Press, 1968); Burrows, *This New Ocean*.

page 375, "sloppy and unsafe": Barbree et al., *Moonshot*, p. 199.

page 377, "Did we lose anybody?": Author interview with Chuck Friedlander.

page 377, "I'll never forget the pain in Al Shepard's eyes": Author interview with Lola Morrow.

page 377, "I hate those empty-slot flyovers": Author interview with Paul Haney.

page 378, "the conquest of space is worth the risk of life": *From the Earth to the Moon* (HBO Studios, 1998).

page 378, A lengthy follow-up report determined . . . : Lewis, *Appointment on the Moon*, p. 388.

page 378, "downright criminal": Burrows, *This New Ocean*, pp. 410–413.

page 378, "But Al was worse": *Moonshot*, Turner Home Video.

page 379, congressional report . . . "overconfidence" and "complacency": Lewis, *Appointment on the Moon*, p. 396.

page 379, "Deke and I insidiously became part of the problem": Shepard, oral history interview, Roy Neal.

page 379, Shepard got even tougher: Ibid.

page 379, "He was mad at the world": Author interview with Gene Cernan.

page 379, "Don't you think you're being a little tough . . .?": *Moonshot*, Turner Home Video.

18: "Captain Shepard? I'm Charles Lindbergh"

pages 384–385, [Josiah Bartlett's story]: Donald Lines Jacobus, ed., *The Shepard Families of New England*, Vol. III (New Haven: The New Haven Colony Historical Society, 1973), p. 52.

page 386, "I convinced myself it would eventually work itself out": Ted Wilbur, "Once a Fighter Pilot," *Naval Aviation News* (1970).

page 388, "aloof" [entire scene]: Author interview with Walter Cronkite.

page 388, "Get me a flight to the moon": Barbree et al., *Moonshot*, p. 253.

page 389, "a stroke of genius": Ibid.

page 390, "the most beautiful, heart-catching sight": Ibid., p. 233.

pages 390–391, made Cooper "furious": Cooper, *Leap of Faith*, p. 178.

page 391, "Deke and I are making crew assignments now": Ibid., p. 180.

page 391, [McDivitt's complaints]: Slayton and Cassut, *DEKE!*, p. 236.

page 392, "What could possibly be the difference": James Lovell and Jeffrey Kluger, *Apollo 13* (New York: Pocket Books, 1995), p. 61.

page 392, "He paid his dues": Author interview with Chris Kraft.

page 392, "How the hell did he pull that one off?": *Moonshot*, Turner Home Video.

page 392, "Al was probably bitter at times . . .": Author interview with Wally Schirra.

page 393, [Slayton on Cooper]: Slayton and Cassut, *DEKE!*, p. 236.

page 393, "tiddlywinks players": Cooper, *Leap of Faith*, p. 178.

page 393, "time for him to move on": Slayton and Cassut, *DEKE!*, p. 236.

page 393, "had little recourse: Cooper, *Leap of Faith*, p. 181.

page 393, "I'm considerably younger than Shepard": "Cooper, Ex-Astronaut, Scores Shepard's Selection as Skipper," *The New York Times* (UPI) (February 5, 1971).

page 393, "He had to have what he wanted to have": Author interview with Gordon Cooper.

page 393, "it took me years to forgive Al . . . I lost the moon": Cooper, *Leap of Faith*, p. 182.

page 394, "aloft in my own thoughts": Pat Hammond, "Shepard Credits Teacher, (Big) Bertha Wiggins," *The New Hampshire Union Leader* (June 24, 1994), p. 1.

page 394, "My chest was beaten and the ground shook": Collins, *Carrying the Fire*, p. x.

page 395, Among the ideas on the table . . . : Kraft, *Flight*, p. 192.

page 396, "a madman with a mission": Kraft, *Flight*, p. 192.

page 396, "If Jack Kennedy had been older and wiser . . .": Ibid.

page 397, [Aldrin peeing in space suit]: Col. Edwin E. "Buzz" Aldrin, with Wayne Warga, *Return to Earth* (New York: Random House, 1973), p. 236.

page 398, diesel locomotives and dogs barking: Ibid., p. 241.

page 399, "big fucking deal" look: Gene Cernan letter to Alan and Louise Shepard.

page 399, "he let me realize what a tremendous man": Author interview with Gene Cernan.

page 399, "storing a few nuts away for the winter": Loudon Wainwright. "The Old Pro Gets His Shot at the Moon," *Life* (July 31, 1970), p. 53.

page 399, "It's something I believe in": John Noble Wilford, "Apollo 14 Crew Is Fit and Ready," *The New York Times* (January 9, 1971), p. 4.

page 400, [Training in Bavaria, Germany]: Author interview with Gene Cernan.

pages 401–402, [Mexican prostitutes]: Ibid.

pages 403–404, [Apollo 13 scenes]: Lovell, *Apollo 13*; Barbree et al., *Moonshot*.

page 404, "quit worrying and get some sleep": Barbree et al., *Moonshot*, p. 270.

page 404, "forlorn and pitiful": Ibid., p. 271.

page 404, "She was a good ship": Ibid., p. 272.

page 404, "Anytime you want Apollo 13 back, Al . . .": Author interview with James Lovell.

page 404, [Louise quiet, shy, and sometimes sickly]: Author interview with Dorel Alco Abbot.

page 405, "What do you expect from a sailor?": Author interviews with Lola Morrow and Bill Dana; Schefter, *The Race*.

page 405, "'How did an asshole like that get a queen like her?'" Author interview with Gene Cernan.

page 407, Shepard got dressed . . . and sneaked out: Author interview with Ed Mitchell.

page 407, "Okay, Al, you win. It's your flight": Cernan, with Davis, *Last Man on the Moon*, p 261.

page 408, "the first and only time I'd seen Alan humble": Author interview with Gene Cernan.

19: "What's wrong with this ship?"

page 410, "I'm going to be leaving town": "It's the Astronaut's Wife Who Suffers Special Agony," Associated Press (February 7, 1971).

page 410, [Louise and Cary Grant]: Author interview with Peter Vanderhoef.

page 410, "I'm constantly aware of the moon these days": "It's the Astronaut's Wife Who Suffers Special Agony," Associated Press (February 7, 1971).

page 410, "Let's get on with it": Barbree et al., *Moonshot*, p. 280.

page 411, "very smooth and strangely quiet": Ibid.

page 412, Shepard told Roosa to "juice it": Ibid., p. 289.

page 412, "It's not working": Robert Godwin, ed., *Apollo 14: The NASA Mission Reports* (Ontario: Apogee Books, 2001).

page 413, "a messy operation": Shepard, interview with Burke; Godwin, *Apollo 14*.

page 413, At the Cape Louise felt closer to Alan: "It's the Astronaut's Wife Who Suffers Special Agony," Associated Press (February 7, 1971).

page 414, "really gave them hell": Author interview with Dorel Alco Abbot.

pages 414–415, "too busy . . . not important": Godwin, *Apollo 14*.

page 415, "uptight" and "snappish": William Hines, "Touchdown Time on Moon," *Chicago Sun-Times* (February 6, 1971).

page 415, "found it difficult to relax": Godwin, *Apollo 14*.

page 415, "Hot damn": Barbree et al., *Moonshot*, p. 294.

page 416, "This is really a wild place": Ibid.

page 416, "the most stark and desolate . . .": Ibid.

page 416, "What's wrong with this ship?": Ibid., p. 297.

page 417, "Done" Ibid., p. 298.

page 419, "We're aware of the ground rules": Barbree et al., *Moonshot*, p. 301.

page 419, "If the radar doesn't kick in . . .": Ibid.

pages 418–420, [Entire radar malfunction moonlanding scene]: Barbree et al., *Moonshot*; Godwin, *Apollo 14.*

page 420, Conrad won $500 from Oriana Fallaci: Andrew Chaikin, *A Man on the Moon* (New York: Penguin Books, 1994), p. 261.

page 421, "very finite . . . so incredibly fragile": Barbree et al., *Moonshot*, p. 310.

page 421, "Now I'm on the moon": Shepard, oral history interview, Roy Neal.

page 422, "We weren't trained to smell the roses": Buzz Aldrin, "What It Feels Like to Walk on the Moon," *Esquire* (June, 2001), p. 90.

page 423, "the only two living creatures on this dead world": Edgar Mitchell and Dwight Williams, *The Way of the Explorer: An Apollo Astronaut's Journey Through the Material and Mystical Worlds* (Audio Partners Publishing Group, 1996, audiotape).

page 423, "Why the hell are we whispering?": Author interview with Ed Mitchell; Shepard, interview with Burke.

page 426, [Apollo 14 scenes]: Chaikin, *A Man on the Moon*; Barbree et al., *Moonshot*; *Moonshot*, Turner Home Video; Kapp, *To the Moon*, audio book; author interview with Ed Mitchell; Godwin, *Apollo 14*; Shepard interviews and oral histories.

page 427, "Good, good, they made it": "Wife Sees Shepard in Promised Land," Associated Press (February 6, 1971).

page 428, "granddaddy of space": Press conference, Houston (January 9, 1971).

page 428, "cut the mustard or you don't": "Alan Shepard: Oldest, Richest of Astronauts," *The Washington Post* (January 3, 1971).

page 429, "the most personally satisfying thing I've ever done": Platt, *Florida Today.*

page 429, "Given a disciplined self": R. M. Henry, "Reaching for the Stars," *All Hands* (April, 1982).

page 429, "old man Moses . . . made his promised land": "Wife Sees Shepard in Promised Land," Associated Press (February 6, 1971).

page 430, "something incomprehensibly big": Mitchell and Williams, *The Way of the Explorer.*

page 430, "I did it, boss": Ibid.

page 431, "divine presence": *The Other Side of the Moon* (Discovery Communications Inc., unreleased review copy).

page 431, "He did his thing, I did my thing": Author interview with Ed Mitchell.

page 431, "first two swings were embarrassing failures": "Dinner Honoring the Apollo 14 Astronauts," *Weekly Compilation of Presidential Documents* (March 8, 1971).

page 432, "As a planet, we are so small": Author interview with Robert B. Williams; Allen, *Yankee.*

page 432, "It's too bad . . .": Allen, *Yankee.*

page 432 drunken night with Lauren Bacall: Author interview with Dorel Abbot.

page 433, "My father's example was he led a good life": Allen, *Yankee.*

page 433, "I was wrong": Allen, *Yankee; Moonshot,* Turner Home Video.

PART III /// AFTER SPACE

20: "When you've been to the moon, where else are you going to go?"

page 437, named in a paternity suit by a Playboy bunny: Tara Weingarten, "Crashing to Earth," *Newsweek,* August 3, 1998, p. 46.

page 437, "somewhat in turbulence ever since": *The Other Side of the Moon* (Discovery Communications Inc., unreleased review copy).

page 438, [Aldrin's nervous breakdown]: Aldrin and Warga, *Return to Earth.*

page 438, "the climax of my life": Weingarten, *Newsweek.*

page 438, "The search goes on . . .": Ibid.

page 439, "Some unfortunate ones didn't have a dream": *The Other Side of the Moon* (Discovery Communications Inc., unreleased review copy).

page 439, He once told a friend: Author interview with Allen Neuharth.

page 440, "to put it in a box, and on a shelf": Shepard, Academy of Achievement.

page 440, "gone to great lengths to maintain my privacy": "People in the News," Associated Press (May 5, 1979).

page 440, "where else are you going to go?": Watson, *The Washington Times.*

page 441, "about broke even on that": Wainwright, *Life* (1971).

page 441, "some good business deals and some bad ones": Wainwright, *Life* (1971); Platt, *Florida Today;* "Alan Shepard: Oldest, Richest of Astronauts," *Washington Post* (January 3, 1971).

page 441, "for my own personal gain": Olive M. Abbott, et al., *From Turnpike to Interstate: The 150 Years of Derry, New Hampshire* (Canaan, New Hampshire: Phoenix Publishing, 1977), p. 90.

page 441, businessmen . . . "like ducks to water": Author interview with Gordon Cooper.

page 442, Shepard . . . experienced "his share of close calls": Ibid.

page 442, "not to use my position as an astronaut": Wainwright, *Life* (1970).

page 442, "I tried to separate the two": Ibid.

page 442, [Molly Ivins on Texas]: Molly Ivins, *Molly Ivins Can't Say That, Can She?* (New York: Random House, 1991).

page 443, "He was quite a salesman": Author interview with Howard Benedict.

page 443, "The business world has smiled upon us": Naval Academy "Class of '45" newsletter (1985).

page 443, "never really a fan" of the stock market: Shepard, unpublished interview with author Robert Sherrod.

page 444, [Shepard's first Kmart]: Ibid.

page 444, "a relatively good investment": Robert Sherrod, unpublished manuscript, NASA archives.

page 445, "The pay is a lot better than going to the moon": Henry, *All Hands* (1982).

page 446, Kraft agreed to put $10,000 down: Author interview with Chris Kraft.

page 446, "Al, I don't trust this guy": Ibid.

page 446, "I haven't seen a dollar of profit yet": Ibid.

page 446, "until I'm pushing up daisies": Ibid.

page 446, "got taken . . . We have nothing": Cathy Gordon, "Potholes and Promises," *Houston Chronicle* (June 21, 1987).

page 447, "He was lucky he didn't go to jail": Author interview with Chris Kraft.

page 448, besides making money: Naval Academy "Class of '45" newsletter (1985).

page 448, "a hell of a lot more famous": Doug Ferguson, "Moon Mulligan," *Houston Chronicle* (July 23, 1998).

page 449, "metabolized a lot of adrenaline in my life": Pat Sullivan, "An Astronaut's Pitch for Pebble Beach," *San Francisco Chronicle* (January 15, 1991).

page 449, "his ability didn't always match his competitiveness": Author interview with Bob Murphy.

page 449, "chicken feed": *NBC Sports Spectacular* (May 17, 1971).

page 450, "the world's best kept secret": "Shepard Admits Three Shots to Sink Moon Hole-in-One," *Philadelphia Bulletin* (May 2, 1971).

page 450, "I've never told anybody": Jaime Diaz, "Shooting for the Moon," *Sports Illustrated* (August 3, 1998).

page 450, Shepard's moon balls were . . . made by Spalding: Ibid.

page 450, "I wonder where my golf ball is": Author interview with Bob Murphy.

21: "I saw a different Alan Shepard, completely different"

page 451, "the question of what bravery is": Mort Sheinman, "Tom Wolfe; the Author of 'The Right Stuff' Blasts Off In This 1979 Interview," *Women's Wear Daily* (September 13, 1999).

pages 452–453, [Louise and *The Right Stuff*]: Author interview with Dorel Alco Abbot.

page 453, "I have nothing to gain and everything to lose": Ibid.

page 453, "none of it was all that accurate": Slayton and Cassut, *DEKE!*, p. 317.

page 453, "poetic license ... great movie": Elisabeth Bumiller and Phil McCombs, "The Right Stuff," *The Washington Post* (October 17, 1983).

page 453, "just fiction": Brenda You, "Alan Shepard Gets Another Shot at Fame," *The Chicago Tribune* (June 16, 1994).

page 453, "What movie?": Watson, *The Washington Times*.

page 453, "nowhere near as tough as I was": Ibid.

page 454, without interviewing any of "the original guys": Jeffrey Weiss, "Alan B. Shepard Jr.," *The Dallas Morning News* (July 10, 1994).

page 455, "old disagreements didn't seem so important": Ibid.

page 455, "Your idea, you do it": Author interview with Henri Landwirth; Landwirth, *Gift of Life*, p. 165.

page 456, [Shepard watching space shuttle explosion]: Author interview with Bob Murphy.

page 456, "a sense of overconfidence, a sense of complacency": Weiss, *The Dallas Morning News*.

page 456, "We thought, as a group . . .": Patt Morrison, "25 Years Later, Mercury Team Launches New Task," *Los Angeles Times* (May 5, 1986).

page 457, secretly gave money to help a child: Author interview with Bobbie Slayton.

page 457, gave one of his secondhand cars: Author interview with John Fasolino.

page 457, his parents' . . . housekeeper's well: Author interview with Hattie Durgin.

page 458, "He didn't take one penny for himself": Author interview with Henri Landwirth.

page 458, "He became passionate about it": Author interview with Howard Benedict.

page 458, "He was very generous": Author interview with Wally Schirra.

page 458, "Al was the one who really persisted": Author interview with John Glenn.

page 459, "Hey, what're you doing?": Author interview with John Fasolino.

page 459, **One of the other twelve moonwalkers once said:** *The Other Side of the Moon* (Discovery Communications Inc., unreleased review copy).

page 459, **"You really end up caring for this planet":** Ibid.

page 460, **"If this will help Deke, I'll do it":** Author interview with Howard Benedict.

page 461, **"He did that for Deke and me":** Author interview with Bobbie Slayton.

page 462, **getting a morning tee time ten minutes before:** Author interview with Doc Abbot.

page 462, **a round with Tiger Woods:** Author interview with Robert Williams.

22: "This is the toughest man I've ever met"

page 463, **ceremony for the *Alan B. Shepard Jr.*:** Author interview with Jack Lengyl.

page 464, **"I'm going to beat this":** Author interview with Robert Williams.

page 465, **[AT&T Pro-Am—not invited back]:** Author interview with Bob Murphy; author interview with Daniel Hruby, AT&T Pro-Am historian.

page 465, **not a candidate for a bone marrow transplant:** Author interview with Mickey Kapp.

page 465, **his twice-monthly "pinking up":** Ibid.

page 465, **traveled the country looking for a cure:** Author interview with Robert Williams.

page 467, **"trying to get along, desperately trying to get along":** Cheryl Arvidson, "Alan Shepard remembered as space hero, First Amendment supporter," *The Freedom Forum* (Web site obituary, July 22, 1998).

page 467, **"Go talk to my doctor":** Transcript of Shepard interview on CNN (June 20, 1998).

page 468, **"a very emotional evening":** Author interview with John Glenn.

page 469, **"That was competition at its best":** Shepard, Academy of Achievement.

page 470, **One astronaut had seven wives in sixteen years:** Cunningham. *The All-American Boys,* p. 187.

page 471, **Louise spoke of how much she missed him:** Author interview with Loraine Meyer.

page 471, **she might not be cut out for widowhood:** Author interview with Dorel Alco Abbot.

page 472, **Laura told a family friend . . . :** Author interview with Robert Williams.

BIBLIOGRAPHY

Primary Interviews

Dorel Alco Abbot, James L. "Doc" Abbot, Andrew Atwell, Robert Baldwin, Foster Ball, Jay Barbree, Jack Barron, Ray Bates, Sam Beddingfield, Howard Benedict, Al Blackburn, Bill Botts, Sherman Brickett, Anne (Shepard) Bullis, Eugene Cernan, William F. Chaires, Laura (Shepard) Churchley, J. T. Cockrill, Gordon Cooper, Wayne Coyne, Walter Cronkite, Bill Dana, Nancy Darling, H. Y. Davidson, Al Deale, Hattie Durgin, Robert Elder, Ike Evans, John Fasolino, Chuck Friedlander, Francis Gallien, Bill Geiger, Paul Gillcrist, John Glenn, Don Gregory, Betty Grissom, Paul Haney, Dick Hardy, Paul Havenstein, Don Hawes, Bill Hines, William House, John Huber, Julie (Shepard) Jenkins, Howard Johnson, Mickey Kapp, Jack King, Wayne Koons, Christopher Kraft, Henri Landwirth, William Lawrence, Jack Lengyl, James Lovell, William McLaughlin, Maxine Messinger, Loraine Meyer, Ed Mitchell, John Mitchell, Lola Morrow, Ralph Morse, Harold Moynihan, Bob Murphy, Al Neuharth, Dee O'Hara, Warren O'Neil, George Overman, Marion Pounder, James "Jig Dog" Ramage, Frank Repp, Larry Richardson, Julian Scheer, Jim Schefter, Walter M. Schirra, Joe Schmitt, Gloria Schwendeman, Hank Searls, Denni Seibert, Richard Sewall, George Sheldon, Don Shelton, Dudley Shepard, Henry Shepard, Tazewell Shepard, Bobbie Slayton, Charles B. Spangler, Tom Spargo, Ralph Stell, James Stockdale, Syd Stockdale, Bill Strong, Dick True, Peter Vanderhoef, Robert Voas, Alice (Shepard) Wackermann, Tamie Watters, Mickey Weisner, Ralph Weymouth, George Whisler, Betty Whisler, Robert Beresford Williams

Books

Abbot, Olive M. et al. *From Turnpike to Interstate: the 150 years of Derry, New Hampshire.* Canaan, New Hampshire: Phoenix Publishing, 1977.

Aldrin, Col. Edwin E. "Buzz", with Wayne Warga. *Return to Earth.* New York: Random House, 1973.

Barbree, Jay, Howard Benedict, Alan Shepard and Deke Slayton. *Moonshot.* Atlanta: Turner Publishing, 1994.

Batchelder, Jean. *History & Heroes of New Hampshire Aviation.* Spring Hill, Florida: Arrow Publishing Co., 1995.

Blackburn, Al. *Aces Wild: The Race for Mach 1.* Scholarly Resources, 1998.

Berg, A. Scott. *Lindbergh.* New York: Berkley Books, 1998.

Burrows, William E. *This New Ocean: The Story of the First Space Age.* New York: Random House, 1998.

Caidin, Martin. *The Cape.* Garden City, New York: Doubleday & Co., 1971.

Caidin, Martin. *Man into Space.* New York: Pyramid Books, 1961.

Carpenter, Scott, and Kristen Stoever. *For Spacious Skies: The Uncommon Journey of a Mercury Astronaut.* New York: Harcourt Inc., 2002.

Chaikin, Andrew. *A Man on the Moon.* New York: Penguin Books, 1994.

Cernan, Eugene, with Don Davis. *Last Man on the Moon.* New York: St. Martin's Press, 1999.

Collins, Michael. *Carrying the Fire: An Astronaut's Journey.* New York: Cooper Square Press, 1974.

Cooper, Gordon, with Bruce Henderson. *Leap of Faith: An Astronaut's Journey into the Unknown.* New York: HarperCollins, 2000.

Cunningham, Walter. *The All-American Boys.* New York: Macmillan Publishing Co., 1977.

Dalek, Robert. *An Unfinished Life: John F. Kennedy, 1917–1963.* Boston: Little Brown & Company, 2003.

Engen, Donald D. *Wings and Warriors: My Life as a Naval Aviator.* Washington, D.C.: Smithsonian Institute Press, 1997.

English, Dave. *Slipping the Surly Bonds—Great Quotations on Flight.* New York: McGraw Hill. 1998.

Fallaci, Oriana. *If the Sun Dies.* New York: Antheum House Inc., 1966 (English translation edition).

Fallaci, Oriana. *The Egotists.* Chicago: Henry Regnery Company, 1963.

Faludi, Susan. *Stiffed: The Betrayal of the American Man.* New York: William Morrow and Co. Inc., 1999.

Fraser, Caroline. *God's Perfect Child: Living and Dying in the Christian Science Church.* New York: Henry Holt and Company, 1999.

Gillcrist, RAdm. Paul T. *Sea Legs.* San Jose: Writer's Showcase, 2000.

Gillcrist, RAdm. Paul T. *Feet Wet: Reflections of a Carrier Pilot*. New York: Pocket Books, 1990.

Glenn, John, with Nick Taylor. *John Glenn: A Memoir*. New York: Bantam Books, 1999.

Godwin, Robert, ed., *Freedom 7: The NASA Mission Reports*. Ontario: Apogee Books, 2001.

Godwin, Robert, ed., *Apollo 14: The NASA Mission Reports*. Ontario: Apogee Books, 2001.

Grissom, Betty, and Henry Still. *Starfall*. New York: Ty Crowell Co., 1974.

Grossnick, Roy, and William J. Armstrong. *United States Naval Aviation: 1910–1995*. Washington, D.C.: Naval Historical Center, 1997.

Halberstam, David. *The Fifties*. New York: Fawcett Columbine, 1994.

Ivins, Molly. *Molly Ivins Can't Say That, Can She?* New York: Random House, 1991.

Jacobus, Donald Lines, ed. *The Shepard Families of New England*. Vol. III. New Haven: The New Haven Colony Historical Society, 1973.

Kennedy, John F. *Profiles in Courage*. New York: HarperCollins, 1956.

Kennedy, Paul. *Pacific Victory*, Vol. 25. New York: Ballantine Books, 1973.

Kraft, Chris. *Flight: My Life in Mission Control*. New York: E. P. Dutton, 2001.

Kranz, Gene. *Failure Is Not an Option*. New York: Simon & Schuster, 2000.

Landwirth, Henri, with J. P. Hendricks. *Gift of Life*. Self-published, privately released, 1996.

Langewiesche, William. *Inside the Sky: A Meditation on Flight*. New York: Vintage Books, 1999.

Langewiesche, Wolfgang. *Stick and Rudder: An Explanation of the Art of Flying*. New York: McGraw Hill, 1944.

Lewis, Richard S. *Appointment on the Moon*. New York: The Viking Press, 1968.

Lindberg, Charles. *We*. Guilford, CT: Lyons Press, 2002.

Lovell, James, and Jeffrey Kluger. *Apollo 13*. New York: Pocket Books, 1995 (paperback edition).

Mailer, Norman. *Of a Fire on the Moon*. Boston: Little Brown & Co., 1969.

Manchester, William. *The Glory and the Dream: A Narrative History of America*. Boston: Little Brown & Co., 1973.

Mertins, Louis. *Robert Frost, Life and Talks-walking*. Univ. Oklahoma, 1965.

Michener, James. *Space*. New York: Fawcett Crest/Ballantine Books, 1982.

Michener, James. *The Bridges at Toko Ri*. New York: Ballatine, 1973 (paperback edition).

Mitchell, Edgar, and Dwight Williams. *The Way of the Explorer: An Apollo Astronaut's Journey Through the Material and Mystical Worlds*. Audio Partners Publishing Group, 1996 (audiotape).

Morrison, Kathleen. *Robert Frost, A Pictorial Chronicle*. New York: Holt, 1974.

O'Leary, Brian. *The Making of An Ex-Astronaut*. Boston: Houghton Mifflin Co., 1970.

Saint-Exupéry, Antoine de. *Wind, Sand and Stars*. New York: Harcourt, 1992.

Schefter, James. *The Race: The Uncensored Story of How America Beat Russia to the Moon*. New York: Doubleday/Random House, 1999.

Schirra, Walter M., with Richard N. Billings. *Schirra's Space*. Annapolis, Maryland: Naval Institute Press/Bluejacket Books, 1995.

Slayton, Donald K. "Deke," with Michael Cassut. *DEKE! U.S. Manned Space: From Mercury to the Shuttle*. New York: Forge Books/A Tom Doherty Associates Book, 1994.

Smaus, Jewel Spangler, and Charles Spangler. *America's First Spaceman*. Garden City, New York: Doubleday & Co., 1962.

Sweetman, Jack. *The U.S. Naval Academy: An Illustrated History*. Annapolis, Maryland: Naval Institute Press, 1995.

Swenson, Loyd S. Jr.; James M. Grimwood, and Charles Alexander. *This New Ocean: A History of Project Mercury*. Houston: NASA History Series, 1989 (Web edition).

Thomas, Shirley. *Men of Space: Profiles of the Leaders in Space Research, Development, and Exploration*, Vol. 3, pp. 182–207. Philadelphia and New York: Chilton Co. Book Division, 1961.

Wakeman, Frederick. *Shore Leave*. New York: Farrar & Rinehart, Inc., 1944.

Wendt, Guenter, with Russell Still. *The Unbroken Chain*. Ontario: Apogee Books, 2001.

Wilford, John Noble. *We Reach the Moon*. New York: Bantam Books, 1969.

Wolfe, Tom. *The Right Stuff*. New York: Bantam Books, 1980 (paperback edition).

———. *We Seven—by the Astronauts Themselves*. New York: Simon and Schuster, 1962.

———. *Spaceflight: A Smithsonian Guide*. New York: Macmillan Publishing, Ligature Books, 1995.

———. *United States Naval Test Pilot School: Historical Narrative and Class Date, 1945–1983*. Annapolis, Maryland: Flshergate Publishing, 1984.

Articles, Reports, Oral Histories, Films, Etc.

Allen, Mel R. "The Disciplined Life," *Yankee*, October 1991.

Altman, Lawrence K. "A Tube Implant Corrected Shepard's Ear Disease," *New York Times*. February 2, 1971.

Berry, Charles. Oral history interviews. NASA Historical Center, 1963 and 1967.

Berry, Charles. Oral history interview. NASA archives, University of Houston, Clear Lake.

Bruning, Fred. "Glenn's Return to Space: A 2nd Launch Into History," *Newsweek*, October 11, 1998.

Carlson, Peter. "Has NASA Lost its Way?", *Washington Post Magazine*, May 30, 1993.

Cheney, Christopher. "The First Astronaut," OpenUniverse.com, May 5, 2001.

Clayton, John. "Carl S. Park Sr. Made His Living in the Skies," *The Union Leader*, September 14, 1998.

Dougherty, Geoff. "Instructor Recalls Hero's First Flight," *St. Petersburg Times*, August 8, 1998.

Felt, Harry D. Oral history interview. U.S. Naval Institute.

Fisher, Allan C. Jr. "Exploring Tomorrow with the Space Agency," *National Geographic*, prepublication version of article, March 14, 1960.

Gordon, Cathy. "Potholes and Promises," *Houston Chronicle*, June 21, 1987.

Griffin, Charles D. Oral history interview. U.S. Naval Institute.

Grimwood, James M., ed. *Project Mercury: A Chronology.* Houston: NASA Historical Branch, 1963.

Haney, Paul. Oral history interview. NASA Historical Center, 1968.

Hyland, John J. Oral history interview. U.S. Naval Institute.

Jackson, Carmault B. "The Flight of Freedom 7," *National Geographic*, September, 1961.

Kapp, Mickey. Oral history interview. NASA Historical Center, 1971.

Kapp, Mickey (producer). *To the Moon.* 6-CD audio book. Lodestone Audio Theater (date unknown).

Lacouture, Capt. John. "You Can Be Good and Be Colorful," *Naval History*, June 2001.

Lawrence, William P. "Reminiscences of Alan Shepard," *Foundation*, journal of the National Museum of Naval Aviation, Spring 1990.

Machat, Mike. "Bob Elder: Naval Aviator," *Wings*, Vol. 31, No. 6, December, 2001.

Mailer, Norman. "Superman Comes to the Supermarket," *Esquire*, September 1960.

Morrison, Patt. "25 Years Later, Mercury Team Launches New Task," *Los Angeles Times*, May 5, 1986.

Powers, John A. "Shorty." Oral history interview. NASA Historical Center, 1968.

Pride, Alfred M. Oral history interview. U.S. Naval Institute.

Radosevich, Walt. Oral history interview with Thomas Saylor, *Oral History Project of the World War II Years*, Concordia University, St. Paul, 2001.

Ramage, James D. Oral history interview. U.S. Naval Institute.

Ryan, Michael. "Yesterday's Heroes: The Astronauts Memorialized in 'The Right Stuff' Have Gone Surprisingly Different Ways," *People*, October 31, 1983.

Sawyer, Paul. Oral history interview. NASA Historical Center, 1972.

Scarr, Lew. "The Space Age Had a Bright Beginning," *San Diego Union-Tribune*, September 1, 1985.

Scheer, Julian. Oral history interview. NASA Historical Center, 1967.

Schudel, Matt. "Rocket Town," *Sunshine* magazine, Oct. 18, 1998.

Selverstone, Marc. "Politics and the Space Program," Presidential Recordings Project. Miller Center of Public Affairs, Winter, 2002.

Sheinman, Mort. "Tom Wolfe: The Author of 'The Right Stuff' Blasts Off in This 1979 Interview," *Women's Wear Daily*, September 13, 1999.

Shepard, Alan B. "The Astronaut's Story of the Thrust into Space," *Life*, Vol. 50, No. 20, May 19, 1961.

Shepard, Alan B. Interview—Academy of Achievement, Hall of Science and Exploration (www.achievement.org), February 1, 1991.

Shepard, Alan B. Interview with Pam Platt, "Shepard Detailed 'Real Stuff' in Florida Today Interview," *Florida Today*, July 22, 1998.

Shepard, Alan B. Unpublished interview with author Robert Sherrod (NASA archives, Washington, D.C.), December 14, 1972.

Shepard, Alan B. Oral history interview, Roy Neal. Johnson Space Center Oral History Project. February 20, 1998.

Shepard, Alan B. Interview transcript, James Burke, BBC TV (at NASA archives), May 17, 1979.

Shepard, Alan B. Oral history interview, Walter Sohier, for the John F. Kennedy Memorial Library, 1964.

Shepard, Alan B. Untitled article, *Voice of America/USIA*, May 23, 1961.

Shepard, Louise. "The Spaceman's Wife: 'Alan Was in His Right Place,' " *Life*, Vol. 50, No. 19, May 12, 1961.

Shepard, Louise. "Just Go Right Ahead," *Life*, Vol. 47, No. 12, September 21, 1959.

Sherrod, Robert. Unpublished manuscript, NASA archives (date unknown).

Slayton, Deke. Oral history interview. NASA Historical Center, 1967.

Temple, David W. "The Car with the Right Stuff," *Car Collector*, August, 2001.

Wainwright, Loudon. "The Old Pro Gets His Shot at the Moon," *Life*, July 31, 1970.

Wainwright, Loudon S. "Shepard: A Cool Customer and a Hot Pilot with an Eye for the Big Picture," *Life*, March 3, 1961, p. 30.

Watson, Jim. "Shepard Sky High on NASA," *The Washington Times*, Aug. 6, 1986.

Wilbur, Ted. "Once a Fighter Pilot," *Naval Aviation News*, 1970.

Williams, Walter. *Go* (unpublished manuscript), NASA archives, 1967.

———. *From the Earth to the Moon* (video), HBO Studios, 1998.

———. *The Other Side of the Moon* (video), Discovery Communications Inc., (unreleased review copy).

———. *Moonshot: The Inside Story of the Apollo Project* (video), Turner Home Video, 1995.

———. *An Oral History of the Corpus Christi Naval Air Station During World War II*, Del Mar College, 1995.

———. *On Guard: USS* Oriskany, *CVA-34, Carrier Air Group 19, 1953–54* (yearbook), Dai Nippon Printing Co., Ltd., 1954.

———. "Former Man on Moon Charged in Real Estate Development," Associated Press, March 8, 1980.

———. *Results of the First U.S. Manned Suborbital Space Flight.* NASA Special Publications, June 6, 1961.

———. *Results of the First United States Manned Orbital Space Flight.* NASA Special Publications, Manned Spacecraft Center, February 20, 1962.

———. *Results of the Second United States Manned Orbital Space Flight.* NASA Special Publications, Manned Spacecraft Center, May 24, 1962.

———. *Results of the Third United States Manned Orbital Space Flight.* NASA Special Publications, Manned Spacecraft Center, October 3, 1962.

———. "Lunar Module Onboard Voice Transcription," Manned Spacecraft Center, NASA. February 1971.

———. "Subject: Alan Shepard," file number 62–106995, Federal Bureau of Investigation. (Note: the FBI conducted an extensive background investigation on Shepard in 1971, at a time when he was under consideration for a presidential appointment. The results of that investigation, along with a 1967 background investigation by the Civil Service Commission—more than 400 pages in all—were obtained by the author through the FBI's Freedom of Information and Privacy Acts.)

ACKNOWLEDGMENTS

Alan Shepard was a diligently private man. His many loyal friends knew and respected that, which makes me all the more grateful to those who nonetheless spoke with me at length, who invited me into their homes, opened up photo albums and scrapbooks, offered a meal, a scotch, a bed—and a story. I hope this book honors their faith in my attempts to tell a great story about a good man.

I'm honored to have had the privilege of spending time with three of the four surviving Mercury 7 astronauts: John Glenn, Wally Schirra, and Gordon Cooper—thank you. Thanks also to the dozens of astronauts, journalists, NASA officials, Navy and Naval Academy men, and family friends who invited me into their homes or offices, particularly these kind people: Walter Cronkite; Chris Kraft; Al Neuharth; Ed Mitchell; Henri Landwirth; Bobbie Slayton; Ralph Morse; Gene Cernan; Mickey Kapp; Lola Morrow; Jack King; Howard Benedict; Jay Barbree; George and Betty Whisler; Jig Dog Ramage; Bob Elder; Dorel Abbot, Sam Beddingfield; Bill Hines; Charles Spangler; Lorraine Meyer; Hattie Durgin; Peter Vanderhoef; Francis Gallien; my good friends Bill and Diane Lawrence; and my new friend Robert Beresford

Williams, and his wife, Carol. Thanks also to the Class of '45, especially Al Blackburn; to my e-mail-and-phone friends, Dee O'Hara, Bill Dana, and Paul Haney; and to USS *Cogswell* crewmen Andrew Atwell, John Huber, Tom Spargo, and, especially, Howard Johnson.

I'm awed by the treasures I found in dusty books and boxes of the libraries, archives, and oral history collections I visited across the country, and am thankful to those working to preserve those bits of our history, the people who kindly showed me where to dig, especially: the inestimable Paul Stillwell and Ann Hassinger at the U.S. Naval Institute; "Cousin" Dave Thompson and Colvin Randall at Longwood Gardens; Steve Garber and Jane Odom at the NASA History Office; Kent, Cindy, and Barbara at the National Archives repository in Fort Worth and the staff of the National Archives in College Park; Shelly Kelly and Anna Keebler at the NASA archives at the University of Houston, Clear Lake; Norman Delaney at Delmar College in Corpus Christi; Glen Swanson at the Johnson Space Center; Gary Lavalley at the Naval Academy library; Kerry Johnson and Robin Perrin at Pinkerton Academy; Hill Goodspeed at the National Museum of Naval Aviation in Pensacola; Nancy Montgomery with the Chief of Naval Air Training in Corpus Christi; and Linda Colton at the FBI's FOIA office.

This book improved with each bit of advice from friends who slogged through sloppy first drafts. Thank you Brian and Cheryl Klam, Katherine and David Reed, Lou King, Mike Hudson, Pauline Trimarco, Victor Yung, Juliette Tower, and, most especially, my Jersey goomba, Jim Haner. Thanks to Buzz Bissinger, Robert Ruby, Bob Timberg, and Richard Ben Cramer for early advice; to Rob Montone and family for loaning me Chez Montone at the lake to write; to Eric Schenck for hiring me when the cash ran low; and to my mom, Pat, and sister, Maura, for inspiration.

I would not have leaped into the abyss without the initial nudge and support from John Seigenthaler at the First Amendment Center and the Freedom Forum. And I'd like to acknowledge a few of the many who provided technical guidance for the paperback: Robert Pearlman and his dedicated crew at CollectSpace.com, Francis French at the Reuben H. Fleet Science Center, Peter King at CBS News, Ted Spitzmiller, and Joel Turpin.

Finally, special thanks to my dad, Phil, the flyer, for attempting to teach me about flight and about life; to my agent, Michael Carlisle, and my friend, Larry Chilnick; to Emily Loose and Caroline Sincerbeaux, for their shrewd, sharp editing; and to the copy editors and designers at Crown Books.

Words can't express how lucky I feel to have worked passionately on this book atop a foundation of undeterred support from my wife, Mary, and sons, Sean and Leo.

INDEX

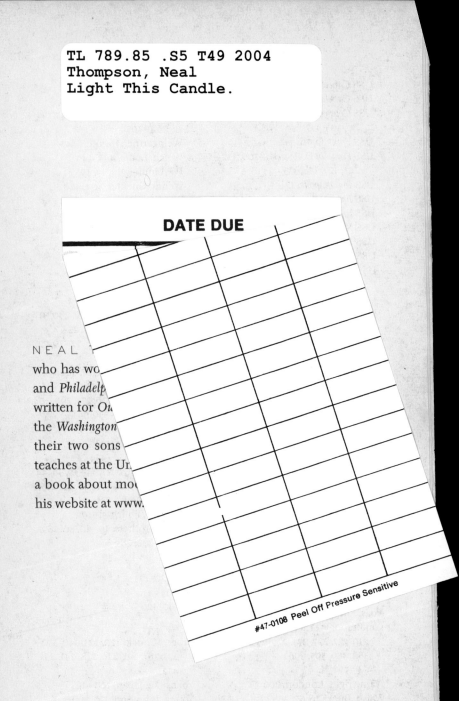

DATE DUE

#47-0108 Peel Off Pressure Sensitive

NEAL
who has wo
and *Philadelp*
written for *Ou*
the *Washington*
their two sons
teaches at the Ur
a book about mo
his website at www.